BEGINNING SPRING

FOREWORDS . . . . **xxvii**

INTRODUCTION . . . . **xxxi**

CHAPTER 1   POJO Programming Model, Lightweight Containers, and
Inversion of Control 1

CHAPTER 2   Dependency Injection with Spring 17

CHAPTER 3   Building Web Applications Using Spring MVC 63

CHAPTER 4   JDBC Data Access with Spring 103

CHAPTER 5   Data Access with JPA Using Spring 137

CHAPTER 6   Managing Transactions with Spring 175

CHAPTER 7   Test-Driven Development with Spring 209

CHAPTER 8   Aspect-Oriented Programming with Spring 237

CHAPTER 9   Spring Expression Language 263

CHAPTER 10   Caching 285

CHAPTER 11   RESTful Web Services with Spring 305

CHAPTER 12   Securing Web Applications with Spring Security 331

CHAPTER 13   Next Stop: Spring 4.0 369

APPENDIX   Solutions to Exercises. 385

INDEX 425

BEGINNING
Spring

BEGINNING

Spring

Mert Çalışkan
Kenan Sevindik

WROX
A Wiley Brand

Beginning Spring

Published by
John Wiley & Sons, Inc.
10475 Crosspoint Boulevard
Indianapolis, IN 46256
www.wiley.com

Copyright © 2015 by John Wiley & Sons, Inc., Indianapolis, Indiana

Published simultaneously in Canada

ISBN: 978-1-118-89292-3
ISBN: 978-1-118-89303-6 (ebk)
ISBN: 978-1-118-89311-1 (ebk)

Manufactured in the United States of America

10 9 8 7 6 5 4 3 2 1

For general information on our other products and services please contact our Customer Care Department within the United States at (877) 762-2974, outside the United States at (317) 572-3993 or fax (317) 572-4002.

Wiley publishes in a variety of print and electronic formats and by print-on-demand. Some material included with standard print versions of this book may not be included in e-books or in print-on-demand. If this book refers to media such as a CD or DVD that is not included in the version you purchased, you may download this material at http://booksupport.wiley.com. For more information about Wiley products, visit www.wiley.com.

Library of Congress Control Number: 2014954686

This is for you, Love.

—MERT ÇALIŞKAN

To my Mom, and to the memory of my Dad...

—KENAN SEVINDIK

ABOUT THE AUTHORS

MERT ÇALIŞKAN is a Principle Software Architect living in Ankara, Turkey. He has more than 10 years of expertise in software development with the architectural design of Enterprise Java web applications. Çalışkan is an open source advocate for software projects such as PrimeFaces, and he is the co-author of *PrimeFaces Cookbook,* first and second editions (Packt Publishing, 2013). He is the founder of AnkaraJUG, which is the most active JUG in Turkey. Çalışkan is part-time lecturer at Hacettepe University about Enterprise Web Applications' Architecture and Web Services. In 2014, he achieved the title of Java Champion. He shares his knowledge at national and international conferences such as JDays 2015, JavaOne 2013, JDC2010, and JSFDays'08. You can follow him on Twitter @mertcal.

KENAN SEVINDIK specializes in architecting and developing enterprise applications using various Java technologies. His experience with Java dates back to 1998 when he started developing Java applets for online education programs at his university. He has been working with Spring Application Framework and Spring Security Framework since their initial phases. Sevindik has a bachelor's degree in computer engineering. Currently he works with Harezmi IT Solutions, where he develops enterprise software and gives training, mentoring, and consulting services about Java, OOP, AOP, Spring, Spring Security, and Hibernate all over the world. You can read his technical writings at http://blog.harezmi.com.tr and reach him at ksevindik@harezmi.com.tr.

ABOUT THE TECHNICAL EDITOR

CHÁD (SHOD) DARBY is an author, instructor, and speaker in the Java development world. As a recognized authority on Java applications and architectures, he has presented technical sessions at software development conferences worldwide. In his fifteen years as a professional software architect, he's had the opportunity to work for Blue Cross/Blue Shield, Merck, Boeing, Red Hat and a handful of startup companies. Chád is a contributing author to several Java books, including *Professional Java E-Commerce* (Wiley, 2001) and *Beginning Java Networking* (Wiley, 2001). Chád has Java certifications from Sun Microsystems and IBM. He holds a B.S. in Computer Science from Carnegie Mellon University. Visit Chád's blog at `www.luv2code.com` to view his free video tutorials on Java. You can also follow him on Twitter `@darbyluvs2code`.

CREDITS

Project Editor
Charlotte Kughen

Technical Editors
Chád Darby
Krishna Srinivasan

Production Editor
Rebecca Anderson

Copy Editor
Kim Cofer

Manager of Content Development and Assembly
Mary Beth Wakefield

Marketing Director
David Mayhew

Marketing Manager
Carrie Sherrill

Professional Technology and Strategy Director
Barry Pruett

Business Manager
Amy Knies

Associate Publisher
Jim Minatel

Project Coordinator, Cover
Patrick Redmond

Proofreader
Nancy Carrasco

Indexer
Johnna VanHoose Dinse

Cover Designer
Wiley

Cover Image
©iStock.com/llandrea

ACKNOWLEDGMENTS

FIRST I WOULD LIKE to thank my friend, Kenan Sevindik, for joining me on this journey. Special thanks go to the creators of the Spring Framework, Rod Johnson and Jürgen Höller, for crowning our book with their Forewords. Without their ideas and inspirations that ignited all of us, this book wouldn't even exist.

I also would like to thank our associate publisher, Jim Minatel; project editor, Charlotte Kughen; technical editors, Chád Darby and Krishna Srinivasan; copy editor, Kim Cofer; and production editor, Rebecca Anderson. These people accompanied us during the entire writing process and made the book publication possible with their support, suggestions, and reviews.

Last but not the least, I would like to thank my mom, my dad, my Tuğçe, and especially my beloved Funda, who gives me her never-ending support and enthusiasm.

—MERT ÇALIŞKAN

FIRST OF ALL, I would like to thank my wife, Betül, for her endless support while I was writing this book. I also would like to thank my colleague, Muammer Yücel, for his encouragement and motivation. Although this book is a direct result of our extensive experience with the Spring Application Framework, it wouldn't be what it is without the help and valuable comments of our project editor, Charlotte Kughen; technical editors, Chád Darby and Krishna Srinivasan; copy editor, Kim Cofer; and production editor, Rebecca Anderson.

—KENAN SEVINDIK

CONTENTS

FOREWORDS   *xxvii*

INTRODUCTION   *xxxi*

CHAPTER 1: POJO PROGRAMMING MODEL, LIGHTWEIGHT CONTAINERS, AND INVERSION OF CONTROL   1

POJO Programming Model   2

Problems of the Old EJB Programming Model   2

Benefits of the POJO Programming Model   7

Lightweight Containers and Inversion of Control (IoC)   8

Lightweight Containers   8

Inversion of Control (IoC)   9

Dependency Injection   10

Setter Injection   11

Constructor Injection   11

Setter or Constructor Injection   12

Summary   12

CHAPTER 2: DEPENDENCY INJECTION WITH SPRING   17

Spring IoC Container   18

Configuration Metadata   18

Configuring and Using the Container   21

Dependency Injection   29

Setter Injection   30

Constructor Injection   31

Circular Dependencies   34

Dependency Resolution Process   35

Overriding Bean Definitions   36

Using the depends-on Attribute   38

Autowiring   39

Bean Lookups   43

Spring-Managed Beans   44

Naming Beans   44

Bean Instantiation Methods   45

Bean Scopes   48

Lazy Initialization   51

Life-Cycle Callbacks 52
Bean Definition Profiles 54
Environment 56
Summary 59

CHAPTER 3: BUILDING WEB APPLICATIONS USING SPRING MVC 63

Learning the Features and Benefits of Spring MVC 64
Using the Dispatcher Servlet Mechanism 65
Defining the Servlet 66
Accessing Servlet Context 67
Creating Your First Spring MVC Application 68
Configuring Spring MVC with Annotations 71
Handling Forms with JSP 73
Configuring the Form Tag Library 73
Understanding the Power of Binding 74
Working with Forms 74
Using Input Elements 75
Entering Dates 76
Selecting from a Drop-Down 77
Selecting with Radio Buttons 78
Selecting with Checkboxes 78
Adding Labels 78
Placing Buttons 79
Styling 79
Exploiting the Power of Annotations 84
@Controller 84
@RequestMapping 84
@ModelAttribute 84
@PathVariable 85
@ControllerAdvice 85
@InitBinder 85
@ExceptionHandler 85
Validating User Input 86
Uploading Files 90
Handling Exceptions 93
Implementing Internationalization (i18n) 95
Using Themes 97
Summary 100

CHAPTER 4: JDBC DATA ACCESS WITH SPRING   **103**

Problems with Using Vanilla JDBC   104
Introducing Spring's JDBC Support   105
    Managing JDBC Connections   105
       Embedded DB Support   108
       Using a Connection-Pooled DataSource   110
       Initializing DB   111
    Configuring and Using Spring's JDBC Support   112
Performing Data Access Operations with Spring   114
    Running Queries   114
    Queries with Named Parameters   117
    Writing Queries Using the IN Clause   118
    Using PreparedStatements within JdbcTemplate   119
    Inserting, Updating, and Deleting Records   121
    Calling Stored Procedures and Stored Functions   124
    Performing Batch Operations   126
    Handling BLOB and CLOB Objects   126
    Accessing Vendor-Specific JDBC Methods   127
    Executing DDL Operations   127
Modeling JDBC Operations as Java Objects   128
    Encapsulating SQL Query Executions   128
    Encapsulating SQL DML Operations   130
    Encapsulating Stored Procedure Executions   131
Exception Handling and Error Code Translation   132
    Common Data Access Exception Hierarchy   132
    Automatic Handling and Translation of SQLException   132
Summary   133

CHAPTER 5: DATA ACCESS WITH JPA USING SPRING   **137**

Brief Introduction to ORM and JPA   138
    Paradigm Mismatch   138
    Building Blocks of an ORM Framework   139
    What JPA Offers   139
    Mapping the Object Model to the Relational Model   140
       Defining Entities   140
       Mapping Attributes to Columns   141
       Creating Associations between Objects   142
       Mapping Java Types to SQL Types   145

Configuring and Using JPA   147
   Performing CRUD Operations on Objects   150
   Querying with Object Query Language   155
Spring's JPA Support   **156**
  Setting Up JPA in Spring Container   156
  Implementing DAOs Based on Plain JPA   161
  Handling and Translating Exceptions   166
  Further JPA Configuration in Spring Environment   167
   JpaDialect   168
   JpaVendorAdapter   168
   JPA and Load Time Weaving   169
   Dealing with Multiple Persistence Units   170
Summary   **171**

CHAPTER 6: MANAGING TRANSACTIONS WITH SPRING   175

Understanding Transaction Management   **176**
Spring's Transaction Abstraction Model   **180**
  Local versus Global Transactions   182
  PlatformTransactionManager Implementations   182
  Advantages of Spring's Abstract Transaction Model   183
Declarative Transaction Management with Spring   **183**
  Isolating the Service Layer from Data Access Technology Details   186
  Customizing Default Transactional Behavior   189
  Using @Transactional on the Class Level   190
  Understanding Transaction Propagation Rules   191
   Propagation REQUIRED   191
   Propagation REQUIRES_NEW   192
   Propagation NESTED   192
   Propagation SUPPORTS   192
   Propagation NOT_SUPPORTED   192
   Propagation NEVER   193
   Propagation MANDATORY   193
  Using <tx:advice> for Declarative Transaction Management   195
**Programmatic Transaction Management
with Spring**   **197**
  Using the PlatformTransactionManager Approach   201
Executing Custom Logic Before or After Transactions   **203**
  Advising Transactional Operations   203
  Executing Logic after Transactions Using TransactionSynchronization   204
Summary   **205**

CHAPTER 7: TEST-DRIVEN DEVELOPMENT WITH SPRING 209

Configuring and Caching ApplicationContext	210
Using XML- and Java-Based Context Configuration in Tests	210
Configuring Context with ApplicationContextInitializer	214
Inheriting Context Configuration	214
ApplicationContext Caching	216
Injecting Dependencies of Test Fixtures	217
Using Transaction Management in Tests	219
Testing Web Applications	222
Context Hierarchies in Tests	225
Testing Request- and Session-Scoped Beans	225
Testing Spring MVC Projects	227
Testing Controllers	227
Testing Form Submit	228
Testing Exception Handlers	230
Printing Mock Request and Response	231
Using Mock Objects and Other Utilities for Testing	231
Spring Provided Mock Objects for Testing	231
Other Utilities and Test Annotations	232
Summary	233

CHAPTER 8: ASPECT-ORIENTED PROGRAMMING WITH SPRING 237

Getting Started with AOP with Spring	239
Becoming Familiar with Types of Advices	243
Before	245
After Returning	245
After Throwing	245
After (Finally)	246
Around	247
Defining Point-Cut Designators	248
The Type Signature Expressions	248
The Method Signature Expressions	249
Other Alternative Point-Cut Designators	249
Wildcards	250
Capitalizing on the Power of Annotations	250
@Before	250
@Pointcut	251
@After	252
@AfterReturning	252

@AfterThrowing 252
@Aspect 253
@Around 253
@DeclareParents 254
Blending AspectJ with Spring 255
Configuring Spring AOP with Annotations 259
Summary 259

CHAPTER 9: SPRING EXPRESSION LANGUAGE 263

Configuring Applications with SpEL 264
Creating a Parser 267
Invoking Methods 270
Calling Constructors 272
Calling Static Methods 272
Working with Variables and Functions 273
#root 273
#this 274
Accessing System Properties and Environment 274
Inline Lists 274
Registering Functions 274
Understanding SpEL Operators 275
Relational Operators 276
Arithmetic Operators 276
Logical Operators 276
Conditional Operators 277
Regular Expression Operator 278
Safe Navigation Operator 278
Collection Selection and Projection 279
Selecting the First and Last Element of a Collection 280
Using Utilities in SpEL 280
Accessing Spring Beans 280
<spring:eval> 281
Expressions in Caching 281
Summary 281

CHAPTER 10: CACHING 285

Building Your First Caching Application 286
Configuring the Cache Manager with a Different Name 289
Configuring the Caching Abstraction with Annotations 289
Working with Cache Annotations 290

@Cacheable   290
  Key Generator   291
  Conditional Caching   291
@CacheEvict   292
@CachePut   292
@Caching   293
Implementing Cache Managers   293
  SimpleCacheManager   293
  NoOpCacheManager   294
  ConcurrentMapCacheManager   294
  CompositeCacheManager   294
Casting Your SpEL on Caches   295
Initializing Your Caches Programmatically   296
Finding Alternative Cache Providers   298
  Ehcache   299
  Guava   302
  Hazelcast   302
Summary   303

CHAPTER 11: RESTFUL WEB SERVICES WITH SPRING   305

Creating Your First REST Web Service   306
Returning Different HTTP Status Codes
from REST Web Service   318
Learning an Annotation-Based
Configuration Alternative   318
Using REST Web Services with XML   320
Using the Exception Handling Mechanism   322
Unit Testing RESTful Services   326
Summary   328

**CHAPTER 12: SECURING WEB APPLICATIONS WITH
SPRING SECURITY**   331

Why Spring Security?   332
Features of Spring Security   333
Configuring and Using Spring Security   334
Understanding the Fundamental Building Blocks of Spring Security   340
Authenticating Users   341
  Unsuccessful Login Flow   342
  Successful Login Flow   342
  Anonymous Authentication   344

Customizing the Login Page 344
Logout Process 346
Accessing UserDetails Using JDBC 346
Encrypting Passwords 349
Remember-Me Support 350
User Session Management 351
Basic Authentication 352
Authorizing Web Requests and Service Method Calls 353
Authorizing Web Requests 353
How Does Authorization Work? 355
Expression-Based Authorization 357
Using JSP Security Tags 358
Authorize Tag 359
Authenticate Tag 359
Authorizing Service Methods 359
Summary 364

CHAPTER 13: NEXT STOP: SPRING 4.0 369

Keeping Up with the Latest: Java 8 and Java EE7 Support 370
Lambda Expressions 370
Method References 373
Bean Validation Integration 374
JSR 310: Date Time Value Type Support 374
Configuring Injection with Conditional Dependency 374
Ordering the Elements of Autowired Collections 377
Repeating Annotations 379
Introducing New Annotations 381
Documenting with @Description 381
Using the @RestController Annotation 382
Summary 382

APPENDIX: SOLUTIONS TO EXERCISES 385

Chapter 1 385
Chapter 2 388
Chapter 3 393
Chapter 4 393
Chapter 5 399
Chapter 6 403
Chapter 7 406
Chapter 8 409

Chapter 9	411
Chapter 10	414
Chapter 11	417
Chapter 12	420
Chapter 13	423
INDEX	*425*

FOREWORD

I have fond memories of Wrox books. The Spring story started 12 years ago from a Wrox book. Before that, I'd contributed chapters to several Wrox books and served as a reviewer on many others.

Some of these memories concern what the imprint has meant to me, but many relate to its philosophy and format, a key reason I was excited to become a Wrox author in 2000. The distinctive format offers an effective structure for imparting knowledge, encouraging the author to highlight important points, and promoting systematic explanation. It emphasizes practical code examples—the most valuable tool for teaching programming.

These virtues are evident in Mert Çalışkan's and Kenan Sevindik's *Beginning Spring*. It's well structured, with plentiful examples that include clear instructions on getting the code running and step-by-step explanations.

Spring—like building enterprise Java applications itself—is a broad subject, making it impossible for an introductory book to cover even the core Spring Framework exhaustively. Mert and Kenan have done a good job in selecting what to focus on. The scope of this book is well chosen to get you productive as a Spring web developer: the core Dependency Injection container; the MVC framework (with a special emphasis on REST); relational data access and transaction management; the use of AOP and Spring EL to customize application behavior; and how Spring 4.0 embraces the important language enhancements in Java 8. Although Spring Security is the only Spring subproject covered, this book provides a solid base on which to build knowledge of the broad Spring ecosystem.

The level of the content is equally well targeted. There's a judicious mix of important background information (for example, the ACID properties of transactions) and specific detail about how to use Spring to get things done. Although this book assumes no knowledge of Spring, it does not waste time covering programming topics better served in more introductory books.

Although I'm no longer personally involved, I continue to observe Spring's progress with pleasure. Reading this book serves as a reminder of why Spring remains so relevant. The core concepts have stood up well over the past 12 years: for example, the consistent, lightweight approach to transaction management and the central principle of Dependency Injection. When you understand the "Spring way," you can master additional Spring technologies quickly.

If you're a Java web developer as yet unfamiliar with Spring, you will find that Spring can make your life much easier, and I recommend this book as a good way to get started with it.

—ROD JOHNSON

FOREWORD

The Java landscape keeps amazing me! Even after 11 years of leading the Spring Framework project, I'm learning about new fields of applications, new scenarios to optimize for, and new system architectures to consider. Software development constantly changes, and Spring doesn't just follow along—Spring keeps pushing. The Spring community often anticipates trends before they become heavily debated; for instance, people had been building microservice architectures with Spring long before the term *microservice* was coined. It is particularly interesting to see how many of the original design decisions behind the framework show their strengths again in 2014: Mechanisms introduced to decouple the framework from the application server infrastructure turn out to be very useful in adapting to modern embedded middleware.

A key mission behind Spring is to keep bringing the latest Java programming model styles to the widest possible range of deployment environments. In the Java community, we tend to put ourselves into straightjackets, not allowing ourselves to use our own current generation of APIs and frameworks. These constraints are primarily due to application server platforms, which contain outdated versions of the JDK and Java EE APIs, lagging behind for way too many years. This situation is particularly critical with Java 8 now: With lambda expressions, the new date-time types, collection streams, and so on, Java 8 has many things to offer that will change your source code style across the codebase. As a community, we need to be able to bring those features into our immediate environments—not just for development, but with full production support.

With Spring 4, we created a new baseline for 2014 and beyond. Spring's comprehensive annotation-oriented programming model is battle-tested, fine-tuned, and as coherent as possible now, and it's designed to be a stable foundation for years to come. We will be extending and refining the framework's functionality in the course of Spring Framework 4.x releases every year, as natural and fully compatible complements to the Spring 4 foundation. We will make a lot of this functionality available to JDK 6+ environments: for updates to existing applications, for deployments to existing data centers, and for corporate environments with conservative JDK policies. At the same time, you will see a strong focus on JDK 8+–oriented functionality with Spring, in particular toward stream-oriented programming and reactive system architectures.

Finally, I have a few personal recommendations to help you get the most out of Spring for your newly started development projects:

➤   First of all, get a good book on core Spring and its design philosophy. With this book, you are beyond that step already.

➤   Don't make compromises up front. Design a clean application architecture based on your understanding of your application's domain.

➤   Start with the latest Java infrastructure that you can possibly bring into production: JDK 8, Spring 4, Tomcat 8, Jetty 9, and so on.

➤ Don't forget to keep updating the frameworks and libraries along with the progress of your own project: Spring, in particular, has been designed for easy upgrades within an application, independent from any server installations.

Beginning Spring focuses on the key principles behind the Spring Framework 4 generation. It is a great way to get started with modern-day Spring development. So free yourself from artificial constraints, and enjoy developing with Spring!

—JÜRGEN HÖLLER

INTRODUCTION

THE SPRING FRAMEWORK IS AN OPEN SOURCE ENTERPRISE APPLICATION framework licensed under Apache License version 2.0, which provides an extensive toolset for building applications that meet the enterprise demands. The idea itself came about because doing development with J2EE (the former version of Java Enterprise Edition) introduced a good deal of complexity in the enterprise world. Creating and deploying beans with Enterprise Java Beans (EJB) was a burden because, to create one bean, you had to create home and component interfaces along with the bean definition. Because the concept of dependency injection was also missing in the EJB world at those times, the lookup approach was the only way to find objects or resources.

The first version of the Spring Framework was based on the code published within *Expert One-on-One J2EE Design and Development without EJB* (Wrox, 2004) by Rod Johnson and Jürgen Höller. The main idea for the book was to reduce this complexity of enterprise application development with EJBs that was introduced to the EE world with J2EE. The first version of Spring was released in 2002, and milestone releases followed in 2004 and 2005. Version 1.0 brought the lightweight application framework along with features including JDBC abstraction, object relational mapping tools support, transaction management, scheduling and mail abstraction implementations, and the Model View Controller (MVC) web framework.

The 2.0 and 3.0 releases introduced important features to the framework, such as AspectJ support and REST support. At the time of writing this book, version 4.0 was released, and it now complies with the specifications provided by Java Enterprise Edition 7 and with Java 8 Standard Edition, which are the latest versions of Java. Within the book we also try to cover the features of the framework that ships with this latest edition.

Spring gained popularity with its core Dependency Injection (DI) pattern, which is also known as Inversion of Control (IoC). Because object-oriented programming introduces relationships between the objects, the DI approach tries to achieve a loose-coupled design by extracting the management of these dependencies to lead to an easy and manageable implementation. Another spectacular feature of Spring is provided by aspect-oriented programming (AOP), which offers an elegant approach to implementing the cross-cutting concerns in your application. Every web application is in need of features such as exception management, authentication and authorization, logging, and caching. The DI and AOP concepts are covered in detail in Chapters 2 and 8, respectively.

With the help of these major features, Spring provides easily testable, reusable code with no vendor lock-in because it can be ported easily between application servers such as WebLogic, JBoss, and Tomcat. With its layered architecture, it addresses different parts of complex enterprise application development.

We can definitely say that the Spring Framework has become the de facto standard for developing Java enterprise applications. In this book you will find all of the major features brought to the enterprise world by the framework.

WHO THIS BOOK IS FOR

As the book's title states, this book covers the Spring Framework on a beginner level, and it touches on intermediate concepts wherever needed. It explains *what* the framework offers and also illustrates the content by showing *how* these features actually work with comprehensive samples. The material presented within the book is suitable for Enterprise application developers who haven't tried the Spring Framework yet or who don't know the details of its core or the subprojects. The book will also be helpful to middle-level management, who will be enlightened about the ingredients of enterprise application development and will get to taste the different flavors of the Spring Framework.

We assume that readers have some knowledge of Java language principles and the ability to develop Java code with integrated development environments (IDEs) such as Eclipse, NetBeans, or others.

This book might not be suitable for people who are not familiar with the Java language and basic object-oriented programming concepts. We also believe that the book might be of no interest for readers who are not keen on the enterprise application development world with Java.

WHAT THIS BOOK COVERS

Spring provides a comprehensive configuration model, both with XML and Java annotations. Throughout the book we demonstrate both annotation-based configuration and XML-based configuration so that we give all the possible configuration scenarios.

The book first focuses on the core concepts and features of the Spring Framework. You take a look at the basic concepts, such as the non-invasive Plain Old Java Object (POJO) programming model approach, and then we define the Dependency Injection pattern (Inversion of Control). Spring also provides a Model View Controller implementation to build web applications; we cover the provided features in detail. The Java Database Connectivity and Java Persistence API features of the Spring Framework are also covered along with the transaction mechanism that it provides. We then focus on what Spring provides for doing test-driven development. Next we cover aspect-oriented programming for giving the reader insight on how Spring handles the implementation for cross-cutting concerns of a system. Spring Expression Languages, caching, and RESTful web services provide extensive features of the Spring Framework, and we cover them with real-world examples that will get you started on development within minutes. Then we dive into Spring Security, which became a de facto standard for applying security constraints on enterprise applications.

The final chapter wraps up the book with the latest features provided by version 4.0 of the framework. We describe the best of the breed because the book covers the major features of Spring by focusing on the latest version of the framework.

The following sections give you just a little bit of detail about what's covered in the 13 chapters of this book.

Dependency Injection and Configuration of Spring

This book covers the core concepts of the Spring Framework such as DI (which is also known as IoC) and its configuration model. The object-oriented programming principles depict having relationships between the objects that are instantiated. The main objective of the DI pattern is to separate the behaviors of those objects from the way that they depend on each other. That way the tenet of loose coupling is achieved with favoring usability and maintainability of the code. The idea of DI originated with Martin Fowler and has become very popular and widely adopted. It's also implemented within popular frameworks such as PicoContainer, Guice, and Spring.

The DI pattern resembles other patterns such as Factory or Strategy. We can say that with the Factory pattern the instantiation of objects is still within the responsibility of the Factory definition, which is your code, but with the DI it's externalized to another component/framework. On the other hand, with the Strategy pattern, the current implementation gets replaced with the help of multiple objects of a same interface, which contain that implementation inside. However, with the DI, the objects that contain those implementations are wired regardless of the implementation defined.

As of version 2.0 of the Spring Framework, the DI mechanism was being configured with the XML schemas along with the support of custom namespaces. As of version 2.5, Spring leveraged the use of Java 5 and the annotations to support auto discovery of components, annotation-driven autowiring of those components, and the life-cycle annotations to hook initialization and destruction callbacks. We cover all of these annotations introduced by the framework.

Spring 4.0

Chapter 13 covers the cutting-edge features of the latest version of Spring. Version 4.0 supports Java 8 with features like lambda expressions and method expressions. It also provides annotation-driven date formatting for the new DateTime API. Version 4.0 also complies with Java EE 7 specifications such as JPA 2.1, JMS 2.0, JTA 1.2, Bean Validation 1.1, and others. We demonstrate these features to give you insight about the best of breed of the most recent version.

Spring Annotations

Spring provides XML-based and annotation-based configuration mainly for dependency injection and also for the other features of the framework. We give the traditional XML configurations with the samples to show the complexity and the burden that they put on the developer. Throughout the book, we favor annotations wherever possible to ease your way and also to make the examples comprehensible in a practical way. We have tried to cover all of the annotations provided by the framework within the samples.

As of Spring 2.5, the JSR-250 Annotations API is also supported. It's the Java Specification Request that has the scope for annotation development, so it makes Spring more compliant with the EE edition of Java.

Spring Persistency Support with JDBC, JPA, and ORM

Spring provides an abstraction to the developers for JDBC database access. It eases development by reducing the boilerplate code for connection management, exception/transaction handling, and preparation and execution of the statements.

Spring doesn't provide a built-in object relational mapping (ORM) framework, but it supports well-known ORM frameworks that comply with the JPA specification, such as Hibernate, EclipseLink, TopLink, and others. The book covers all these features regarding JDBC, JPA, and ORM with step-by-step working samples.

Spring Expression Language (SpEL)

Spring Expression Language (SpEL) is a powerful expression language for navigating through object graphs at run time. All of the SpEL expressions can be defined in XML configurations or with annotations. The syntax used with SpEL resembles Unified EL, but it provides more enhanced features.

SpEL can be used to perform property or bean injections and method invocations. It also supports mathematical and relational operators along with regular expressions. SpEL can be easily used with other subprojects of Spring, such as Security or Caching. It's also technology-agnostic, so it can be used separately without depending on the Spring context. We cover each of these features with self-contained working samples.

Spring Transaction Management and AOP

Data integrity is one of the key points of every system that deals with the data. System behavior such as incorrect account balances, lost orders, or missing entries in a document will definitely be considered unacceptable by the system's users. Transaction management provides a way to achieve integrity on the data. Spring provides extensive transaction management to ensure this data integrity and consistency for enterprise applications. Chapter 6 uses sample code to show how Spring provides declarative and programmatic transaction mechanisms, the differences in local and global transactions, propagation rules on the transactions, and the commit/rollback architecture of the framework.

To implement the cross-cutting concerns, Spring AOP provides easy definition of the elements of AOP with XML configuration, but it also supports the AspectJ framework annotations to easily configure the application.

Spring MVC and Developing RESTful Web Services

With the Model View Controller (MVC) pattern, the enterprise application can be clearly defined with three layers. Model is the part of the application that handles the logic for the application data. View is the part that handles the display of the data, and Controller is the part that handles the user interaction. Spring provides an MVC subproject to handle the HTTP requests by reducing the boilerplate code needed for accessing request parameters, validations, and conversations and model updates. It also provides a convenient way to define RESTful web services to be used with cutting-edge user-interface frameworks to provide more responsive web applications.

Spring Security

Spring Security is the subproject that provides first-class authentication and authorization support for Java-based enterprise applications. The project first started as codename Acegi and then merged into the Spring portfolio. The project conforms to the Servlet API, so it's easy to integrate it with a

Java EE–based web application. It also provides optional integration with other Spring frameworks, such as MVC, so it gives consistent usage on its features. In Chapter 12 we provide some neat examples for these feature foundations.

Spring Cache

By starting with version 3.1, Spring Framework provides a transparent caching abstraction for enterprise applications by employing various caching frameworks, such as Ehcache and Hazelcast, in the backend.

The main objective of caching is to reduce the execution of targeted methods by caching the results of method returns with their executed parameters.

> **NOTE** The Spring Framework is a comprehensive toolset that cannot be covered in a beginner-level book with all of its subprojects and the whole set of their features. This book might not be suitable for readers who seek a show-down of Spring subprojects with an end-to-end explanation.
>
> This book also focuses on version 4.0.5.RELEASE of the framework, which is the most recent version at the time of writing. Thus the older versions of the framework are not covered with their features in this book.

WHAT YOU NEED TO RUN THE SAMPLES

To run the samples that reside in the book you will need

➤ **Java Development Kit (JDK) 8.0**

➤ **Maven project build and management tool:** You can find all the samples given in the book at www.wrox.com/go/beginningspring on the Download Code tab with the Maven-based project structure.

> **NOTE** Maven demands that the Java Development Kit be installed on your local environment instead of the Java Runtime Environment.

➤ **A Java web container:** For running the web project samples given throughout the book we've used Tomcat 8.0.12 and Jetty version 9.2.3.

➤ **A Java IDE:** The samples given in the book are implemented with Eclipse IDE, but because Maven is used for the project structure, you could build the samples with other IDEs such as NetBeans or IntelliJ IDEA without any difficulty.

CONVENTIONS

To help you get the most from the text and keep track of what's happening, we've used a number of conventions throughout the book.

TRY IT OUT

The Try It Out is an exercise you should work through, following the text in the book.

1. They usually consist of a set of steps.

2. Each step has a number.

3. Follow the instructions in the steps to complete the activity.

How It Works

After each Try It Out, the code you've typed is explained in detail.

> **WARNING** *Boxes like this one hold important, not-to-be forgotten information that is directly relevant to the surrounding text.*

> **NOTE** *Notes, tips, hints, tricks, and asides to the current discussion are offset and placed in italic like this.*

As for styles in the text:

➤ We *highlight* new terms and important words when we introduce them.

➤ We show filenames, URLs, and code within the text like so: `persistence.properties`.

➤ We present code in two different ways:

```
We use a monofont type with no highlighting for most code examples.
```

```
We use bold to emphasize code that's particularly important in the present
context.
```

Source Code

As you work through the examples in this book, you may choose either to type in all the code manually or to use the source code files that accompany the book. All of the source code used in this book is available for download at `www.wrox.com/go/beginningspring`. You will find that the code snippets from the source code are accompanied by a download icon and note indicating the name of the program so you know it's available for download and can easily locate it in the download file. Once at the site, simply locate the book's title (either by using the Search box or by using one of the title lists) and click the Download Code link on the book's detail page to obtain all the source code for the book.

> **NOTE** *Because many books have similar titles, you may find it easiest to search by ISBN; this book's ISBN is 978-1-118-89292-3.*

After you download the code, just decompress it with your favorite compression tool. Alternatively, you can go to the main Wrox code download page at `http://www.wrox.com/dynamic/books/download.aspx` to see the code available for this book and all other Wrox books.

ERRATA

We make every effort to ensure that there are no errors in the text or in the code. However, no one is perfect, and mistakes do occur. If you find an error in one of our books, like a spelling mistake or faulty piece of code, we would be very grateful for your feedback. By sending in errata you may save another reader hours of frustration and at the same time you will be helping us provide even higher quality information.

To find the errata page for this book, go to `http://www.wrox.com` and locate the title using the Search box or one of the title lists. Then, on the book details page, click the Book Errata link. On this page you can view all errata that has been submitted for this book and posted by Wrox editors. A complete book list including links to each book's errata is also available at `www.wrox.com/misc-pages/booklist.shtml`.

If you don't spot "your" error on the Book Errata page, go to `www.wrox.com/contact/techsupport.shtml` and complete the form there to send us the error you have found. We'll check the information and, if appropriate, post a message to the book's errata page and fix the problem in subsequent editions of the book.

P2P.WROX.COM

For author and peer discussion, join the P2P forums at `p2p.wrox.com`. The forums are a web-based system for you to post messages relating to Wrox books and related technologies and interact with other readers and technology users. The forums offer a subscription feature to e-mail you topics of interest of your choosing when new posts are made to the forums. Wrox authors, editors, other industry experts, and your fellow readers are present on these forums.

At `http://p2p.wrox.com` you will find a number of different forums that will help you not only as you read this book, but also as you develop your own applications. To join the forums, just follow these steps:

1. Go to `p2p.wrox.com` and click the Register link.

2. Read the terms of use and click Agree.

3. Complete the required information to join as well as any optional information you wish to provide and click Submit.

4. You will receive an e-mail with information describing how to verify your account and complete the joining process.

> **NOTE** You can read messages in the forums without joining P2P, but in order to post your own messages, you must join.

Once you join, you can post new messages and respond to messages other users post. You can read messages at any time on the web. If you would like to have new messages from a particular forum e-mailed to you, click the Subscribe to this Forum icon by the forum name in the forum listing.

For more information about how to use the Wrox P2P, be sure to read the P2P FAQs for answers to questions about how the forum software works as well as many common questions specific to P2P and Wrox books. To read the FAQs, click the FAQ link on any P2P page.

BEGINNING

Spring

1

POJO Programming Model, Lightweight Containers, and Inversion of Control

WHAT YOU WILL LEARN IN THIS CHAPTER:

- ➤ Problems of the old EJB programming model that triggered the birth of POJO movement

- ➤ Advantages of the POJO programming model

- ➤ What a container is and what services it provides to its deployed applications

- ➤ Lightweight containers and what makes a container lightweight

- ➤ What Inversion of Control (IoC) means and its importance for applications

- ➤ Relationship between IoC and dependency injection

- ➤ Dependency injection methods, setter and constructor injection

- ➤ Advantages and disadvantages of those different dependency injection methods

The *Plain Old Java Object* (POJO) movement started around the beginning of the 2000s and quickly became mainstream in the enterprise Java world. This quick popularity is certainly closely related with the open source movement during that time. Lots of projects appeared, and most of them helped the POJO programming model become mature over time. This chapter first closely examines how things were before the POJO programming model existed in the enterprise Java community and discusses the problems of the old Enterprise JavaBeans (EJB) programming model. It's important that you understand the characteristics of the POJO programming model and what it provides to developers.

The second half of the chapter focuses on containers and the inversion of control patterns that are at the heart of the lightweight containers we use today. You learn what a container is, what services it offers, and what makes a container lightweight. You also learn how the inversion of control pattern arises and its close relationship with dependency injection terms. The chapter concludes with an examination of two different dependency injection methods and their pros and cons.

POJO PROGRAMMING MODEL

POJO means Plain Old Java Objects. The name was first coined by Martin Fowler, Rebecca Parsons, and Josh MacKenzie to give regular Java objects an exciting-sounding name. It represents a programming trend that aims to simplify the coding, testing, and deployment phases of Java applications—especially enterprise Java applications.

You'll have a better understanding of what problems the POJO programming model solves if you first understand what problems the old EJB programming model had.

Problems of the Old EJB Programming Model

The Enterprise JavaBeans (EJB) technology was first announced around 1997. It offered a distributed business component model combined with a runtime platform that provided all the necessary middleware services those EJB components needed for their execution. It was a main specification under the J2EE specification umbrella at the time.

Many people were really excited by the promise of the EJB technology and J2EE platform. EJBs were offering a component model that would let developers focus only on the business side of the system while ignoring the middleware requirements, such as wiring of components, transaction management, persistence operations, security, resource pooling, threading, distribution, remoting, and so on. Developers were told that services for middleware requirements could be easily added into the system whenever there was any need of them. Everything seemed good and very promising on paper, but things didn't go well in practice.

The EJB 2.x specification required that the component interface and business logic implementation class extend interfaces from the EJB framework package. These requirements created a tight coupling between the developer-written code and the interface classes from the EJB framework package. It also required the implementation of several unnecessary callback methods, such as `ejbCreate`, `ejbPassivate`, and `ejbActivate`, which are not directly related to the main design goal of EJB.

To develop an EJB component, developers had to write at least three different classes—one for home, one for remote interfaces, and one for business objects, as shown here:

```
public interface PetClinicService extends EJBObject {
  public void saveOwner(Owner owner) throws RemoteException;
}


public interface PetClinicServiceHome extends EJBHome {
  public PetClinicService create() throws RemoteException, CreateException;
```

```
  }

  public class PetClinicServiceBean implements SessionBean {
    private SessionContext sessionContext;
    public void ejbCreate() {
    }
    public void ejbRemove() {
    }
    public void ejbActivate() {
    }
    public void ejbPassivate() {
    }
    public void setSessionContext(SessionContext sessionContext) {
      this.sessionContext = sessionContext;
    }
    public void saveOwner() throws java.rmi.RemoteException {
      //implementation of saving owner instance...
    }
  }
```

The preceding code snippet shows the minimum amount of code that needs to be written in order to create an EJB component with only one method using the EJB2 application programming interface (API). Although the remote interface defined the public API of the business object class to the outside world, a non-mandatory requirement in the specification asked that the business object class implementation not depend on the remote interface directly. When developers obeyed this warning, however, they were opening up a possibility that business object class implementation and its public API remote interface would become unsynchronized whenever the method declarations were modified in one of those classes. The solution was to introduce a fourth interface, which was implemented by the business object class and extended by the remote interface to keep the remote interface and the business object class implementation synchronized while not violating this non-mandatory requirement.

There were actually two interfaces that defined the public API of the business object class: the remote and local interfaces. Local interfaces were introduced to the EJB specification when people realized that remote interfaces were causing unnecessary performance overheads in systems in which there were no physically separated layers, and there was no direct access to the EJB layer from another client in the architecture, except through servlets. However, when developers needed to make EJB components remotely available they had to create a remote interface for them. Although there was no direct dependency between the business object class and its remote interface, all public methods of the business object implementation class had to throw `RemoteException`, causing the business object implementation class to depend on EJB and remoting technologies.

Testability was one of the biggest problems of the old EJB programming model. It was almost impossible to test session and entity beans outside the EJB container; for example, inside an integrated development environment (IDE) using JUnit. This is because dependencies of those session beans were satisfied through local or remote interfaces, and it was very hard—but not impossible—to test session beans in a standalone environment. When it came time to run or test entity beans outside the container, things were more difficult because the entity bean classes had to be abstract and their concrete implementations were provided by the EJB container at deployment time. Because of such difficulties, people tried to access the EJBs deployed in the container and test them using in-container test frameworks, such as Cactus. Nevertheless, such solutions were far from the simplicity and speed of running tests within a standalone environment by right-clicking and selecting Run As JUnit Test.

The deployment process was another time-consuming and error-prone phase of the EJB programming model. Developers used deployment descriptor files in XML format to deploy developed EJB components, but configuring their middleware requirements, such as transaction semantics, security requirements, and so on, caused those files to become several hundred lines long. Developers usually were trying to maintain the files by hand, and it was quite easy to make simple typos in package or class names, and those errors wouldn't be noticed until deployment time.

The following code snippet contains two EJB definitions, one depending on the other, and it includes a container-managed transaction configuration as well. Imagine how things can go wrong when you have dozens of other EJB definitions, each having its own dependencies, transaction management, security configurations, and so on:

```xml
<ejb-jar>
    <display-name>PetClinicEJB2</display-name>
    <enterprise-beans>
        <session>
            <ejb-name>PetClinicService</ejb-name>
            <home>com.example.PetClinicServiceHome</home>
            <remote>com.example.PetClinicService</remote>
            <ejb-class>com.example.PetClinicServiceImpl</ejb-class>
            <session-type>Stateless</session-type>
            <transaction-type>Container</transaction-type>
            <resource-ref>
                <res-ref-name>jdbc/ds</res-ref-name>
                <res-type>javax.sql.DataSource</res-type>
                <res-auth>Container</res-auth>
            </resource-ref>
        </session>
        <message-driven>
            <ejb-name>MessageSubscriber</ejb-name>
            <ejb-class>com.example.MessageSubscriber</ejb-class>
            <transaction-type>Container</transaction-type>
            <message-destination-type>javax.jms.Topic</message-destination-type>
            <ejb-ref>
                <ejb-ref-name>ejb/PetClinicService</ejb-ref-name>
                <ejb-ref-type>Session</ejb-ref-type>
                <home>com.example.PetClinicServiceHome</home>
                <remote>com.example.PetClinicService</remote>
                <ejb-link>PetClinicService</ejb-link>
            </ejb-ref>
        </message-driven>
    </enterprise-beans>

    <assembly-descriptor>
        <container-transaction>
            <method>
                <ejb-name>PetClinicService</ejb-name>
                <method-name>saveOwner</method-name>
            </method>
            <trans-attribute>Required</trans-attribute>
```

```
        </container-transaction>
    </assembly-descriptor>
</ejb-jar>
```

One very common task while coding EJBs was to access the Java Naming and Directory Interface (JNDI) context in the J2EE environment and perform object lookups so that necessary dependencies to other EJBs and `DataSource` instances could be satisfied. However, this was causing the EJB component to become tightly coupled with the container, and unit testing was hard to perform because of this environmental dependency. The following code snippets show how an EJB home object and `javax.sql.DataSource` are looked up from a JNDI repository:

```
try {
    InitialContext context = new InitialContext();
    PetClinicServiceHome petClinicServiceHome = (PetClinicServiceHome)
        context.lookup("java:/comp/env/ejb/PetClinicService");
    PetClinicService petClinicService = petClinicServiceHome.create();
    //you can now access business methods of the component...
} catch (NamingException e) {
    throw new RuntimeException(e);
}


try {
    InitialContext context = new InitialContext();
    DataSource ds = (DataSource)context.lookup("java:/comp/env/jdbc/ds");
    //you can now obtain JDBC Connections via DataSource object...
} catch (NamingException e) {
    throw new RuntimeException(e);
}
```

Actually, JNDI lookup can be considered an early form of dependency injection, but, due to its pull-based nature, it was difficult to isolate components during unit testing because of the dependency to the JNDI context.

Another problem of the old EJB programming model was that it diverted developers toward the procedural programming style. Application behavior in this style of programming is mainly handled within some methods, while data from and to those methods is carried with dumb domain model objects. Unfortunately, data and behavior are separated from each other and are not in a cohesive form in such a case. This is definitely a divergence from the object-oriented programming perspective in which one of the important characteristics is encapsulation of data together with the related behavior. After all, you are using an object-oriented programming language called Java, and you want to take advantage of all its abilities, don't you?

The main reason for such a paradigm shift, while using an object-oriented language, was the EJB programming model. People usually were developing session- and message-driven beans that were stateless, monolithic, and heavyweight components in which all the business logic was implemented with data access operations inside them. Entity EJBs were expected to represent the domain model, but they had some subtle deficiencies that prevented them from being used at all. For example, inheritance support was too limited, and recursive calls within entity beans were not supported; it was not possible to transfer the entity bean instances as session and message-driven bean method inputs and return values, and so on.

People might think that procedural style is not a big problem for scenarios in which business logic is simple. However, things don't stay simple in real-life enterprise application projects. As new require-ments come along, things become more complex and written code grows to be more and more of a maintenance headache. The pro-cedural style of programming that was promoted by the old EJB programming model caused the creation and use of dumb domain objects, which were acting purely as data transfer objects between the application layers and the network. Martin Fowler coined the term *anemic domain model* for such problematic domain objects. Anemic blood is missing vital ingredients; similarly, an anemic domain model is also limited to only data transfer and persistence-related operations, and it contains hardly any behavioral code. Unfortunately, the old EJB programming model was not able to enforce operating on a fine-grained and rich object model behind a coarse-grained component model.

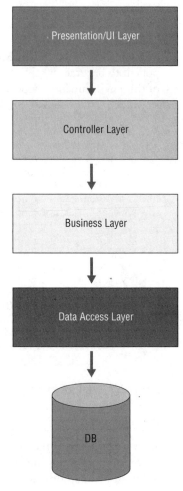

Enterprise applications usually have layered architectures. They are mainly composed of the web, service, and data access layers. Figure 1-1 shows those logical layers and the relationships between each.

Each layer should only know and interact with the layer just beneath it. That way, upper layers aren't affected by changes made within other layers upon which they don't directly depend. It also becomes possible to easily replace layers because only one layer depends on another, and only that dependent layer will have to be changed if there is a need.

It is a desirable and correct approach to divide the system into sev-eral logical layers. However, this doesn't mean that there should always be a one-to-one correspondence between physical layers. Unfortunately, having an EJB container caused those web and ser-vice layers to work using remote method invocation (RMI), which is practically equivalent to having separate physical layers. Hence, servlet and JavaServer Pages (JSP) components in the web layer have complex and performance-degrading interactions with the EJB com-ponents in the service layers. Apart from inefficient network interac-

FIGURE 1-1

tion, developers also experienced class- and resource-loading issues. The reason for these issues were that the EJB container used a different `ClassLoader` instance than the web container.

Figure 1-2 shows a typical physical layering of a J2EE application. The application server has separate web and EJB containers. Therefore, although they are located in the same server instance, web components have to interact with EJB components as if they are in different phys-ical servers using RMI. It is observed in many enterprise Java applications that RMI calls from the web to the service layers create an unnecessary performance cost over time when the web and EJB layers are located in the same physical machine, and the EJB layer is only accessed from the web layers. As a result, local interfaces were introduced to get rid of RMI between those layers.

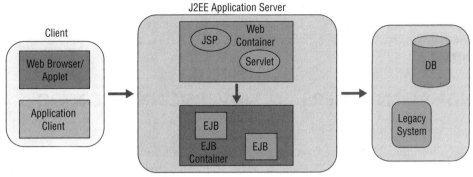

FIGURE 1-2

The "write once and run everywhere" slogan was very popular at those times, and people expected it to be true among J2EE environments as well. However, there were lots of missing and open issues in EJB and J2EE specifications, so many enterprise projects had to develop solutions specific to their application servers. Every application server had its own legacy set of features, and you had to perform server-specific configurations, or code against a server-specific API to make your application run in the target environment. Actually, the slogan had turned into "write once and debug everywhere," and this was a common joke among J2EE developers.

Most of the aforementioned problems were addressed in the EJB 3 and EJB 3.1 specifications. The most important point during those improvements is that the POJO programming model was taken as a reference by those newer EJB specifications. Session and message-driven beans are still available but much simpler now, and entity beans are transformed into POJO-based domain objects with the Java Persistence API (JPA). It is now much easier to implement, test, and deploy them. The EJB programming model has become more and like the POJO programming model over time.

Certainly, the biggest contribution to improve the EJB component model and J2EE environment has come from POJO-based, lightweight frameworks, such as Hibernate and Spring. We can safely say that the EJB programming model mostly was inspired by those frameworks, especially Spring.

Benefits of the POJO Programming Model

The most important advantage of the POJO programming model is that coding application classes is very fast and simple. This is because classes don't need to depend on any particular API, implement any special interface, or extend from a particular framework class. You do not have to create any special callback methods until you really need them.

Because the POJO-based classes don't depend on any particular API or framework code, they can easily be transferred over the network and used between layers. Therefore, you don't need to create separate data transfer object classes in order to carry data over the network.

You don't need to deploy your classes into any container or wait for long deployment cycles so that you can run and test them. You can easily test your classes within your favorite IDE using JUnit. You don't need to employ in-container testing frameworks like Cactus to perform integration unit tests.

The POJO programming model lets you code with an object-oriented perspective instead of a pro-cedural style. It becomes possible to reflect the problem domain exactly to the solution domain. Business logic can be handled over a more fine-grained model, which is also richer in terms of behavioral aspects.

LIGHTWEIGHT CONTAINERS AND INVERSION OF CONTROL (IOC)

Despite all the difficulties and disadvantages of the old EJB programming model, there were still some attractive points in the platform that caused many people to develop enterprise Java applica-tions and deploy them into J2EE application servers. It was very important that several middleware services crucial for applications to work were readily provided by the J2EE environment, and devel-opers were able to utilize them in their applications. For example, the following actions are indepen-dent from business logic, and it's important that they are provided by a J2EE platform:

➤ Handling database connections outside the application codebase

➤ Enabling pooling capabilities, if necessary

➤ Performing transaction management with declarative means

➤ Working with a ready-to-use transaction management infrastructure

➤ Creating and wiring of components in the application

➤ Applying security constraints on the system

➤ Dealing with thread and scheduling issues

Lightweight Containers

Some people were developing their applications without using EJBs while still leveraging many of those middleware features mentioned earlier. On the other hand, they usually perceived that they had to deploy their application to a full-featured J2EE application server only so that they could leverage those middleware services. This was quite a wrong opinion at the time. It is technically pos-sible to develop an enterprise application without using a container at all. In that case, however, you need to handle the creating and wiring of components and implement required middleware services yourself. These tasks will definitely distract you from dealing solely with business requirements of the system, and delay the completion time of it.

Therefore, in practice it is much better to have an environment by which all those components will be created and wired and those required middleware services will be provided. Such an environ-ment is called a *container.* The Java EE platform provides several such containers, each specialized with services required by a particular layer in the application. For example, the Servlet container creates and manages components of the web layer of an application, such as Servlets, JSPs, Filters, and so on. The EJB container, on the other hand, focuses on the business layer of the application and manages the EJB components of it. Similar to the Java EE platform, the Spring Container is also a container in which components of an application are created, wired with each other, and the middleware services are provided in a lightweight manner.

When we talk about containers, it is expected that any container should be capable of providing several basic services to components managed in its environment. According to the seminal book *Expert One-on-One J2EE Development Without EJB* by Rod Johnson and Jürgen Höller (Wrox, 2004), those expected services can be listed as follows:

- ➤ Life-cycle management
- ➤ Dependency resolution
- ➤ Component lookup
- ➤ Application configuration

In addition to those features, it will be very useful if the container is able to provide following middleware services:

- ➤ Transaction management
- ➤ Security
- ➤ Thread management
- ➤ Object and resource pooling
- ➤ Remote access for components
- ➤ Management of components through a JMX-like API
- ➤ Extendibility and customizability of container

A *lightweight container* includes all of these features, but doesn't require application code to depend on its own API. That is, it doesn't have invasive character, its startup time is very fast, it doesn't need to be deployed into a full-featured Java EE application server to be able to provide those services, and deploying components into it is a trivial process. The Spring Application Framework is one of the most prominent lightweight containers in the enterprise world.

Inversion of Control (IoC)

One of the most important benefits containers that provide with components they manage is pluggable architecture. Components implement some interfaces, and they also access services provided by other components they need through similar interfaces. They never know concrete implementation classes of their services. Therefore, it becomes very easy to replace any component in the system with a different implementation. The job of a container is to create those components and their dependent services and wire them together.

Dependent components are never instantiated using a new operator within component classes. They are injected into the component by the container instance at run time. Hence, control of dependencies is moved out of components to the container. This pattern, therefore, is called *Inversion of Control*, or IoC for short. IoC is an important concept in frameworks generally, and is best understood through the Hollywood principle of "Don't call us; we'll call you."

IoC is one of the fundamental features that is expected to be provided by any container. It has basically two forms: dependency lookup and dependency injection.

In *dependency lookup*, the container provides callback methods to the components it manages, and the components interact with the container and acquire their dependencies explicitly within those callback methods. In such a scenario, there is usually a lookup context that is used to access dependent components and other resources managed by the container.

In *dependency injection*, components are provided with suitable constructors or setter methods so that the container can inject dependent components. There is hardly ever an explicit lookup performed within components. Most of the time dependencies are injected during creation of components through those methods.

The method used during the early years of J2EE corresponds to dependency lookup. The lookup context mentioned earlier was also called the JNDI context in this environment. EJB components and other resources such as JDBC DataSource and JMS ConnectionFactory were accessed through that JNDI context. Figure 1-3 depicts explicit interaction of various parts with the JNDI repository in the J2EE platform via JNDI API.

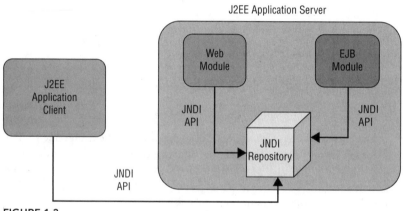

FIGURE 1-3

With the advent of the Spring Application Framework and other lightweight IoC frameworks, the dependency injection method has become popular. In this scenario, how components are instantiated and what dependent components they need are defined using a container's own configuration mechanism. It is the job of the container to process this configuration information to instantiate necessary components and wire up their dependencies at run time. During the evolution process of J2EE toward Java EE, explicit dependency lookup using JNDI has been transformed into the implicit dependency injection method. Today, when IoC is mentioned, it is usually understood as dependency injection among developers.

DEPENDENCY INJECTION

The fundamental principle of dependency injection is that application objects should not be responsible for looking up the resources or collaborators on which they depend. Instead, an IoC container should handle object creation and dependency injection, resulting in the externalization of resource lookup from application code to the container.

Dependency injection has several benefits to the overall system. First of all, lookup logic is completely removed from application code, and dependencies can be injected into the target component in a pluggable manner. Components don't know the location or class of their dependencies. Therefore, unit testing of such components becomes very easy because there is no environmental dependency like the JNDI context, and dependent components can easily be mocked and wired up to the component in the test case. Configuration of the application for different environments also becomes very easy and achievable without code modification because no concrete class dependencies exist within components. There is no dependence on the container API. Code can be moved from one container to another, and it should still work without any modification in the codebase. There is no requirement to implement any special interfaces at all. Written classes are just plain Java objects, and it is not necessary to deploy those components to make them run.

Two dependency injection methods can be used. One is constructor injection, and the other is setter injection. A good container should be able to support both at the same time, and should allow mixing them.

Setter Injection

The setter methods are invoked immediately after the object is instantiated by the container. The injection occurs during the component creation or initialization phase, which is performed much earlier in the process than handling business method calls. Thus, there are no threading issues related with calling those setter methods. Setter methods are part of the JavaBean specification, so that they allow the outside world to change collaborators and property values of components. Those JavaBean properties are also used to externalize simple properties such as int or boolean values. This simplifies the code and makes it reusable in a variety of environments.

The most important advantage of setter injection is that it allows re-configurability of the component after its creation. The component's dependencies can be changed at run time. Many existing classes can already be used with standard JavaBean-style programming. In other words, they offer getter and setter methods to access their properties. For example, Jakarta Commons DBCP DataSource provides a commonly used DataSource implementation, and it can be managed via its JavaBean properties within the container. It's possible to use the standard JavaBeans property-editor mechanism for type conversions whenever necessary. For example, a String value given in configuration can easily be converted into a necessary typed value, or a location can be resolved into a resource instance, and so on. If there is a corresponding getter for each setter, it becomes possible to obtain the current state of the component and save it to restore for a later time. If the component has default values for some or all of its properties, it can be configured more easily using setter injection. You can still optionally provide some dependencies of it as well.

The biggest disadvantage of setter injection is that not all necessary dependencies may be injected before use, which leaves the component in a partially configured state. In some cases, the order of invocation of setter methods might be important, and this is not expressed in the component's contract. Containers provide mechanisms to detect and prevent such inconsistencies in component states during their creation phase.

Constructor Injection

With constructor injection, beans express their dependencies via constructor arguments. In this method, dependencies are injected during component creation. The same thread safety applies for constructor injection as well. You can also inject simple properties such as int or boolean values as constructor arguments.

The biggest advantage of constructor injection is that each managed component in the container is guaranteed to be in a consistent state and ready to use after it is created. Another good point is that the amount of code written with constructor injection will be slightly less compared to the code written when setter injection is used.

The biggest disadvantage of constructor injection is that it won't be possible to reconfigure components after their creation unless they provide a setter for those properties given as constructor arguments. Having several overloaded constructors for different configuration options might be confusing or even unavailable most of the time. Concrete inheritance can also be problematic unless you are careful about overriding all of the constructors in the superclass.

Setter or Constructor Injection

Both methods have advantages as well as disadvantages, and it is not possible to use only one method for any application. You might have classes especially written by third parties that don't have constructors that accept suitable arguments for your configuration case. Therefore, you might first create a component with an available constructor that accepts arguments close to your needs, and then inject other dependencies with setter methods. If the components need to be reconfigurable at run time, having setters for their specific properties will be mandatory in that case. IoC containers are expected to allow developers to mix the two types of dependency injection methods for the same component within the application configuration.

SUMMARY

In this chapter, you first learned the problems of the old-school EJB programming model that caused many enterprise Java projects to fail completely—or at least fail to satisfy their promises to some degree. The main problems of the old EJB programming model was that developers had to write several interfaces to create a business component, tight coupling between EJB and J2EE technologies was necessary, you couldn't run components outside the J2EE platform, there was difficulty in unit testing outside the container, long and complex develop-package-deploy-test cycles were required, and the characteristics and limitations of J2EE technologies required promotion of the procedural style of programming. Then you found out how those problems led to the creation of the POJO programming model, how the POJO programming model solves the problems of the EJB programming model, and how the POJO programming model helped J2EE to evolve into the new Java EE environment.

This chapter discussed why so many people insisted on using J2EE technologies and tried to deploy their enterprise applications despite all those obstacles in the J2EE environment. After identifying the attractive points of the J2EE platform, we defined what a container is, listed fundamental features a container should offer to its applications, and identified what makes a container lightweight by looking at its characteristics.

The last part of the chapter focused on what IoC is, and what any container should offer as its core services. We discussed how IoC helps make applications more modular and pluggable. The chapter wrapped up with an explanation of dependency injection, which is a form of IoC, and its two different types: setter injection and constructor injection.

EXERCISES

You can find possible solutions to the following exercises in Appendix A.

1. Investigate the in-container test frameworks available today. What are their biggest advantages and disadvantages compared to testing outside the container?

2. What IoC method is used by the new EJB programming model today?

3. Which dependency injection method can handle "circular dependencies" and which cannot?

▶ WHAT YOU LEARNED IN THIS CHAPTER

TOPIC	KEY POINTS
POJO	Plain Old Java Objects, a term devised to infer Java classes that don't depend on any environment-specific classes or interfaces, and don't need any special environment to run in.
EJB	Enterprise JavaBeans, the distributed business component model of the J2EE platform.
J2EE, Java EE	Java 2 Enterprise Edition, an umbrella specification that brings several different technologies together and forms the enterprise Java environment. Java Enterprise Edition (Java EE) is its newer name after Java release 5.
Container, EJB Container, Web Container	An environment in which components are created and wired together in addition to utilizing middleware services offered by the container.
Middleware services	Requirements that appear in every application, independent of business requirements such as transaction, persistence, security, remoting, threading, connection and resource pooling, caching, validation, and clustering.
Home interface	Special interface that needs to be implemented in the old EJB programming model so that clients can obtain a handle of an EJB component remotely.
Remote interface	An interface that needs to be provided in the EJB programming model so that clients can invoke business functions of an EJB component remotely.
Local interface	Similar to the remote interface but derived for efficient interaction between the web layer and the EJB layer, which sit together in the same application server and JVM.
Callback methods	Methods that are implemented in the business implementation class of the EJB component and invoked by the container to let the component interact with the environment.
JNDI context	Context available in every Java EE environment in which objects are managed with their names and attributes and are accessible using JNDI.
Inversion of Control (IoC)	Pattern that represents control of managing dependencies in a component whose dependency management is taken out of it and given to the environment—in other words, the container.
Dependency lookup	A form of IoC that is based on callback methods, invoked by a container at specific phases, and lets a component look up its dependencies using a lookup context, like the JNDI context in the J2EE environment.

TOPIC	KEY POINTS
Dependency injection	A second and more popular form of IoC in which components define their dependencies and the container wires them during component creation time.
Setter injection	Dependency injection method that uses JavaBean specification setter methods.
Constructor injection	Dependency injection method that uses constructors.

2

Dependency Injection with Spring

WHAT YOU WILL LEARN IN THIS CHAPTER:

➤ Configuring and using Spring Container

➤ Using different types of configuration metadata to configure Spring Container

➤ Understanding dependency resolution

➤ Learning the advantages and disadvantages of autowiring

➤ Performing explicit bean lookups in Spring Container

➤ Learning different bean instantiation methods

➤ Understanding scoped beans and available scopes

➤ Learning how lazy bean creation works

➤ Understanding life-cycle callbacks

➤ Using bean definition profiles to create conditional bean configurations

CODE DOWNLOAD *The wrox.com code downloads for this chapter are found at* www.wrox.com/go/beginningspring *on the Download Code tab. The code is in the Chapter 2 download and individually named according to the names throughout the chapter.*

This chapter explains how you can apply dependency injection using the Spring Application Framework. You first look at different formats of configuration metadata necessary for the Spring Container to create and wire up objects in the system. The chapter includes examples for XML-, annotation-based, and Java-based configuration metadata formats. The chapter covers the two dependency injection methods in detail—setter injection and constructor injection—and explains how the dependency resolution process works in the container. You find out how you can override bean definitions, learn what autowiring means, and discover different modes of autowiring that are available in the container.

The lifetimes of Spring-managed beans can be different according to their scope definitions. This chapter lists the scopes supported by the Spring Container and explains how different scopes behave in the system. You can create Spring beans either during startup (*eager initialization*), or delay their creation until they are needed in the system (*lazy initialization*). In this chapter you find out how those bean initialization methods work, the pros and cons of each, and the different bean instantiation methods provided by the Spring Container.

The chapter wraps up with coverage of new features, such as bean definition profiles and environment abstraction introduced in Spring 3.1, which helps you conditionally handle bean definitions according to the runtime platform of the application or its environment.

SPRING IOC CONTAINER

The core of the Spring Application Framework is its Inversion of Control (IoC) Container. Its job is to instantiate, initialize, and wire up objects of the application, as well as provide lots of other features available in Spring throughout an object's lifetime. The objects that form the backbone of your application, and are managed by Spring Container, are called *beans*. They are ordinary Java objects—also known as POJOs—but they are instantiated, assembled by the Spring Container, and managed within it.

Configuration Metadata

The Spring Container expects information from you to instantiate beans and to specify how to wire them together. This information is called *configuration metadata*. Together with this configuration metadata, the Spring Container takes classes written in the application and then creates and assembles beans in it. Figure 2-1 depicts this process.

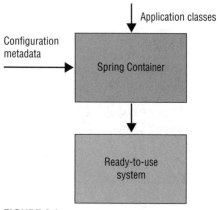

FIGURE 2-1

The traditional form of configuration metadata is XML; however, it is not the only form. Annotation-based and Java-based configuration metadata options are also available. The nice thing is that the Spring Container is independent of the configuration metadata format. You can use any format you like and even mix them together in the same application. The following code is an example of XML configuration metadata:

```xml
<?xml version="1.0" encoding="UTF-8"?>
<beans xmlns="http://www.springframework.org/schema/beans"
    xmlns:xsi="http://www.w3.org/2001/XMLSchema-instance"
    xsi:schemaLocation="http://www.springframework.org/schema/beans
    http://www.springframework.org/schema/beans/spring-beans.xsd">

    <bean id="accountService" class="com.wiley.beginningspring.ch2.~CA
        AccountServiceImpl">
          <property name="accountDao" ref="accountDao"/>
    </bean>

    <bean id="accountDao" class="com.wiley.beginningspring.ch2.~CA
        AccountDaoInMemoryImpl">
          <!-- dependencies of accountDao will be defined here -->
    </bean>

</beans>
```

In this code, all beans are defined within the `<beans>` element, and each bean is defined using the `<bean>` element. Beans have names defined with the `id` attribute. They are accessed using their names either from the application or from another bean definition in the configuration metadata. In the preceding example, the `accountService` bean has a property called `accountDao`, and this property is satisfied with the `accountDao` bean defined in the configuration.

The next code snippet is an example of annotation-based configuration metadata:

```java
@Service("accountService")
public class AccountServiceImpl implements AccountService {
    private AccountDao accountDao;

    @Autowired
    public void setAccountDao(AccountDao accountDao) {
        this.accountDao = accountDao;
    }
}

@Repository("accountDao")
public class AccountDaoInMemoryImpl implements AccountDao {

}
```

Here, beans are defined using Java annotations. The `@Service` and `@Repository` annotations are used to define two beans. They are actually a more specialized form of the `@Component` annotation. The `@Autowired` annotation is used to specify bean dependency that will be injected by the Spring Container at run time. Annotation-based configuration metadata was introduced with Spring 2.5.

The following code snippet exemplifies Java-based configuration metadata:

```
@Configuration
public class Ch2BeanConfiguration {

    @Bean
    public AccountService accountService() {
        AccountServiceImpl bean = new AccountServiceImpl();
        bean.setAccountDao(accountDao());
        return bean;
    }

    @Bean
    public AccountDao accountDao() {
        AccountDaoInMemoryImpl bean = new AccountDaoInMemoryImpl();
        //depedencies of accountDao bean will be injected here...
        return bean;
    }
}
```

You define beans in a Java class annotated with @Configuration. Within that class each public method marked with the @Bean annotation corresponds to a bean definition. Beans are instantiated by invoking an appropriate constructor from their concrete classes, then their dependencies are obtained by calling other bean definition methods, and those obtained dependencies are injected into the bean. Java-based configuration metadata was introduced with Spring 3.0.

In a big project, it's a good idea to divide configuration metadata into several different files so that it can be managed easily and can be managed by different developers at the same time. This division usually reflects the layers of the application. You create a separate bean definition file or class for each layer in the application, and you also create some additional bean definition files or classes for other container-specific configuration tasks as well. Therefore, for a typical web application project that's developed using Spring, it is very common to see bean definition files or classes similar to these:

➤ Beans that operate in the web/presentation layer of the application are defined in the beans-web.xml file or ConfigurationForWeb class.

➤ Beans that operate in the service/business layer of the application are defined in the beans-service.xml file or the ConfigurationForService class.

➤ Beans that operate in the data access layer of the application are defined in the beans-dao.xml file or the ConfigurationForDao class.

➤ Beans that are necessary for several container-specific features to be activated are defined in the beans-config.xml file or the ConigurationForConfig class.

➤ Beans that are used for security requirements of the application are defined in the beans-security.xml file or the ConfigurationForSecurity class.

Your application doesn't have to have this exact collection of files. The number and granularity of configuration metadata files varies according to the architecture and specific requirements of the target application. However, the files in this list are a good starting point, and you can always add new ones and divide existing ones according to your needs.

Configuring and Using the Container

The Spring Container is also a Java object, which is created in the application at some specific point and then allowed to manage the rest of the application. You can instantiate the Spring Container in basically two different ways. In standalone applications, you use the programmatic approach. In web applications, on the other hand, the declarative approach is preferable with the help of some configuration within the web.xml file.

The following Try It Out shows how the Spring Container can be created and used in a standalone environment using Java-based configuration. We try to employ a simple form of layered architecture by defining beans corresponding to each layer illustrated in the Figure 2-2:

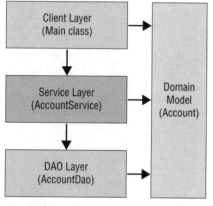

FIGURE 2-2

In a layered architecture, each layer only talks to the layer beneath it, and they don't know the real implementations of the beans they use from the layer they interact. Such an architectural approach helps developers to make the application more modular and testable as well. Developers can create different implementations corresponding to each layer, and they can replace them without causing any problem in the upper layers as long as they stick with the contract declared by the interfaces in each layer. Maintenance of the application also becomes easier because they only need to fix the layer in which the problem exists. The only other layer that can be affected by this problem and its fix might be the layer that is just one level above it.

TRY IT OUT   Creating and Using the Spring Container in a Standalone Environment with Java-Based Configuration

In this Try It Out, you create and use an ApplicationContext with Spring's Java-based configuration in the standalone environment. You can find the source code within the project named java-based-configuration in the spring-book-ch2.zip file. To begin, follow these steps:

1. Create a Maven project with the following command:

```
mvn archetype:generate -DarchetypeGroupId=org.apache.maven.archetypes
    -DgroupId=com.wiley.beginningspring -DartifactId=spring-book-ch2
```

2. Add the following Spring dependencies to your `pom.xml` file if they are not already available there:

```xml
<dependency>
    <groupId>org.springframework</groupId>
    <artifactId>spring-context</artifactId>
    <version>4.0.5.RELEASE</version>
</dependency>
```

3. Create a package named `com.wiley.beginning.spring.ch2`, and then create the following Java classes in it:

```java
public class Account {
    private long id;
    private String ownerName;
    private double balance;
    private Date accessTime;

    //getters & setters...
}

public interface AccountDao {
    public void insert(Account account);
    public void update(Account account);
    public void update(List<Account> accounts);
    public void delete(long accountId);
    public Account find(long accountId);
    public List<Account> find(List<Long> accountIds);
    public List<Account> find(String ownerName);
    public List<Account> find(boolean locked);
}

public class AccountDaoInMemoryImpl implements AccountDao {

    private Map<Long,Account> accountsMap = new HashMap<>();

    {
        Account account1 = new Account();
        account1.setId(1L);
        account1.setOwnerName("John");
        account1.setBalance(10.0);

        Account account2 = new Account();
        account2.setId(2L);
        account2.setOwnerName("Mary");
        account2.setBalance(20.0);

        accountsMap.put(account1.getId(), account1);
        accountsMap.put(account2.getId(), account2);

    }


    @Override
    public void update(Account account) {
        accountsMap.put(account.getId(), account);
```

```
        }

        @Override
        public Account find(long accountId) {
            return accountsMap.get(accountId);
        }

        //other method implementations
    }

    public interface AccountService {
        public void transferMoney(
            long sourceAccountId, long targetAccountId, double amount);
        public void depositMoney(long accountId, double amount) throws Exception;
        public Account getAccount(long accountId);
    }

    public class AccountServiceImpl implements AccountService {
        private AccountDao accountDao;

        public void setAccountDao(AccountDao accountDao) {
            this.accountDao = accountDao;
        }

        @Override
        public void transferMoney(
            long sourceAccountId, long targetAccountId, double amount) {
            Account sourceAccount = accountDao.find(sourceAccountId);
            Account targetAccount = accountDao.find(targetAccountId);
            sourceAccount.setBalance(sourceAccount.getBalance() - amount);
            targetAccount.setBalance(targetAccount.getBalance() + amount);
            accountDao.update(sourceAccount);
            accountDao.update(targetAccount);
        }

        @Override
        public void depositMoney(long accountId, double amount) throws Exception {
            Account account = accountDao.find(accountId);
            account.setBalance(account.getBalance() + amount);
            accountDao.update(account);
        }

        @Override
        public Account getAccount(long accountId) {
            return accountDao.find(accountId);
        }
    }
```

4. Create the following Java-based bean definition class:

```
@Configuration
public class Ch2BeanConfiguration {

    @Bean
    public AccountService accountService() {
```

```
            AccountServiceImpl bean = new AccountServiceImpl();
            bean.setAccountDao(accountDao());
            return bean;
        }

        @Bean
        public AccountDao accountDao() {
            AccountDaoInMemoryImpl bean = new AccountDaoInMemoryImpl();
            //depedencies of accountDao bean will be injected here...
            return bean;
        }
    }
```

5. Create a Main class with the main method and instantiate the Spring Container by giving the Java-based configuration class you created in the previous step as the constructor argument:

```
public class Main {

    public static void main(String[] args) {
        AnnotationConfigApplicationContext applicationContext =
new AnnotationConfigApplicationContext(Ch2BeanConfiguration.class);

    }
}
```

6. Access the accountService bean from within the Spring Container, and use it like so:

```
        AccountService accountService = applicationContext.getBean("accountService",
AccountService.class);

        System.out.println("Before money transfer");
        System.out.println("Account 1 balance :" + accountService.getAccount(1).getBalance());
        System.out.println("Account 2 balance :" + accountService.getAccount(2).getBalance());

        accountService.transferMoney(1, 2, 5.0);

        System.out.println("After money transfer");
        System.out.println("Account 1 balance :" + accountService.getAccount(1).getBalance());
        System.out.println("Account 2 balance :" + accountService.getAccount(2).getBalance());
```

How It Works

You first created a domain class named Account. Then you created the AccountDao interface with the AccountDaoInMemoryImpl class—which corresponds to the DAO layer—and the AccountService interface with the AccountServiceImpl class—which corresponds to the service layer. AccountService declares a transferMoney method, which moves a given amount between two Account objects identified by their accountIds. The AccountServiceImpl class needs to first obtain those two Account objects and update them after the money transfer operation. Therefore, AccountServiceImpl has a dependency to the AccountDao interface, which declares methods to perform basic persistence operations on a given Account, and finder methods to find Account instances using some query parameters.

You then created a Spring bean definition class named `Ch2BeanConfiguration` and marked it with the `org.springframework.context.annotation.Configuration` annotation. This annotation tells Spring that this class contains configuration metadata as well as itself as a bean. Within the configuration class, you created two factory methods marked with the `org.springframework.context.annotation.Bean` annotation. Those methods are called by the Spring Container during bootstrap, and their returning values are treated as Spring-managed beans. The method name is accepted as the bean name by default. Within a factory method, you created a bean using its concrete class and returned it after setting its necessary dependencies by calling its setter methods. Dependencies can also be given as constructor arguments.

Notice that the return type of the factory methods are defined as interfaces instead of concrete classes. Using interfaces is not mandatory, but it's very useful to let the system easily be configured with different bean implementation classes. For example, you can add another bean definition with a new configuration metadata that returns a Java Database Connectivity (JDBC) implementation of the `AccountDao` interface, and your `AccountService` bean keeps working without any change in its implementation or in its bean definition.

You might notice that the `AccountDao` dependency of the `AccountService` bean is obtained by calling the `accountDao()` method within the `AccountService()` method. If other factory methods were also calling the `accountDao()` method several times, wouldn't there be more than one `accountDao` bean instance in the system, and wouldn't it be a problem if you wanted to have only one instance of those beans as the common case for service and repository beans as well? The answer to these questions is no, there won't be several bean instances for a bean definition in the system. By default, each bean has a single instance, which is called *singleton scope*. (Bean scopes are covered in more detail later in this chapter.) At this point, it is enough to know that there will be only one instance of the `accountDao` bean, and several different method calls won't cause any more instances to be created. Spring handles this by extending the `@Configuration` classes dynamically at run time and overriding factory methods with the `@Bean` annotation. Therefore, several calls to a factory method either from within the class or from another `@Configuration` class won't cause any new bean instances to be created after the first call. For consecutive calls, the same bean instance will be returned from factory methods.

The next step was to create the Spring Container instance. As mentioned earlier, it is also a Java object that manages other objects in your application. The `org.springframework.context` `.ApplicationContext` interface represents the Spring Container; in fact, the terms the Spring Container and `ApplicationContext` are often used interchangeably. Several different implementations of the `ApplicationContext` interface are available, distinguished by how and from where those `ApplicationContext` instances process bean configuration metadata files or classes. The `org` `.springframework.context.annotation.AnnotationConfigApplicationContext` class is used to process Java-based configuration metadata classes. Although you have provided only one, you can also provide several configuration classes as input arguments to the `AnnotationConfigApplicationContext` class.

Spring Container (or `ApplicationContext`) is ready to use right after its creation. At this point you may get beans from the Spring Container and use them to fulfill your system requirements. The process of obtaining Spring-managed beans is called "bean lookups." You find out more about bean lookups later in this chapter. Here, it is enough to say that you can obtain a reference to any bean using its name. The `ApplicationContext.getBean()` method is used to perform bean lookups. The type argument next to the bean name is given so that a returned bean instance will be downcasted to that type automatically. After obtaining a reference to the bean, it is possible to invoke any method of the bean contract. You invoked the `transferMoney()` method by giving `accountIds` and `amount` as input parameters.

You can also create XML-based configuration metadata and use it as well. Follow along with the next Try It Out activity to see how it's done.

TRY IT OUT **Creating and Using the Spring Container in a Standalone Environment with XML-Based Configuration**

In this Try It Out, you create a Spring Container using XML-based configuration metadata. You can find the source code within the project named `xml-based-configuration` in the `spring-book-ch2.zip` file. You can continue from the project you created for the earlier Try It Out. To begin, follow these steps:

1. Create an XML bean definition file named `ch2-beans.xml` in the `com.wiley.beginningspring` `.ch2` package with the following content:

```
<?xml version="1.0" encoding="UTF-8"?>
<beans xmlns="http://www.springframework.org/schema/beans"
    xmlns:xsi="http://www.w3.org/2001/XMLSchema-instance"
    xsi:schemaLocation="http://www.springframework.org/schema/beans
    http://www.springframework.org/schema/beans/spring-beans.xsd">

    <bean id="accountService" class="com.wiley.beginningspring.ch2.↵
      AccountServiceImpl">
        <property name="accountDao" ref="accountDao"/>
    </bean>

    <bean id="accountDao" class="com.wiley.beginningspring.ch2.↵
      AccountDaoInMemoryImpl">

    </bean>

</beans>
```

2. Modify the `main` method in the `Main` class and instantiate the Spring Container by giving the XML bean definition file as the constructor argument:

```
public class Main {

    public static void main(String[] args) {
        ClassPathXmlApplicationContext applicationContext = new↵
ClassPathXmlApplicationContext("/com/wiley/beginningspring/ch2/ch2-beans.xml");

    }

}
```

3. Access the `accountService` bean from within the Spring Container, and use it in the same way you did in the previous Try It Out:

```
AccountService accountService = applicationContext.getBean↵
  ("accountService", AccountService.class);

System.out.println("Before money transfer");
System.out.println("Account 1 balance :" + accountService.getAccount(1).↵
```

```
        getBalance());
    System.out.println("Account 2 balance :" + accountService.getAccount(2).↵
        getBalance());

    accountService.transferMoney(1, 2, 5.0);

    System.out.println("After money transfer");
    System.out.println("Account 1 balance :" + accountService.getAccount(1).↵
        getBalance());
    System.out.println("Account 2 balance :" + accountService.getAccount(2).↵
        getBalance());
```

How It Works

You created the `ApplicationContext` instance with an XML bean definition file. In this case,
`org.springframework.context.support.ClassPathXmlApplicationContext` is used to load the
XML configuration metadata files, which reside in the classpath of the application. After creating
`ApplicationContext`, you performed a bean lookup by calling the `ApplicationContext.getBean()`
method and obtained the `accountService` bean. After obtaining the bean, you used it in the same way
as in the previous example.

The next Try It Out gives you the final example about container configuration, which uses Java
annotations. You are going to achieve the same results as before.

TRY IT OUT   Creating and Using the Spring Container in a Standalone
Environment with a Java Annotation-Based Configuration

In this Try It Out, you create the Spring Container using Java annotation-based configuration metadata. The
source code is within the project named `annotation-based-configuration` in the `spring-book-ch2.zip`
file. You can continue from the project you created for the earlier Try It Out. To begin, follow these steps:

1.   Put the `org.springframework.stereotype.Service` and `org.springframework.stereotype`
`.Repository` annotations on top of the `AccountServiceImpl` and `AccountDaoInMemoryImpl`
classes, respectively:

```
@Service
public class AccountServiceImpl implements AccountService {
//...
}

@Repository
public class AccountDaoInMemoryImpl implements AccountDao {
//...
}
```

2.   Put the `org.springframework.beans.factory.annotation.Autowired` annotation on top of
the `setAccountDao()` method in the `AccountServiceImpl` class:

```
@Service
public class AccountServiceImpl implements AccountService {
```

```java
    private AccountDao accountDao;


    @Autowired
    public void setAccountDao(AccountDao accountDao) {
        this.accountDao = accountDao;
    }
//...
}
```

3. Create an XML-based Spring bean configuration file named `ch2-beans.xml` in the `com.wiley` `.beginningspring.ch2` package with the following content:

```xml
<?xml version="1.0" encoding="UTF-8"?>
<beans xmlns="http://www.springframework.org/schema/beans"
    xmlns:xsi="http://www.w3.org/2001/XMLSchema-instance"
    xmlns:context="http://www.springframework.org/schema/context"
    xsi:schemaLocation="http://www.springframework.org/schema/beans
    http://www.springframework.org/schema/beans/spring-beans.xsd
        http://www.springframework.org/schema/context
    http://www.springframework.org/schema/context/spring-context-4.0.xsd">

    <context:component-scan base-package="com.wiley.beginningspring.ch2"/>

</beans>
```

4. Modify the `main` method in the `Main` class and instantiate the Spring Container by giving the bean definition file as the constructor argument:

```java
public class Main {

    public static void main(String[] args) {
        ClassPathXmlApplicationContext applicationContext = new
ClassPathXmlApplicationContext("/com/wiley/beginningspring/ch2/ch2-beans.xml");

    }

}
```

5. Access the `accountServiceImpl` bean from within the Spring Container, and use it in the same way you did in the previous Try It Out:

```java
        AccountService accountService = applicationContext.getBean
          ("accountServiceImpl", AccountService.class);

        System.out.println("Before money transfer");
        System.out.println("Account 1 balance :" + accountService.getAccount(1).
          getBalance());
        System.out.println("Account 2 balance :" + accountService.getAccount(2).
          getBalance());

        accountService.transferMoney(1, 2, 5.0);

        System.out.println("After money transfer");
        System.out.println("Account 1 balance :" + accountService.getAccount(1).
```

```
        getBalance());
    System.out.println("Account 2 balance :" + accountService.getAccount(2).↵
        getBalance());
```

How It Works

You used the `@Service` and `@Repository` annotations to define your Spring-managed beans. They both extend from the `org.springframework.stereotype.Component` annotation. The `@Service` annotation has no special meaning apart from defining a bean from the class it used on top. `@Repository`, on the other hand, enables additional functionality related to Spring data access, which is explained in Chapter 5. By default, the bean names are derived from simple class names with a lowercase initial character. Therefore, your beans have the names `accountServiceImpl` and `accountDaoInMemoryImpl`, respectively. It is also possible to give a specific name with a value attribute in those annotations.

`org.springframework.beans.factory.annotation.Autowired` is used to tell Spring that the specified dependency should be satisfied from within the container if it's available. Therefore, Spring first looks at the input argument type of the setter method onto which the `@Autowired` annotation is placed. It then tries to find a Spring managed bean with that type in the container, and injects it into the target bean by invoking the setter method. You can read about autowiring in detail in the "Autowiring" section later in this chapter.

Spring tries to identify classes that have the `@Component` annotation and its derivations during bootstrap by scanning classes that exist in the classpath. However, you first need to enable this component scan process and narrow the classpath so that the bootstrap doesn't take too much time. Unrelated classes aren't included in the bean creation process, either. Therefore, you put the `<context:component-scan/>` element into the bean configuration file. However, you first need to enable the context namespace capability by adding its schema location directives into the `<beans>` element on top. The Spring namespace feature was introduced in Spring 2.5 to ease the bean definition and configuration process within the container. Each Spring module has its own namespace support and provides several namespace elements for different purposes. The `<context:component-scan/>` element's role is to scan classes in the classpath, create beans with related annotations, and inject their dependencies.

In the last part, you again used `ClasspathXmlApplicationContext` to create the Spring Container and gave `ch2-beans.xml` as the constructor argument into it. It loads the specified XML configuration files from the classpath and performs bootstrap. The container becomes ready to use right after its creation. At this point, you looked up the `accountServiceImpl` bean and used its methods as before.

For Java-based configuration, the `<context:component-scan/>` namespace element has its `org.springframework.context.annotation.ComponentScan` annotation counterpart. It is used at the type level.

DEPENDENCY INJECTION

Chapter 1 defined dependency injection as moving the creation of dependent components out of code and managing them within an IoC Container. Chapter 1 also mentioned two types of dependency injection methods—setter injection and constructor injection—and listed their pros and cons in the application. This chapter explains in detail how dependency injection is performed within the Spring Container.

Setter Injection

Setter injection is performed after a bean instance is created. All properties defined in the configuration metadata of the bean are injected by calling setter methods corresponding to those properties. It is possible to inject other bean dependencies and primitive values, strings, classes, enums, and so on.

References to other beans are specified with the `ref` attribute of the `<property>` element. For example:

```
<bean id="accountService" class="com.wiley.beginningspring.ch2.AccountServiceImpl">
    <property name="accountDao" ref="accountDao"/>
</bean>
```

The `AccountService` bean needs a bean with the type `AccountDao`. Therefore we specified the `accountDao` bean name in the `ref` attribute. If there is no bean with the `accountDao` name in the container, the bootstrap process fails. You can have several property elements in a bean definition, each for a different dependency in the bean, and you don't need to follow any specific order among them.

It is also possible to specify dependency with a `<ref bean=""/>` child element of the `<property>` element as shown in the following code snippet. You can use either the short form or the long form without any difference:

```
<bean id="accountService" class="com.wiley.beginningspring.ch2.AccountServiceImpl">
    <property name="accountDao">
        <ref bean="accountDao"/>
    </property>
</bean>
```

To inject dependency values other than bean references, like `int`, `Boolean`, `String`, `Enum`, and so on, you can use the `value` attribute of the `<property>` element as shown here:

```
<bean id="account1" class="com.wiley.beginningspring.ch2.Account">
    <property name="id" value="1" />
    <property name="ownerName" value="John" />
    <property name="balance" value="10.0"/>
    <property name="locked" value="false" />
</bean>

<bean id="account2" class="com.wiley.beginningspring.ch2.Account">
    <property name="id" value="2" />
    <property name="ownerName" value="Mary" />
    <property name="balance" value="20.0"/>
    <property name="locked" value="false" />
</bean>
```

Spring handles necessary type conversions as much as possible. For example, a `"false"` String value is converted to a `boolean` type and injected into a locked property, or a `"20.0"` String value is first converted into a double and then injected into the `balance` property. Spring achieves this with its built-in property editors, and you can add custom editors to handle other type conversions that Spring cannot handle by default.

Spring allows you to inject `Collection` or `Map` values as well. Their elements can be either straight values, such as `Integer`, `Boolean`, `String` and so on, or references to other beans in the container.

The following code snippet shows how a `Map` typed property can be populated. Similar to a `<map>` element, you can use the `<set>`, `<list>`, or `<array>` elements to populate `Collection` typed properties (and arrays as well):

```
<bean id="accountDao" class="com.wiley.beginningspring.ch2.AccountDaoInMemoryImpl">
    <property name="accountsMap">
        <map>
            <entry key="1" value-ref="account1"/>
            <entry key="2" value-ref="account2"/>
        </map>
    </property>
</bean>
```

Constructor Injection

Constructor injection is performed during component creation. Dependencies are expressed as constructor arguments, and the container identifies which constructor to invoke by looking at types of those constructor arguments specified in the bean definition. The following Try It Out shows how Spring beans can be configured using constructor injection.

TRY IT OUT   Configuring Beans Using Constructor Injection

In this Try It Out, you configure the beans in the Spring Container using constructor injection. You can find the source code within the project named `constructor-injection` in the `spring-book-ch2.zip` file. You can continue from the project you created for the earlier Try It Out. To begin, follow these steps:

1. Change your `AccountServiceImpl` class so that it has the following constructor, which expects an object of type `AccountDao`:

```
public class AccountServiceImpl implements AccountService {
    private AccountDao accountDao;

    public AccountServiceImpl(AccountDao accountDao) {
        this.accountDao = accountDao;
    }
//...
}
```

2. Your `accountService` bean definition using constructor injection should look like this:

```
<?xml version="1.0" encoding="UTF-8"?>
<beans xmlns="http://www.springframework.org/schema/beans"
    xmlns:xsi="http://www.w3.org/2001/XMLSchema-instance"
    xsi:schemaLocation="http://www.springframework.org/schema/beans
    http://www.springframework.org/schema/beans/spring-beans.xsd">

    <bean id="accountService" class="com.wiley.beginningspring.ch2.↵
        AccountServiceImpl">
        <constructor-arg ref="accountDao"/>
    </bean>

    <bean id="accountDao" class="com.wiley.beginningspring.ch2.↵
```

```
        AccountDaoInMemoryImpl">
    </bean>

</beans>
```

3.   Modify the `main` method in the `Main` class and instantiate the Spring Container by giving the XML bean definition file as the constructor argument:

```
public class Main {

    public static void main(String[] args) {
        ClassPathXmlApplicationContext applicationContext = new↵
ClassPathXmlApplicationContext("/com/wiley/beginningspring/ch2/ch2-beans.xml");

    }

}
```

4.   Access the `accountService` bean from within the Spring Container, and use it in the same way you did in the previous Try It Out:

```
AccountService accountService = applicationContext.getBean↵
    ("accountService", AccountService.class);

System.out.println("Before money transfer");
System.out.println("Account 1 balance :" + accountService.getAccount(1).↵
    getBalance());
System.out.println("Account 2 balance :" + accountService.getAccount(2).↵
    getBalance());

accountService.transferMoney(1, 2, 5.0);

System.out.println("After money transfer");
System.out.println("Account 1 balance :" + accountService.getAccount(1).↵
    getBalance());
System.out.println("Account 2 balance :" + accountService.getAccount(2).↵
    getBalance());
```

How It Works

There can be several constructors in the bean definition class. The Spring Container looks at the `<constructor-arg/>` elements in the bean definition, identifies types of dependencies specified using the `<constructor-arg/>` elements, and then tries to find a suitable constructor using Java reflection. The order of the `<constructor-arg/>` elements is not important. After the suitable constructor is identified, Spring Container invokes it by giving dependencies as input argument values.

The rest of the example is completely the same as before. You created `ApplicationContext`, performed bean lookup using the `getBean()` method, and invoked the `moneyTransfer()` method of the `accountService` bean.

Similar to setter injection, you can also provide straight values like `int`, `Boolean`, `String`, `Enum`, and so on, in addition to references to other beans. The `<constructor-arg>` element accepts the `value` attribute to inject those values. The necessary conversions are handled by the Spring Container.

When several `<constructor-arg>` elements are available in a bean definition, their placement order is not important. Spring tries to find a suitable constructor by comparing types of dependencies with argument types of available constructors in the bean class. This can sometimes cause problems. For example, say you have the following three classes: Foo, Bar, and Baz. The Foo class has two constructors that accept objects from the other two types:

```
public class Foo {

    private Bar bar;
    private Baz baz;

    public Foo(Bar bar, Baz baz) {
        this.bar = bar;
        this.baz = baz;
    }

    public Foo(Baz baz, Bar bar) {
        this.bar = bar;
        this.baz = baz;
    }
}

public class Bar {

}

public class Baz {

}
```

When you attempt to create a bean configuration as follows, the Spring Container fails to instantiate the foo bean because it won't be able to identify which constructor to invoke:

```
<bean id="foo" class="com.wiley.beginningspring.ch2.Foo">
    <constructor-arg ref="bar"/>
    <constructor-arg ref="baz"/>
</bean>

<bean id="bar" class="com.wiley.beginningspring.ch2.Bar"/>

<bean id="baz" class="com.wiley.beginningspring.ch2.Baz"/>
```

You need to help the Spring Container a bit, so that it can choose one constructor and create the bean instance using it. You do this by giving an `index` attribute for each `<constructor-arg>` element in the bean definition:

```
<bean id="foo" class="com.wiley.beginningspring.ch2.Foo">
    <constructor-arg ref="bar" index="0"/>
    <constructor-arg ref="baz" index="1"/>
</bean>
```

In a bean definition, you can use both setter injection and constructor injection. Indeed, this type of usage is very common in real-world projects. Beans are first created by invoking suitable constructors based on `<constructor-arg/>` elements, and then other dependencies are injected specified by `<property>` elements:

```
public class Foo {

    private Bar bar;
    private Baz baz;

    public Foo(Bar bar) {
        this.bar = bar;
    }

    public void setBaz(Baz baz) {
        this.baz = baz;
    }
//...
}
```

```xml
<bean id="foo" class="com.wiley.beginningspring.ch2.Foo">
    <constructor-arg ref="bar"/>
    <property name="baz" ref="baz"/>
</bean>
```

Circular Dependencies

One disadvantage of constructor injection is that it cannot handle circular dependencies. If, for example, you have two beans, a and b, and they both have dependencies to each other through their constructors, the Spring Container is not able to instantiate those two beans:

```
public class A {
    private B b;

    public A(B b) {
        this.b = b;
    }
}

public class B {
    private A a;

    public B(A a) {
        this.a = a;
    }
}
```

```xml
<bean id="a" class="com.wiley.beginningspring.ch2.A">
    <constructor-arg ref="b"/>
</bean>

<bean id="b" class="com.wiley.beginningspring.ch2.B">
    <constructor-arg ref="a"/>
</bean>
```

This is because, while the first bean is being created, it expects the second bean to be injected into itself. However, the second bean is also in the creation phase and expecting the first bean as its dependency as well. This results in a `BeanCurrentlyInCreationException` in the application. Setter injection, on the other hand, is able to handle circularity. Although Spring allows circular dependencies using setter injection, some of its other features won't be available for those beans that have circular dependencies. Therefore, in general, it is not advisable to have circular dependencies in your configuration.

Dependency Resolution Process

The Spring Container's bootstrap process can be divided into roughly two main phases. In the first phase, the container processes configuration metadata and builds up bean definitions that exist in the metadata. At this step, it also validates those bean definitions. For example, it checks whether the correct bean references are given to the <property> or <constructor-arg> elements, and so on. However, at this step, beans are not created, and their properties are not injected. In the second phase, bean creations are performed, and then dependency injections are performed. Actually, not all beans are created; only singleton-scoped beans are created during the container bootstrap process. Later in this chapter, the "Bean Scopes" section discusses scopes in detail. The creation of a bean actually triggers a bunch of other dependent beans to be created as well. Those other beans also trigger creation of their dependencies, and so on.

A bean is not injected as a dependency before it is first fully created and its own dependencies are injected. Therefore, you can be sure that bean dependencies that are injected into a bean are fully configured and ready to use within the target bean. An exception for this is related to circular dependencies. As mentioned earlier, circular dependencies can be handled by setter injection, but there's one big deficiency because of the nature of circularity. Circular dependencies need to be injected before they are fully configured. For example, Figure 2-3 illustrates a circular dependency between two bean definitions:

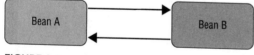

FIGURE 2-3

Let's assume you configured bean a so that bean b is injected into it via setter injection, and bean b is also configured so that bean a is injected into it via setter injection as well. In that case, the Spring Container first creates bean a and then goes to bean definition b to inject it into the bean a and tries to create bean b as well. However, at this step, it notices that bean b has a dependency to bean a, which is already in the creation phase. This time, it returns back to the bean definition a and takes bean a instance to inject it into the bean b. However, dependencies of bean a may not have been fully populated or its creation step is not finished yet. As a result, bean b will have a reference to bean a, which may not be fully configured. Because of this limitation, Spring highly discourages having circular dependencies in an application configuration.

Overriding Bean Definitions

It is possible to override a bean definition in the Spring Container. Beans have identities. Names of the beans define their identities. If you create a bean definition with a name that is already given to some other bean definition, the second definition overrides the first one.

The Spring Container provides two different forms of the bean override mechanism. The first is on the bean configuration metadata file level. It is possible to divide configuration metadata into several different files or classes, and then you can specify them together during creation of `ApplicationContext`. In that case, the Spring Container merges all those bean definitions coming from different configuration sources. During this merge, the order of configuration sources given to the container becomes important. If two bean definitions with the same name are in two different configuration sources, the bean definition coming from the second one in the given order overrides the first one. This type of bean override is only possible if bean definitions with the same name are placed into different configuration metadata sources. Spring doesn't allow redefining a bean in the same configuration metadata file or class. The following Try It Out exemplifies how you override beans in Spring Container.

TRY IT OUT Overriding Bean Definitions

In this Try It Out, you configure the beans in the Spring Container using constructor injection. The source code is within the project named bean-definition-override in the spring-book-ch2.zip file. You can continue from the project you created for the earlier Try It Out. To begin, follow these steps:

1. Create the following `Foo` class:

```
public class Foo {
    private String name;

    public String getName() {
        return name;
    }

    public void setName(String name) {
        this.name = name;
    }
}
```

2. Create two `@Configuration` classes, both with bean factory methods that create two `foo` beans with the same name as follows:

```
@Configuration
public class Configuration1 {
    @Bean
    public Foo foo() {
        Foo foo = new Foo();
        foo.setName("my foo");
        return foo;
    }
```

```
    }

@Configuration
public class Configuration2 {
    @Bean
    public Foo foo() {
        Foo foo = new Foo();
        foo.setName("your foo");
        return foo;
    }
}
```

3. Modify the `main` method in the `Main` class, and instantiate `ApplicationContext` with the previously created `@Configuration` classes:

```
public class Main {

    public static void main(String[] args) {
        AnnotationConfigApplicationContext applicationContext =
            new AnnotationConfigApplicationContext(
                Configuration1.class, Configuration2.class);
    }

}
```

4. Access the `foo` bean available in `ApplicationContext`, and call its `getName()` method to see which definition is used to create the bean instance:

```
Foo foo = applicationContext.getBean(Foo.class);
System.out.println(foo.getName());
```

5. Change the order of the `@Configuration` classes during `ApplicationContext` instantiation and retry the previous step:

```
AnnotationConfigApplicationContext applicationContext =
    new AnnotationConfigApplicationContext(
            Configuration2.class, Configuration1.class);
```

How It Works

You created two `@Configuration` classes, each with the same `foo()` bean factory methods, but one is creating the `foo` bean with the name `my foo`, and the other is creating it with the name `your foo`. Then you passed them into `AnnotationConfigApplicationContext` as constructor arguments to create `ApplicationContext`.

The Spring Container gets all configuration metadata sources and merges bean definitions in those sources. Here, you have two `foo()` methods with the `@Bean` annotation coming from the `Configuration1` and `Configuration2` classes. By looking at the order in which they are fed into the `ApplicationContext` constructor, you can deduce that Spring makes use of the `foo()` method defined in the `Configuration2` class in the first try and ignores the other `foo()` method completely.

When you call the `getBean()` method of `ApplicationContext` by giving `Foo.class` as the method parameter, you can tell the container to give you the bean with this type. The Spring Container looks at the type and returns the appropriate bean instance if there is one, and only one, bean instance with that type. If there were two it would fail with an exception.

In the second try you flipped the order of the `@Configuration` classes given into the `ApplicationContext` constructor, and this time the returned `Foo` instance is created by the method that resides in the `Configuration1` class because it was the second one in the argument list.

The second form of bean override is on the container level. `ApplicationContext` can have the parent `ApplicationContext`, and it is possible to have two bean instances with the same name coexisting in both parent and child `ApplicationContext` instances. In that case, when you refer to the bean with the repeating name, Spring provides the bean defined in the child `ApplicationContext`. `ApplicationContext` hierarchies are common for web applications. Chapter 4 describes how Spring is configured and used in web applications. In short, parent `ApplicationContext` in a web application is usually created using `org.springframework.web.context.ContextLoaderListener`, and child `ApplicationContext` is created by Spring MVC `DispatcherServlet`. `DispatcherServlet` identifies the `ApplicationContext` instance created by the `ContextLoaderListener` if it's available, and it uses it as the parent `ApplicationContext` during its own `ApplicationContext` instance creation.

Using the depends-on Attribute

If bean a directly or indirectly depends on bean b, it is certain that the Spring Container will first create bean b—guaranteed. However, if you have two bean definitions that have no dependency on each other, either directly or indirectly, the order of their creation is internal to the Spring Container. You cannot be sure that bean b will always be created before bean a. Sometimes, you have beans that have no dependency on each other, but they require a specific bean creation order among them. For example, a bean that performs a Java Virtual Machine (JVM)-level initialization needs to be created before some other beans that expect this initialization to be performed when they are being initialized. In such scenarios, you can specify that bean b should be created before bean a using the depends-on attribute of the `<bean>` element in an XML-based configuration:

```
<bean id="a" class="com.wiley.beginningspring.ch2.A" depends-on="b,c"/>
```

You can list several bean names in the depends-on attribute. The depends-on attribute also plays a role during the bean destruction phase as well as during the bean initialization phase. In the case of singleton beans only, the beans listed in the depends-on attribute are destroyed after the bean that has the depends-on attribute. The bean destroy phase is discussed later in this chapter in the "Life-Cycle Callbacks" section.

For Java- and annotation-based configurations, the `org.springframework.context.annotation.DependsOn` annotation is used for the same purpose. When the `@DependsOn` annotation is used on the class level, it is processed during component scanning and the bean defined with it is created after the beans specified within the `@DependsOn` annotation. Otherwise, it is simply ignored. When it is used on the method level with the `@Bean` annotation, it takes effect during Java-based configuration.

Autowiring

You don't have to explicitly define dependencies in your bean definitions; you can let the Spring Container inject them to your beans automatically. This is called *autowiring*. It is useful especially during development because bean definitions need to be updated as the codebase evolves. Autowiring has three modes: `byType`, `byName`, and `constructor`.

In autowiring `byType`, Spring investigates properties of a bean definition by looking at its class via Java reflection and tries to inject available beans in the container to the matching properties by their types. It performs injection by calling setter methods of those properties. In XML-based configuration, autowiring is enabled with the `autowire` attribute of the `<bean>` element:

```
<bean id="accountService" class="com.wiley.beginningspring.ch2.AccountServiceImpl"
    autowire="byType"/>

<bean id="accountDao" class="com.wiley.beginningspring.ch2.↵
    AccountDaoInMemoryImpl"/>
```

If more than one bean instance autowiring candidates are suitable for injection to a specific property, dependency injection fails. The Spring Container needs a bit of help from you to decide which one to inject. One way is to exclude other beans from autowiring candidates, and the remaining bean is injected by the container. You can use the `autowire-candidate` attribute of the `<bean>` element for this purpose:

```
<bean id="accountService" class="com.wiley.beginningspring.ch2.AccountServiceImpl"
    autowire="byType"/>

<bean id="accountDao" class="com.wiley.beginningspring.ch2.AccountDaoInMemoryImpl"
    autowire-candidate="false"/>

<bean id="accountDaoJdbc"
    class="com.wiley.beginningspring.ch2.AccountDaoJdbcImpl"/>
```

The other option is to use autowiring mode `byName` if you have several candidate beans. In that case, the container tries to match the property name with the bean name that it will be injected into:

```
<bean id="accountService" class="com.wiley.beginningspring.ch2.AccountServiceImpl"
    autowire="byName"/>

<bean id="accountDao" class="com.wiley.beginningspring.ch2.↵
    AccountDaoInMemoryImpl"/>

<bean id="accountDaoJdbc" class="com.wiley.beginningspring.ch2.↵
    AccountDaoJdbcImpl"/>
```

What happens if there is no candidate bean in the Spring Container? In that case, no bean is injected into the property, and its default value (most probably null) is left unchanged.

The third mode is `constructor`. It is very similar to `byType`, but in this case the Spring Container tries to find beans whose types match with constructor arguments of the bean class. Again, if there is more than one candidate bean for an argument, Spring fails to inject the argument.

Autowiring in a Java-based bean configuration is very similar to XML-based configuration. The following Try It Out is an example.

> **TRY IT OUT** Autowiring with a Java-Based Bean Configuration

In this Try It Out, you configure the beans using autowiring in the Spring Container. The source code is within the project named `java-based-autowiring` in the `spring-book-ch2.zip` file. You can continue from the project you created for the earlier Try It Out. To begin, follow these steps:

1. Create the `AccountDaoJdbcImpl` class, which implements the `AccountDao` interface, and leave all method bodies empty:

```
public class AccountDaoJdbcImpl implements AccountDao {
//...
}
```

2. Add an `accountDaoJdbc()` factory method with the `@Bean` annotation in the `Ch2Configuration` class, create a bean instance from `AccountDaoJdbcImpl`, and return it from this method:

```
@Bean
public AccountDao accountDaoJdbc() {
    AccountDaoJdbcImpl bean = new AccountDaoJdbcImpl();
    return bean;
}
```

3. Add the `autowire` attribute with the `Enum` value `Autowire.AUTOWIRE_BY_TYPE` to the `@Bean` annotation of the `accountService()` factory method in the `Ch2Configuration` class. Don't forget to remove the line that performs explicit dependency injection within the `accountService()` method:

```
@Bean(autowire=Autowire.BY_TYPE)
public AccountService accountService() {
    AccountServiceImpl bean = new AccountServiceImpl();
    return bean;
}
```

4. Try to run the `main` method and observe the result.

5. Change the `autowire` value to `Autowire.AUTOWIRE_BY_NAME` and retry running the `main` method:

```
@Bean(autowire=Autowire.BY_NAME)
public AccountService accountService() {
    AccountServiceImpl bean = new AccountServiceImpl();
    return bean;
}
```

How It Works

You first created another implementation of the `AccountDao` interface called `AccountDaoJdbcImpl` and created a second bean using it. Removing the explicit `accountDao` injection in the `accountService()` method and putting the `autowire` attribute in the `@Bean` annotation enabled autowiring in the container.

However, the container failed during bootstrap because it identified two candidate beans with the AccountDao type, which can be auto-injected into the accountDao property of the accountService bean. After changing the autowire mode to byName, the container was able to inject the accountDao bean into the target property because their names matched.

You can also trigger autowiring without adding the autowire attribute into the @Bean annotation. When you place the org.springframework.beans.factory.annotation.Autowired annotation onto the setter method of the accountDao property of AccountServiceImpl, the container automatically tries to inject a suitable dependency. If there is more than one candidate, it fails as expected. In that case, you need to tell the container which specific bean it should auto-inject into the target bean. Spring provides the org.springframework.beans.factory.annotation.Qualifier annotation for this purpose. When you place the @Qualifier annotation together with the @Autowired and @Bean annotations, autowiring behavior turns into byName mode:

```
public class AccountServiceImpl implements AccountService {
    private AccountDao accountDao;

    @Autowired
    @Qualifier
    public void setAccountDao(AccountDao accountDao) {
        this.accountDao = accountDao;
    }
//...
}

@Configuration
public class Ch2BeanConfiguration {

    @Bean
    @Qualifier
    public AccountDao accountDao() {
        AccountDaoInMemoryImpl bean = new AccountDaoInMemoryImpl();
        //depedencies of accountDao bean will be injected here...
        return bean;
    }
//...
}
```

The @Qualifier annotation accepts a String value that helps you to change the default qualifier value, which is the bean name, into something different. That way, any other bean whose name doesn't match with the property name can be autowired based on the qualifier value.

Annotation-based bean configuration also makes use of the @Autowired and @Qualifier annotations to enable autowiring. Use of the @Autowired and @Qualifier annotations is the same as in Java-based configuration. However, if you want to assign a specific qualifier value other than the bean name, you need to place the @Qualifier annotation on top of the class with the @Component annotation.

Another nice feature related to autowiring in Java- and annotation-based configurations is that you can also place @Autowired on fields. This removes the necessity of having setter methods for setter injection. In such a case, the Spring Container performs dependency injection by direct field access using the Java Reflection API.

Autowiring is only for dependencies to other beans. It doesn't work for straight values, such as int, boolean, String, Enum, and so on. For such properties, you can use the org.springframework.beans.factory.annotation.Value annotation either on the field level or on the setter method level. The @Value annotation accepts a String value to specify the value to be injected into the built-in Java typed property. Necessary type conversion is handled by the Spring Container. The @Value annotation can also be used for expression-driven dependency injection. In other words, you can place Spring expressions or placeholders in it, and the container evaluates the expression or placeholder and injects the obtained value from the expression evaluation or placeholder resolution.

In the following code snippet, the name attribute of the foo bean is set to the value obtained from the evaluation of the SpEL expression (see Chapter 9 for more information about SpEL):

```
@Component
public class Foo {

    @Value("#{systemProperties.fooName}")
    private String name;

    public String getName() {
        return name;
    }

    public void setName(String name) {
        this.name = name;
    }
}
```

In addition to SpEL expressions, you can also give placeholders to the @Value annotation:

```
@Component
public class Foo {

    @Value("${fooName}")
    private String name;

    public String getName() {
        return name;
    }

    public void setName(String name) {
        this.name = name;
    }
}
```

${fooName} is a placeholder variable that is resolved by a special Spring infrastructural bean that is configured with the <context:property-placeholder/> namespace element. This namespace element has a location attribute that accepts a list of Properties files that exist in a filesystem or classpath location. Within those `Properties` files are key/value pairs, and values of keys match with placeholders used in the bean configuration injected into the property:

```
<context:property-placeholder location="classpath:application.properties"/>
```

Bean Lookups

In any Spring-enabled application, the aim should be increasing the number of Spring-managed beans as much as possible and decreasing the number of other objects that are outside the control of the Spring Container. For beans that are managed within the Spring Container, except for the marginal use cases, there is no need for explicit dependency lookup. Their dependencies are specified in bean definitions and are injected by the container during bean creation time. Figure 2-4 illustrates how the Spring Container's beans are obtained by the objects outside the control of Spring Container.

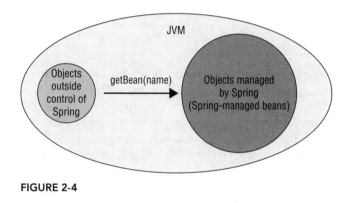

FIGURE 2-4

However, no matter how hard you try, you come to a point at which you need to access beans from other objects not under control of the Spring Container. In such cases, those objects should first obtain a reference to the `ApplicationContext` instance in the environment. For standalone applications, this is a task that should be handled by the developers explicitly. For example, they can assign the `ApplicationContext` instance to a static variable that is globally accessible right after its creation. For web applications, Spring provides a utility class called `org.springframework.web.context.support.WebApplicationContextUtils`, which has methods that return the `ApplicationContext` of the web application. In any case, after obtaining a reference to the `ApplicationContext` instance, you can perform explicit bean lookups via various `getBean()` methods available in the `ApplicationContext` interface.

At times you also need to perform explicit bean lookups within Spring-managed beans as well. There can be various reasons for this requirement. For example, one requirement is accessing a prototype-scoped bean from a singleton-scoped bean. Another example is that your bean may need to invoke a specific method provided by a type that is also implemented by several other Spring-managed beans in the application, but that bean has no direct dependency on those other beans. In any case, the same rule applies here as well. You first need a reference to the `ApplicationContext` instance in the Spring-managed bean as well so that its `getBean()` method can be invoked to perform bean lookup. Spring provides the `org.springframework .context.ApplicationContextAware` interface for this purpose:

```
public interface ApplicationContextAware extends Aware {
    void setApplicationContext(ApplicationContext applicationContext)
            throws BeansException;
}
```

If your bean class implements this interface, the Spring Container injects itself into the bean instance during its creation. That way, your bean has access to its container. For Java- and annotation-based configuration, you don't even have to implement that interface. It is enough just to place the `@Autowired` annotation either on the field level or on the setter method for the injection to happen.

SPRING-MANAGED BEANS

As stated in the beginning of the chapter, Java objects created and managed by Spring are called beans. They are simply POJOs, but they are managed within the Spring Container. Therefore, it is very common to call them Spring-managed beans. The roots of this term date back to the beginning of the POJO movement and the early days of the framework. Creators of the Spring Application Framework wanted to differentiate POJOs managed within their containers from Enterprise Java Beans (EJBs) managed by the EJB container, so they called them Spring "managed" beans in contrast to EJBs that are "managed" by the EJB container.

Naming Beans

Beans are identified by their names. They have at least one name. If developers don't assign them one, the Spring Container assigns an internal name. Beans are referenced by their names, either from other bean definitions, or from the application code via explicit lookup. In XML-based configuration, the `id` attribute is used to assign a name to a bean. You cannot duplicate a name in the same XML file. However, it is possible to give another bean definition the same name in a second XML file. In that case, the bean override mechanism comes into play.

You can assign a bean more than one name in its definition and you can use the `Name` attribute for that purpose. You can use spaces, commas, and semicolons to separate several names given to a bean definition within the `name` attribute. Use of special characters such as commas and semicolons is not allowed in the `id` attribute:

```
<bean name="accountDao,accountDaoInMemory"
      class="com.wiley.beginningspring.ch2.AccountDaoInMemoryImpl"/>
```

Names other than the first one are called *aliases*. You can also give aliases to beans in a place other than their bean definitions. You use the `<alias>` element for this purpose:

```
<bean id="accountDaoInMemory" class="com.wiley.beginningspring.ch2.~CA
    AccountDaoInMemoryImpl"/>

<alias name="accountDaoInMemory" alias="accountDao"/>
```

> **TIP** *Bean aliasing is especially useful to configure already-existing configuration metadata sources that expect some beans with specific names to exist in the container.*

The annotation-based configuration @Component and its derivatives accept a String value as the bean name. If the name isn't given, a simple class name with a lowercase first character becomes the bean name by default:

```
@Service("accountService")
public class AccountServiceImpl implements AccountService {
//...
}
```

In a Java-based configuration, the @Bean annotation has a name attribute, which allows more than one name to be given as a bean name. If no value is set, the factory method name becomes the bean name:

```
@Configuration
public class Ch2BeanConfiguration {

    @Bean(name={"accountDao,accountDaoInMemory"})
    public AccountDao foo() {
        AccountDaoInMemoryImpl bean = new AccountDaoInMemoryImpl();
        //depedencies of accountDao bean will be injected here...
        return bean;
    }
//...
}
```

Bean Instantiation Methods

The most common way to create beans is to invoke one of the constructors available in their classes. For example, the Foo class has the following default no arg constructor and a constructor accepting the String name argument. Therefore, it is possible to create bean instances from the Foo class by calling either of those two constructors in bean definitions:

```
public class Foo {
    private String name;

    public Foo() {
    }

    public Foo(String name) {
```

```
        this.name = name;
    }

    public String getName() {
        return name;
    }

    public void setName(String name) {
        this.name = name;
    }
}


<bean id="foo1" class="com.wiley.beginningspring.ch2.Foo">
    <property name="name" value="foo1"/>
</bean>

<bean id="foo2" class="com.wiley.beginningspring.ch2.Foo">
    <constructor-arg value="foo2"/>
</bean>
```

The second option for creating beans is to invoke the static or instance factory methods that are available. For example, the FooFactory class has two factory methods in the following code snippet. The createFoo3() method has a static modifier. Therefore, it can be invoked without having a FooFactory instance available at run time. The second factory method, createFoo4(), has no static modifier. Therefore, it can only be invoked if there is an instance of FooFactory available at run time:

```
public class FooFactory {

    public static Foo createFoo3() {
        Foo foo = new Foo();
        foo.setName("foo3");
        return foo;
    }

    public Foo createFoo4() {
        Foo foo = new Foo();
        foo.setName("foo4");
        return foo;
    }
}
```

In XML bean configuration, the <bean> element has a factory-method attribute that accepts a static factory method name as an argument value. The Spring Container, when the factory-method attribute is available, doesn't attempt to create a bean instance using the class attribute but instead invokes the static factory method specified in the factory-method attribute in that class:

```
<bean id="foo3" class="com.wiley.beginningspring.ch2.FooFactory"
        factory-method="createFoo3"/>
```

To create a `Foo` instance using the instance factory method, the `<bean>` element has the `factory-bean` attribute in addition to the `factory-method` attribute. That way, you can refer to the factory bean in which the instance factory method resides:

```
<bean id="fooFactory" class="com.wiley.beginningspring.ch2.FooFactory"/>

<bean id="foo4" factory-bean="fooFactory" factory-method="createFoo4"/>
```

In annotation-based configuration, first the `FooFactory` class needs to be annotated with the `@Component` element. That way it becomes a regular Spring-managed bean. After that, the static and instance factory methods in the `fooFactory` bean are annotated with the `@Bean` annotation. This is very similar to Java-based configuration. In Java-based configuration, it is enough to replace `@Component` with the `@Configuration` annotation, and the rest will be the same:

```
@Component
public class FooFactory {

    @Bean(name="foo3")
    public static Foo createFoo3() {
        Foo foo = new Foo();
        foo.setName("foo3");
        return foo;
    }

    @Bean(name="foo4")
    public Foo createFoo4() {
        Foo foo = new Foo();
        foo.setName("foo4");
        return foo;
    }
}
```

The final option for bean creation is to use Spring's own `FactoryBean` interface:

```
public class FooFactoryBean implements FactoryBean<Foo> {

    @Override
    public Foo getObject() throws Exception {
        Foo foo = new Foo();
        foo.setName("foo5");
        return foo;
    }

    @Override
    public Class<?> getObjectType() {
        return Foo.class;
    }

    @Override
    public boolean isSingleton() {
        return true;
    }
```

```
    }
    <bean id="foo5" class="com.wiley.beginningspring.ch2.FooFactoryBean"/>
```

It is a special interface, and the Spring Container detects bean definition classes that implement this interface at run time. If the bean class is of type `FactoryBean`, the bean is created by calling its `getObject()` method. The type of the created bean is the type returned from `getObjectType()`, not the `FactoryBean` implementation class. It is also commonly used by the Spring Framework itself.

Bean Scopes

The lifetime of beans created by the Spring Container is called *bean scope*. By default, all beans created by the Spring Container have singleton scope. In other words, only one bean instance is created for a bean definition, and that instance is used by the container for the whole application lifetime. This scope is very appropriate for beans that correspond to layers such as controller, service, and data access object (DAO). They are usually stateless instances that serve several different requests at the same time:

```
    <bean id="commandManager" class="com.wiley.beginningspring.ch2.CommandManager"
        scope="singleton">
    </bean>
```

You can use the `scope` attribute of the `<bean>` element to specify the scope of a bean definition. Because its value is `singleton` by default, you don't need to use it for singleton-scoped beans.

The second scope supported by Spring is `prototype`. It is very similar to creating an object using the `new` operator in Java code. Beans with the prototype scope are created whenever they are accessed in the container, either from other bean definitions via bean reference, or from within the application code with explicit bean lookup using the `ApplicationContext.getBean()` method:

```
    <bean id="command" class="com.wiley.beginningspring.ch2.Command" scope="prototype">

    </bean>
```

Sometimes a singleton-scoped bean may depend on a prototype-scoped bean, and it may expect to deal with a new instance whenever it uses the prototype-scoped bean in its method calls. Bean dependencies, however, are injected at bean creation time, and because the singleton-scoped bean is created and its dependencies are injected only once in its lifetime, its prototype scope dependency is created once at that time and injected into it. After that time, no new prototype instance is created and injected into that singleton-scoped bean. Practically, prototype scope in that case behaves like singleton scope. To overcome this limitation, you have to give up the dependency injection feature provided by the Spring Container and perform explicit bean lookup within the singleton scope instance whenever you need a new prototype instance.

```
    public class CommandManager implements ApplicationContextAware {
        private ApplicationContext applicationContext;
```

```
        public void execute() {
            createCommand().execute(new CommandContext());
        }

        @Override
        public void setApplicationContext(ApplicationContext applicationContext)
                throws BeansException {
            this.applicationContext = applicationContext;
        }

        private Command createCommand() {
            return applicationContext.getBean(Command.class);
        }
    }
}
```

Those two scopes have always existed in the Spring Framework. In Spring 2.5, additional scopes for web applications have been introduced with a custom scope mechanism so that developers can also introduce new scope types as necessary.

New scopes, introduced in Spring 2.5, are `request` and `session`. They can only be used in web applications. Attempting to use them in a standalone application causes the Spring Container not to bootstrap. A request-scoped bean is created every time a new web request arrives at the application, and that same bean instance is used throughout the request. A session-scoped bean, as you may have already guessed, is created each time a new HTTP Session is created, and that instance stays alive as the session stays alive.

```
<beans xmlns="http://www.springframework.org/schema/beans"
    xmlns:xsi="http://www.w3.org/2001/XMLSchema-instance"
    xmlns:aop="http://www.springframework.org/schema/aop"
    xsi:schemaLocation="http://www.springframework.org/schema/aop
    http://www.springframework.org/schema/aop/spring-aop-4.0.xsd
        http://www.springframework.org/schema/beans
    http://www.springframework.org/schema/beans/spring-beans.xsd">

    <bean id="userPreferences" class="com.wiley.beginningspring.ch2.~CA
        UserPreferences">
        <aop:scoped-proxy/>
    </bean>

</beans>
```

When you define request- and session-scoped beans, you have to place the `<aop:scoped-proxy/>` element as a child element in the `<bean>` element. `<aop:scoped-proxy>` is available in the aspect oriented programming (AOP) namespace, and you can see how that namespace is activated in the earlier XML snippet. This directive causes the Spring Container to generate a class extending from the bean definition class dynamically at run time, and a proxy object is created using that dynamically generated class. The proxy object is then injected to other beans referencing the scoped bean in the container. At run time, when a method call arrives to that proxy object, Spring tries to obtain a real target bean instance in the current request or session. If there is an existing bean, it is used to handle method invocation. Otherwise, a new instance is created and used for that request or session.

Two modes of proxy object creation exist. The Spring Container can either create a proxy class by extending from the bean definition class, or it can use the interface-based proxy mechanism available in Java to implement interfaces that are already implemented by a target bean definition class. By default, it uses a class-generation mechanism. You can change this behavior with the `proxy-target-class` attribute of the `<aop:scoped-proxy/>` element.

Table 2-1 summarizes the built-in scopes supported by the Spring Application Framework.

TABLE 2-1: Built-In Scopes Supported by Spring Application Framework

SCOPE NAME	SCOPE DEFINITION
`singleton`	Only one instance from a bean definition is created. It is the default scope for bean definitions.
`prototype`	Every access to the bean definition, either through other bean definitions or via the `getBean(..)` method, causes a new bean instance to be created. It is similar to the `new` operator in Java.
`request`	Same bean instance throughout the web request is used. Each web request causes a new bean instance to be created. It is only valid for web-aware `ApplicationContexts`.
`session`	Same bean instance will be used for a specific HTTP session. Different HTTP session creations cause new bean instances to be created. It is only valid for web-aware `ApplicationContexts`.
`globalSession`	It is similar to the standard HTTP Session scope (described earlier) and applies only in the context of portlet-based web applications.

If you are using Spring MVC to handle web requests, you need to do nothing to make request- and session-scoped beans work properly. However, if your user interface (UI) technology is something like JSF or Vaadin, in which requests are passing out of Spring MVC, you have to add the following `ServletRequestListener` definition in your `web.xml` file so that request- and session-scoped beans can work properly:

```
<web-app>

  <listener>
     <listener-class>
        org.springframework.web.context.request.RequestContextListener
     </listener-class>
  </listener>

  //...
</web-app>
```

In annotation- and Java-based configuration, the `org.springframework.context.annotation.Scope` annotation is used to specify the scope of the current bean definition either on the class level or on the factory method level. The `@Scope` annotation expects the `String` value that identifies the scope of the bean definition. It can also accept a second argument, which can change the proxy-generation mode:

```java
@Component
@Scope("protoype")
public class Command {
//...
}


@Component
@Scope(value="session",proxyMode=ScopedProxyMode.INTERFACES)
public class UserPreferences {
//...
}
```

Lazy Initialization

The Spring Container, by default, creates beans during its startup. This is called *eager bean initialization*. Its advantage is that you can see configuration errors as early as possible. For example, in XML-based configuration you may have had a typo in the class attribute of a bean definition, or you may refer to an unavailable bean definition. On the other hand, it may slow down the bootstrap process if you have lots of bean definitions or some special beans, such as Hibernate `SessionFactory` or JPA `EntityManagerFactory`, whose initialization may take a considerable amount of time. Some beans may only be required for specific use cases or alternative scenarios, and are not needed for other times. In such cases, eager initialization may result in unnecessary heap memory consumption as well.

Spring also supports *lazy bean initialization*. If beans are configured by developers to be created lazily, the container delays their creation until they are really needed. Their creation is triggered either by a reference made from another bean that is already being created or by an explicit bean lookup performed from within application code.

In XML-based configuration, you can use the `lazy-init` attribute in the `<bean>` element to define a bean as lazy. To define all beans as lazy in an XML file, you can use the `default-lazy-init` attribute of the `<beans>` element. Lazy behavior defined on the XML file level can be overridden on the bean definition level as well.

```xml
<beans xmlns="http://www.springframework.org/schema/beans"
    xmlns:xsi="http://www.w3.org/2001/XMLSchema-instance"
    xsi:schemaLocation="http://www.springframework.org/schema/beans
http://www.springframework.org/schema/beans/spring-beans.xsd"
    default-lazy-init="true">

    <bean id="accountService" class="com.wiley.beginningspring.ch2.~CA
        AccountServiceImpl">
        <property name="accountDao" ref="accountDao"/>
    </bean>

    <bean id="accountDao" class="com.wiley.beginningspring.ch2.~CA
        AccountDaoInMemoryImpl"
```

```
            lazy-init="false">

    </bean>
</beans>
```

In annotation- and Java-based configuration, you can use the `org.springframework.context.annotation.Lazy` annotation to enable lazy behavior. If the `@Lazy` attribute with a value of true is present on the class level together with the `@Component` annotation, or on the factory method level with the `@Bean` annotation, that bean definition is lazy:

```
@Service("accountService")
@Lazy(true)
public class AccountServiceImpl implements AccountService {
//...
}

@Configuration
public class Ch2BeanConfiguration {

    @Bean
    @Lazy(true)
    public AccountService accountService() {
        AccountServiceImpl bean = new AccountServiceImpl();
        return bean;
    }
//...
}
```

The advantage of lazy bean creation is that it speeds container bootstrap time and has a smaller memory footprint. On the other hand, if bean configuration errors exist in the metadata, they may remain unnoticed until their scenarios are tested.

Take care while you are defining beans as lazy. If one of their depending beans, either directly or indirectly, is defined as eager, your lazy definition won't have any effect. Eager bean definition is processed during startup, so it triggers processing lazy bean definition as well.

Life-Cycle Callbacks

Beans can define callback methods, which can be invoked by the container at specific points during their lifetime. Those points are after their instantiation and just before termination of their defined scopes. They are also called init and destroy methods. You have several different ways to define and invoke such life-cycle callback methods.

XML-based configuration `<bean>` elements have `init-method` and `destroy-method` attributes that accept method names in the bean class as attribute values:

```
public class Foo {
    public void init() {
        System.out.println("init method is called");
    }
```

```
        public void destroy() {
            System.out.println("destroy method is called");
        }
}

<bean id="foo" class="com.wiley.beginningspring.ch2.Foo"
        init-method="init" destroy-method="destroy"/>
```

The `init` method is invoked by the container after the bean is created, and its properties are injected. Because the bean instance is ready to use, you can perform anything within the init method in which the bean's properties are involved. The destroy method is invoked just before the end of a bean's lifetime. Because the lifetime of beans is changeable according to their scopes, the invocation of destroy methods may be occur at different times. For example, the destroy methods of singleton-scoped beans are invoked at the shutdown of the whole Spring Container. The destroy methods of request-scoped beans are invoked at the end of the current web request, and the destroy methods of session-scoped beans are invoked at HTTP session timeout or invalidation. Prototype-scoped beans, on the other hand, are not tracked after their instantiation; therefore, their destroy methods cannot be invoked.

Method names can be anything. There is no restriction; however, methods should return void and accept nothing as input arguments. They can throw any type of exception.

Spring also supports the JSR-250 Common Java annotations `javax.annotation.PostConstruct` and `javax.annotation.PreDestroy`. When they are placed on top of `init` and `destroy` methods, they are invoked at bean creation and destruction times as well. There is no restriction on the names of those methods. The method names can be anything as long as they are annotated properly. To activate processing of JSR-250 annotations, you need to add the `<context:annotation-config/>` namespace element in your configuration metadata file for XML- and annotation-based configurations:

```
public class Bar {
    @PostConstruct
    public void init() throws Exception {
        System.out.println("init method is called");
    }

    @PreDestroy
    public void destroy() throws RuntimeException {
        System.out.println("destroy method is called");
    }
}

<bean class="com.wiley.beginningspring.ch2.Bar"/>

<context:annotation-config/>
```

There is a third option for life-cycle callback methods. The Spring Framework provides two special interfaces called `org.springframework.beans.factory.InitializingBean` and `org.springframework.beans.factory.DisposableBean`. They declare `afterPropertiesSet()` and `destroy()` methods, respectively. If a bean implements the `InitializingBean` interface, the

Spring Container calls its `afterPropertiesSet()` method just after injection of its properties. Similarly, if a bean implements the `DisposableBean` interface, its destroy method is called just before the bean's destruction time—in other words, at the end of its scope:

```java
public class Baz implements InitializingBean, DisposableBean {

    @Override
    public void afterPropertiesSet() throws Exception {
        System.out.println("init method invoked");
    }

    @Override
    public void destroy() throws Exception {
        System.out.println("destroy method invoked");
    }

}

<bean class="com.wiley.beginningspring.ch2.Baz"/>
```

Bean Definition Profiles

Sometimes you need to define beans according to the runtime environment. For example, you may use different databases for development and production environments. During development, you may prefer to use a lightweight, possibly in-memory database, such as H2, to quickly test your codebase. In a production environment, on the other hand, you may prefer a more enterprise-level product, such as Oracle, DB2, or MySQL. In some other related case, you may define your own `javax.sql.DataSource`-typed bean for the development environment, or you may prefer to access the `DataSource` object managed by the application server that provides some connection pooling capabilities. Prior to Spring 3.1, you had to handle such platform- or environment-specific bean definition issues as discussed next.

Because you can't have two bean definitions with the same name in a single configuration metadata file, you had to first create two different bean configuration metadata files in which your bean definitions for that specific environment or platform should exist. For example, you would create a `dataSource-dev.xml` file with a `dataSource` bean definition that provides JDBC connections to a lightweight, in-memory H2 database:

```xml
<?xml version="1.0" encoding="UTF-8"?>
<beans xmlns="http://www.springframework.org/schema/beans"
    xmlns:xsi="http://www.w3.org/2001/XMLSchema-instance"
    xsi:schemaLocation="http://www.springframework.org/schema/beans
    http://www.springframework.org/schema/beans/spring-beans.xsd">

    <bean id="dataSource"
class="org.springframework.jdbc.datasource.SingleConnectionDataSource">
        <property name="driverClassName" value="org.h2.Driver"/>
        <property name="url" value="jdbc:h2:mem:test"/>
        <property name="username" value="sa"/>
```

```
        <property name="password" value=""/>
    </bean>

</beans>
```

For a production environment, you might have had another file called `dataSource-prod.xml` in which another `dataSource` bean was defined. But this time, instead of being created by the application, it was obtained from the application server's JDBC context through JNDI lookup:

```
<?xml version="1.0" encoding="UTF-8"?>
<beans xmlns="http://www.springframework.org/schema/beans"
    xmlns:xsi="http://www.w3.org/2001/XMLSchema-instance"
    xsi:schemaLocation="http://www.springframework.org/schema/beans
    http://www.springframework.org/schema/beans/spring-beans.xsd">

    <bean id="dataSource" class="org.springframework.jndi.JndiObjectFactoryBean">
        <property name="jndiName" value="java:comp/env/jdbc/DS"/>
    </bean>

</beans>
```

At this point, you need one of those two `dataSource` bean definitions selectively to be processed according to the target runtime environment. If, for example, the target runtime environment is development or test, the `dataSource-dev.xml` file should be loaded by the container; otherwise, `dataSource-prod.xml` should be loaded. For this purpose, you usually created a third bean configuration file with an import element that imports one of those two configuration metadata sources according to the value of some platform-specific value:

```
<?xml version="1.0" encoding="UTF-8"?>
<beans xmlns="http://www.springframework.org/schema/beans"
    xmlns:xsi="http://www.w3.org/2001/XMLSchema-instance"
    xmlns:context="http://www.springframework.org/schema/context"
    xsi:schemaLocation="http://www.springframework.org/schema/beans
    http://www.springframework.org/schema/beans/spring-beans.xsd
        http://www.springframework.org/schema/context
    http://www.springframework.org/schema/context/spring-context-4.0.xsd">

    <context:property-placeholder/>

    <import resource="classpath:/dataSource-${targetPlatform}.xml"/>

    <bean id="jdbcTemplate" class="org.springframework.jdbc.core.JdbcTemplate">
        <property name="dataSource" ref="dataSource" />
    </bean>
</beans>
```

In the preceding code snippet, the `${targetPlatform}` placeholder is resolved either from the operating system's environment variables or from JVM's system properties (for example, it can be specified as the `-DtargetPlatform=dev` JVM argument). In either case, if it exists, the placeholder is replaced with the value, and the configuration metadata file is resolved according to that value.

Bean definition profiles were introduced in Spring 3.1. In XML-based configuration, profile support enables having a `<beans>` element within another `<beans>` element:

```xml
<?xml version="1.0" encoding="UTF-8"?>
<beans xmlns="http://www.springframework.org/schema/beans"
    xmlns:xsi="http://www.w3.org/2001/XMLSchema-instance"
    xsi:schemaLocation="http://www.springframework.org/schema/beans
    http://www.springframework.org/schema/beans/spring-beans.xsd">

    <bean id="jdbcTemplate" class="org.springframework.jdbc.core.JdbcTemplate">
        <property name="dataSource" ref="dataSource"/>
    </bean>

    <beans profile="dev,test">
        <bean id="dataSource"
            class="org.springframework.jdbc.datasource.SingleConnectionDataSource">
            <property name="driverClassName" value="org.h2.Driver" />
            <property name="url" value="jdbc:h2:mem:test" />
            <property name="username" value="sa" />
            <property name="password" value="" />
        </bean>
    </beans>

    <beans profile="prod">
      <bean id="dataSource" class="org.springframework.jndi.JndiObjectFactoryBean">
            <property name="jndiName" value="java:comp/env/jdbc/DS" />
      </bean>
    </beans>
</beans>
```

Child `<beans>` elements should be defined at the end of the parent `<beans>` element. In other words, there cannot be any `<bean>` elements after a child `<beans>` element within a parent `<beans>` element. The `<beans>` element has the `profile` attribute. It can have comma-separated profile values. Beans defined within a child `<beans>` element are only created if any value given in profile attribute is specified among active profile values during the container bootstrap process. You can specify active profile values for your application in various ways. One easy way is to specify them as the `-Dspring.profiles.active` JVM argument value. For web applications, you can also specify them as `spring.profiles.active` context-param. Spring also has a default profile values concept. If active profile values are not specified, and if default profile values are available, they are used as active profile values. Methods to specify default profile values are very similar to specifying active profile values. You can specify them either with the `-Dspring.profiles.default` JVM argument or with `spring.profiles.default` context-param.

In annotation- and Java-based configuration, you can use the `org.springframework.context .annotation.Profile` annotation on either the type or method level to specify that related beans will only be created if the specified profiles are the active ones.

Environment

Spring 3.1 introduced a new `org.springframework.core.env.Environment` interface to represent the environment in which your applications run. It enables you to manage profiles and properties information used by the application. The following Try It Out shows you how the application `Environment` instance can be accessed and configured at run time.

TRY IT OUT   Configuring the Application Environment at Run Time

In this Try It Out, you configure the beans using the bean profile feature of the Spring Container and activate one of those profiles defined in the bean configuration class. The source code is within the project named `configuring-environment` in the `spring-book-ch2.zip` file. You can continue from the project you created for the earlier Try It Out. To begin, follow these steps:

1. You should have a `Foo` class with the following content if you have already worked through the "Overriding Bean Definitions" Try It Out. Otherwise, create a class `Foo` with the following content:

```java
public class Foo {

    private String name;

    public String getName() {
        return name;
    }

    public void setName(String name) {
        this.name = name;
    }

}
```

2. Create an `@Configuration` class, and add two factory methods as follows:

```java
@Configuration
public class Ch2Configuration {

    @Bean
    @Profile("dev")
    public Foo devFoo(@Value("${name}") String name) {
        Foo foo = new Foo();
        foo.setName("dev " + name);
        return foo;
    }

    @Bean
    @Profile("prod")
    public Foo prodFoo(@Value("${name}") String name) {
        Foo foo = new Foo();
        foo.setName("prod " + name);
        return foo;
    }

}
```

3. Add a static bean factory method in the configuration class, which will enable the property place-holder resolve mechanism:

```java
@Bean
public static PropertySourcesPlaceholderConfigurer propertyPlaceHolderConfigurer() {
```

```
            return new PropertySourcesPlaceholderConfigurer();
      }
```

4. Modify the `main` method in the `Main` class and create `ApplicationContext` using `AnnotationConfigApplicationContext`, which loads the configuration class as follows:

```
public class Main {

      public static void main(String[] args) {
            AnnotationConfigApplicationContext applicationContext =
                  new AnnotationConfigApplicationContext();
            applicationContext.register(Ch2Configuration.class);
      }

}
```

5. Call the `getEnvironment()` method to obtain the `Environment` instance, and set the active profile value `"dev"` via its `setActiveProfiles()` method:

```
            ConfigurableEnvironment environment = applicationContext.getEnvironment();
            environment.setActiveProfiles("dev");
```

6. Call the `getPropertySources()` method of the environment instance to obtain `MutablePropertySources`, and add a new `MapPropertySource` into it, which will serve as the name placeholder from its `Map` object given as the constructor argument:

```
            MutablePropertySources propertySources = environment.getPropertySources();
            propertySources.addLast(new MapPropertySource("mapSource",
                  Collections.singletonMap("name", (Object)"my foo")));
```

7. Call the `AbstractApplicationContext.refresh()` method to initialize the Spring Container, obtain the `foo` bean via bean lookup, and print its name to the console:

```
            applicationContext.refresh();

            Foo foo = applicationContext.getBean(Foo.class);
            System.out.println(foo.getName());
```

How It Works

You added the `devFoo()` and `prodFoo()` bean factory methods in the `Ch2Configuration` class. Those methods are marked with the `@Profile` annotation, so that the `devFoo()` method is invoked to create the `foo` bean instance if the dev value is available among active profiles. Otherwise, the `prodFoo()` method is invoked if the prod value is available among them. In addition, those methods also accept `String` input arguments, which are annotated with the `@Value` annotation that has the `${name}` placeholder as the value. This means that name placeholder should be resolved from the application environment, and its value should be used as the input method argument.

To activate the placeholder resolve mechanism, you added a static bean factory method in which you created a bean instance from the `org.springframework.context.support` `.PropertySourcesPlaceholderConfigurer` class. The reason for making that bean factory bean method is that the returned bean instance is a special infrastructural bean that is used to process placeholders defined in configuration metadata files or classes and replace those placeholders with the values of properties found in `PropertySources`. Therefore, that bean instance should be instantiated without creating an instance of the configuration class. The other option to activate the property placeholder mechanism would be to use the `<context:property-placeholder/>` namespace element in an XML-based configuration file as was shown in the "Bean Definition Profiles" section. You can then import that XML metadata file from the configuration class using the type-level `org.springframework.context.annotation.ImportResource` annotation by specifying the location of the metadata file on top of the configuration class. That way, it is also possible to mix up different metadata sources while configuring the Spring Container.

In step 4, you created a new Spring Container instance using the `AnnotationConfigApplicationContext` class. However, you didn't give the configuration class as the constructor argument as you previously did in other examples. This is because you don't want the container to be initialized when its constructor is just invoked; you want to preconfigure it before its initialization. Therefore, the `ApplicationContext` instance is obtained using the default no arg constructor. You specified the configuration class that is used as the metadata source by calling the `AnnotationConfigApplicationContext.register()` method.

The `AbstractApplicationContext.getEnvironment()` method returns the `org.springframework` `.core.env.ConfigurableEnvironment` instance, which is a subtype of the `Environment` interface. The `ConfigurableEnvironment` can be used to specify active or default profile values as well as change the configuration of the `org.springframework.core.env.PropertySource` instances, which are used to resolve property placeholders in the configuration metadata. The `ConfigurableEnvironment.getPropertySources()` method returns `org.springframework.core` `.env.MutablePropertySources`, which allows additional `PropertySource` instances to be registered with a specific order or removes other instances as well. You created a `MapPropertySource` instance that accepts a `java.util.Map` object as the source of its properties.

When configuration of the container was finished, you called the `AbstractApplicationContext` `.refresh()` method. Invocation of this method initializes the Spring Container and causes beans to be created and so on. When the container was ready to use, you performed a bean lookup using the `getBean()` method to obtain a reference to the `foo` bean, and used that bean instance to see its name value in the console.

SUMMARY

This chapter explained how dependency injection using setter methods and constructors can be performed within the Spring Container. Both setter injection and constructor injection have their pros and cons. You looked at those in detail with the provided examples. The Spring Framework supports different configuration metadata formats to give information about beans that will be created and wired up together within the container. You learned about those three different configuration metadata formats—namely XML-, annotation-, and Java-based formats—and you worked through some code examples. The chapter explained what the `<context:component-scan/>` element performs and described the `@Component` annotation and its derivatives `@Service`, `@Repository`, and `@Controller`, which are used to define beans in annotation-based configuration. You also saw how the `@Configuration` and `@Bean` annotations are used to create Java-based metadata. You learned about circular dependencies and why they can only be handled with setter injection, but you also found out why it is better if you completely avoid having them in your applications.

The chapter explained what autowiring means and covered different modes that are available in the container. It also defined eager and lazy initializations and discussed their advantages and disadvantages. You were introduced to different bean instantiation methods and saw examples of static and instance factory methods using both XML- and annotation-based configuration methods. The chapter also introduced Spring's own `FactoryBean` interface. You learned that Spring-managed beans can interact with the `ApplicationContext` whenever necessary by injecting a container into themselves, and you discovered that the life-cycle callback methods are invoked at specific times during their lifetimes by the container.

Spring beans are identified by their unique names, and you learned that beans can have more than one name defined in the container. You saw how to override bean definitions in the container metadata. You've been introduced to scoping and different scopes—namely `singleton`, `prototype`, `request`, and `session`, which are provided by the Spring Container—and their characteristics. Finally, you looked at bean definition profiles that can be used to define beans according to the runtime environment, and how `Environment` abstraction (which is introduced in Spring 3.1) can help you configure active profiles and placeholder variables specific to the application.

EXERCISES

You can find possible solutions to the following exercises in Appendix A.

1. The `<context:component-scan>` element supports extending the bean scanning mechanism outside the `@Component` annotations. The `<context:include-filter/>` child element is available for this purpose. Create a sample application in which beans are defined with `<context:component-scan/>`, but without using the `@Component` annotations. Instead, beans should be discovered by scanning the package in which bean classes are placed.

2. Create a bean class that implements the `InitializingBean` interface and also create two other init methods, one of them named `init` and annotated with `@PostConstruct` and the other named `initialize` and defined as `init-method` in the XMLconfiguration. Examine in which order those methods will be invoked while the bean is being instantiated.

3. Try to create two beans depending on each other with the Java-based configuration using setter injection. What happens?

▶ WHAT YOU LEARNED IN THIS CHAPTER

TOPIC	KEY POINTS
Configuration metadata	Information about beans that need to be created and wired together to form a working system using the Spring Container.
IoC Container	Dependency injection container in which beans are created and wired up together in addition to various other services being applied to them.
`@Component`, `@Service`, `@Repository`, `@Controller` annotations	Annotations that are used to define Spring-managed beans.
`<beans>` element and `@Configuration` annotation	Root XML element for XML-based configurations under which individual `<bean>` elements are defined. Annotation applied to the Java class in which beans are defined with factory methods.
`<bean>` element and `@Bean` annotation	XML element and Java annotation used to define individual beans.
`autowire` attribute and `@Autowired` annotation	XML attribute and Java annotation used to enable dependency injection without any definition.
`<context:component-scan/>`	XML namespace element that enables annotation-based configuration with `@Component` annotations.
`ClasspathXmlApplicationContext`, `AnnotationConfigApplicationContext`	Spring `ApplicationContext` implementations used to create containers with XML-, annotation-, and Java-based metadata.
Bean name, bean aliasing	Identifier of beans defined in the container, assigning several names to a bean definition.
`depends-on` attribute and `@DependsOn` annotation	XML attribute and Java annotation to specify order during bean creation among several bean definitions.
`lazy-init` attribute and `@Lazy` annotation	XML attribute and Java annotation to specify instantiation time of a bean.
`scope` attribute and `@Scope` annotation	XML attribute and Java annotation to specify the lifetime of a bean instance.
`singleton`, `prototype`, `request`, and `session` scopes	Bean scopes supported by the Spring Container.
`FactoryBean` interface	Special interface provided by Spring, which is used to create beans.

continues

(continued)

TOPIC	KEY POINTS
`factory-bean` and `factory-method` attributes	XML attributes that are used to create beans with static and instance factory methods.
`init-method` and `destroy-method` attributes	XML attributes to specify life-cycle methods in a bean definition.
`InitializingBean`, `DisposableBean` interfaces	Special interfaces provided by Spring, which are used to define life-cycle callbacks.
`@PostConstruct` and `@PreDestroy` annotations	JSR-250 annotations that are used to define life-cycle callbacks.
`profile` attribute and `@Profile` annotation	XML attribute and Java annotation used to create conditional bean definition groups.
`spring.profiles.active` and `spring.profiles.default`	Spring properties that are used to specify active and default profile values for the run time.
`Environment`, `ConfigurableEnvironment`	Spring interfaces that abstract the environment in which an application works.
`PropertySource` and `MutablePropertySources`	Spring interfaces that are used to provide property key/value pairs from various sources.

3

Building Web Applications Using Spring MVC

WHAT YOU WILL LEARN IN THIS CHAPTER:

- ➤ Learning the features and benefits of Spring MVC
- ➤ Using the Dispatcher Servlet mechanism
- ➤ Creating your first Spring MVC application
- ➤ Configuring Spring MVC with annotations
- ➤ Handling forms with JSP
- ➤ Exploiting the power of annotations
- ➤ Validating user input
- ➤ Uploading files
- ➤ Handling exceptions
- ➤ Implementing Internationalization (i18n)
- ➤ Using themes

> **CODE DOWNLOAD** *The wrox.com code downloads for this chapter are found at* www.wrox.com/go/beginningspring *on the Download Code tab. The code is in the Chapter 3 download and individually named according to the names throughout the chapter.*

It's viable to say that the World Wide Web has become the ultimate knowledge base ever built. Of course, the web's creators didn't foresee that it would become an enormous organization. The beginning of this information era first started with the need to share data between the teams attending the experiments at CERN Labs. They all needed to share the data in a common way, and the data needed to be accessed with a common format. To provide this communication link, Tim Berners Lee, a computer scientist who was working for CERN at the time, came up with the idea of the World Wide Web with its three core elements: *HTML* (HyperText Markup Language), *HTTP* (HyperText Transfer Protocol), and *URI* (Uniform Resource Identifier).

So, that's where it all began. Nowadays we, as the programmers, are building enterprise web applications by using other kinds of frameworks, but they all depend on those three founding elements. The technologies have evolved over the years to become more sophisticated as the need for enterprise applications has increased.

The Spring Framework provides features for achieving enterprise web development, and *Spring MVC* is the subproject that gathers these implementations under its hood. This chapter focuses on Spring MVC, which complies with the *Model View Controller* pattern that is widely used among the web application development frameworks.

LEARNING THE FEATURES AND BENEFITS OF SPRING MVC

Spring MVC is a layered Java web development framework. The Model View Controller pattern offers a layered architecture in which each layer provides an abstraction on top of the other. *Model* is the representation of the domain-specific information that the application uses. *View* is the representation of the domain model with user interface elements, like input elements and buttons, which interact with the model. *Controller* is the part that interprets the user's input and transforms it into the model to be shown to the user again after the transformation. The main flow diagram for the MVC pattern is shown in Figure 3-1.

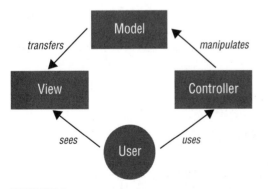

FIGURE 3-1

Spring MVC is an action-based MVC framework. The framework itself highlights the request/response characteristic of the HTTP protocol, where each request by the user states an action to be performed within the framework. This is achieved by mapping each request URI to an executable method. Request parameters are also mapped to the arguments of this method. The alternative approach to an action-based framework is a component-based one in which the user interface is built up by components—similar to thick client applications—and with the users' interaction with these components, events get fired that are handled on an HTTP request/response basis.

Because Spring MVC is a subproject of Spring, it fully integrates with Spring's core features, such as the *dependency injection* mechanism. You can easily configure and use annotation-based definitions for the controllers. Later sections of this chapter discuss controllers, and you can read more about dependency injection in Chapter 2.

Spring MVC provides a binding mechanism to extract the data from the user request, converts it to the predefined data format, and maps it to a model class to construct an object. Spring MVC achieves this binding mechanism by easily matching the request parameter names to the properties of the Java classes, which makes the web development very easy and straightforward.

Spring MVC is view-agnostic. You are not forced to use, say, JSP for the view layer. You can use other view technologies such as Velocity templates, Tiles, Freemarker, and XSLT. That's why Spring MVC introduces its model architecture and avoids working directly with HTTP servlet requests to prevent binding itself directly to them. Spring MVC is also non-invasive because the business logic code is separate from the framework itself.

Spring MVC provides an easy way to test its components because there is no need for a servlet container to do the integration testing. You find out more about testing the MVC projects in the "Testing Spring MVC Projects" section of Chapter 7 with the help of mock implementations and fluent builder APIs provided by the `spring-test` subproject.

Using in-house solutions for building enterprise web projects is always an option, but using frameworks that have proven themselves to the community by becoming de-facto standards is a better approach for doing the enterprise web development. Stay tuned until the end of the chapter to get the best of breed.

USING THE DISPATCHER SERVLET MECHANISM

We can say that the core element of Spring MVC is the *Dispatcher Servlet*, which is the main servlet that handles all requests and dispatches them to the appropriate channels. With the Dispatcher Servlet, Spring MVC follows the *Front Controller* pattern that provides an entry point for handling all requests of web applications. Figure 3-2 shows this flow diagram.

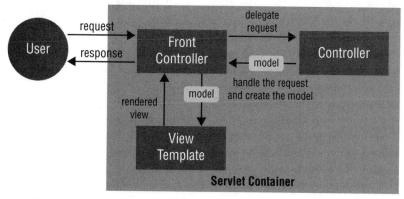

FIGURE 3-2

The Dispatcher Servlet cooperates with *handler mappings* and *view resolvers* to determine which business logic to execute upon user request and what to render at the end of the flow to return to the user. HandlerMapping is an interface to be implemented by handler mapping objects that provide a bridge between the mapping and the handler objects. ViewResolver is also an interface to be implemented by the view resolver objects that resolve the views by name. Here's the detailed definition of the execution:

1.   With a user's HTTP request, Dispatcher Servlet decides which controller to execute by communicating with handler mapping. Then Dispatcher Servlet invokes the actual handler method via Handler Adapter, forwards the request, and expects a model and a view in return.

2.   The handler method within the controller is invoked for the business logic. The method sets the model data, which is passed to the view and returns the view name to the Dispatcher Servlet, which will be rendered to the user as a response.

3.   Dispatcher Servlet integrates with a view resolver to pick up the appropriate view based on the resolver configuration.

4.   Dispatcher Servlet passes the model to the view, and the view gets rendered on the browser.

The default implementations for handler mapping, handler adapter, and view resolver are stored in the DispatcherServlet.properties file that resides under the org.springframework.web .servlet package of the spring-webmvc subproject. The "Creating Your First Spring MVC Application" section describes the ways of adding the subproject as a dependency to your project.

Spring MVC offers various handler mappings to integrate with your application. ControllerClassNameHandlerMapping uses convention over configuration to map a requested URL to the controller class. It takes the class name, trims the Controller part if it exists, and returns what remains of the class name by lowercasing the first character and prefixing it with /. BeanNameUrlHandlerMapping is the default implementation used by the Dispatcher Servlet along with the DefaultAnnotationHandlerMapping. BeanNameUrlHandlerMapping maps the URL requests to the name of the beans. So if the user requests /hello, the servlet dispatches it to the HelloController class automagically.

Defining the Servlet

Definition of the Dispatcher Servlet occurs in the deployment descriptor file of the web application, which is the web.xml file. The following is a sample definition for the servlet:

```
<servlet>
     <servlet-name>springmvc</servlet-name>
     <servlet-class>
        org.springframework.web.servlet.DispatcherServlet
     </servlet-class>
     <load-on-startup>1</load-on-startup>
</servlet>

<servlet-mapping>
     <servlet-name>springmvc</servlet-name>
     <url-pattern>*.mvc</url-pattern>
</servlet-mapping>
```

Here, servlet-mapping contains the definition of url-pattern to route any URL requested with the .mvc extension through itself in order to act as a gateway. During the initialization phase of the servlet, it looks for a configuration XML file to get Spring's application context, which is an implementation of WebApplicationContext, up and running. WebApplicationContext is an interface that extends the famous ApplicationContext to provide the web-centric features. A naming convention is used by default for the resolver mechanism of this configuration file. The servlet looks for the configuration file named {servlet-name}-servlet.xml under the WEB-INF folder by default. Because the servlet-name is defined as springmvc, the springmvc-servlet.xml file will be resolved first. Of course, the location of the file can be changed easily. The contextConfigLocation servlet initialization parameter provides this feature:

```xml
<servlet>
    <servlet-name>springmvc</servlet-name>
    <servlet-class>
        org.springframework.web.servlet.DispatcherServlet
    </servlet-class>
    <load-on-startup>1</load-on-startup>
    <init-param>
        <param-name>contextConfigLocation</param-name>
        <param-value>classpath:springmvc-servlet.xml</param-value>
    </init-param>
</servlet>
```

Here, the configuration file is resolved from the classpath of the application according to the definition stated in the highlighted code.

> **NOTE** With Servlet 3.1, it's also possible to define the servlets within web-fragment.xml files to introduce the pluggability to your application. So having multiple modules within your application, where each contains a fragment of the servlet definitions named as web-fragment.xml, rather than having a complete definition of web.xml, can achieve this.

Accessing Servlet Context

The beans that are registered within the WebApplicationContext can also access the *Servlet Context* by implementing the ServletContextAware interface shown here:

```java
package org.springframework.web.context;

public interface ServletContextAware extends Aware {
    void setServletContext(ServletContext servletContext);
}
```

This could be useful when you need to access configurations, such as context initialization parameters of the web application.

CREATING YOUR FIRST SPRING MVC APPLICATION

We have defined some of the bits, now let's create a Maven-based web application to demonstrate the architecture of Spring MVC. This example first configures the Maven dependencies by adding them to the pom.xml file, adding the servlet definition into the web.xml file, and finally defining the application context XML file for the configuration of Spring MVC. As a last step, a Controller class and a JSP are defined.

The application renders a `Hello Reader!` message to the user when a URL is accessed through the browser. The following Try It Out explains the steps.

TRY IT OUT Hello World Spring MVC Application

Use the following steps to create your first Spring MVC application that will output a message on JSP. You can find this project named as basic in the downloaded zip file.

1. Create an empty Maven web application project from the archetype maven-archetype-webapp. Add the spring-webmvc dependency to your pom.xml file. At the time of writing this book the latest version of Spring subprojects is 4.0.5.RELEASE:

    ```
    <dependency>
        <groupId>org.springframework</groupId>
        <artifactId>spring-webmvc</artifactId>
        <version>4.0.5.RELEASE</version>
    </dependency>
    ```

2. spring-webmvc depends on the spring-core, spring-beans, spring-context, and spring-web subprojects, so add them as dependencies to the project:

    ```
    <dependency>
        <groupId>org.springframework</groupId>
        <artifactId>spring-core</artifactId>
        <version>4.0.5.RELEASE</version>
    </dependency>

    <dependency>
        <groupId>org.springframework</groupId>
        <artifactId>spring-beans</artifactId>
        <version>4.0.5.RELEASE</version>
    </dependency>

    <dependency>
        <groupId>org.springframework</groupId>
        <artifactId>spring-context</artifactId>
        <version>4.0.5.RELEASE</version>
    </dependency>

    <dependency>
        <groupId>org.springframework</groupId>
        <artifactId>spring-web</artifactId>
        <version>4.0.5.RELEASE</version>
    </dependency>
    ```

3. Define the Dispatcher Servlet with its URL mapping in `web.xml`:

```xml
<web-app version="3.1" xmlns="http://xmlns.jcp.org/xml/ns/javaee"
        xmlns:xsi="http://www.w3.org/2001/XMLSchema-instance"
        xsi:schemaLocation="http://xmlns.jcp.org/xml/ns/javaee
    http://xmlns.jcp.org/xml/ns/javaee/web-app_3_1.xsd">

    <servlet>
        <servlet-name>springmvc</servlet-name>
        <servlet-class>
            org.springframework.web.servlet.DispatcherServlet
        </servlet-class>
        <load-on-startup>1</load-on-startup>
    </servlet>

    <servlet-mapping>
        <servlet-name>springmvc</servlet-name>
        <url-pattern>*.mvc</url-pattern>
    </servlet-mapping>
</web-app>
```

You defined the `web.xml` compatible with Servlet 3.1 as shown in the namespace definitions. If you are not using a Java EE7 container you can define the `web.xml` compatible with Servlet 3.0 as shown here:

```xml
<web-app xmlns="http://java.sun.com/xml/ns/javaee"
    xmlns:xsi="http://www.w3.org/2001/XMLSchema-instance"
    xsi:schemaLocation="http://java.sun.com/xml/ns/javaee
            http://java.sun.com/xml/ns/javaee/web-app_3_0.xsd"
    version="3.0">
...
</web-app>
```

4. Create the `springmvc-servlet.xml` file for application context configuration:

```xml
<?xml version="1.0" encoding="UTF-8"?>
<beans xmlns="http://www.springframework.org/schema/beans"
        xmlns:xsi="http://www.w3.org/2001/XMLSchema-instance"
        xmlns:context="http://www.springframework.org/schema/context"
        xsi:schemaLocation="http://www.springframework.org/schema/beans
    http://www.springframework.org/schema/beans/spring-beans-4.0.xsd
    http://www.springframework.org/schema/context
    http://www.springframework.org/schema/context/spring-context-4.0.xsd">

    <context:component-scan base-package="com.wiley.beginningspring.ch3" />
    <context:annotation-config />

    <bean class="org.springframework.web.servlet.view.InternalResourceViewResolver">
        <property name="prefix" value="/WEB-INF/pages/" />
        <property name="suffix" value=".jsp" />
    </bean>
</beans>
```

5. Create a simple controller that adds a hello message to the model data and returns the name of the UI page, `helloReader.jsp`, to show the message:

```
@Controller
public class HelloReaderController {

    @RequestMapping(value = "/hello")
    public ModelAndView sayHello() {
        ModelAndView mv = new ModelAndView();
        mv.addObject("message", "Hello Reader!");
        mv.setViewName("helloReader");
        return mv;
    }
}
```

6. Create the JSP file named `helloReader` under the `/WEB-INF/pages` folder:

```
<html>
<body>
    ${message}
</body>
</html>
```

7. Run the `mvn package` command to create a war file. Deploy your application on the web container and request `http://localhost:8080/hello.mvc` to see the output as shown in Figure 3-3.

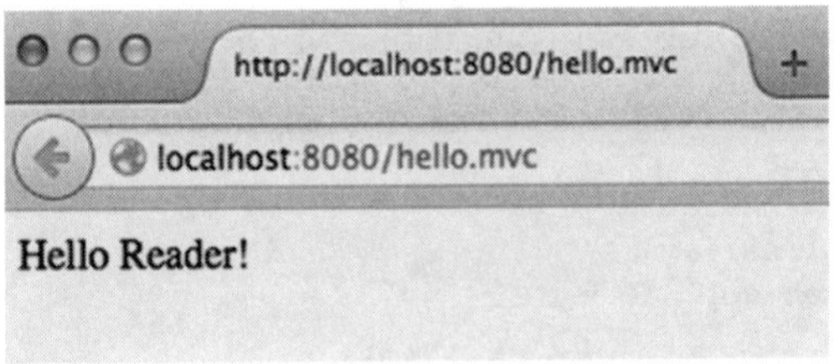

FIGURE 3-3

How It Works

The `springmvc-servlet.xml` file configures Spring's application context, and it's being picked up with this naming convention: {servletname}-servlet.xml. Within the configuration file, the `<context:component-scan>` tag states that all the beans that reside under the package `com.wiley.beginningspring.ch3` will be registered to the application context automatically. The `<context:annotation-config/>` tag activates the annotations that are defined in the beans, which are already registered within the context of the application.

> **NOTE** *Prior to Spring 3.2, the* `<mvc:annotation-driven/>` *tag needed to be declared in the XML configuration file to configure the dispatch of requests to the controller classes. It registers the* `DefaultAnnotationHandlerMapping` *and* `AnnotationMethodHandlerAdapter` *beans to the application context to handle the requests. Starting from version 3.2, this configuration was deprecated for the registration part. As of Spring 4.0, it's not necessary to register the* `DefaultAnnotationHandlerMapping` *and* `AnnotationMethodHandlerAdapter` *beans anymore because they are registered by default. But the configuration is still needed for enabling annotation-driven configuration, such as using* `@DateTimeFormat` *on a date field, so keep that in mind and use it where necessary.*

You defined the Dispatcher Servlet with the URL mapping as `*.mvc`. When the user requests the URL `http://localhost:8080/hello.mvc`, the `DispatcherServlet` is executed because it's mapped to the URLs suffixed with `.mvc`. It handles the incoming request and decides which controller should handle this request with the help of handler mapping—in the example, the `RequestMappingHandlerMapping` class. With Spring version 3.2, `DefaultAnnotationHandlerMapping` was deprecated in favor of `RequestMappingHandlerMapping`. The controller is the part that interprets the user input and transforms it into the model. (It's the C in the MVC pattern.)

Handler mapping matches the requested URL with the handler methods annotated with `@RequestMapping`. It compares the request path of the URL with the `value` attribute of the annotation. The values of `@RequestMapping` annotations are parsed and stored, and Dispatcher Servlet accesses them while handling the requests. `@RequestMapping` can be defined on the class level also, to map all the methods of a controller to a URL. We'll get to the details of the annotation in "Exploiting the Power of Annotations" section.

The handler method of the matching controller, `sayHello`, creates an instance of the `ModelAndView` class, sets the object to be passed to the view with a key (`message`), sets the name of the view (`helloReader`), and returns it for the servlet to resolve the view that will be rendered to the user as the response. An instance of the `ModelAndView` class could also be passed to the handler method. The signature of the handler methods annotated by `@RequestMapping` is very flexible. You can read the details of it in the "Exploiting the Power of Annotations" section.

`ModelAndView` is a holder class for both the model and view. `Model` is represented as a map that collects key/value pairs, and `View` is an interface that represents a web interaction.

Now it's the servlet's turn to resolve which view will be rendered to the user. It uses the `InternalResourceViewResolver` class as the default implementation for its view resolution strategy. This means that the user interface page that will be navigated from the controller will be picked up with this view-resolving mechanism. The `InternalResourceViewResolver` class extends `UrlBasedViewResolver`, which provides `prefix` and `suffix` properties. In the example, you defined `prefix` as `/WEB-INF/pages/` and `suffix` as `.jsp`. So the view name set by the handler method will be prefixed and suffixed with these values to get the JSP.

> **TIP** It's a good practice to place all the view files in a folder under the `WEB-INF` folder to prevent direct access of the pages via URL.

CONFIGURING SPRING MVC WITH ANNOTATIONS

It's also possible to do the application context configuration with annotations instead of an XML file. To demonstrate, you convert the XML configuration that is given in the "Creating Your First Spring MVC Application" section into an annotation-based one.

First you need to create a configurator class. The class will have the @Configuration annotation, stating that it could contain one or more methods annotated with @Bean. You'll use the @Bean annotation to declare a Spring bean explicitly by returning an instance of the appropriate class—InternalResourceViewResolver in this case—because you defined a bean of it in the XML configuration.

For scanning components starting with a given base package you also need to use the @ComponentScan annotation that does the same job with XML configuration's <context:component-scan> tag.

The whole definition of the configurator class is the following:

```
@Configuration
@ComponentScan(basePackages = {"com.wiley.beginningspring.ch3"})
public class AppConfig {

    @Bean
    public InternalResourceViewResolver getInternalResourceViewResolver() {
        InternalResourceViewResolver resolver = new InternalResourceViewResolver();
        resolver.setPrefix("/WEB-INF/pages/");
        resolver.setSuffix(".jsp");
        return resolver;
    }
}
```

You should reconfigure the definition of the Dispatcher Servlet to load the application context via class definition. With this approach the contextClass parameter refers to the org.springframework.web.context.support.AnnotationConfigWebApplicationContext class, which is an implementation of ApplicationContext. This class uses the contextConfigLocation parameter to get the class annotated with @Configuration; in this example, it is the fully qualified name of the AppConfig class. The following code snippet is the new servlet definition:

```
<servlet>
    <servlet-name>springmvc</servlet-name>
    <servlet-class>
        org.springframework.web.servlet.DispatcherServlet
    </servlet-class>
    <init-param>
        <param-name>contextClass</param-name>
        <param-value>
org.springframework.web.context.support.AnnotationConfigWebApplicationContext
        </param-value>
    </init-param>
    <init-param>
        <param-name>contextConfigLocation</param-name>
        <param-value>
            com.wiley.beginningspring.ch3.config.AppConfig
        </param-value>
    </init-param>
    <load-on-startup>1</load-on-startup>
</servlet>
```

HANDLING FORMS WITH JSP

Every web application needs to interact with forms to retrieve data from users by wrapping the input fields with forms. Spring MVC provides form handling with its custom JSP form tag library in an elegant way.

The form tag library supports creating the views with its custom tags, which also provide the binding with the model classes. So the parameters in the HTTP requests submitted by the browser are mapped to the model with the binding ability of the framework. This section covers how to use these tags in detail.

The form tag library offers many tags from input elements such as checkboxes, radio buttons, combo boxes, and so on, to output elements for displaying informational data such as labels and errors.

Following is a list of tags. These custom tags correspond with the HTML tags that render matching output. We'll go through them with examples later in this section.

- ➤ `form`
- ➤ `input`
- ➤ `password`
- ➤ `hidden`
- ➤ `select`
- ➤ `option`
- ➤ `options`
- ➤ `radiobutton`
- ➤ `radiobuttons`
- ➤ `checkbox`
- ➤ `checkboxes`
- ➤ `textarea`
- ➤ `errors`
- ➤ `label`
- ➤ `button`

Configuring the Form Tag Library

The form tag library needs some configuration to be used within the pages. You should add the definition of the tag library to the pages; the examples use `mvc` as the prefix for the library definition:

```
<%@taglib uri="http://www.springframework.org/tags/form" prefix="mvc" %>
```

The form tag library descriptor file, `spring-form.tld`, resides under the `META-INF` folder of the `spring-webmvc` subproject. By adding the project as a Maven dependency (as described in the "Hello World Spring MVC Application" Try It Out) you will be ready to use it directly.

For each tag definition in the tag library, the `dynamic-attributes` tag is set to `true`. This means that attributes that do not exist in the tag definition can still be defined and used because they will be rendered as pass-through attributes, so you will see them in the HTML output as you defined in the tags.

Spring MVC also provides another tag library for handling internationalization of the messages, selecting resources from themes, and so on. The name of the tag library descriptor file for this is `spring.tld`, and it also resides under the `META-INF` folder of the `spring-webmvc` subproject. Definition of the tag library is shown here:

```
<%@ taglib uri="http://www.springframework.org/tags" prefix="spring" %>
```

The `message` and `theme` tags of the tag library are explained with examples in the "Implementing Internationalization (i18n)" and "Using Themes" sections, respectively.

Now it's time to move on to the binding ability of the input tags. This is one of the most important concepts of Spring MVC.

Understanding the Power of Binding

Spring MVC provides powerful binding between its view and the model layer. The user sends the data through the views, and they are automatically bound to the model. Because each interaction of the user is an HTTP request on the web, Spring MVC binds the request parameters to the *Command object*, which is a POJO/Java bean whose values are populated by the input of the user. The Command object is synonymous with the *Form object* and the *Form-Backing object*; you may also see these definitions online.

The main element for enabling the binding in the view layer is the `path` attribute of the tags. `path` refers to the property of the class that is defined in a model. Here's an example:

```
<mvc:input path="name" />
```

In the example, `path` refers to the `name` property of a class—let's say `User`. The value input by the user is automatically set to the `name` property of the `User` class instance. If the property of a class defined by the `path` attribute does not exist, Spring MVC throws out the error `org.springframework.beans.NotReadablePropertyException`, stating that the property is not readable or has an invalid getter/setter method. `path` is a required attribute for most of the tags, so you must define it to get the tag working. One exception is the `errors` tag, for which the `path` attribute is not required. You can read more details about this in the "Handling Exceptions" section.

So `path` knows about the property but not the Command object itself. To better understand how the values are set to the model automagically, you should take a look at the `form` tag in the next section.

Working with Forms

The `form` tag renders an HTML `form`. By default, a form executes a `GET` method to a given `action`. This means that the data input by the user will be sent to a URL stated within the `form`. The `form` tag might contain one or more tags inside—such as input fields, radio buttons, or checkboxes—to retrieve data from its user. We cover them one by one in this section.

To help with the binding, the `form` tag exposes a binding path to its inner tags with the `modelAttribute` attribute of the form, which states under which name this model class will be exposed to the view. So `modelAttribute` points to the model class, and `path` attributes of the input tags defined inside that form point to the properties of the same model class. That's how the input tags know about the model class; when it gets bound to a form, it is commonly called the Command object as previously defined.

By default, the value of the `modelAttribute` is `command`, but it's a good practice to set a specific name to it rather than `command`. We mostly use the same name with the class—for example, if we have the `User` class, the value for the `modelAttribute` is set to `user`. You can also use the `commandName` attribute to set the reference name. But it's a former usage that is supported with the versions of the framework prior to 4.0, so the examples stick with the `modelAttribute`. The following code snippet gives a sample `form` tag definition. Notice that in it `mvc` is used as the prefix for the tags:

```
<mvc:form modelAttribute="user" action="result.mvc">
    <table>
        <tr>
            <td><mvc:label path="name">Name</mvc:label></td>
            <td><mvc:input path="name" /></td>
        </tr>
        <tr>
            <td><mvc:label path="lastname">Last Name</mvc:label></td>
            <td><mvc:input path="lastname" /></td>
        </tr>
        <tr>
            <td colspan="2">
                <input type="submit" value="Submit" />
            </td>
        </tr>
    </table>
</mvc:form>
```

In this example, the form definition contains two input elements and a button element to submit the form.

Using Input Elements

You defined the `form` tag and the way to bind the model to the view; now you find out how to retrieve the user data. Let's first start with the `input` tag, which renders an HTML `input` tag with the `type` attribute set to `text`. This enables the user to input free-form text. Here is a simple definition for the tag that was mentioned previously:

```
<mvc:input path="name" />
```

Here, the binding to the model is done with the `path` attribute, and the input is set to the `name` property of a model class. The HTML `input` tag rendered in the output uses the value of the `path` attribute for its `id` and `name` attributes if they are not explicitly specified. This rule also applies for most of the user input tags of the Spring MVC tag library.

As of Spring version 3.1, HTML5 types such as `date`, `color`, and `email` can be used with the `type` attribute. Spring MVC leverages the use of HTML5 where possible.

To render a text area rather than an input, you can use the `textarea` tag. The following example binds the `detail` property of a model class to the tag:

```
<mvc:textarea path="detail" />
```

To have a password field rendered on the view, you can use the `password` tag to render an HTML `input` tag with the `type` attribute set to `password`. A sample usage is given in the next snippet, which binds to the `password` property of a model class with the `path` attribute:

```
<mvc:password path="password" />
```

The `showPassword` attribute of the tag states that the HTML tag rendered in the view will have the submitted data in the `value` attribute (`true`), or it will have the value of the attribute as `""`, which is an empty string (`false`). The latter is the default value.

Entering Dates

With version 4.0 of Spring, it's possible to use the `java.time` package of JDK 8. The annotation-driven date formatting enables the usage of the JSR310 Date-Time API, and it enables you to replace the `java.util.Date`/`java.util.Calendar` or `joda-time` project classes.

You will use the `@DateTimeFormat` annotation on the `java.time.LocalDate` typed property of a model class without the need of any extra configuration. Following is a sample JSP snippet and field definition from the model class:

```
<mvc:input path="birthDate" />

@DateTimeFormat(pattern="yyyy-MM-dd")
private LocalDate birthDate;
```

Under the hood the `Jsr310DateTimeFormatAnnotationFormatterFactory` class automatically handles these fields, and by default it applies to short date and short time, which would be like 6/30/09 7:03 AM. Of course, you can specify customized formatting with the help of the `iso` and `pattern` attributes.

Supported class types of the new JDK8 date-time features are shown in Table 3-1.

TABLE 3-1: The List of Supported Class Types

CLASS TYPE	ANNOTATION	FORMAT
java.time.LocalDate	@DateTimeFormat(iso = ISO.DATE)	yyyy-MM-dd
java.time.LocalTime	@DateTimeFormat(iso = ISO.TIME)	HH:mm:ss.SSSZ
java.time .LocalDateTime	@DateTimeFormat(iso = ISO .DATE_TIME)	yyyy-MM- dd'T'HH:mm:ss.SSSZ
java.time .OffsetDateTime	@DateTimeFormat(iso = ISO .DATE_TIME)	yyyy-MM- dd'T'HH:mm:ss.SSSZ
java.time.OffsetTime	@DateTimeFormat(iso = ISO.TIME)	HH:mm:ss.SSSZ
java.time .ZonedDateTime	@DateTimeFormat(iso = ISO .DATE_TIME)	yyyy-MM- dd'T'HH:mm:ss.SSSZ

> **NOTE** To process `@DateTimeFormat` annotations, define `<mvc:annotation-driven/>` in Spring's application context configuration file.

Selecting from a Drop-Down

To select data from a drop-down, you can use the `select` tag, which renders an HTML `select` tag. The following example displays a list of countries and selects one of them:

```
<mvc:select path="country" items="${countries}" />
```

Here, the selected data is bound to the `country` property of a model class with a `path` attribute. The `items` attribute refers to the collection, array, or map of objects that will be used to generate the HTML `option` tags within the `select`. You can set the `countries` list as an object to a `ModelAndView` instance in the controller. You are setting three countries with the `countries` key in the following sample:

```
final String[] countries = { "Turkey", "United States", "Germany" };
modelAndView.addObject("countries", countries);
```

If the list bound by the `items` attribute contains objects of a POJO—instead of `String`, for instance—you can use the `itemLabel` and `itemValue` attributes to determine what will be displayed to the user and what will be set as the value of the `option` tag, respectively.

> **NOTE** To enable `multiple` select within the drop-down, set the `multiple` attribute to `true`.

Another way to add options to the `select` tag is to use the `option` or `options` tags by nesting them within the `select`. Use `option` to add one element and `options` to add one or more elements into the drop-down. You can also use them together as shown here:

```
<mvc:select path="country">
    <mvc:option value="" label="--Select--"></mvc:option>
    <mvc:options items="${countries}"></mvc:options>
</mvc:select>
```

> **NOTE** The `items` attribute overrides the usage of the `option` tag. But if the `items` attribute and the `options` tag are used together, the content of both is merged and rendered together to the user in the drop-down.

Selecting with Radio Buttons

Spring MVC provides the `radiobutton` and `radiobuttons` tags that render an HTML `input` tag with the `type` attribute set to `radio`. In the following example, two radio buttons are defined for selecting gender. Here the `path` attribute is set to the `gender` property of a model class:

```
<mvc:radiobutton path="gender" label="Female" value="F" />
<mvc:radiobutton path="gender" label="Male" value="M" />
```

The `value` attribute defines what will be submitted and the `label` attribute states what will be shown to the user. The example is submitting the string values `F` and `M`. You can also use the `radiobuttons` tag to bind a list of values, as shown in the following example. `items` defines an array of `enum` values and adds it as an object to an instance of `ModelAndView`:

```
<mvc:radiobuttons path="gender" items="${genders}" />

public enum Gender {
        MALE,
        FEMALE;
}

modelAndView.addObject("genders", Gender.values());
```

Selecting with Checkboxes

The `checkbox` and `checkboxes` tags render the HTML `input` tag with the `type` attribute set to `checkbox`. You use them in a similar way as the radio buttons. In the following example a `Boolean` value is bound to the `checkbox` tag with its `path` attribute:

```
<mvc:checkbox path="nonSmoking" />
```

It's also possible to bind an array of strings to the `checkboxes` tag with the `items` attribute.

Adding Labels

The `label` tag renders the HTML5 `label` tag, which refers to an HTML `input` tag. While building up forms, it's essential to use the labels to identify what will be input by the user. In the following example, a label and an input box are bound to the `name` property of a model class:

```
<mvc:label path="name">Name</mvc:label>
<mvc:input path="name" />
```

The tag itself wraps the text value that will be displayed—in the example, it's `Name`. To refer to the `input` element in HTML, the value of the `path` is used for the `for` attribute of the `label` tag. But `label` also contains the attribute `for`, so if it's defined it overrides the value given with the `path` attribute in HTML output.

Placing Buttons

The `button` tag renders an HTML5 `button` tag. It's possible to put content, such as text or images, within the `button` tag. It's suggested to use the HTML `input` tag with `type` set to `submit` instead of the `button` tag when a form will be submitted because different browsers may submit different values. You should wrap the text of the button with the tags as shown here:

```
<mvc:button>Submit</mvc:button>
```

Styling

Styling for the tags is provided by three main attributes: `cssClass`, `cssStyle`, and `cssErrorClass`. `cssClass` is the equivalent of the HTML `class` attribute; `cssStyle` is the equivalent of the HTML `style` attribute; and `cssErrorClass` is also the equivalent of the HMTL `class` attribute, but it's only rendered when errors exist in the application.

You can find detailed examples of using the styles in the "Validating User Input" section. The following Try It Out walks you through an example of handling a user registration form.

TRY IT OUT Handling a User Registration Form

Use the following steps to create an application that demonstrates the usage input fields like text field, text area, combo box, radio button, and checkbox. You can find this project named as `formelements` in the downloaded zip file.

1. Create an empty Maven web application project from the archetype `maven-archetype-webapp`. Add `spring-webmvc` and its subproject dependencies to your `pom.xml` file. At the time of writing this book the latest version for Spring projects is `4.0.5.RELEASE`:

```xml
<dependency>
    <groupId>org.springframework</groupId>
    <artifactId>spring-webmvc</artifactId>
    <version>4.0.5.RELEASE</version>
</dependency>

<dependency>
    <groupId>org.springframework</groupId>
    <artifactId>spring-core</artifactId>
    <version>4.0.5.RELEASE</version>
</dependency>

<dependency>
    <groupId>org.springframework</groupId>
    <artifactId>spring-beans</artifactId>
    <version>4.0.5.RELEASE</version>
</dependency>

<dependency>
    <groupId>org.springframework</groupId>
    <artifactId>spring-context</artifactId>
    <version>4.0.5.RELEASE</version>
</dependency>
```

```
<dependency>
    <groupId>org.springframework</groupId>
    <artifactId>spring-web</artifactId>
    <version>4.0.5.RELEASE</version>
</dependency>
```

2. Define the Dispatcher Servlet with its URL mapping in your web.xml:

```
<web-app version="3.1" xmlns="http://xmlns.jcp.org/xml/ns/javaee"
        xmlns:xsi="http://www.w3.org/2001/XMLSchema-instance"
        xsi:schemaLocation="http://xmlns.jcp.org/xml/ns/javaee
  http://xmlns.jcp.org/xml/ns/javaee/web-app_3_1.xsd">

    <servlet>
        <servlet-name>springmvc</servlet-name>
        <servlet-class>
            org.springframework.web.servlet.DispatcherServlet
        </servlet-class>
        <load-on-startup>1</load-on-startup>
    </servlet>

    <servlet-mapping>
        <servlet-name>springmvc</servlet-name>
        <url-pattern>*.mvc</url-pattern>
    </servlet-mapping>
</web-app>
```

3. Create the springmvc-servlet.xml file for application context configuration:

```
<?xml version="1.0" encoding="UTF-8"?>
<beans xmlns="http://www.springframework.org/schema/beans"
        xmlns:xsi="http://www.w3.org/2001/XMLSchema-instance"
        xmlns:context="http://www.springframework.org/schema/context"
        xmlns:mvc="http://www.springframework.org/schema/mvc"
        xsi:schemaLocation="http://www.springframework.org/schema/beans
    http://www.springframework.org/schema/beans/spring-beans-4.0.xsd
    http://www.springframework.org/schema/context
    http://www.springframework.org/schema/context/spring-context-4.0.xsd
    http://www.springframework.org/schema/mvc
    http://www.springframework.org/schema/mvc/spring-mvc-4.0.xsd">

    <context:component-scan base-package="com.wiley.beginningspring.ch3" />
    <context:annotation-config />
    <mvc:annotation-driven />

    <bean class="org.springframework.web.servlet.view.InternalResourceViewResolver">
        <property name="prefix" value="/WEB-INF/pages/" />
        <property name="suffix" value=".jsp" />
    </bean>
</beans>
```

4. Create the UserController class:

```
@Controller
public class UserController {
```

```java
    private static final String[] countries = { "Turkey",
        "United States", "Germany" };

    @RequestMapping(value = "/form")
    public ModelAndView user() {
        ModelAndView modelAndView =
            new ModelAndView("userForm", "user", new User());
        modelAndView.addObject("genders", Gender.values());
        modelAndView.addObject("countries", countries);

        return modelAndView;
    }

    @RequestMapping(value = "/result")
    public ModelAndView processUser(User user) {
        ModelAndView modelAndView = new ModelAndView();
        modelAndView.setViewName("userResult");
        modelAndView.addObject("u", user);
        return modelAndView;
    }
}
```

5. Create the userForm.jsp page under the /WEB-INF/pages folder:

```jsp
<%@ page contentType="text/html; charset=ISO-8859-1" %>
<%@taglib uri="http://www.springframework.org/tags/form" prefix="mvc" %>
<html>
<head>
    <title>Spring MVC Form Handling</title>
</head>
<body>

<h2>User Registration Form</h2>
<mvc:form modelAttribute="user" action="result.mvc">
    <table>
        <tr>
            <td><mvc:label path="name">Name</mvc:label></td>
            <td><mvc:input path="name" /></td>
        </tr>
        <tr>
            <td><mvc:label path="lastname">Last Name</mvc:label></td>
            <td><mvc:input path="lastname" /></td>
        </tr>
        <tr>
            <td><mvc:label path="password">Password</mvc:label></td>
            <td><mvc:password path="password" /></td>
        </tr>
        <tr>
            <td><mvc:label path="detail">Detail</mvc:label></td>
            <td><mvc:textarea path="detail" /></td>
        </tr>
        <tr>
            <td><mvc:label path="birthDate">Birth Date</mvc:label></td>
            <td><mvc:input path="birthDate" /></td>
        </tr>
```

```
        <tr>
            <td><mvc:label path="gender">Gender</mvc:label></td>
            <td><mvc:radiobuttons path="gender" items="${genders}" /></td>
        </tr>
        <tr>
            <td><mvc:label path="country">Country</mvc:label></td>
            <td><mvc:select path="country" items="${countries}" /></td>
        </tr>
        <tr>
            <td><mvc:label path="nonSmoking">Non Smoking</mvc:label></td>
            <td><mvc:checkbox path="nonSmoking" /></td>
        </tr>
        <tr>
            <td colspan="2">
                <input type="submit" value="Submit" />
            </td>
        </tr>
    </table>
</mvc:form>
</body>
</html>
```

6. Create the `userResult.jsp` page under the `/WEB-INF/pages` folder:

```
<%@ page contentType="text/html; charset=ISO-8859-1" %>
<%@taglib uri="http://www.springframework.org/tags/form" prefix="mvc" %>
<html>
<head>
    <title>Spring MVC Form Handling</title>
</head>
<body>
    <h2>User Registration Result</h2>
    <table>
        <tr>
            <td>Name</td>
            <td>${u.name}</td>
        </tr>
        <tr>
            <td>Last name</td>
            <td>${u.lastname}</td>
        </tr>
        <tr>
            <td>Password</td>
            <td>${u.password}</td>
        </tr>
        <tr>
            <td>Detail</td>
            <td>${u.detail}</td>
        </tr>
        <tr>
            <td>Birth Date</td>
            <td>${u.birthDate}</td>
        </tr>
        <tr>
```

```
            <td>Gender</td>
            <td>${u.gender}</td>
        </tr>
        <tr>
            <td>Country</td>
            <td>${u.country}</td>
        </tr>
        <tr>
            <td>Non-Smoking</td>
            <td>${u.nonSmoking}</td>
        </tr>
    </table>
</body>
</html>
```

7. Run the `mvn package` command to create a war file. Deploy your application on the web container and request `http://localhost:8080/form.mvc`. Fill up the form and submit it to see the output as shown in Figure 3-4.

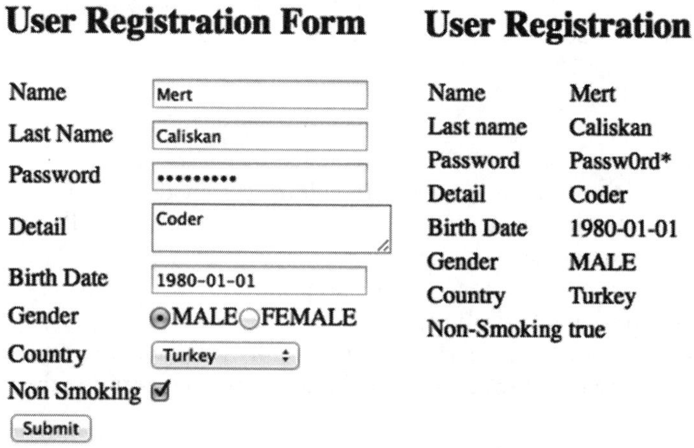

User Registration Form

Name	Mert
Last Name	Caliskan
Password	••••••••
Detail	Coder
Birth Date	1980-01-01
Gender	⦿MALE◯FEMALE
Country	Turkey ◆
Non Smoking	☑

Submit

User Registration Result

Name	Mert
Last name	Caliskan
Password	Passw0rd*
Detail	Coder
Birth Date	1980-01-01
Gender	MALE
Country	Turkey
Non-Smoking	true

FIGURE 3-4

How It Works

When the user requests `/form.mvc`, the `user()` method is invoked and an empty `User` instance is set into a `ModelAndView` instance along with the name of the view—`userForm`. The genders and countries are also set to the model in the `user()` method, and they are accessed from the JSP with `${genders}` and `${countries}`, respectively.

The location of the `userForm` JSP is resolved with the help of the `InternalResourceViewResolver` definition. The `modelAttribute` of the form definition is set with the same value while creating the `ModelAndView` instance in the `user()` method. When the user submits the form to `/result.mvc`, the `processUser()` method is invoked because the value of the `@RequestMapping` matches with the `/result`. The user instance is passed as an argument to the `processUser()` method with the submitted values. The binding takes care of the type conversion in here. The view name is set as `userResult` to a `ModelAndView` instance. The retrieved user is also set to the model with the u key value. It is accessed in the `userResult` page and the properties of the user are printed out as shown in Figure 3-4.

EXPLOITING THE POWER OF ANNOTATIONS

As of version 2.5, Spring MVC leveraged the use of annotations to define the controllers. This section covers some of the annotations.

@Controller

`@Controller` is the main annotation that indicates the annotated class serves as a Controller of the MVC framework. The Dispatcher Servlet scans classes annotated with it to map the web requests to the methods annotated with `@RequestMapping`. `@Controller` inherits from the `@Component` annotation like other Spring annotations, such as `@Service` and `@Repository`.

@RequestMapping

`@RequestMapping` is the annotation that is used to map the user's requests to handler classes or methods. It can be applied on the class level and also on the method level. The methods annotated with this annotation are allowed to have a very flexible signature. It can take HTTP Servlet request/response objects, HTTP Session objects, `InputStream`/`OutputStream` objects, `PathVariable`/`ModelAttribute` annotated parameters, `BindingResult` objects, and many others. You can refer to the Javadoc of the class for the full documentation at `http://docs.spring.io/spring/docs/4.0.5.RELEASE/javadoc-api/org/springframework/web/bind/annotation/RequestMapping.html`. Read more about the use of the annotation in the "Handling Forms with JSP" section.

@ModelAttribute

This annotation binds a return value to a parameter with a key to be exposed to the view. It can be applied on the method level or on a method's argument.

At the method level, it can easily help to load the reference data. In the "Handling a User Registration Form" Try It Out, you were loading the genders into the model by setting an object to it with a key. You can define a new method to set the gender values into the model with a key as shown here:

```
@ModelAttribute("genders")
public Gender[] genders() {
    return Gender.values();
}
```

At the method's argument level, the handler method gets a reference to the object, which contains the data entered by the user with a form:

```
@RequestMapping(value = "/process")
public ModelAndView doSomeStuff(@ModelAttribute("value") MyObject object) {
...
}
```

The signature for the methods annotated with @ModelAttribute is also flexible like the handler methods annotated with @RequestMapping. You can refer to the Javadoc of @RequestMapping for full documentation at http://docs.spring.io/spring/docs/4.0.5.RELEASE/javadoc-api/org/springframework/web/bind/annotation/RequestMapping.html.

@PathVariable

This annotation binds a method parameter to a URI template. It's helpful to execute the handler method by retrieving data from the user via a request URL. So you can fetch the user data with the given userid with @PathVariable and show it to the requested user in the handler method as shown here:

```
@RequestMapping(value = "/view/{userid}")
public ModelAndView fetchUser(@PathVariable String userid) {
...
}
```

Here the name of the method parameter matches the template so the example didn't define the value to the annotation, but you could also define it as @PathVariable("userid"). The @PathVariable argument can be of any type, such as int, Date, String, and so on.

@ControllerAdvice

This annotation enables you to centralize the code in one place and share it across the controllers. A class annotated with @ControllerAdvice can contain methods with the @ExceptionHandler, @InitBinder, and @ModelAttribute annotations, and they will be applied to all the methods with the @RequestMapping annotation in the application. To see the @ControllerAdvice annotation in detail, refer to the "Handling Exceptions" section.

@InitBinder

This annotation determines the methods that initialize the WebDataBinder. It supports features such as turning off automatic data binding from request parameters to model objects or registering custom editors for parsing the date fields.

@ExceptionHandler

This annotation defines the method that will handle the exceptions that occur in the controller class in which it is defined. The detailed explanation and usage of the annotation are described in the "Handling Exceptions" section.

VALIDATING USER INPUT

Spring MVC supports integration with the JSR349 Bean Validation API, which offers extensive features for validating the data through the layers of an application. Because the view layer is the first layer that interacts with the user, doing the validation process at this point will make the data more stable and less error prone. With the help of Bean Validation you can easily apply validation metadata onto your model classes and reflect the possible error outcomes to the user via the appropriate view. The metadata can easily be defined with annotations, hence the validations will be much easier to define. The following snippet is the `User` domain class to which some of the validation annotations have been applied—such as the following:

➤ The `@Size` annotation that sets length of the username between 3 and 20

➤ The `@Email` annotation that validates the input with an appropriate regular expression for an e-mail

➤ The `@CreditCardNumber` that validates the input number with the *Luhn algorithm*

> **NOTE** *Luhn algorithm is a simple modulus-10 checksum formula that can be used to validate a variety of identification numbers.*

➤ The `@Pattern` that validates the password according to a regular expression such as the first character must be a letter and it must contain at least 4 characters and no more than 15 characters

For the sake of space, getter and setter methods are omitted in the code:

```
public class User {
    @Size(min=3, max=20)
    String username;

    @Email
    String email;

    @CreditCardNumber
    String ccNumber;

    @Pattern(regexp = "^[a-zA-Z]\\w{3,14}$")
    String password;

    //getters & setters
}
```

To enable the validation, you need to add an implementation of a Bean Validation to your project. For the example, we have chosen the `Hibernate Validator` framework to provide the validation features. At the time of writing, the latest version of the Hibernate Validator project was 5.1.1.Final; you can easily add it as a Maven dependency like the one given in the following example. Hibernate Validator also adds the Bean Validation API as a transitive dependency to the project so you don't need to take care of it explicitly:

```
<dependency>
    <groupId>org.hibernate</groupId>
    <artifactId>hibernate-validator</artifactId>
    <version>5.1.1.Final</version>
</dependency>
```

> **NOTE** *You can find the list annotations provided by the Hibernate Validator and JSR 349 Bean Validation API at* `http://docs.jboss.org/hibernate /validator/5.1/reference/en-US/html_single/ #section-builtin-constraints.`

Because you defined the model, you can move on with the JSP that will contain the form. The `form` you defined in the page contains four input elements for the properties of the `User` class, respectively, and it also contains four `errors` tags to display the possible errors that might occur for each input field. The form submits to a method with a request mapping `/result`:

```jsp
<%@ page contentType="text/html; charset=ISO-8859-1" %>
<%@taglib uri="http://www.springframework.org/tags/form" prefix="mvc" %>
<html>
<head>
    <title>Spring MVC Form Validation</title>
    <style type="text/css">
        .formFieldError { background-color: #FFC; }
    </style>
</head>
<body>

<h2>User Registration Form</h2>
<mvc:form modelAttribute="user" action="result.mvc">
    <table>
        <tr>
            <td><mvc:label path="username">User Name</mvc:label></td>
            <td><mvc:input path="username" cssErrorClass="formFieldError" /></td>
            <td><mvc:errors path="username" /></td>
        </tr>
        <tr>
            <td><mvc:label path="email">E-Mail</mvc:label></td>
            <td><mvc:input path="email" cssErrorClass="formFieldError" /></td>
            <td><mvc:errors path="email" /></td>
        </tr>
        <tr>
            <td><mvc:label path="ccNumber">Credit Card Number</mvc:label></td>
            <td><mvc:input path="ccNumber" cssErrorClass="formFieldError" /></td>
            <td><mvc:errors path="ccNumber" /></td>
        </tr>
        <tr>
            <td><mvc:label path="password">Password</mvc:label></td>
            <td><mvc:password path="password" cssErrorClass="formFieldError" /></td>
            <td><mvc:errors path="password" /></td>
        </tr>
        <tr>
```

```
            <td colspan="3">
                <input type="submit" value="Submit" />
            </td>
        </tr>
    </table>
</mvc:form>
</body>
</html>
```

For each `errors` tag you set the name of the property of the model class to its `path` attribute. But for the `errors` tag the `path` attribute is not required. If it's omitted, you will not see an error message next to the related input field. If you want to display all the errors in one place you can set the value of the `path` to `*` and put an `errors` tag on top of the form. This example also defines a style-sheet class `formFieldError` and sets the `cssErrorClass` attribute of each input field to it. With this error class, when validation fails for an input field, the background color of the field will be set to yellow.

The controller method that handles the form submit is shown here:

```
@RequestMapping(value = "/result")
public ModelAndView processUser(@Valid User user, BindingResult result) {
    ModelAndView modelAndView = new ModelAndView();
    modelAndView.addObject("u", user);

    if (result.hasErrors()) {
        modelAndView.setViewName("userForm");
    }
    else {
        modelAndView.setViewName("userResult");
    }

    return modelAndView;
}
```

The validation of the user is being triggered by the `@Valid` annotation that you set on the `user` method parameter. The annotation gets applied recursively to the properties of the class. If this annotation is missing, the bean validation will not be invoked.

The `processUser` method takes an extra parameter named `result`, which is an instance of `BindingResult`. This parameter is used for checking whether any validation errors occurred during the mapping of request parameters to the domain class properties, with the method `result.hasErrors()`. You are setting the view according to this condition to stay on the input page for showing the errors to the user.

> **NOTE** *If the method parameter of type* `BindingResult` *is omitted while using the* `@Valid` *annotation on the model attribute, you might encounter the following problem while submitting the form:*
> `HTTP 400 - The request sent by the client was syntactically incorrect.` *Make sure that the method parameter of the* `BindingResult` *is not missing.*

If you submit the form with empty input fields, you get the output shown in Figure 3-5.

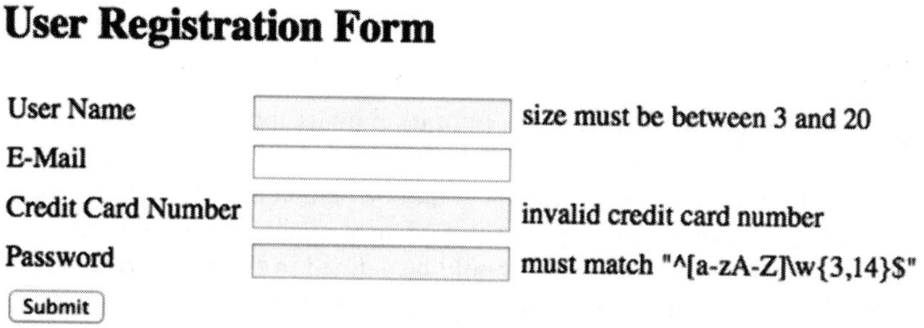

User Registration Form

User Name   [   ]   size must be between 3 and 20

E-Mail   [   ]

Credit Card Number [   ]   invalid credit card number

Password   [   ]   must match "^[a-zA-Z]\w{3,14}$"

[Submit]

FIGURE 3-5

The shaded box styling is coming from the `cssErrorClass` attribute. The error messages displayed in Figure 3-5 are set as default by the framework. To modify them you can set new messages through annotations, such as for the password field:

```
@Pattern(regexp = "^[a-zA-Z]\\w{3,14}$", message = ⌐
    "first character must be a letter and it must contain at least ⌐
    4 characters and no more than 15 characters")
String password;
```

With this approach, the message makes more sense compared to the old one, but it still lacks internationalization because the message itself is hardcoded.

To configure the validation, first you need to add the `LocalValidatorFactoryBean` and `ReloadableResourceBundleMessageSource` bean definitions into your web application's context. You also need to define the validator in the `annotation-driven` tag of the `mvc` namespace:

```
<mvc:annotation-driven validator="validator" />

<bean id="messageSource"
class="org.springframework.context.support.ReloadableResourceBundleMessageSource">
    <property name="basename" value="classpath:messages" />
</bean>

<bean id="validator"
class="org.springframework.validation.beanvalidation.LocalValidatorFactoryBean">
    <property name="validationMessageSource" ref="messageSource"/>
</bean>
```

Here, `ReloadableResourceBundleMessageSource` refers to a properties file that contains the messages as key/value pairs. The file should reside under the classpath of the application with the basename `messages` as stated in the preceding code. If you are using Maven as your build tool, you can create the properties file under the `src/main/resources` folder. The file could be differentiated according to the locale such as `messages_en_US.properties` for a U.S. locale or `messages_tr_TR.properties` for a Turkish locale, or you can just define it as `messages.properties`.

Now you can define the key for the message in annotation like this:

```
@Pattern(regexp = "^[a-zA-Z]\\w{3,14}$", message = "{error.password}")
String password;
```

With this approach, you need to add a message key to each annotation by wrapping it with a curly bracket. Another intuitive option is to define the key value according to the annotation, model attribute, and the pathname used. The notation for a key like this would be `AnnotationName.ModelAttributeName.PathName`. Let's sample this for a field. For the `password` field, which is marked with the `@Pattern` annotation, the key value that should be defined in the properties file will be `Pattern.user.password`. This approach is non-obtrusive compared to the previous ones because there is no hardcoded information in the code.

> **NOTE** If both the annotation's message attribute and implicit key definition are applied to a field, the implicit definition takes precedence over the annotation's message attribute.

> **NOTE** At the time of writing, Hibernate Validator does not provide full support for validating the `java.time.LocalDate` type of JDK8. Keep that in mind while applying validation metadata on the model classes.

UPLOADING FILES

Spring provides two ways to process file upload, one with the *Commons FileUpload* multipart request process and the other one with the *Servlet 3.1* multipart request process. By default, Spring does not handle any multipart requests, so to enable the file upload, you need to define some configuration.

To enable multipart handling you first need to define a multipart resolver in the web application's context, which `DispatcherServlet` can access. The bean name should be given as `multipartResolver`. The multipart resolver can either be specific to Commons FileUpload as shown here:

```
<bean id="multipartResolver"
  class="org.springframework.web.multipart.commons.CommonsMultipartResolver" />
```

or it can be specific to Servlet 3.1, like this:

```
<bean id="multipartResolver"
  class="org.springframework.web.multipart.↵
    support.StandardServletMultipartResolver" />
```

> **NOTE** *If you do not provide any configuration for the multipart resolvers of Spring, you might encounter some unexpected behaviors in your code—for example, the uploaded file could be* `null` *or you can get the exception* `java.lang.IllegalArgumentException: Expected MultipartHttpServletRequest: is a MultipartResolver configured?` *in the application's console log.*

When `DispatcherServlet` detects a file upload request, it delegates the job to one of the multipart resolvers that you declared. Then the resolver parses the request into multipart files and parameters to create an instance of the `MultipartHttpServletRequest`.

While using the Commons FileUpload approach, you can configure the upload process by defining properties to the resolver. With Servlet 3.1, you need to configure the upload process within the definition of the `DispatcherServlet` by the tag `multipart-config`.

`CommonsMultipartResolver` contains the following configuration parameters:

➤ `uploadTempDir` to set the temporary directory where uploaded files are saved. The default value is the servlet container's temporary directory for the web application.

➤ `maxUploadSize` to set the maximum allowed size (in bytes) before uploads get refused. The default value is -1, which states that there is no limit.

➤ `maxInMemorySize` to set the maximum allowed size (in bytes) before uploaded files are saved to the temporary folder. The default value is 10240, which is also in bytes.

The final configuration would be as follows:

```
<bean id="multipartResolver"
    class="org.springframework.web.multipart.commons.CommonsMultipartResolver">
        <property name="uploadTempDir" value="/tmp" />
        <property name="maxUploadSize" value="1048576" />
        <property name="maxInMemorySize" value="524288" />
</bean>
```

The `multipart-config` tag contains the following inner tag definitions:

➤ `location` to set the directory location where uploaded files will be stored

➤ `max-file-size` to set the maximum size limit (in bytes) for uploaded files. The default value is -1, which states that there is no limit.

➤ `max-request-size` to set the maximum size limit (in bytes) for multipart/form-data requests. The default value is -1, which states that there is no limit.

➤ `file-size-threshold` to set the maximum allowed size (in bytes) before uploaded files are saved to the temporary folder. The default value is 0, which states that container should never write bytes to disk.

The following snippet is a sample configuration with the definition of `DispatcherServlet`:

```
<servlet>
    <servlet-name>springmvc</servlet-name>
    <servlet-class>
        org.springframework.web.servlet.DispatcherServlet
    </servlet-class>
    <load-on-startup>1</load-on-startup>
    <multipart-config>
        <location>/tmp</location>
        <max-file-size>1048576</max-file-size>
        <max-request-size>2097152</max-request-size>
        <file-size-threshold>524288</file-size-threshold>
    </multipart-config>
</servlet>
```

> **NOTE** *If any of these limits is exceeded, Spring throws* `MultipartException` *with detailed information stating under what circumstances the multipart requests were rejected.*

To use the Commons FileUpload resolver, you also need to add it as a dependency to your project. At the time of writing the current latest version available for the project was 1.3.1. Here is the Maven dependency definition that you can use to fetch the artifact:

```
<dependency>
    <groupId>commons-fileupload</groupId>
    <artifactId>commons-fileupload</artifactId>
    <version>1.3.1</version>
</dependency>
```

After handling the configuration with Servlet 3.1, you can define the view with a `form` that has the `enctype` attribute set to `multipart/form-data` to handle the multipart requests of the user. You define a model class, named `User`, and set the model attribute of the form to `user`. The user class contains a property that is a type of `MultipartFile`. After submitting the form, you retrieve the file in the controller class set to this `MultipartFile` property. Then you can extract the `byte[]` out of it and do whatever you need to do, like persisting the file in a folder or in the database.

The following is the definition of the `User` class:

```
public class User {

    private String name;
    private MultipartFile file;

    public String getName() {
        return name;
    }
    public void setName(String name) {
        this.name = name;
    }
```

```java
        public MultipartFile getFile() {
            return file;
        }
        public void setFile(MultipartFile file) {
            this.file = file;
        }
    }
```

Here's an example for the view definition:

```html
<mvc:form modelAttribute="user" action="upload.mvc" enctype="multipart/form-data">
    <table>
        <tr>
            <td>Name</td>
            <td><mvc:input path="name" /></td>
        </tr>
        <tr>
            <td>Choose File</td>
            <td><mvc:input type="file" path="file" /></td>
        </tr>
        <tr>
            <td colspan="2"><input type="submit" value="Submit" /></td>
        </tr>
    </table>
</mvc:form>
```

The following snippet gives the controller method for handling the file upload. It puts username and file size data back into the model and sends it back to the view:

```java
@RequestMapping(value = "/upload")
public ModelAndView processUser(User user) throws IOException {
    ModelAndView modelAndView = new ModelAndView();
    modelAndView.setViewName("fileUpload");
    modelAndView.addObject("userName", user.getName());
    modelAndView.addObject("fileLength", user.getFile().getBytes().length);
    return modelAndView;
}
```

HANDLING EXCEPTIONS

Spring MVC provides a well-defined exception handling mechanism to manage unhandled exceptions thrown by the application. It offers a *controller-based* approach in which methods that handle the exceptions can be defined with the @ExceptionHandler annotation in the controller classes. To detail the scenario, the following example implements a custom exception class, named UserNotFoundException, which extends Exception:

```java
public class UserNotFoundException extends Exception {
    public UserNotFoundException(String name) {
        super("User not found with name: " + name);
    }
}
```

For simplicity, this exception will be thrown when the user searches for a user with a key that doesn't exist in the hash map, which simulates that the user cannot be found in the system. If the user searches for a specific key, such as johndoe, a more generic exception is thrown, which is treated in a global controller. You read more about that later at the end of this section.

```
@Controller
public class UserController {

    private Map<String, User> users = new HashMap<String, User>();

    @PostConstruct
    public void setup() {
        users.put("mert", new User("Mert", "Caliskan"));
        users.put("kenan", new User("Kenan", "Sevindik"));
    }

    @RequestMapping(value = "/form")
    public ModelAndView user() {
        return new ModelAndView("userForm", "user", new User());
    }

    @RequestMapping(value = "/result")
    public ModelAndView processUser(String name) throws Exception {
        ModelAndView modelAndView = new ModelAndView();
        User user = users.get(name);
        if ("johndoe".equals(name)) {
            throw new Exception();
        }
        if (user == null) {
            throw new UserNotFoundException(name);
        }
        modelAndView.addObject("u", user);
        modelAndView.setViewName("userResult");

        return modelAndView;
    }

    @ExceptionHandler
    public ModelAndView handleException(UserNotFoundException e) {
        ModelAndView modelAndView = new ModelAndView("errorUser");
        modelAndView.addObject("errorMessage", e.getMessage());
        return modelAndView;
    }
}
```

The handler method annotated with @ExceptionHandler is also defined in UserController. This annotation can take the classes of the exception as its value parameter, such as @ExceptionHandler(UserNotFoundException.class). If no class definition is provided within the parenthesis, the handler intercepts the exceptions listed in its method arguments list as in the example.

Because handling exceptions should be treated in one common central place, a global method that could handle exceptions would make more sense, and Spring MVC provides another annotation to achieve this: `@ControllerAdvice`. A class annotated with `@ControllerAdvice` can contain methods with the `@ExceptionHandler`, `@InitBinder`, and `@ModelAttribute` annotations, and they will be applied to all the methods with the `@RequestMapping` annotation in the application. So the more generic exceptions such as `SQLException` or `IOException` can easily be handled in a global controller. For simplicity, the example uses the `java.lang.Exception` class in the `processUser` method when the user searches for the keyword `johndoe`. The global controller with the method that handles this exception is given in the following snippet. It just takes the user to a more generic error page named `errorGlobal.jsp`:

```
@ControllerAdvice
public class GlobalExceptionHandler {

    @ExceptionHandler(Exception.class)
    public ModelAndView handleException() {
        return new ModelAndView("errorGlobal");
    }
}
```

IMPLEMENTING INTERNATIONALIZATION (i18n)

Spring MVC supports the *internationalization* (*i18n*) of a web application, which states that the application should support multiple languages. The `DispatcherServlet` configures multilanguage support according to the client's locale by delegating the job to the provided locale resolvers in the application.

To initialize the locale resolver, the `DispatcherServlet` looks for a Spring bean named `localeResolver` in its application context. If no bean exists with the given name, the `AcceptHeaderLocaleResolver` bean is configured for use.

The `AcceptHeaderLocaleResolver` bean extracts the locale information from the HTTP request header with the key `accept-language`. This is the locale information directly sent by the client's browser. A better approach for handling the locale information is to store it within the user's session. The `SessionLocaleResolver` class stores this information in a session with a predefined session attribute name.

To demonstrate locale support, you create a view with two links that point to different locales as shown in Figure 3-6.

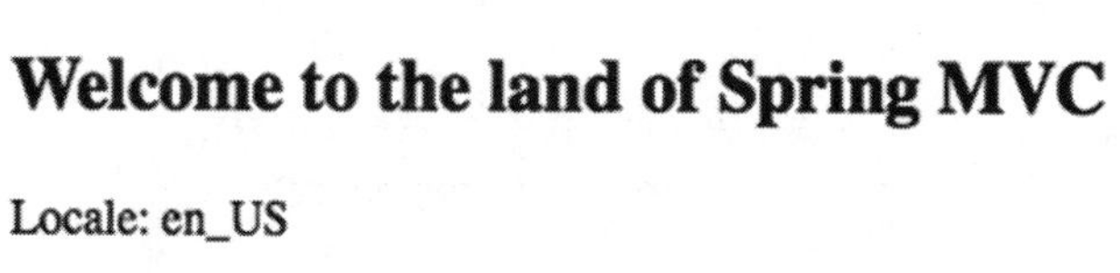

Language : English - Turkish

Welcome to the land of Spring MVC

Locale: en_US

FIGURE 3-6

When the user clicks one of the locale links, it sets the locale name as a request parameter that triggers the `LocaleChangeInterceptor` for execution:

```
<%@ taglib prefix="spring" uri="http://www.springframework.org/tags"%>
<html>
<head>
    <title>Spring MVC Internationalization</title>
</head>
<body>
    Language :
    <a href="?lang=en_US">English</a> - <a href="?lang=tr_TR">Turkish</a>
    <h2>
        <spring:message code="welcome" />
    </h2>
    Locale: ${pageContext.response.locale}
</body>
</html>
```

The `message` tag from the Spring tag library is used in the page to display a message from the resource bundle. The code attribute is set to the key value that is defined in the properties file.

The following snippet is from the application context configuration file for defining the locale resolver and locale change interceptor:

```
<bean id="localeResolver"
        class="org.springframework.web.servlet.i18n.SessionLocaleResolver"/>

<bean id="messageSource"
class="org.springframework.context.support.ReloadableResourceBundleMessageSource">
        <property name="basename" value="classpath:messages" />
</bean>

<mvc:interceptors>
    <bean id="localeChangeInterceptor"
        class="org.springframework.web.servlet.i18n.LocaleChangeInterceptor">
        <property name="paramName" value="lang" />
    </bean>
</mvc:interceptors>
```

The default locale could be set to `SessionLocaleResolver` with the `defaultLocale` property to provide a fallback handler if no locale information is found in the user's session—that is, the first request to the page. If `defaultLocale` is also not defined, the resolver parses `accept-language` from the request header to set the locale and store it in session.

> **NOTE** *You should define the* `SessionLocaleResolver` *bean with the exact bean name* `localeResolver`*.*

localeChangeInterceptor is wrapped by the <mvc:interceptors> tag. This tag lists the ordered set of interceptors that intercept HTTP requests handled by controllers. The paramName property is the key value that is used to set the locale in the JSP.

The messageSource bean sets the path for locating properties files—in the example the basename attribute sets them to be found under the classpath of the application with the name messages. If you are using Maven as your build tool, you can locate the properties file under the src/main/resources folder of the project. The files could be differentiated according to the locale, such as messages_en_US.properties for a U.S. locale or messages_tr_TR.properties for a Turkish locale, or you can just define it as messages.properties.

An alternative way to change the locale is to use the CookieLocaleResolver class, which searches for a cookie on the client and sets the locale if a cookie is found. It's feasible to use this resolver for applications that don't manage user sessions and act stateless. You can define the resolver like this:

```
<bean id="localeResolver"
    class="org.springframework.web.servlet.i18n.CookieLocaleResolver" />
```

> **NOTE** Spring 4.0 introduced the LocaleContextResolver interface, which extends LocaleResolver to support rich locale contexts. The TimeZoneAwareLocaleContext type is one of these enriched locale contexts that stores the locale and also the time zone.

USING THEMES

For a better user experience, Spring MVC provides theming support with a grouping of static resources, such as images, styles, and so on. Theme architecture features three main mechanisms: theme-aware resource bundles, theme resolvers, and theme change interceptors. This section covers these with an example that switches between two themes.

The theme-aware resource bundle is an implementation of ThemeSource that loads properties files from the classpath. A properties file lists all the theme resources with key/value pairs. The key is a name to the resource, and the value is the URI to access the resource. Here is the content of the dark.properties file that's used in the example:

```
style=css/dark.css
```

Here, style is the key value and css/dark.css is the locator path of the appropriate style sheet. You can prefix the properties files with a given value, such as theme-dark.properties or theme-light.properties by setting the basenamePrefix property to theme of the resource bundle definition.

The theme resolver determines which theme name will be resolved and which theme-aware resource bundle will be used by the application. To initialize it, the DispatcherServlet looks for a Spring bean named themeResolver in its application context. If no bean exists with the given name, the FixedThemeResolver bean is configured for use.

`FixedThemeResolver` is an implementation that uses a default theme for an application, and the theme cannot be set to another one. If no theme name is specified, the default theme name is set to `theme`. A better approach to store the theming information is to use the user's session. The `SessionThemeResolver` class stores this information in session with a predefined session attribute name. We also give the definition of it within this section.

The example demonstrates the theme support by creating a view with two links—Light and Dark—that point to two different themes as shown in Figure 3-7.

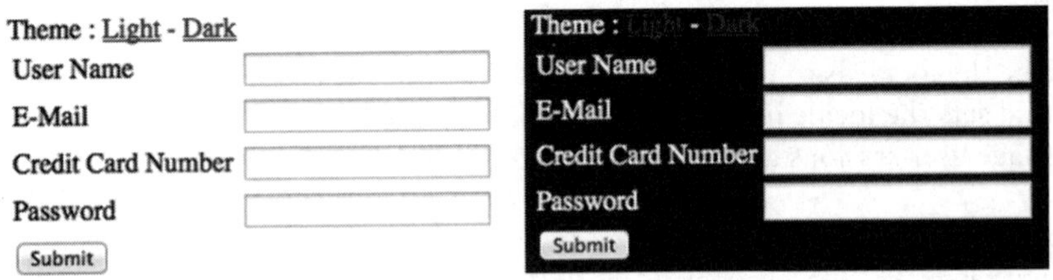

FIGURE 3-7

When the user clicks one of the theme links, the theme name is set as the request parameter and that triggers the `ThemeChangeInterceptor` for execution. Here is the content of the JSP:

```
<%@ page contentType="text/html;charset=ISO-8859-9" %>
<%@taglib uri="http://www.springframework.org/tags/form" prefix="mvc" %>
<%@taglib uri="http://www.springframework.org/tags" prefix="spring" %>
<html>
<head>
    <title>Spring MVC Themes</title>
    <link rel="stylesheet" href="<spring:theme code="style"/>" type="text/css" />
</head>
<body>
Theme :
<a href="?theme=light">Light</a> - <a href="?theme=dark">Dark</a>
<br/>
<mvc:form modelAttribute="user" action="result.mvc">
    <table>
        <tr>
            <td><mvc:label path="username">User Name</mvc:label></td>
            <td><mvc:input path="username" /></td>
            <td><mvc:errors path="username" /></td>
        </tr>
        <tr>
            <td><mvc:label path="email">E-Mail</mvc:label></td>
            <td><mvc:input path="email" /></td>
            <td><mvc:errors path="email" /></td>
        </tr>
        <tr>
            <td><mvc:label path="ccNumber">Credit Card Number</mvc:label></td>
            <td><mvc:input path="ccNumber" /></td>
            <td><mvc:errors path="ccNumber" /></td>
        </tr>
```

```
    <tr>
        <td><mvc:label path="password">Password</mvc:label></td>
        <td><mvc:password path="password" /></td>
        <td><mvc:errors path="password" /></td>
    </tr>
    <tr>
        <td colspan="3">
            <input type="submit" value="Submit" />
        </td>
    </tr>
  </table>
</mvc:form>
</body>
</html>
```

As shown in the preceding snippet, the theme is set to the HTML link tag within the href attribute by using the theme tag from the Spring tag library href attribute of a tag. The code attribute of the theme tag specifies the key value that is defined in the theme properties file, which is style in the example.

The snippet from the application context configuration file for defining the Theme Resolver and the theme change interceptor is shown here:

```
<bean id="themeSource"
      class="org.springframework.ui.context.support.ResourceBundleThemeSource" />

<bean id="themeResolver"
      class="org.springframework.web.servlet.theme.SessionThemeResolver">
      <property name="defaultThemeName" value="dark" />
</bean>

<mvc:interceptors>
    <bean id="themeChangeInterceptor"
      class="org.springframework.web.servlet.theme.ThemeChangeInterceptor">
        <property name="paramName" value="theme"/>
    </bean>
</mvc:interceptors>
```

SessionThemeResolver sets the default theme that will be used at the user's first request with the defaultThemeName property.

> **NOTE** The SessionThemeResolver bean should be defined with the exact bean name themeResolver.

themeChangeInterceptor is wrapped by the <mvc:interceptors> tag. This tag lists the ordered set of interceptors that intercept HTTP requests handled by controllers. The paramName property is the key value that is used to set the theme in the JSP.

An alternative way to change the theme is to use the `CookieThemeResolver` class, which searches for a cookie on the client and sets the theme if a cookie is found. It's feasible that you can use this resolver for applications that don't manage user sessions and act stateless. You can define the resolver like this:

```
<bean id="themeResolver"
      class="org.springframework.web.servlet.theme.CookieThemeResolver" />
```

SUMMARY

In this chapter, you learned what the Model View Controller pattern is all about and how Spring MVC provides features that comply with this pattern. The chapter started with the definition of the Dispatcher Servlet, which acts as a gateway for all MVC-based applications, and then created the simplest application with the framework.

The chapter then gave the alternative annotation-based configuration that is provided for the Spring MVC. The next topic was handling forms in a web application with the tags provided by Spring MVC. The chapter detailed how the binding mechanism works and how the flow between the views and the controllers is constructed with the help of the model.

Examples in the chapter show the validation of the user input with the integration of the Bean Validation API to Spring MVC. You saw the ways to handle exceptional cases in an application. The examples are configured with the Spring MVC–based application with Servlet 3.1 and also with Commons FileUpload so that it can handle the file uploads.

The chapter wrapped up by showing you how to integrate internationalization and theming into your web application so that the user can switch between locales and themes.

EXERCISES

You can find possible solutions to these exercises in Appendix A.

1. Which Spring annotation should be used to support Java 8's `java.time.LocalDateTime`?

2. What's the best approach for handling locale changes in a Spring MVC–based application that doesn't manage user sessions and works as stateless?

3. Define a global exception handler that will handle all exceptions that would derive from the `RuntimeException` class and that will redirect to the view `uppsie.mvc`.

▶ WHAT YOU LEARNED IN THIS CHAPTER

TOPIC	KEY POINTS
Model View Controller	A design pattern where *model* represents the domain-specific information, *view* represents the domain model with user interface elements, and *controller* is the part that interprets the input by the user and transforms it into the model to be shown to the user via the *view*.
Dispatcher Servlet	The main servlet that handles HTTP requests and dispatches those requests to appropriate channels with the help of *handler mappings* and *view resolvers*.
HandlerMapping	The interface that is used to determine which handler method will be executed according to the user's request. The Dispatcher Servlet uses its implementations to decide on which controller to execute.
ViewResolver	The interface that resolves a view according to its view name. The Dispatcher Servlet uses its implementations to determine the view to be shown to the user.
Command object	A POJO/Java bean whose values are populated by the input of the user through a form. It's synonymous with the Form object and Form-Backing object.
spring-form.tld	The form tag library descriptor file that contains input tags, such as form, input, radiobutton, checkbox, and output tags, such as label and errors.
path	The attribute of the form tags for enabling the binding between the view layer and the model.
@Controller	The annotation that marks the classes, which will serve as controllers of the MVC concept.
@RequestMapping	The annotation that is used to map user requests to handler classes or methods.
@ModelAttribute	Binds a return value to a parameter with a key to be exposed to the view. It can be applied on the method level or on a method's argument.
@ExceptionHandler	Defines the annotated method that will handle the exceptions that occur in the controller class in which the method is defined.

continues

(continued)

TOPIC	KEY POINTS
`@ControllerAdvice`	The annotation that allows you to centralize the code in one place and share it across the controllers.
`BindingResult`	The interface that represents the binding results. It can be used to retrieve the validation errors that occur on the model.
`StandardServletMultipartResolver`	The Servlet 3.1 implementation of the `MultipartResolver` interface. It gets configured as a Spring bean.
`CommonsMultipartResolver`	The Commons FileUpload implementation of the `MultipartResolver` interface. It gets configured as a Spring bean.
`AcceptHeaderLocaleResolver`	The implementation that extracts the locale information from the HTTP request header with the `accept-language` key.
`SessionLocaleResolver`	The implementation that stores the locale information in session with a predefined session attribute name.
`FixedThemeResolver`	The implementation that uses a default theme for an application and the theme cannot be set to another one.
`SessionThemeResolver`	The implementation that stores theme information in session with a predefined session attribute name.
`@ContextConfiguration`	The annotation that defines the location configuration file, which will be loaded for building up the application context.
`@WebAppConfiguration`	The annotation that defines that the application context will be a web application context, which will be loaded by `@ContextConfiguration`.
`MockMvc`	The main implementation class that is used in tests. It's built up with a `WebApplicationContext`, and it performs the mock HTTP request operations.

4

JDBC Data Access with Spring

WHAT YOU WILL LEARN IN THIS CHAPTER:

➤ Problems with using vanilla JDBC access

➤ Advantages of Spring's JDBC support

➤ Configuring and using Spring's JDBC support

➤ Properly handling and translating SQLExceptions and SQL error codes

➤ Configuring and managing connections and initializing the database

➤ Performing queries and batch operations, updating databases, accessing native JDBC methods, and calling stored procedures

➤ Modeling JDBC operations as Java objects

> **CODE DOWNLOAD** *The wrox.com code downloads for this chapter are found at* www.wrox.com/go/beginningspring *on the Download Code tab. The code is in the Chapter 4 download and individually named according to the names throughout the chapter.*

You can use various data access technologies to perform persistence operations, and JDBC is among the first used in enterprise applications. However, using JDBC directly has some drawbacks, and this chapter first focuses on the problems of using vanilla JDBC. The starting point of using Spring JDBC support is to define a `DataSource` bean, and you learn about several different methods for creating a `DataSource` within your application or obtaining one managed by your application server through JNDI lookup. This chapter also explains how to initialize a database by populating data during system bootstrap.

Later in the chapter you are introduced to Spring's JDBC support. The chapter explains and gives examples of several of its uses, such as executing queries; data manipulation operations like insert, update, and delete using Spring's infamous `JdbcTemplate` class; calling stored procedures and stored functions; and performing batch operations. You also see how Spring tries to help you handle checked `SQLExceptions` and translate them into a common data access exception hierarchy provided by Spring.

PROBLEMS WITH USING VANILLA JDBC

Almost every application has to deal with data at some point in its lifetime, and enterprise applications mostly keep their data stored in relational databases. The relational database world has SQL for querying and dealing with persistent data in databases, but, unfortunately, there is no standard way of accessing and executing SQL operations on those databases. You have to follow different ways to connect to a database system; execute SQL operations; fetch and process query results; and demarcate transactions compared to any other database system in the market if you use a proprietary API.

When developing enterprise applications using Java became popular, developers needed an API to work with those relational databases. At that time, the designers of Java introduced an API, called the Java Database Connectivity (JDBC) API, to help Java programmers easily connect, work with, and abstract away all differences among those databases.

According to the JDBC 4.0 specification, JDBC 4 drivers must support ANSI SQL 2003. Thus, as long as you use a JDBC 4–compliant driver then you can use ANSI SQL 2003 in a portable fashion. However, it is important to note that JDBC doesn't completely abstract away the differences in SQL notations across different database vendors. If a developer, for example, wants to use DB-specific SQL-like "decode" on Oracle, he can do that because the Oracle JDBC driver supports it. But this is tied to Oracle, and the Oracle-specific SQL will not work anywhere else. In general, you need to write your SQL statements specific to your relational database vendor. However, it provides a standardized API to connect, execute SQL operations, fetch and process query results, demarcate transactions, and properly close up database resources, such as connections.

When we are working with JDBC, we almost always follow a similar pattern in our data access layer:

```
try {
    //obtain database connection
    //start a transaction
    //create and execute the query
    //process query result
    //commit the transaction
} catch (SQLException e) {
    //handle SQL exceptions, perform transaction rollback
} finally {
    //close db resources like connections, statements
}
```

The preceding (partly) pseudo-code block shows a recurring pattern. We start working with JDBC by obtaining a database connection using database connection URL and database authentication credentials. When a connection is obtained, if necessary, we start a transaction and create a statement object to execute our SQL. If the SQL operation returns a result set, we create a `while` loop to iterate over this result set, and process each row returned from the database. We need to perform those operations within a `try-catch-finally` block so that if an error occurs in any of those steps listed earlier, we can handle the error within the `catch` block. It is best practice to close the open connection and any other resources within the `finally` block. Failing that leads to a resource leak that would impact the performance of the application.

Unfortunately, this boilerplate code scatters every point in our data access layer, and things get more painful in the long term if teams don't pull up that repetitive code to a common place, like a utility class. If they instead employ a copy-paste approach, maintenance becomes a nightmare; adding or changing existing logic has the potential to cause already existing parts to fail easily. Although database errors are mostly unrecoverable, people are forced to code to handle them. Inappropriate SQL exception handling operations appear; connections are left open, which causes database resources to exhaust; and out-of-memory problems occur in the application. People spend considerable amounts of time converting data obtained as rows and columns into a more object-oriented form, such as a network of objects, to use in their business logic. More importantly, even though persistence operations have no relation with the core of the business logic, a lot of time is spent dealing with data persistence operations, and they are mixed with the business logic.

INTRODUCING SPRING'S JDBC SUPPORT

One of the main reasons Spring has become so popular in the enterprise Java world is probably its extensive data access support, and JDBC is definitely at the center of that. Spring provides data access operations performed with JDBC using three main approaches:

➤ Using Template Method pattern-based utility classes, namely `JdbcTemplate` and `NamedParameterJdbcTemplate`, to perform JDBC operations more easily by removing repetitive data access code blocks in the application, properly handling resource cleanups, and so on.

➤ Using database metadata to simplify queries using classes such as `SimpleJdbcInsert` and `SimpleJdbcCall`. That way you need to provide only a table or stored procedure name and a map of parameters corresponding to column names to perform an SQL operation.

➤ Using `MappingSqlQuery`, `SqlUpdate`, and `StoredProcedure` classes to represent database operations as reusable Java objects so that you can use them over and over again by providing only different query parameters each time.

Managing JDBC Connections

To start working with JDBC and utilizing Spring's JDBC support, you first need to obtain a database connection. You have basically two ways to obtain database connections within the JDBC API. The first option is to use `DriverManager`, and the other is to use `DataSource`. `DataSource` is preferable because it is a generalized connection factory that enables you to hide database connection parameters, connection pooling, and transaction management issues from the application. (See the following Try It Out for an example of using `DataSource` to obtain a database connection.)

Spring uses `DataSource` to obtain a connection to the underlying database. Actually, Spring owns several implementations of the `DataSource` interface, in addition to providing mechanisms to access `DataSources` defined and managed by application servers through JNDI.

TRY IT OUT   Configuring DataSource to Obtain JDBC Connections

You can find the source code within the project named `configuring-datasource` in the `spring-book-ch4.zip` file.

In this Try It Out, you configure a `DataSource` object to obtain a JDBC connection. To begin, follow these steps:

1. Create a Maven project with the following Maven command:

```
mvn archetype:generate -DarchetypeGroupId=org.apache.maven.archetypes
    -DgroupId=com.wiley.beginningspring -DartifactId=spring-book-ch4
```

2. Add the following Spring `<dependency>` elements into your `pom.xml`:

```
<dependency>
    <groupId>org.springframework</groupId>
    <artifactId>spring-jdbc</artifactId>
    <version>4.0.5.RELEASE</version>
</dependency>

<dependency>
    <groupId>org.springframework</groupId>
    <artifactId>spring-context</artifactId>
    <version>4.0.5.RELEASE</version>
</dependency>
```

3. Use an H2 database. Add the following `<dependency>` element into your `pom.xml`:

```
<dependency>
    <groupId>com.h2database</groupId>
    <artifactId>h2</artifactId>
    <version>1.3.175</version>
</dependency>
```

4. Find the `org.h2.tools.Console` class of the H2 database from the project classpath, and run it as a Java application within your IDE. When it runs, the browser automatically appears on your screen with the database console. Select Generic H2 Server and log in to it using `sa` as the username with an empty password.

5. Prepare the database schema. You are going to create an ACCOUNT table with the following data definition language (DDL) statement. You can execute it from your database console:

```
CREATE TABLE ACCOUNT (
    ID BIGINT IDENTITY PRIMARY KEY,
    OWNER_NAME VARCHAR(255),
    BALANCE DOUBLE,
    ACCESS_TIME TIMESTAMP,
    LOCKED BOOLEAN
)
```

6. Create a Spring bean configuration class as follows, and define a *dataSource* bean using the
    `org.springframework.jdbc.datasource.DriverManagerDataSource` class:

```
@Configuration
public class Ch4Configuration {
    @Bean
    public DataSource dataSource() {
        DriverManagerDataSource dataSource = new DriverManagerDataSource();
        dataSource.setDriverClassName("org.h2.Driver");
        dataSource.setUrl("jdbc:h2:tcp://localhost/~/test");
        dataSource.setUsername("sa");
        dataSource.setPassword("");
        return dataSource;
    }
}
```

7. You can now create a `Main` class having a `main` method with the following contents:

```
public class Main {
    public static void main(String[] args) throws SQLException {
        AnnotationConfigApplicationContext applicationContext =
        new AnnotationConfigApplicationContext(Ch4Configuration.class);
        DataSource dataSource =
            applicationContext.getBean("dataSource", DataSource.class);

        Connection connection = dataSource.getConnection();
        System.out.println(connection.isClosed());
        connection.close();
        System.out.println(connection.isClosed());
    }
}
```

How It Works

H2 is a simple, lightweight, file-based database implementation that you can easily run in your environment. You first added its library into your classpath as a Maven dependency and ran it using its `org.h2.tools.Console` main class. The H2 database console application immediately launches a browser window so that you can log in to the database.

You defined a `dataSource` bean using Spring's `DriverManagerDataSource` class. The `DriverManagerDataSource` class is a simple implementation of the `javax.sql.DataSource` interface. It returns a new connection every time the `getConnection()` method is called. This is primarily for test and standalone environments. You need to feed it some configuration parameters—`driverClassName`, `url`, `username`, and `password` properties—so that it can connect to the H2 database.

To test your `dataSource` bean configuration, you created a `Main` class with a `main` method, which basically loads your `Configuration` class and obtains the `dataSource` bean from `ApplicationContext`. Inside the `main` method you called `DataSource.getConnection()` to obtain a `Connection` and check whether it is open.

Another implementation of the `javax.sql.DataSource` interface, called `org.springframework.jdbc.datasource.SingleConnectionDataSource`, is also suitable for test and standalone environments.

It reuses the same connection over and over again. You could have defined the `dataSource` bean using `SingleConnectionDataSource` class as well:

```
public class Ch4Configuration {
    @Bean
    public DataSource dataSource() {
        SingleConnectionDataSource dataSource = new SingleConnectionDataSource();
        dataSource.setSuppressClose(true);
        dataSource.setDriverClassName("org.h2.Driver");
        dataSource.setUrl("jdbc:h2:tcp://localhost/~/test");
        dataSource.setUsername("sa");
        dataSource.setPassword("");
        return dataSource;
    }
}
```

Setting the `supressClose` property to `true` causes a proxy `Connection` instance to be returned, which intercepts `close()` method calls. This is important if your data access technology or framework calls the `close()` method.

DO NOT USE DRIVERMANAGERDATASOURCE IN YOUR PRODUCTION ENVIRONMENT

`DriverManagerDataSource` has no connection-pooling capability. Therefore, it tries to open a new physical JDBC `Connection` whenever it is asked for it. Opening JDBC connections is an expensive process, so it's better to use another `DataSource` implementation that provides connection-pooling capability. C3P0 or Apache Commons DBCP libraries are good open source candidates for this purpose. Application servers also let you configure `DataSource` instances with connection-pooling capability, and you can access configured `DataSource` instances from within Spring Container via JNDI lookup.

You can find more information about the C3P0 connection pool library and download it at `http://sourceforge.net/projects/c3p0`.

You can find more information about the Apache Commons DBCP connection pool library and download it at `http://commons.apache.org/proper/commons-dbcp/`.

Embedded DB Support

Spring has nice support for easily creating and using lightweight database instances, and it provides the `EmbeddedDatabase` interface for this purpose. Currently, it supports implementations for H2, HSQL, and Derby for development and testing, but you can also create your custom implementation, as well. The `EmbeddedDatabase` interface extends the `javax.sql.DataSource` interface. Therefore, it can also be defined and used as an ordinary *dataSource* bean. You can create and initialize an embedded database engine using XML-based configuration as follows:

```xml
<?xml version="1.0" encoding="UTF-8"?>
<beans xmlns="http://www.springframework.org/schema/beans"
    xmlns:xsi="http://www.w3.org/2001/XMLSchema-instance"
    xmlns:jdbc="http://www.springframework.org/schema/jdbc"
    xsi:schemaLocation="http://www.springframework.org/schema/beans
        http://www.springframework.org/schema/beans/spring-beans.xsd
        http://www.springframework.org/schema/jdbc
        http://www.springframework.org/schema/jdbc/spring-jdbc-4.0.xsd">

    <jdbc:embedded-database id="FileName_dataSource" type="H2">
        <jdbc:script location="classpath:schema.sql"/>
        <jdbc:script location="classpath:data.sql"/>
    </jdbc:embedded-database>

</beans>
```

Libraries of the database instance you specified in the `type` attribute must exist in the project classpath. For example, if you specify H2 as a database, `h2.jar` must be available in the project classpath. You need to add JDBC schema namespace support of Spring to be able to use the `<jdbc:embedded-database/>` element in the preceding code within the XML configuration file.

It is also possible to perform this configuration programmatically, as shown in the following JUnit4 unit test code:

```java
public class EmbeddedDataSourceTest {
    private DataSource dataSource;

    @Before
    public void setUp() {
        dataSource = new EmbeddedDatabaseBuilder()
                .setType(EmbeddedDatabaseType.H2)
                .addScript("classpath:schema.sql")
                .addScript("classpath:data.sql").build();
    }

    @Test
    public void testDataAccessLogic() throws SQLException {
        Connection connection = dataSource.getConnection();
        Assert.assertFalse(connection.isClosed());
        connection.close();
    }

    @After
    public void tearDown() {
        ((EmbeddedDatabase)dataSource).shutdown();
    }
}
```

> **NOTE** You can populate your embedded database with SQL scripts, which can be given as input parameters. You need to create `schema.sql` and `data.sql` script files within your root classpath for the preceding test class to work.

Using a Connection-Pooled DataSource

For enterprise Java production environments, it is more suitable to use a DataSource instance that has connection-pooling capabilities. DataSource instances managed by application servers usually have this feature. However, you can easily define a connection-pooled DataSource bean from a third-party connection-pooling library, such as C3P0 or Apache Commons DBCP, as follows:

```
@Configuration
public class Ch4ConfigurationForPooledDS1 {

    @Bean(destroyMethod="close")
    public DataSource dataSource() {
        BasicDataSource dataSource = new BasicDataSource();
        dataSource.setDriverClassName("org.h2.Driver");
        dataSource.setUrl("jdbc:h2:tcp://localhost/~/test");
        dataSource.setUsername("sa");
        dataSource.setPassword("");
        return dataSource;
    }
}

@Configuration
public class Ch4ConfigurationForPooledDS2 {

    @Bean(destroyMethod="close")
    public DataSource dataSource() throws Exception {
        ComboPooledDataSource dataSource = new ComboPooledDataSource();
        dataSource.setDriverClass("org.h2.Driver");
        dataSource.setJdbcUrl("jdbc:h2:tcp://localhost/~/test");
        dataSource.setUser("sa");
        dataSource.setPassword("");
        return dataSource;
    }
}
```

You must add the following dependency elements into your pom.xml file to create the bean definitions shown in the preceding code:

```
<dependency>
    <groupId>commons-dbcp</groupId>
    <artifactId>commons-dbcp</artifactId>
    <version>1.4</version>
</dependency>

<dependency>
    <groupId>com.mchange</groupId>
    <artifactId>c3p0</artifactId>
    <version>0.9.2.1</version>
</dependency>
```

If you want to use a DataSource instance managed by an application server, you can access it via JNDI lookup using JEE schema namespace support of Spring as follows:

```xml
<?xml version="1.0" encoding="UTF-8"?>
<beans xmlns="http://www.springframework.org/schema/beans"
    xmlns:xsi="http://www.w3.org/2001/XMLSchema-instance"
    xmlns:jee="http://www.springframework.org/schema/jee"
    xsi:schemaLocation="http://www.springframework.org/schema/beans
        http://www.springframework.org/schema/beans/spring-beans.xsd
        http://www.springframework.org/schema/jee
        http://www.springframework.org/schema/jee/spring-jee-4.0.xsd">

    <jee:jndi-lookup jndi-name="jdbc/pooledDS" id="FileName_dataSource"/>

</beans>
```

Initializing DB

It is also quite easy to initialize a database using some SQL scripts during application startup time using Spring:

```xml
<?xml version="1.0" encoding="UTF-8"?>
<beans xmlns="http://www.springframework.org/schema/beans"
    xmlns:xsi="http://www.w3.org/2001/XMLSchema-instance"
    xmlns:jdbc="http://www.springframework.org/schema/jdbc"
    xsi:schemaLocation="http://www.springframework.org/schema/beans
        http://www.springframework.org/schema/beans/spring-beans.xsd
        http://www.springframework.org/schema/jdbc
        http://www.springframework.org/schema/jdbc/spring-jdbc-4.0.xsd">

    <jdbc:initialize-database data-source="dataSource">
        <jdbc:script location="classpath:schema.sql"/>
        <jdbc:script location="classpath:data.sql"/>
    </jdbc:initialize-database>

</beans>
```

You assign your `DataSource` bean name to the `data-source` attribute, and the initialization step is executed after `DataSource` bean creation.

It is important to note that the preceding initialization scripts will work every time the application is started. If you only want to perform this initialization once then you must either execute them outside the application—for example, using a database tool like SQL Plus—or you can run the initialization conditionally as follows:

```xml
<jdbc:initialize-database data-source="dataSource"
    enabled="#{systemProperties.INIT_DB}">
        <jdbc:script location="classpath:schema.sql"/>
        <jdbc:script location="classpath:data.sql"/>
    </jdbc:initialize-database>
```

The `<initialize-database>` element has the `enabled` attribute, which can have either a `true` or `false` value. Initialization happens only if the `enabled` attribute value is `true`. In the preceding code snippet, the `enabled` attribute value is a Spring Expression that queries for the `INIT_DB` property among system properties or environment variables. You can define the Java system property with `-DINIT_DB=true` while running the application with the `java` command.

Configuring and Using Spring's JDBC Support

The core class of Spring's JDBC support is `JdbcTemplate`. It simplifies the use of JDBC and helps to avoid common errors. `JdbcTemplate` can be used to execute SQL queries or insert, update, and delete statements. It executes core JDBC workflow, initiating iteration over `ResultSets` and catching JDBC exceptions and translating them to the generic, more informative `DataAccessException` hierarchy defined by Spring. Application code only needs to provide SQL and `ResultSet` processing logic if necessary. The following Try It Out shows you how to configure and use `JdbcTemplate`.

TRY IT OUT Configuring and Using Spring JdbcTemplate

You can find the source code within the project named `configuring-and-using-jdbctemplate` in the `spring-book-ch4.zip` file.

In this Try It Out, you first create an `Account` domain class and an `AccountDao` interface to define persistence operations that will be performed over those `Account` objects. Second, you define a `JdbcTemplate` bean and inject it into your `accountDao` bean to perform data access operations later. You can continue from the project you created for the earlier Try It Out. To begin, follow these steps:

1. Create an `Account` domain class, and `AccountDao` interface to define persistence operations that will be performed over those `Account` objects:

```
public class Account {
    private long id;
    private String ownerName;
    private double balance;
    private Date accessTime;
    private boolean locked;

    //getters & setters...
}


public interface AccountDao {
    public void insert(Account account);
    public void update(Account account);
    public void update(List<Account> accounts);
    public void delete(long accountId);
    public Account find(long accountId);
    public List<Account> find(List<Long> accountIds);
.... public List<Account> find(String ownerName);
    public List<Account> find(boolean locked);
}
```

2. Create an `AccountDaoJdbcImpl` class that implements the previously defined `AccountDao` interface. You can leave method bodies empty or return a null value for the moment. You implement them one by one in the following sections.

```
public class AccountDaoJdbcImpl implements AccountDao {

    private JdbcTemplate jdbcTemplate;

    public void setJdbcTemplate(JdbcTemplate jdbcTemplate) {
        this.jdbcTemplate = jdbcTemplate;
    }

    //method implementations...
}
```

3. Define the jdbcTemplate bean using the org.springframework.jdbc.core.JdbcTemplate class and satisfy its DataSource dependency using the previously defined dataSource bean:

```
@Configuration
public class Ch4Configuration {
    @Bean
    public JdbcTemplate jdbcTemplate() {
        JdbcTemplate jdbcTemplate = new JdbcTemplate();
        jdbcTemplate.setDataSource(dataSource());
        return jdbcTemplate;
    }
```

4. Define your accountDao bean using the AccountDaoJdbcImpl class and inject the jdbcTemplate bean into it:

```
    @Bean
    public AccountDao accountDao() {
        AccountDaoJdbcImpl accountDao = new AccountDaoJdbcImpl();
        accountDao.setJdbcTemplate(jdbcTemplate());
        return accountDao;
    }
}
```

5. You can now perform a lookup to the accountDao bean in the main method:

```
public class Main {
    public static void main(String[] args) {
        AnnotationConfigApplicationContext applicationContext =
            new AnnotationConfigApplicationContext(Ch4Configuration.class);
        AccountDao accountDao = applicationContext.getBean(AccountDao.class);
    }
}
```

How It Works

JdbcTemplate is defined as a Spring-managed bean. It is thread safe and can be shared across different data access objects; therefore, it is defined as a singleton. The main dependency it needs is a DataSource object, and you already created a DataSource bean in the previous example. You injected that bean into the jdbcTemplate.

At the last step, you injected the `jdbcTemplate` bean into your `accountDao` bean, which is defined using the `AccountDaoJdbcImpl` class. You can now use the `JdbcTemplate` instance within `AccountDaoJdbcImpl` to perform various data access operations.

PERFORMING DATA ACCESS OPERATIONS WITH SPRING

This section mainly focuses on using `JdbcTemplate` and its more specialized form, `NamedParameterJdbcTemplate`, to show how various data access operations can be performed. However, this section also includes information about other classes provided by Spring as well. For example, `SimpleJdbcCall` is used to simplify queries using database metadata. `MappingSqlQuery`, `SqlUpdate`, and `StoredProcedure` classes are used to show how SQL operations can be modeled as Java objects and used over and over again.

Running Queries

`JdbcTemplate` offers various methods with overloaded versions to execute queries and handle results as different types of objects in your application. You usually make use of the `query(..)`, `queryForObject(..)`, `queryForList(..)`, `queryForMap(..)`, and `queryForRowSet(..)` methods with several different overloaded versions of them that accept different input arguments such as query string, query input parameter values, their types, result object type, and so on. You can use any version suitable for your specific query at hand. The following Try It Out demonstrates how to run queries with `JdbcTemplate`.

TRY IT OUT Running Queries with JdbcTemplate

You can find the source code within the project named `running-queries-with-jdbctemplate` in the `spring-book-ch4.zip` file.

In this Try It Out, you implement the `find(long accountId)` method of the `AccountDaoJdbcImpl` class using `JdbcTemplate`. You can continue from the place you left off in the previous Try It Out. To begin, follow these steps:

```
@Override
public Account find(long accountId) {
```

1. Use the `JdbcTemplate.queryForObject(..)` method for this purpose. It expects an SQL query, an `org.springframework.jdbc.core.RowMapper` object, and a varargs `Object` as query input parameters, if any exist:

```
return jdbcTemplate.queryForObject(
    "select id,owner_name,balance,access_time,locked from account where id = ?",
    new RowMapper<Account>() {
```

2. Create an anonymous class from the `RowMapper` interface with the `Account` generic type parameter. Its `mapRow(..)` method returns an `Account` object:

```
                @Override
                public Account mapRow(ResultSet rs, int rowNum) throws SQLException {
```

3. Create an `Account` instance inside the `mapRow(..)` method and populate its properties with values obtained from the `ResultSet` object given as the input parameter to the `mapRow(..)` method:

```
                    Account account = new Account();
                    account.setId(rs.getLong("id"));
                    account.setOwnerName(rs.getString("owner_name"));
                    account.setBalance(rs.getDouble("balance"));
                    account.setAccessTime(rs.getTimestamp("access_time"));
                    account.setLocked(rs.getBoolean("locked"));
                    return account;
                }

            }, accountId);
    }
```

4. Insert sample account data into the database with the following SQL statement:

```
    insert into account (id,owner_name,balance,access_time,locked) values ~CA
        (100,'john doe',10.0,'2014-01-01',false);
```

5. Now you can use the `accountDao` bean to fetch the account record within the `main` method:

```
    public class Main {
        public static void main(String[] args) {
            AnnotationConfigApplicationContext applicationContext =
                new AnnotationConfigApplicationContext(Ch4Configuration.class);
            AccountDao accountDao = applicationContext.getBean(AccountDao.class);

            Account account = accountDao.find(100L);

            System.out.println(account.getId());
            System.out.println(account.getOwnerName());
            System.out.println(account.getBalance());
            System.out.println(account.getAccessTime());
            System.out.println(account.isLocked());
        }
    }
```

How It Works

`JdbcTemplate` implements the Template Method pattern. The Template Method pattern, in general, tries to encapsulate the main steps of an algorithm, enabling the developer to change individual parts of it by passing them via method parameters.

You have already seen the following pseudocode block in the section that discussed the problems of using vanilla JDBC. If you closely examine the recurring code block, you see that only two parts within this code block change across different data access methods. The first one is the executed query and its parameters; the second one is the result set processing logic. If the query returns a list of rows, you need to set up a `while` loop, and process each row by iterating over the result set.

```
try {
    //obtain database connection
    //start a transaction
    //create and execute the query
    //process query result
    //commit the transaction
} catch (SQLException e) {
    //handle SQL exceptions, perform transaction rollback
} finally {
    //close db resources like connections, statements
}
```

You pass result set processing logic into the template method using callback objects. Callback objects usually have one known method in which data access–specific result set processing logic is implemented. Callbacks are usually implemented as anonymous classes and immediately passed into the template method as an input parameter, and then the template method calls their well-known method whenever necessary.

JdbcTemplate, as an implementation of the Template Method pattern, encapsulates all of the earlier data access logic within its query execution methods. The query(..) and queryForObject(..) methods of JdbcTemplate follow exactly the same approach. They accept query string, query parameters, and callback object of type RowMapper as input parameters.

RowMapper is used to map each row returned in a ResultSet to a result object. It is usually used as an input parameter given to JdbcTemplate, but it can also be used as your parameter of a stored procedure. Its mapRow(ResultSet rs, int rowNum) method is called within a while loop inside JdbcTemplate for each row in the ResultSet, converting them into corresponding result objects.

RowMapper implementations are stateless and reusable. Therefore, it is always good practice to create a RowMapper implementation for each different domain object and use it in several different places.

Input arguments with the org.springframework.jdbc.core.ResultSetExtractor interface are also accepted as input arguments by several JdbcTemplate.query(..) methods. However, that interface is mainly used within the JDBC framework itself. Hence, it is almost always better to use RowMapper instead.

Another interface called org.springframework.jdbc.core.RowCallbackHandler is also used to process the ResultSet on a per-row basis. Compared to the other two interfaces, RowCallbackHandler implementations are stateful. They keep the result state for later use. For example, you can implement a RowCallbackHandler to count rows or create an XML document from the ResultSet.

The queryForList(..) and queryForMap(..) methods use a simpler approach. The queryForList(..) method executes the query and returns a List whose elements are Map with column names as keys. The queryForMap(..) method, on the other hand, returns Map as a result; again keys of the Map are column names. It is useful if you don't have a corresponding domain object that can be used for row mapping.

The `queryForRowSet(..)` method returns `org.springframework.jdbc.support.rowset`
`.SqlRowSet`, which is a disconnected version of the `ResultSet` object. You can access your data
after your connection is closed. It is actually a mirror interface for `javax.sql.RowSet`. Its main
advantage over `RowSet` is that it doesn't throw an `SQLException`, so you don't have to deal with
checked `SQLExceptions` in your code. It also extends the `java.io.Serializable` interface; therefore, its implementations usually can be stored and retrieved later on.

Queries with Named Parameters

Instead of using the classic "?" placeholder, you can use named parameters, each starting with a
column, within your SQL statements, as shown in the following Try It Out. Spring provides `org`
`.springframework.jdbc.core.namedparam.NamedParameterJdbcTemplate` for this purpose.
`NamedParameterJdbcTemplate` actually wraps up `JdbcTemplate`, so almost all the hard work is
actually done by `JdbcTemplate`.

TRY IT OUT   Using Named Parameters within Queries

You can find the source code within the project named `using-namedparameters` in the
`spring-book-ch4.zip` file.

In this Try It Out, you use named parameters within a query instead of the positional parameters used
in the preceding example. You can continue from the place you left at the previous Try It Out. To
begin, follow these steps:

1. Add a property with type `NamedParameterJdbcTemplate` in `AccountDaoJdbcImpl`, and initialize
   it within the `setJdbcTemplate(..)` method as follows:

   ```
   public class AccountDaoJdbcImpl implements AccountDao {

       private JdbcTemplate jdbcTemplate;
       private NamedParameterJdbcTemplate namedParameterJdbcTemplate;

       public void setJdbcTemplate(JdbcTemplate jdbcTemplate) {
           this.jdbcTemplate = jdbcTemplate;
           namedParameterJdbcTemplate = new NamedParameterJdbcTemplate(jdbcTemplate);
       }
   ```

2. Instead of using `JdbcTemplate`, use `NamedParameterJdbcTemplate` to implement the
   `AccountDaoJdbcImpl.find(String ownerName)` method:

   ```
   @Override
   public Account find(String ownerName) {
       return namedParameterJdbcTemplate.queryForObject(
   "select id,owner_name,balance,access_time,locked from account where owner_name = ~CA
       :ownerName",
    Collections.singletonMap("ownerName", ownerName),
   ```

3. The `RowMapper` parameter is an instance created from an anonymous class. You implement its
   `mapRow(..)` method, and create and return the `Account` instance whose properties are obtained
   from the `ResultSet` given to the `mapRow(..)` method:

```
        new RowMapper<Account>() {
                @Override
                public Account mapRow(ResultSet rs, int rowNum) throws SQLException {
                    Account account = new Account();
                    account.setId(rs.getLong("id"));
                    account.setOwnerName(rs.getString("owner_name"));
                    account.setBalance(rs.getDouble("balance"));
                    account.setAccessTime(rs.getTimestamp("access_time"));
                    account.setLocked(rs.getBoolean("locked"));
                    return account;
                }
        });
    }
}
```

4.   Use the `accountDao` bean to fetch the account records within the `main` method:

```
public class Main {
    public static void main(String[] args) {
        AnnotationConfigApplicationContext applicationContext =
            new AnnotationConfigApplicationContext(Ch4Configuration.class);
        AccountDao accountDao = applicationContext.getBean(AccountDao.class);

        Account account = accountDao.find("john doe").get(0);

        System.out.println(account.getId());
        System.out.println(account.getOwnerName());
        System.out.println(account.getBalance());
        System.out.println(account.getAccessTime());
        System.out.println(account.isLocked());
    }
}
```

How It Works

You can pass in named parameters using either an ordinary `Map` or an `org.springframework.jdbc` `.core.namedparam.SqlParameterSource` instance. The `SqlParameterSource` interface has several different implementations. `MapSqlParameterSource` is one of them. It actually wraps up an ordinary `Map` within it, so keys are named parameter names, and values are named parameter values. You can also use a `BeanPropertySqlParameterSource` implementation as well. This implementation wraps a JavaBean object, and properties of that JavaBean object are used as named parameter values.

Writing Queries Using the IN Clause

SQL supports running queries based on an expression that includes a variable number of input parameter values. For example, you can write a query like SELECT FROM ACCOUNT WHERE ID IN (1,2,3,4,5). Unfortunately, JDBC doesn't directly support this feature, so you cannot declare a variable number of placeholders in your query. To overcome this limitation, you can either write several different versions of your query with a different number of input parameter values, or generate your SQL query with a variable number of input parameters dynamically at run time. Spring's `JdbcTemplate` and `NamedParameterJdbcTemplate` classes handle this for you. They enable to pass in input parameters of type `List` of primitive values, and they generate the query dynamically at run time with the exact number of placeholders by looking at the size of the `List` object. The following code snippet shows an implementation of the `AccountDaoJdbcImpl.find(List <Long> accountIds)` method:

```java
@Override
public List<Account> find(List<Long> accountIds) {
    SqlParameterSource sqlParameterSource =
        new MapSqlParameterSource("accountIds", accountIds);
    return namedParameterJdbcTemplate.query(
        "select * from account where id in (:accountIds)", sqlParameterSource,
        new RowMapper<Account>() {

        @Override
        public Account mapRow(ResultSet rs, int rowNum) throws SQLException {
            Account account = new Account();
            account.setId(rs.getLong("id"));
            account.setOwnerName(rs.getString("owner_name"));
            account.setBalance(rs.getDouble("balance"));
            account.setAccessTime(rs.getTimestamp("access_time"));
            account.setLocked(rs.getBoolean("locked"));
            return account;
        }

    });
}
```

> **WARNING** You need to be careful because the SQL standard doesn't support more than 100 placeholders as query parameters in the IN clause. Therefore, your query may fail depending on the database you are using. Each database vendor has its own max limit. For example, Oracle supports 1,000. If your input List size exceeds this limit, you need to split your List elements into appropriate chunks, and execute the query several times for each group separately.

Using PreparedStatements within JdbcTemplate

When you execute a query using `java.sql.Statement`, the database first gets the query string, and then parses, compiles, and computes an execution plan for it before the execution. If you are executing the same query many times, this preprocess step might be a performance bottleneck. The preprocess phase is performed only once if you use `java.sql.PreparedStatement`. Therefore, it will probably yield better execution times. The other advantage of using `PreparedStatements` over creating query strings dynamically each time is protecting the system against SQL injection attacks. Because query parameters are not given during query construction, queries executed with `PreparedStatements` are safer to use. `JdbcTemplate` query methods support executing queries using `PreparedStatement` objects. The following Try It Out demonstrates how to use `PreparedStatements`.

TRY IT OUT   Using PreparedStatements within JdbcTemplate

You can find the source code within the project named using-preparedstatements in the spring-book-ch4.zip file.

In this Try It Out, you implement the AccountDaoJdbcImpl.find(Boolean locked) method using java.sql.PreparedStatment. You can continue from the place you left at the previous Try It Out. To begin, follow these steps:

1. JdbcTemplate.query(..) methods expect the org.springframework.jdbc.core.PreparedStatementCreator instance to obtain a PreparedStatement. Spring provides the org.springframework.jdbc.core.PreparedStatementCreatorFactory class that efficiently helps you create multiple PreparedStatement objects with different parameters based on an SQL statement and a single set of parameter declarations:

```
@Override
public List<Account> find(boolean locked) {
    PreparedStatementCreatorFactory psCreatorFactory =
    new PreparedStatementCreatorFactory(
        "select * from account where locked = ?",new int[]{Types.BOOLEAN});
```

2. You can now invoke the query(..) method with the PreparedStatementCreator instance obtained using the previously mentioned PreparedStatementCreatorFactory object and RowMapper parameters:

```
    return jdbcTemplate.query(psCreatorFactory.newPreparedStatementCreator(
            new Object[]{locked}),
```

3. The RowMapper parameter is an instance created from an anonymous class. Implement its mapRow(..) method, and then create and return the Account instance whose properties are obtained from the ResultSet given to the mapRow(..) method:

```
new RowMapper<Account>() {
        @Override
        public Account mapRow(ResultSet rs, int rowNum) throws SQLException {
            Account account = new Account();
            account.setId(rs.getLong("id"));
            account.setOwnerName(rs.getString("owner_name"));
            account.setBalance(rs.getDouble("balance"));
            account.setAccessTime(rs.getTimestamp("access_time"));
            account.setLocked(rs.getBoolean("locked"));
            return account;
        }

    });
}
```

How It Works

You first need to create the factory object and initialize it by giving SQL and parameter type declarations. After that you can use its newPreparedStatementCreator(..) methods to create actual `PreparedStatementCreator` instances by giving input parameter values to those method calls.

`PreparedStatementCreator` implementations are responsible for providing SQL and any necessary parameters. It is also possible for them to implement the `org.springframework.jdbc.core` `.SqlProvider` interface. By implementing this interface, the `PreparedStatementCreator` implementations can expose the SQL used for `PreparedStatement` creation to the outside, resulting in better contextual information in case of exceptions.

`JdbcTemplate.query(..)` methods also accept an instance from the `org.springframework.jdbc` `.core.PreparedStatementSetter` interface in order to be used as a callback interface. It is used to set parameter values on the `PreparedStatement` object provided by `JdbcTemplate`. `JdbcTemplate` creates `PreparedStatement`, and this callback is responsible only for setting parameter values:

```
@Override
public List<Account> find(final boolean locked) {
    return jdbcTemplate.query(
        "select * from account where locked = ?", new PreparedStatementSetter() {

        @Override
        public void setValues(PreparedStatement ps) throws SQLException {
            ps.setBoolean(1, locked);
        }
    }, new RowMapper<Account>() {

        @Override
        public Account mapRow(ResultSet rs, int rowNum) throws SQLException {
            Account account = new Account();
            account.setId(rs.getLong("id"));
            account.setOwnerName(rs.getString("owner_name"));
            account.setBalance(rs.getDouble("balance"));
            account.setAccessTime(rs.getTimestamp("access_time"));
            account.setLocked(rs.getBoolean("locked"));
            return account;
        }
    });
}
```

If you need to create `PreparedStatement`s manually, it might be the only case to implement the `PreparedStatementCreator` interface; otherwise, it is almost always easier and better to use the `PreparedStatementSetter` interface.

Inserting, Updating, and Deleting Records

`JdbcTemplate` has several overloaded `update(..)` methods that each accepts different parameters such as an SQL statement, input parameter values, their types, and so on. They can be used to perform data manipulation language (DML) operations like inserting, updating, or deleting rows in the database (see the following Try It Out for an example).

TRY IT OUT Inserting, Updating, and Deleting Records Using JdbcTemplate

You can find the source code within the project named `inserting-updating-deleting-records` in the `spring-book-ch4.zip` file. In this Try It Out, you implement insert, update, and delete methods of the `AccountDaoJdbcImpl` class using `JdbcTemplate`. You can continue from the place you left off in the previous Try It Out. To begin, follow these steps:

1. The primary key of the account table is autogenerated, so you need to obtain it after the insert operation. Use the `org.springframework.jdbc.support.KeyHolder` interface that Spring provides for this purpose:

```java
@Override
public void insert(Account account) {
    PreparedStatementCreatorFactory psCreatorFactory =
      new PreparedStatementCreatorFactory(
        "insert into account(owner_name,balance,access_time,locked) values(?,?,?,?)",
            new int[] { Types.VARCHAR, Types.DOUBLE, Types.TIMESTAMP,
                Types.BOOLEAN });
    KeyHolder keyHolder = new GeneratedKeyHolder();
    int count=jdbcTemplate.update(
            psCreatorFactory.newPreparedStatementCreator(new Object[] {
                account.getOwnerName(), account.getBalance(),
                account.getAccessTime(), account.isLocked() }), keyHolder);
```

2. Create the following exception to throw if the insert operation fails:

```java
public class InsertFailedException extends DataAccessException {
    public InsertFailedException(String msg) {
        super(msg);
    }
}
```

3. Check the returned value from the `update(..)` method and throw `InsertFailedException`:

```java
if(count != 1) throw new InsertFailedException("Cannot insert account");
```

4. Set the `id` value obtained from `keyHolder` to the `Account` instance:

```java
account.setId(keyHolder.getKey().longValue());
}
```

5. Create the following exception to throw if the update operation fails:

```java
public class UpdateFailedException extends DataAccessException {
    public UpdateFailedException(String msg) {
        super(msg);
    }
}
```

6. Next perform the update operation in a similar way:

```java
@Override
public void update(Account account) {
    int count = jdbcTemplate
            .update(
```

```
        "update account set (owner_name,balance,access_time,locked) = (?,?,?,?) where id=?",
                    account.getOwnerName(), account.getBalance(),
                    account.getAccessTime(), account.isLocked(),
                    account.getId());
    if(count != 1) throw new UpdateFailedException("Cannot update account");
}
```

7. Create the following exception to throw if the delete operation fails:

```
public class DeleteFailedException extends DataAccessException {
    public DeleteFailedException(String msg) {
        super(msg);
    }
}
```

8. Use the `JdbcTemplate.update(..)` method to perform the delete operation as well, and throw `DeleteFailedException` if the delete is unsuccessful:

```
@Override
public void delete(long accountId) {
    int count = jdbcTemplate.update("delete account where id = ?",accountId);
    if(count != 1) throw new DeleteFailedException("Cannot delete account");
}
```

9. You can now create a new account, update its balance, and finally delete it within the `main` method.

```
Account account = new Account();
account.setOwnerName("Joe Smith");
account.setBalance(20.0);
account.setAccessTime(new Date());
account.setLocked(false);

accountDao.insert(account);

account = accountDao.find(account.getId());

System.out.println(account.getId());
System.out.println(account.getOwnerName());
System.out.println(account.getBalance());
System.out.println(account.getAccessTime());
System.out.println(account.isLocked());

account.setBalance(30.0);

accountDao.update(account);

account = accountDao.find(account.getId());
System.out.println(account.getBalance());

accountDao.delete(account.getId());

List<Account> accounts = accountDao.find(Arrays.asList(account.getId()));

System.out.println(accounts.size());
```

How It Works

All insert, update, and delete SQL operations are performed with `update(..)` methods of `JdbcTemplate`. Because you needed to obtain the autogenerated primary key value at the end of the insert operation, you first created a `PreparedStatementCreatorFactory` so that you can obtain a `PreparedStatementCreator`, and instantiated a `KeyHolder` from the `GeneratedKeyHolder` class. After the update operation you called the `keyHolder.getKey()` method to fetch an autogenerated value, and set it to the `Account`'s *id* property.

You defined exceptions to throw when the related data access operation fails. Spring provides an abstract base class `org.springframework.dao.DataAccessException`. You use it to create a common base to handle various kinds of data access exceptions that occur while using different data access technologies through Spring Data Access support.

All those insert, update, and delete DML operations are performed using the `update(..)` method of the `JdbcTemplate`. You need to check the returned value from the `update(..)` methods. The returned value gives the number of records that are affected by executed DML operations. If an unexpected number returns, you should throw an appropriate exception to indicate this error to the upper layer in your application.

Calling Stored Procedures and Stored Functions

You can call stored procedures and stored functions defined in your database using Spring's `org.springframework.jdbc.core.simple.SimpleJdbcCall` and `org.springframework.jdbc.object.StoredProcedure` classes. See the following Try It Out for an example.

TRY IT OUT Calling Stored Procedures with SimpleJdbcCall

You can find the source code within the project named `calling-storedprocedures` in the `spring-book-ch4.zip` file.

In this Try It Out, you call a stored procedure available in the database using `SimpleJdbcCall`. You can continue from the place you left off in the previous Try It Out. To begin, follow these steps:

1. Create a `SimpleJdbcCall` instance:

```
SimpleJdbcCall simpleJdbcCall = new SimpleJdbcCall(jdbcTemplate);
```

2. Specify a procedure name to be executed and declare its input and output parameters:

```
simpleJdbcCall
        .withProcedureName("concat")
        .withoutProcedureColumnMetaDataAccess()
        .declareParameters(
                new SqlParameter("param1", Types.VARCHAR),
                new SqlParameter("param2", Types.VARCHAR))
```

3. If your procedure/function returns a `ResultSet`, you can assign a name to it and specify `RowMapper` to process it as follows:

```
.returningResultSet("result",new SingleColumnRowMapper<String>(String.class));
```

4. Compile the procedure by calling its `compile()` method:

```
simpleJdbcCall.compile();
```

5. After compiling the `SimpleJdbcCall` instance, create a `Map` to pass input parameters and call its `execute(..)` method:

```
Map<String, Object> paramMap = new HashMap<String, Object>();
paramMap.put("param1", "hello ");
paramMap.put("param2", "world!");
Map<String,Object> resultMap = simpleJdbcCall.execute(paramMap);
```

6. Access the result `List` via the `result` key from within the `Map` that's returned, and iterate over the `List` with a `for` loop:

```
List<String> resultList = (List<String>) resultMap.get("result");
for(String value:resultList) {
    System.out.println(value);
}
```

How It Works

`SimpleJdbcCall` expects a `DataSource` or `JdbcTemplate` instance to operate. However, it is better to initialize it with a `JdbcTemplate` instance to benefit from the automatic exception translation feature that Spring provides. You can use it to invoke both stored procedures and stored functions in a very similar way. You set the procedure name by calling the `withProcedureName(..)` method. If it is a function, you can call the `withFunctionName(..)` method instead. `SimpleJdbcCall` can obtain names of in and out parameters by looking at database metadata, so that you don't need to declare them explicitly. Currently, Spring supports Derby, DB2, MySQL, MS SQL, Oracle, and Sybase. You can still declare parameters by yourself, for example, if you have a parameter like `ARRAY` or `STRUCT` that cannot be mapped to a Java class automatically, or your database might not be among the supported databases for Spring's metadata lookup functionality. To disable automatic metadata discovery, you can call `withoutProcedureColumnMetaDataAccess()` as shown earlier.

You can declare input parameters with `SqlParameter`, output parameters with `SqlOutParameter`, and input-output parameters with `SqlInOutParameter` classes. They all accept the name assigned to the parameter defined. Otherwise it becomes an anonymous parameter definition, and when calling a stored procedure or stored function the order of parameter values becomes important. If you've assigned names, you can create a `Map` to give input parameter values during execution. If your procedure or function returns a `ResultSet`, you can assign it a name to access it later from the returned result `Map`, and specify a `RowMapper` instance to process the `ResultSet` by calling `returningResultSet(..)`. If this `ResultSet` is defined as an out parameter of type `ref cursor`, the name given must be the same as the out parameter declared with `SqlOutParameter` in the parameter-declaration step.

Before execution, as the last step, you invoke the `compile()` method. By calling compile, a `java.sql.CallableStatement` is created in the back end and prepared for execution. You execute the procedure by calling `execute(..)`, and input parameters are given within a `Map`. If it is a stored function, you can also invoke it by calling its `executeFunction(..)`. When the execution is completed, it returns a `Map` in which any return value(s) are contained. If it is a function, it will return a function result instead of the result `Map`.

Performing Batch Operations

You can group several update operations and execute them together within a single `PreparedStatement` object created by `JdbcTemplate`. This is called *batching*. Batch operations reduce the number of round trips to the database and help you improve data access performance of the application. `JdbcTemplate` has several `batchUpdate(..)` methods for this purpose:

```java
@Override
public void update(final List<Account> accounts) {
    int[] counts = jdbcTemplate.batchUpdate(
"update account set(owner_name,balance,access_time,locked)=(?,?,?,?) where id=?",
 new BatchPreparedStatementSetter() {

            @Override
            public void setValues(PreparedStatement ps, int i) throws SQLException {
                Account account = accounts.get(i);
                ps.setString(1, account.getOwnerName());
                ps.setDouble(2, account.getBalance());
                ps.setTimestamp(3, new Timestamp(account.getAccessTime().getTime()));
                ps.setBoolean(4, account.isLocked());
                ps.setLong(5, account.getId());
            }

            @Override
            public int getBatchSize() {
                return accounts.size();
            }
    });
    int i = 0;
    for(int count:counts) {
        if(count == 0) throw new UpdateFailedException("Row not updated :" + i);
        i++;
    }
}
```

The preceding code snippet illustrates how you can perform batch update by implementing the `AccountDaoJdbcImpl.update(List<Account> accounts)` method. You need to create a `BatchPreparedStatementSetter` instance to set parameter values of each update operation to be executed within a single `PreparedStatement`, and this is usually provided as an anonymous class object. It has two methods: one is `getBatchSize()`, which returns the number of operations performed in the batch, and the other is `setValue(..)`, within which you set the parameters of each row.

Handling BLOB and CLOB Objects

You can store binary data–like images, videos, or documents that have large sizes. Such data is called *large object* (LOB)—more specifically, *binary large object* (BLOB) if it is binary data or *character large object* (CLOB) if it is textual data. Spring provides the `org.springframework .jdbc.support.lob.LobHandler` and `org.springframework.jdbc.support.lob.LobCreator` interfaces to deal with LOB values.

The org.springframework.jdbc.support.lob.DefaultLobHandler class implements the LobHandler interface. You can use it to access LOB values from the result set:

```
LobHandler lobHandler = new DefaultLobHandler();
byte[] binaryContent = lobHandler.getBlobAsBytes(rs, 1);
String textualContent = lobHandler.getClobAsString(rs, 2);
```

By calling its getLobCreator() method, you can obtain the LobCreator instance as well and use it to set LOB values in the PreparedStatement:

```
jdbcTemplate.update(
    "update account set (owner_photo,account_desc) = (?,?) where id = ? ",
    new PreparedStatementSetter() {

    @Override
    public void setValues(PreparedStatement ps) throws SQLException {
        LobCreator lobCreator = lobHandler.getLobCreator();
        lobCreator.setBlobAsBytes(ps, 1, binaryContent);
        lobCreator.setClobAsString(ps, 2, textualContent);
        ps.setInt(3,accountId);
    }
});
```

Accessing Vendor-Specific JDBC Methods

You may sometimes need to access vendor-specific features that are available only in your database implementation and which you cannot access over the standard JDBC API. DataSource implementations usually wrap Connection, Statement, and ResultSet objects with their own implementations. Therefore, you need a mechanism to extract wrapped native instances. Spring provides the NativeJdbcExtractor interface for this purpose. You can select an implementation of it according to your runtime environment, although most of the time the SimpleNativeJdbcExtractor class is enough. You just need to set it in your JdbcTemplate:

```
Connection con = jdbcTemplate.getDataSource().getConnection();
Connection nativeCon = jdbcTemplate.
        getNativeJdbcExtractor().getNativeConnection(con);
//you can now access your vendor specific features over native connection...
```

Executing DDL Operations

Various execute(..) methods provided by JdbcTemplate enable you to execute DDL operations like the CREATE TABLE and ALTER TABLE statements in addition to implementing arbitrary data access operations within Spring's managed JDBC environment:

```
jdbcTemplate.execute(
"CREATE TABLE ACCOUNT (ID BIGINT IDENTITY PRIMARY KEY,
    OWNER_NAME VARCHAR(255), BALANCE DOUBLE,
    ACCESS_TIME TIMESTAMP, LOCKED BOOLEAN,
    OWNER_PHOTO BLOB, ACCOUNT_DESC CLOB)");
```

That way, your data access operations still participate in Spring's managed transactions, and SQLException conversion takes place automatically. Those execute(..) methods can return a result object: for example, a domain object, a collection of domain objects, or nothing, which is the case when DDL operations are executed.

MODELING JDBC OPERATIONS AS JAVA OBJECTS

Spring JDBC provides support for accessing databases in a more object-oriented manner. For example, you can define an object that represents a specific SQL query, then execute it and obtain the result as a list of business objects whose properties are mapped with corresponding column names. You can also represent insert, update, and delete SQL operations, or call stored procedures as Java objects in a similar way, and reuse those objects over and over again.

Encapsulating SQL Query Executions

You can encapsulate any arbitrary SQL query as a Java object using Spring. It provides the abstract MappingSqlQuery class for this purpose. The primary advantage of using this technique is that it helps you to encapsulate SQL queries as Java objects and reuse them in several different places. Such query objects are thread safe and can be shared by several other DAO objects in your application. The following Try It Out shows you how to encapsulate SQL queries using MappingSQLQuery.

TRY IT OUT Encapsulating SQL Queries Using MappingSqlQuery

You can find the source code within the project named encapsulating-sql-queries in the spring-book-ch4.zip file.

In this Try It Out, you create a class to encapsulate the SQL query and then use it within the DAO bean. You can continue from the place you left off with the Try It Out. To begin, follow these steps:

1. Create a class named AccountByIdQuery that extends from the MappingSqlQuery abstract class. Provide the type of object that will be returned as the query result:

```
public class AccountByIdQuery extends MappingSqlQuery<Account> {
```

2. Create a constructor that accepts DataSource as an input parameter:

```
public AccountByIdQuery(DataSource dataSource) {
```

3. Pass in a DataSource object and the SQL query to be executed to the super class:

```
super(dataSource,
    "select id,owner_name,balance,access_time,locked from account where id = ?");
```

4. Declare any input parameters, and, as the last step, call the compile() method in the constructor:

```
declareParameter(new SqlParameter(Types.BIGINT));
compile();
}
```

5. Implement the `mapRow(..)` method, create an `Account` instance by getting property values from the `ResultSet` and return the populated `Account` instance from the `mapRow(..)` method:

```java
@Override
protected Account mapRow(ResultSet rs, int rowNum) throws SQLException {
    Account account = new Account();
    account.setId(rs.getLong("id"));
    account.setOwnerName(rs.getString("owner_name"));
    account.setBalance(rs.getDouble("balance"));
    account.setAccessTime(rs.getTimestamp("access_time"));
    account.setLocked(rs.getBoolean("locked"));
    return account;
}
```

6. Add a property with the `MappingSqlQuery` type to the `AccountDaoJdbcImpl` class:

```java
private MappingSqlQuery<Account> accountByIdQuery;

public void setAccountByIdQuery(MappingSqlQuery<Account> accountByIdQuery) {
    this.accountByIdQuery = accountByIdQuery;
}
```

7. Define a bean for this `AccountByIdQuery` and inject `DataSource` as the constructor argument. Next, inject this `MappingSqlQuery` bean into the `accountDao` bean:

```java
@Configuration
public class Ch4Configuration {
    @Bean
    public DataSource dataSource() {
        DriverManagerDataSource dataSource = new DriverManagerDataSource();
        dataSource.setDriverClassName("org.h2.Driver");
        dataSource.setUrl("jdbc:h2:tcp://localhost/~/test");
        dataSource.setUsername("sa");
        dataSource.setPassword("");
        return dataSource;
    }

    @Bean
    public JdbcTemplate jdbcTemplate() {
        JdbcTemplate jdbcTemplate = new JdbcTemplate();
        jdbcTemplate.setDataSource(dataSource());
        return jdbcTemplate;
    }

    @Bean
    public MappingSqlQuery<Account> accountByIdQuery() {
        AccountByIdQuery query = new AccountByIdQuery(dataSource());
        return query;
    }

    @Bean
    public AccountDao accountDao() {
        AccountDaoJdbcImpl accountDao = new AccountDaoJdbcImpl();
        accountDao.setJdbcTemplate(jdbcTemplate());
        accountDao.setAccountByIdQuery(accountByIdQuery());
```

```
        return accountDao;
    }

}
```

8. Call the `accountbyIdQuery.findObject(..)` method inside the `AccountDaoJdbcImpl`
`.find(long accountId)` method as follows:

```
@Override
public Account find(long accountId) {
    return accountByIdQuery.findObject(accountId);
}
```

How It Works

The first step in implementing such a reusable query object is to pass an available *dataSource* bean into
its super constructor together with an SQL query statement. After this step, you need to provide it with
SQL parameters using `SqlParameter` instances by calling its `declareParameter(..)` method. The
final step in the constructor is to call the `compile()` method. At this point your query statement is prepared and becomes ready for use. After the compilation phase, the query object is thread safe and can
be shared among several different data access objects in the application. `AccountDaoJdbcImpl` defines
a property with the `MappingSqlQuery` type, and your `accountByIdQuery` bean is injected into it.
It can then be used within the `find(..)` method of the DAO object to fetch `Account` using the given
accountId input parameter.

Encapsulating SQL DML Operations

The `SqlUpdate` class is used to encapsulate insert, update, and delete operations as reusable Java
objects. Those Java objects can be defined as Spring-managed beans, injected into several DAO
beans, and can be used for persistence operations:

```
public class AccountInsert extends SqlUpdate {
    public AccountInsert(DataSource dataSource) {
        super(dataSource,
        "insert into account(owner_name,balance,access_time,locked) values(?,?,?,?)");
            setParameters(new SqlParameter[] {
                    new SqlParameter(Types.VARCHAR),
                    new SqlParameter(Types.DOUBLE),
                    new SqlParameter(Types.TIMESTAMP),
                    new SqlParameter(Types.BOOLEAN) });
            setReturnGeneratedKeys(true);
            setGeneratedKeysColumnNames(new String[]{"id"});
            compile();
    }
}
```

The preceding code snippet gives an example of how you can extend `SqlUpdate` to encapsulate the
insert SQL operation as a Java object. Similar to `MappingSqlQuery`, you give a `DataSource` bean
and SQL insert statement as constructor parameters to the `super(..)` call of the `AccountInsert`

class. After defining input parameters of the SQL insert statement and generated key values, if any, you call the `compile()` method to make the insert object ready for use.

The following classes are for encapsulation of update and delete SQL operations as well. They both look very similar to the `AccountInsert` class:

```
public class AccountUpdate extends SqlUpdate {
    public AccountUpdate(DataSource dataSource) {
        super(dataSource,
    "update account set (owner_name,balance,access_time,locked)=(?,?,?,?) where id=?");
        setParameters(new SqlParameter[] {
                new SqlParameter(Types.VARCHAR),
                new SqlParameter(Types.DOUBLE),
                new SqlParameter(Types.TIMESTAMP),
                new SqlParameter(Types.BOOLEAN),
                new SqlParameter(Types.BIGINT) });
        compile();
    }
}

public class AccountDelete extends SqlUpdate {
    public AccountDelete(DataSource dataSource) {
        super(dataSource, "delete account where id = ?");
        setParameters(new SqlParameter[] {new SqlParameter(Types.BIGINT) });
        compile();
    }
}
```

To use those insert, update, and delete objects, you can define them as ordinary Spring beans, inject them into other beans—for example, your `accountDao` bean—and call their `update(..)` methods by passing any necessary input parameter values.

Encapsulating Stored Procedure Executions

You can use the `StoredProcedure` class to encapsulate stored procedure or stored function executions in a very similar way to how you used the `SqlUpdate` class previously:

```
public class ConcatStoredProcedure extends StoredProcedure {
    public ConcatStoredProcedure(DataSource dataSource) {
        setDataSource(dataSource);
        setSql("concat");
        declareParameter(new SqlParameter("param1",Types.VARCHAR));
        declareParameter(new SqlParameter("param2",Types.VARCHAR));
        compile();
    }

    public String execute(String param1, String param2) {
        Map<String,Object> inParams = new HashMap<String,Object>();
        inParams.put("param1", param1);
        inParams.put("param2", param2);
        Map<String, Object> map = execute(inParams);
        List<Map> list = (List<Map>) map.get("#result-set-1");
        return list.get(0).values().iterator().next().toString();
    }
}
```

The `StoredProcedure` class is an abstract class; therefore, you need to extend it and set its `sql` property together with in and out parameters before calling the `compile()` method. You also need to add a public method so that it calls one of its protected `execute(..)` methods and extracts and returns the result.

```
ConcatStoredProcedure storedProcedure =
    applicationContext.getBean(ConcatStoredProcedure.class);

String result = storedProcedure.execute("hello ", "world!");

System.out.println(result);
```

EXCEPTION HANDLING AND ERROR CODE TRANSLATION

Spring tries to encapsulate data access logic and abstracts away its technical details from the rest of the application. You can use different technologies in your data access layer, and even mix several of them in your application at the same time. Each data access technology has its own exception types, and what Spring does here is to handle technology-specific exceptions—such as `SQLException` for direct JDBC access, `HibernateException` used by native Hibernate, or `EntityException` used by JPA—and translate them into its own exception hierarchy.

Spring JDBC also processes SQL error codes and state information and tries to map those SQL-specific error codes to more meaningful exceptions.

Common Data Access Exception Hierarchy

All the exceptions thrown by the Spring JDBC are subclasses of `DataAccessException`, which is a type of `RuntimeException`, so you don't need to handle it explicitly. Any checked `SQLException` when thrown by the underlying JDBC API will be mapped to any of the subclasses of the `DataAccessException` framework. As a result, you are relieved from the burden of handling checked exceptions, and technology-specific details won't leak to the upper layers as well. If you need to handle data access exceptions in any of those layers, you can simply create a `try-catch` block, and it will be enough to just catch Spring's `DataAccessException`. For example, if a violation of integrity constraint occurs while you perform insert or update using Spring JDBC, it handles the `SQLException` and decides to throw `org.springframework` `.dao.DataIntegrityViolationException` by examining the SQL error code contained in the `SQLException`. The original `SQLException` is also included while rethrowing `DataIntegrityViolationException`. In a similar way, assume that you use Hibernate over Spring ORM support to perform similar inserts and updates in the database. When Hibernate throws `org.hibernate.exception.ConstraintViolationException`, Spring ORM support handles the `HibernateException` and decides to rethrow this exception by wrapping with `DataIntegrityViolationException`. You can always access the original exception thrown by the specific data access technology and examine it through the `DataAccessException` instance.

Automatic Handling and Translation of SQLException

Spring's JDBC support provides `SQLExceptionTranslator` to perform automatic translation of `SQLException` into a Spring-specific `DataAccessException`. The `SQLExceptionTranslator` class is actually an interface, and it has several implementations.

The default implementation used by Spring is `SQLErrorCodeSQLExceptionTranslator`, which uses vendor-specific error codes. Error codes are obtained from the `SQLErrorCodesFactory` class. This factory class loads an `sql-error-codes.xml` file from the project classpath. Error code mappings are defined separately for each database. Spring identifies the database product name from the `DatabaseMetadata` obtained from the JDBC `Connection`. This file is by default located under `org.springframework.jdbc.support` package; however, it can be overridden through a file with the same name located in the root classpath or `WEB-INF/classes` folder.

You also can extend the `SQLErrorCodeSQLExceptionTranslator` class and override its `customTranslate(..)` method. Within this method, you can check the error code, which you can obtain through the `SQLException.getErrorCode()` method, and return a `DataAccessException` instance specific to your needs.

Another common implementation of the `SQLExceptionTranslator` interface is `SQLStateSQLExceptionTranslator`, which uses SQL state information in the `SQLException` thrown. It looks at the first two digits of the SQL error code, and tries to diagnose the problem. It cannot diagnose all problems, but its main advantage is portability. It doesn't depend on a special database vendor to translate error codes. Actually, `SQLErrorCodeSQLExceptionTranslator` uses `SQLStateSQLExceptionTranslator` as a fallback.

`JdbcTemplate` by default creates and uses `SQLErrorCodeSQLExceptionTranslator` if the *dataSource* dependency of `JdbcTemplate` is satisfied; otherwise, it uses `SQLStateSQLExceptionTranslator`. As a result, if your data access object is using `JdbcTemplate`, you will have automatic exception translation capability by default. You can also set your custom `SQLErrorCodeSQLExceptionTranslator` by calling the `JdbcTemplate.setExceptionTranslator(..)` method as well.

SUMMARY

In this chapter, you learned what sorts of problems and deficiencies might occur within your codebase if you try to use JDBC without any preparation. You also learned the general steps that repeatedly arise while working with the JDBC API. The chapter explained the Template Method pattern as a cure to this recurring problem in the system. It also mentioned the `javax.sql.DataSource` concept and how it is used to obtain database connections. You learned several different ways of defining `DataSource` beans within the Spring environment, together with a facility to initialize the database during startup.

You learned that `JdbcTemplate` is the central point in Spring JDBC support and how to perform queries and execute insert, update, and delete operations using it. You also saw how those query results and return values of data manipulation operations can be processed. The chapter provided some examples that showed you how to use the `RowMapper` interface as a callback to handle query results and transform rows into Java objects. You were also introduced to `NamedParameterJdbcTemplate`, which helps you write queries using named parameters. The chapter explained several advantages of using `PreparedStatement` objects over `Statement` objects and showed you how to create `PreparedStatement` instances and execute them using `JdbcTemplate`. You saw how to call stored procedures and stored functions defined in the database and process their `ResultSet` objects, which are usually returned as cursors. The chapter provided a brief explanation and code examples about batch SQL processing, executing DDL statements, how to access vendor-specific features of your JDBC driver, and dealing with BLOB and CLOB data types.

Near the end of the chapter you saw some classes provided by Spring—MappingSqlQuery, SqlUpdate, and StoredProcedure—so that you can encapsulate your queries and data manipulation operations. You also saw stored procedures as Java objects and how to call those classes. Then you found out how Spring handles checked SQLExceptions and automatically translates them into its own data access exception hierarchy by looking at SQL error codes and SQL states.

EXERCISES

You can find possible solutions to the following exercises in Appendix A.

1. Define a new method called findByOwnerAndLocked(String ownerName, boolean locked) in the AccountDao interface and implement it within the AccountDaoJdbcImpl class using the named parameter support of Spring.

2. Define beans for the AccountInsert, AccountUpdate, and AccountDelete classes; inject them into the accountDao bean; and then change the implementation of the insert, update, and delete methods of AccountDaoJdbcImpl so that it will use those new beans for its SQL operations.

3. Add a new property called byte[] ownerPhoto into the Account domain class, and a corresponding BLOB column with the name owner_photo. Modify the AccountByIdQuery, AccountInsert, and AccountUpdate classes so that they will handle this new property.

▶ WHAT YOU LEARNED IN THIS CHAPTER

TOPIC	KEY POINTS
DataSource	JDBC Connection factory object that abstracts away database connection–specific details
DriverManagerDataSource	Spring's DataSource implementation that returns a new SQL Connection each time its getConnection method is called
jee:jndi-lookup	Namespace element that you can use to obtain application server–managed DataSource instances
JdbcTemplate	Template Method pattern implementation of Spring to support working with JDBC
RowMapper	Callback interface to process ResultSet row values, and convert each row into a Java object
NamedParameterJdbcTemplate	Spring's class to support named parameters
SqlParameterSource	Interface to pass named parameter values into NamedParameterJdbcTemplate
PreparedStatementCreator and PreparedStatementCreatorFactory	Interface to create PreparedStatement objects and factory method to create instances from default implementation
MappingSqlQuery	Abstract class provided by Spring to encapsulate SQL queries as Java objects
SimpleJdbcCall	Class that you use to invoke stored procedures and stored functions
SqlUpdate	Concrete class to encapsulate insert, update, and delete SQL operations
StoredProcedure	Abstract class to encapsulate calling stored procedures and stored functions
LobHandler & LobCreator	Interfaces to deal with BLOB and CLOB data types
NativeJdbcExtractor	Interface to extract native Connection, Statement, and ResultSet instances specific to database vendors
SQLExceptionTranslator	Interface to translate checked SQLException instances to Spring's unchecked DataAccessException instances
SQLErrorCodeSQLExceptionTranslator	Default implementation of SQLExceptionTranslator that looks up SQL error code values for exception translation

5

Data Access with JPA Using Spring

WHAT YOU WILL LEARN IN THIS CHAPTER:

➤ Introducing the ORM world

➤ Learning the role of JPA and what Spring offers

➤ Configuring and using Spring's JPA support

➤ Making use of PersistenceContext and PersistenceUnit annotations

➤ Learning the role of JpaDialect and load-time weaving in JPA configuration

➤ Properly handling and translating ORM exceptions

CODE DOWNLOAD *The wrox.com code downloads for this chapter are found at* www.wrox.com/go/beginningspring *on the Download Code tab. The code is in the Chapter 5 download and individually named according to the names throughout the chapter.*

Object-oriented programs deal with hierarchies of objects. They create objects; make associations between objects; modify their attributes; and so on. At some point they need to store states of those objects so that those objects can later be restored with the saved state. This state is usually kept in relational databases as records in tables. Enterprise applications, therefore, use data access strategies; for example, Java Database Connectivity (JDBC) fetches the data in a relational database, processes it in the application layer, and shows it to their users, or it accepts some data from a user, processes it again, and stores it in the database using JDBC. Hence, some sort of translating between objects and relational data is continuously performed in such systems. Object-relational mapping (ORM) tools try to automate this translation process and let developers focus only on the object model.

The Java Persistence API (JPA) is the Java EE specification that defines how such object-relational mapping tools and frameworks should handle persistence-related tasks in Java applications. It defines what features they should offer to their users, and tries to standardize persistence operations that could be performed in those applications. This chapter discusses what JPA offers in brief detail. It also gives examples of persistence operations that are performed over objects, and discusses Spring's role in facilitating use of JPA as a data access technology in enterprise Java applications.

BRIEF INTRODUCTION TO ORM AND JPA

ORM stands for object-relational mapping. It is a general term for data access technologies that try to handle persistent data on the application side. It is placed between the business layer and the database. By doing so, the database becomes more isolated from applications, and it is expected that developers will be able to think in a more object-oriented way and focus more on business logic.

The object world is composed of objects associated with each other either with composition or with inheritance hierarchies. Attributes inside objects are used to hold their current states. The relational world, on the other hand, is composed of tables, columns inside those tables, and foreign keys among those tables that create relationships between the tables. At first sight, those two worlds look similar to each other, and you might think that it is an easy job to bridge between them. Unfortunately, it is not an easy job to sit between the business layer and the database and translate the object model to the relational model and vice versa. There is a paradigm mismatch. The following section looks at what constitutes that mismatch.

Paradigm Mismatch

The first problem is that objects have associations with other objects, and those associations have direction information as well. If an association is *unidirectional*, that means that it is only possible to navigate from the source object to the target object, but not the other way around. On the other hand, if an association is *bidirectional*, it is possible to navigate from both sides to the other. In the relational world, associations among tables are represented with foreign keys. However, they don't keep any direction information.

The second problem is granularity. There can be no exact one-to-one map between a class and a table. For example, a user table can consist of columns that hold data about a user, and his home address as well. However, you might model your objects so that you have two separate classes: one for the user and the other for his address. As object-oriented enthusiasts we tend to make our object model more fine grained, but database gurus try to decrease the number of joins among tables; therefore, they tend to combine related data in one table.

The third problem is related to inheritance and polymorphic behavior. You can create object hierarchies that involve several different types, and you can establish associations against abstract types, which results in relationships of objects with more than one concrete type at run time. On the other hand, the relational world has no concept of inheritance. You can only create foreign key relationships between tables. You can map several different types in a hierarchy with different numbers of tables in the database. Handling polymorphic associations is also problematic because, to create a polymorphic association, you might have to create foreign key relationships to several different tables from a table. All of those foreign keys represent that same polymorphic association on the object side.

Finally, traversal of the object network on demand and the data-fetch approach in the relational world are not a good fit for one another. In the object world, relationships are traversed node by node. This means the state of the target object is needed only when you attempt to access it. However, in the relational world, best practice is to decrease the number of SQL queries by joining tables so that all of the data needed for the execution of the current scenario is fetched with a minimum number of queries. This results in a performance improvement. This obviously conflicts with on-demand traversal of the object network and causes memory problems on the application side. If you try to fetch data table by table, on the other hand, you have performance problems on the database side.

Building Blocks of an ORM Framework

In short, an ORM framework tries to solve the problems explained in the preceding section. Therefore, a full-fledged ORM tool should offer the following facilities:

➤ Metadata mapping between the object model and the relational model

➤ A Create, Read, Update, Delete (CRUD) API for operations that need to be performed over objects

➤ An object query language

➤ Different fetch strategies and object network traversal facilities to improve memory usage and performance of data fetch times

What JPA Offers

The Java Persistence API, or JPA for short, is for handling persistence operations in Java. It tries to standardize ORM features and functionalities in the enterprise Java world. It defines an API for mapping the object model with the relational model, CRUD operations that can be performed on objects, an object query language, and a criteria API to fetch data over an object graph.

Several JPA implementations are available, such as Hibernate, OpenJPA, DataNucleus, EclipseLink, and so on. Hibernate is one of the most popular options. EclipseLink is the reference implementation for JPA. However, this book uses Hibernate in the examples.

JPA has several benefits over using proprietary ORM tools directly. It provides automatic metadata discovery, standardized and simplified configuration, and standardized data access support. As a result, switching between different JPA implementations is much easier than switching between different proprietary ORM tools, and ORM knowledge within the Java community becomes more homogenized and widespread.

Mapping the Object Model to the Relational Model

Any ORM tool tries to map the object model to the relational model. This mapping is a must to perform other runtime operations—such as performing CRUD operations or querying data with an object query language—using the tool. Object relational mapping occurs between the following:

➤ Classes and tables

➤ Attributes of a class and columns in a table

➤ Object associations and foreign keys

➤ Java types and SQL types

Defining Entities

An object that has a corresponding record on the database side with its own primary key is called an *entity*. There is usually a one-to-one mapping between an entity class and its corresponding database table. However, an entity may be mapped to more than one table as well. The following code illustrates how an entity class is defined:

```
@Entity
@Table(name="users")
public class User {

    @Id
    @GeneratedValue
    private Long id;

}
```

Entity classes should be top-level classes. They don't have to extend from special super classes or implement any interfaces. You don't need to make them serializable, either. They should have at least a package visible default no arg constructor, and they should not be marked as final. This is because some ORM providers may extend from entity classes to create corresponding proxy classes at run time. You don't need to create public getter/setter methods for persistent fields. ORM providers can access persistent field values directly. That way, you can put business logic into your getters and setters. Your public methods should also be not marked as final because of the proxying operation mentioned earlier.

JPA provides Java annotations for mapping purposes. Those annotations are in the `javax` `.persistence` package. The `@Entity` annotation defines that the `User` class is a persistent type that has a corresponding table. The `@Table` annotation specifies the name of the table. If not specified, the class name is used. Each entity in the JPA configuration should have a unique name. By default, it is equal to the simple name of the class. If there happens to be more than one class with the same name but they are in different packages, you need to distinguish among their names with the `name` attribute value in the `@Entity` annotation.

The `@Id` annotation marks the primary key attribute. The name of the primary key column matches the name of the property. If the column name is different, you can use the `@Column` annotation to change its name. Primary keys can be composed of more than one column, and they contain meaningful values for the business. Those primary keys are called *natural primary keys*. However, having a single primary key column and assigning it totally meaningless value in terms of the business perspective is a more popular solution, and it has several benefits over the natural key approach. Such primary keys are called *surrogate* or *synthetic primary keys*, and the application doesn't deal with producing their values. Instead their values are assigned by the JPA vendor during new record insertion. The @GeneratedValue annotation tells JPA that the application won't deal with assigning values, and the JPA vendor should handle it instead.

There are different ID-generation strategies that can be used by the JPA vendor to assign values to surrogate primary keys. Identity, sequence, and UUID are some examples of those ID-generation strategies. The javax.persistence.GenerationType enum type has values that are supported by all JPA vendors. The ID-generation strategy of an entity class is specified with the strategy attribute of the @GeneratedValue annotation. If it's not specified, the JPA vendor uses the default strategy of the underlying database provider. For example, it will be SEQUENCE for Oracle or IDENTITY for MySQL.

Mapping Attributes to Columns

By default, any attribute defined in a class is assumed to be persistent. In other words, JPA seeks a corresponding column in the table. If you want an attribute not to be considered as persistent, you can either mark it with the @Transient annotation or with the transient modifier.

For example, the following code snippet shows several attributes with or without JPA annotations. The username field is persistent by default. The password field is also persistent, but JPA annotations are used to customize its mapping. The selected attribute, on the other hand, is marked with the transient modifier. Therefore, it is ignored by the JPA provider.

```
private String username;

@Basic(optional=false)
@Column(name="passwd",nullable=false,length=128)
private String password;

private transient Boolean selected;
```

If you don't use any annotation over attributes, they are mapped with table columns with names equal to the attributes' names. If you want to differentiate between attribute and column names, you can use the @Column annotation as shown in the preceding code. You can also change other attributes of a column, such as its nullability, length, unique constraint, and so on.

You can place JPA annotations either on fields or getter methods of those fields. This identifies the access strategy of JPA during entity loading, persisting, and so on. If you prefer *field-level access*, JPA doesn't need getters/setters to access values of persistent fields in the entity, instead it sets and gets values directly on fields via the Reflection API. In addition, it becomes easier to see and examine JPA configuration in a large Java class, and getter/setter methods are freed to be used for business purposes as well.

JPA determines the access strategy by looking at the location of @Id annotation. If it is used on a field, access strategy is field level, otherwise it is getter. If you prefer *getter-level access*, JPA performs data access via getter and setter methods instead. In that case, you need to provide public getter/setter methods for those persistent fields.

Access strategy in an entity class cannot be changed. However, it can be different among entities.

Creating Associations between Objects

You can examine associations between objects from different perspectives. *Multiplicity* and *directionality* are two perspectives explained in this section. Multiplicity defines the number of associated instances on each side of the association. Directionality defines the direction from which that association is navigable—that is, from which instance you should start so that you can reach the other side of the navigation.

There can be several different types of associations between objects in terms of multiplicity:

➤ One-to-one (1:1)

➤ Many-to-one (M:1)

➤ One-to-many (1:M)

➤ Many-to-many (M:N)

One-to-One Associations

In one-to-one associations, two objects are associated only with each other. For example, if a user has only one address, there can be a 1:1 association between user and address:

```
@Entity
public class User {

    //...

    @OneToOne
    @JoinColumn(name="address_id")
    private Address address;
}

@Entity
public class Address {
    //...
}
```

The @OneToOne annotation is used for this purpose. @JoinColumn specifies the foreign key relationship between tables corresponding to the User and Address entities. It is the column in the user table that references the address table.

Many-to-One Associations

In many-to-one associations several objects can refer to the same instance. For example, an employee and company relationship is an M:1 association. In other words, there can be several employees working for a company:

```
@Entity
public class Employee {
```

```
    //...

    @ManyToOne(optional=false)
    @JoinColumn(name="company_id")
    private Company company;
}

@Entity
public class Company {
    //...
}
```

The @ManyToOne annotation is used here. @JoinColumn is again used to specify the foreign key relationship between two tables. The *optional=false* attribute means this association is required by the Employee type; that is, the Employee instance cannot exist without being associated with a Company instance.

One-to-Many Associations

In one-to-many associations, an instance can have a relationship with more than one object of the same type. Let's say a student has several books, and those books only belong to one student. Hence, the student/book relationship is considered to be 1:M:

```
@Entity
public class Student {
    //...

    @OneToMany
    @JoinColumn(name="student_id")
    private Set<Book> books = new HashSet<Book>();
}

@Entity
public class Book {
    //...
}
```

The @OneToMany annotation creates a 1:M relationship between the Student and Book entities. A type from the Java Collection API is used to define the variable type. You can use Set, List, Collection, and Map types, each with different semantics that you need to consider before deciding on which one to use during the analysis or design phase. @JoinColumn is again used to specify the foreign key column. However, this time its value indicates the column that exists in the table of the Book entity.

Many-to-Many Associations

In many-to-many associations, several objects of a type can refer to several other objects of another type. For example, products can be placed in more than one category, and in any category there can be several different types of products. Therefore, a product and category relationship is an M:N relationship:

```
@Entity
public class Product {
    // ...
    @ManyToMany
```

```
        @JoinTable(name = "product_catalog", joinColumns = @JoinColumn(
        name = "product_id"), inverseJoinColumns = @JoinColumn(name = "catalog_id"))
        private Set<Catalog> catalogs = new HashSet<Catalog>();
}

@Entity
public class Catalog {
    //...
}
```

The annotation for creating an M:N relationship is @ManyToMany, as you may easily guess. However, this example used @JoinTable instead of @JoinColumn because several instances on each side can be associated with an instance on the other side. Therefore, you cannot keep association data in a column that is referring to the other side's table. Instead, you need an intermediate table, called an *association table*, between those two tables, that contains references to primary key columns in each table. In this example, the association table is named product_catalog, and the joinColumns and inverseJoinColumns attributes specify column names that exist in the product_catalog table and references to primary keys of product and catalog tables, respectively.

Directionality in Associations

You also need to take into account the direction of associations between objects. Two possibilities exist:

➤ Unidirectional

➤ Bidirectional

In unidirectional associations, navigation is only possible from one side to the other—that is, only from the source object of the association to the target object. For bidirectional associations, navigation is possible in both directions. You can start from either node, and reach the other node in the association. A bidirectional one-to-many association is actually a many-to-one association from the other side, and vice versa.

In the following code, for example, we added a one-to-one association from the Address entity to the User entity, which already has an association from User to Address. At this stage, the User-Address association becomes bidirectional. We can start navigating the object tree from either node and can reach the other side:

```
@Entity
public class User {

    //...

    @OneToOne
    @JoinColumn(name="address_id")
    private Address address;
}
@Entity
public class Address {

    //...

    @OneToOne(mappedBy="address")
```

```
        private User user;
}
```

In terms of managing associations between two `User` and `Address` instances, it is enough for the JPA to look at only one of those two attributes. It looks at the value of the attribute specified with the `mappedBy` attribute during run time so that a new association is created, or an already existing association between two instances is removed. Except for the `@ManyToOne` annotation, all other multiplicity annotations have a `mappedBy` attribute. By looking at its value, JPA identifies the attribute that it looks at to manage association between two entities. The side on which `mappedBy` is used can be seen as a mirror, or read-only. Setting a value on this mirror property has no effect on creating or removing associations.

Mapping Java Types to SQL Types

Java has its own types, such as primitives, wrapper types for primitives, `String`, `Date`, `Enum`, `BigInteger`, `BigDecimal`, and so on. Databases, on the other hand, have their own SQL types as well, such as `char`, `varchar`, `number`, `bigint`, `clob`, `blob`, `datetime`, and so on. The JPA tries to map a Java type to the most appropriate SQL type. However, developers sometimes intervene.

Table 5-1 shows how Java types are mapped to the corresponding SQL types. The column in the middle shows the corresponding ORM types used in XML-based mapping metadata. However, they are not needed when Java annotation-based mappings are used because the JPA provider is able to find the corresponding SQL type just by looking at the Java type of the persistent field.

TABLE 5-1: Java - SQL Type Mappings Table

JAVA TYPE	ORM TYPE	SQL TYPE
int / java.lang.Integer	integer	INTEGER
long / java.lang.Long	long	BIGINT
short / java.lang.Short	short	SMALLINT
float / java.lang.Float	float	FLOAT
double / Java.lang.Double	double	DOUBLE
java.math.BigDecimal	big_decimal	NUMERIC
java.lang.String	character	CHAR(1)
java.lang.String	string	VARCHAR
byte / java.lang.Byte	byte	TINYINT
boolean / java.lang.Boolean	boolean	BIT
boolean / java.lang.Boolean	yes_no	CHAR(1)
boolean / java.lang.Boolean	true_false	CHAR(1)

continues

TABLE 5-1 *(continued)*

JAVA TYPE	ORM TYPE	SQL TYPE
java.util.Date / java.sql.Date	date	DATE
java.util.Date / java.sql.Time	time	TIME
java.util.Date / java.sql.Timestamp	timestamp	TIMESTAMP
java.util.Calendar	calendar	TIMESTAMP
java.util.Calendar	calendar_date	DATE
byte[]	binary	VARBINARY
java.lang.String	text	CLOB
java.sql.Clob	clob	CLOB
java.sql.Blob	blob	BLOB
java.lang.Serializable	serializable	VARBINARY
java.lang.Class	class	VARCHAR
java.util.Locale	locale	VARCHAR
java.util.Timezone	timezone	VARCHAR
java.util.Currency	currency	VARCHAR

For example, Java has the java.util.Date type for handling date values. It contains the date value in millisecond precision. However, SQL has three different types for handling temporal values: date, time, and timestamp. date only keeps the year, month, and day parts. time keeps the hour, minute, and second parts. timestamp keeps the date and time together with nanosecond precision. By default, JPA maps attributes with the java.util.Date type to timestamp. However, according to your requirements and available SQL column type in the database, you may need to specify a different temporal SQL type. You do this with @Temporal annotation (as shown in the following code snippet), and you can specify which TemporalType should be used in the mapping. DATE, TIME, and TIMESTAMP are available values for TemporalType:

```
@Temporal(TemporalType.DATE)
private Date birthDate;
```

By default, JPA handles Java enum types and maps them with ordinal values to the database columns with numeric SQL types. However, you can change that. If you want the name of the enum value to be persisted, you can use the @Enumerated annotation with the EnumType.STRING attribute value:

```
@Enumerated(EnumType.STRING)
private Gender gender;
```

The `String` Java type is by default mapped to `varchar` on the SQL side, and `varchar` has an upper limit that can be unsuitable for fields in which a large amount of character data is to be kept. In that case, you can change the type mapping using the `@Lob` annotation. From now on, the description value will be kept in a column with the SQL type `CLOB`:

```
@Lob
private String description;
```

There can be attributes having more than one value in entities. For example, an entity may have several telephone numbers, each of which can be stored in text form. If there was only one telephone number, it could have been stored in a `String` attribute corresponding to a `varchar` column in an entity table. However, as there might be more than one telephone number of an entity, you need another table to store telephone number values of each entity. Such associations are called as collection values. They can be mapped with the `@ElementCollection` annotation. The table in which collection values are kept is specified with `@CollectionTable` annotation:

```
@ElementCollection
@CollectionTable(name="user_phone_numbers",joinColumns=@JoinColumn(name="user_id"))
private Set<String> telephoneNumbers = new HashSet<>();
```

ORM mapping is much more detailed and deeper than explained here. However, this amount of mapping information is enough to introduce you to JPA. Now, you can focus on the runtime part of ORM. The ORM mapping metadata briefly explained earlier is very crucial for ORM's runtime functionality. Mappings should be made correctly so that the ORM tool runs properly at run time.

Configuring and Using JPA

To perform runtime operations, you first need to configure JPA. The examples here use Hibernate as the JPA provider. We are going to use Hibernate version 4.3.1.Final, which implements JPA version 2.1 in our examples.

Check out how it is done with the following Try It Out.

TRY IT OUT Configuring JPA and Hibernate

You can find the source code within the project named `configuring-jpa` in the `spring-book-ch5` `.zip` file.

In this Try It Out, you configure Hibernate to use as the JPA provider. To begin, follow these steps:

1. Create a Maven project with the following Maven command:

```
mvn archetype:generate -DarchetypeGroupId=org.apache.maven.archetypes
    -DgroupId=com.wiley.beginningspring -DartifactId=spring-book-ch5
```

2. Add the necessary dependencies to the `pom.xml` file:

```
<dependency>
    <groupId>org.springframework</groupId>
    <artifactId>spring-orm</artifactId>
```

```
    <version>4.0.5.RELEASE</version>
</dependency>

<dependency>
    <groupId>org.springframework</groupId>
    <artifactId>spring-context</artifactId>
    <version>4.0.5.RELEASE</version>
</dependency>
```

3. In order to use Hibernate as the JPA provider, also add the following dependencies into pom.xml:

```
<dependency>
    <groupId>org.hibernate</groupId>
    <artifactId>hibernate-core</artifactId>
    <version>4.3.1.Final</version>
</dependency>

<dependency>
    <groupId>org.hibernate</groupId>
    <artifactId>hibernate-entitymanager</artifactId>
    <version>4.3.1.Final</version>
</dependency>
```

4. The example uses the H2 database. If its dependency is not already added, add the following <dependency> element to the pom.xml file:

```
<dependency>
    <groupId>com.h2database</groupId>
    <artifactId>h2</artifactId>
    <version>1.3.175</version>
</dependency>
```

5. Create a META-INF/persistence.xml file with the following content. That file should be located under the root classpath of the project:

```
<?xml version="1.0" encoding="UTF-8"?>
<persistence version="2.0"
    xmlns="http://java.sun.com/xml/ns/persistence"
    xmlns:xsi="http://www.w3.org/2001/XMLSchema-instance"
    xsi:schemaLocation="http://java.sun.com/xml/ns/persistence
    http://java.sun.com/xml/ns/persistence/persistence_2_0.xsd">
    <persistence-unit name="test-jpa" transaction-type="RESOURCE_LOCAL">
        <properties>
        <property name="hibernate.connection.driver_class" value="org.h2.Driver"/>
        <property name="hibernate.connection.url" value="jdbc:h2:tcp://localhost/↵
                ~/test"/>
            <property name="hibernate.connection.username" value="sa" />
            <property name="hibernate.connection.password" value="" />
            <property name="hibernate.dialect" value="org.hibernate.dialect.H2Dialect"/>
        <property name="hibernate.hbm2ddl.auto" value="update" />
        </properties>
    </persistence-unit>
</persistence>
```

6. Find the `org.h2.tools.Console` class of the H2 database from the project classpath, and run it as a Java application from your integrated development environment (IDE). When it runs, the browser automatically appears with the database console.

7. Create a `Main` class having a `main` method, and load the persistence unit with the `test-jpa` name. If it runs successfully, it means that you have successfully configured your JPA environment:

```java
public class Main {

    public static void main(String[] args) {
        EntityManagerFactory entityManagerFactory =
            Persistence.createEntityManagerFactory("test-jpa");
        System.out.println(entityManagerFactory.isOpen());
    }
}
```

How It Works

`META-INF/persistence.xml` is the main entry point for the JPA configuration. There can be several different JPA configurations in an application, and different JPA providers can co-exist at the same time. Each configuration is called a *persistence unit*, and each persistence unit has its own name. That name is used to access the configuration at run time.

Transactions are crucial in order for JPA to operate. Transactions group several data access operations and help you to execute them together as a single unit. Either all of them succeed, with changes reflected to the database, or none of them succeed. In the case of failure, no change happens in the database. JPA has two transactional modes: one is RESOURCE_LOCAL and the other is JTA. The first means local transaction—only a single database is involved in data access operations—and the second one means global transaction, in which there can be several databases on which the data access operations are performed. You can read more about transactions in Chapter 6. This example uses local transactions; we set the RESOURCE_LOCAL value to the `transaction-type` attribute of the `<persistence-unit>` element.

The JPA provider can connect to the database in different ways. It can use a `javax.sql.DataSource` instance, or it can open connections directly with `DriverManager`. For the sake of simplicity, this example uses the second option and provides the following Hibernate properties for connection management:

```xml
<property name="hibernate.connection.driver_class" value="org.h2.Driver" />
<property name="hibernate.connection.url" value="jdbc:h2:tcp://localhost/~/test"/>
<property name="hibernate.connection.username" value="sa" />
<property name="hibernate.connection.password" value="" />
```

ORM tools are laid on top of the database layer, and they can operate with different databases. With the help of a JDBC driver class, they identify the currently operating database and generate the necessary SQL statements suitable for that database at run time. A dialect class is used to create correct SQL for the specific database at hand. The following property defines which dialect class is to be used by Hibernate:

```xml
<property name="hibernate.dialect" value="org.hibernate.dialect.H2Dialect" />
```

Actually, providing a dialect is optional if the connection is managed directly by Hibernate. Because Hibernate can understand which database is used by looking at the JDBC driver class, it can then deduce the corresponding dialect class by itself. However, if you had used the `DataSource` approach to obtain connections, Hibernate has no clue for guessing correct dialect; therefore, it becomes compulsory to provide it explicitly.

JPA auto-detects mapping metadata in the classpath and loads it. Hibernate also provides a means to automatically create or update the database schema with the help of that mapping metadata. The following `<property>` element tells Hibernate that it should update the schema to synchronize it with the mapping metadata:

```
<property name="hibernate.hbm2ddl.auto" value="update" />
```

Allowing Hibernate to create or update the database schema is great for development and test environments. However, it shouldn't be used during production. By default, it does nothing, but you can also give a `none` value to disable schema creation or the update facility.

The last step is to check whether that persistence unit configuration is loaded. The `javax.persistence.Persistence` class offers a method to create an `EntityManagerFactory` by giving the persistence unit name as the input argument:

```
EntityManagerFactory entityManagerFactory =
    Persistence.createEntityManagerFactory("test-jpa");
```

The `EntityManagerFactory` instance, which is obtained for the corresponding persistence unit, is usually created once and used throughout the application lifetime. Therefore, it is common practice to execute the preceding code within a class statically, and assign the returned instance to a static variable so that it can be accessed from anywhere in the application code.

Performing CRUD Operations on Objects

JPA provides a CRUD API to perform data access and manipulation operations that is used to operate on entities at run time. You can use that API to select an entity by using its type and primary key value, insert a new entity into the table, update its changed attributes, or delete it. Those operations are provided by the JPA `EntityManager`. `EntityManager` is called a *persistence context* because it's available at run time. The persistence context is the bridge between application and database run times. Using persistence context, you can solely operate on entities, load them, change their states, persist new ones, or delete already loaded ones. It helps you to manage transactions and so on. Have a look at some of those CRUD methods offered by `EntityManager` with an example.

TRY IT OUT   Using JPA to Persist Entities and Create Associations

You can find the source code within the project named `configuring-and-using-jdbctemplate` in the `spring-book-ch5.zip` file.

In this Try It Out, you first create two persistent entities called `Student` and `Book`, and you associate those two classes. Later, you create an `EntityManager` and an active transaction to persist some `Student` and `Book` instances. You can continue from where you left off with the previous Try It Out. To begin, follow these steps:

1. First, create the following `Book` entity class:

```java
@Entity
public class Book {
    @Id
    @GeneratedValue
    private Long id;

    private String name;

    public String getName() {
        return name;
    }

    public void setName(String name) {
        this.name = name;
    }

    public Long getId() {
        return id;
    }
}
```

2. Create the following `Student` entity class. There will be a unidirectional 1:M association between those two classes:

```java
@Entity
public class Student {
    @Id
    @GeneratedValue
    private Long id;

    private String firstName;

    private String lastName;

    @OneToMany(cascade=CascadeType.ALL)
    @JoinColumn(name="student_id")
    private Set<Book> books = new HashSet<Book>();

    public Long getId() {
        return id;
    }
    public String getFirstName() {
        return firstName;
    }
    public void setFirstName(String firstName) {
        this.firstName = firstName;
    }
    public String getLastName() {
        return lastName;
    }
    public void setLastName(String lastName) {
        this.lastName = lastName;
    }
    public Set<Book> getBooks() {
```

```
        return books;
    }
}
```

3. Create a new `EntityManager` by using an `EntityManagerFactory` instance in the `main` method:

```
public class Main {

    public static void main(String[] args) {
        EntityManagerFactory entityManagerFactory =
            Persistence.createEntityManagerFactory("test-jpa");
        EntityManager entityManager = entityManagerFactory.createEntityManager();
```

4. Start a new transaction from `EntityManager`:

```
        EntityTransaction transaction = entityManager.getTransaction();
        transaction.begin();
```

5. Create a new `Student` instance and two `Book` instances:

```
        Student student = new Student();
        student.setFirstName("John");
        student.setLastName("Doe");
         Book book1 = new Book();
        book1.setName("Book 1");
         Book book2 = new Book();
        book2.setName("Book 2");
```

6. Add those books into the `Student`'s collection, and persist the student using `EntityManager`:

```
        student.getBooks().add(book1);
        student.getBooks().add(book2);

        entityManager.persist(student);
```

7. Commit the transaction and close the `EntityManager` instance:

```
        transaction.commit();
        entityManager.close();
    }
}
```

How It Works

The `Student` and `Book` classes are defined as persistent entities using the `@Entity` annotation. Their ID property is marked as a primary key with the `@Id` annotation. The primary key is automatically generated during an entity persist operation, as indicated with `@GeneratedValue`, and how it is to be produced is determined according to the specific database vendor. Several different primary-key generation strategies exist, such as *identity*, autoincrement, sequence, *uuid*, and so on. Not all databases support all methods, and each database has a default strategy assigned within its dialect. Because the example uses the H2 database and `@GeneratedValue` has no strategy defined, the primary-key generation strategy is `sequence` by default. If you were using MySQL, it would be autoincrement, and so on.

The 1:M association between `Student` and `Book` is defined with the `@OneToMany` annotation, and the foreign key is on the `student_id` column of the `Book` table.

When the application is run, Hibernate automatically creates the Student and Book tables and a foreign key relationship between those two tables. Figure 5-1 shows how those tables would look as an entity-relationship (ER) diagram.

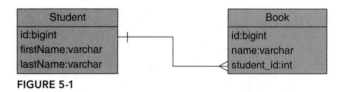

FIGURE 5-1

There is an attribute called `cascade` defined in the `@OneToMany` annotation. Its purpose is to instruct JPA to repeat the persistence context operation performed on the source entity—such as persist, merge, or delete—on the target entity of the association as well. For example, it helps JPA to decide what it will do with the books of a student when the student entity is persisted, updated, or deleted. As a result, you don't have to explicitly deal with each of those books associated with the student entity. This is called *transitive persistence* in the ORM world, and it is one of the very useful features of JPA. In this example you gave the `CascadeType.ALL` value to that attribute. This means that any JPA operation performed on the source entity, in this case the `Student` instance, is repeated on each of the `Book` instances one by one.

This example creates an `EntityManager` and an `EntityTransaction` instance, respectively. It is crucial that you execute insert, delete, and update operations of JPA within an available active transaction. Otherwise, it will fail with an exception. Later, the fourth and fifth steps create a `Student` with two separate `Book` instances. The `entityManager.persist(student);` statement will persist `Student` and `Book` entities in the database. You don't need to call `persist` on each `Book` instance separately because of the `cascade` attribute value defined in the mapping.

At the end of the scenario you have to commit the transaction if everything goes well up to that point. You do this with the `transaction.commit();` statement. It is also important not to keep the `EntityManager` instance open too long because it may cause state data problems for the current session, and you should call `entityManager.close();` at the end of the scenario.

If you inspect the H2 database contents via its console at this point, you will see student and book records inserted in the related tables.

After being able to persist entities together with their associations, you can now try to find, update, and delete entities via the JPA API in the following Try It Out.

TRY IT OUT Using JPA to Find, Update, and Delete Entities

You can find the source code within the project named `configuring-and-using-jdbctemplate` in the `spring-book-ch5.zip` file.

In this Try It Out, you use the EntityManager API to query a database for entities and then update and delete those entities. You can continue from where you left off with the previous Try It Out. To begin, follow these steps:

1. It is just enough to remove the lines between the transaction begin and commit operations in the preceding example:

```
public static void main(String[] args) {
    EntityManagerFactory entityManagerFactory =
        Persistence.createEntityManagerFactory("test-jpa");
    EntityManager entityManager = entityManagerFactory.createEntityManager();
    EntityTransaction transaction = entityManager.getTransaction();
    transaction.begin();
```

2. Find `Student` and the second `Book` instances using their primary key values via `EntityManager`:

```
Student student = entityManager.find(Student.class, 1L);
Book book2 = entityManager.getReference(Book.class, 2L);
```

3. Change the student's `firstName`:

```
student.setFirstName("Joe");
```

4. Delete the second book using `EntityManager`:

```
entityManager.remove(book2);
```

5. Commit the transaction and close the `EntityManager` instance:

```
transaction.commit();
entityManager.close();
}
```

How It Works

The JPA API provides two different finder methods to load entities from databases using their persistent classes and their primary key values: the `find(..)` and `getReference(..)` methods of `EntityManager`. Those two methods look very similar in terms of loading specified entity instances. However, there is an important difference between those two. The `entityManager.find(Student .class,1L);` method call causes the specified entity to be fetched and returned immediately if it exists in the database. If there is no corresponding record in the database, it returns null. The second method, `getReference(..)`, does not access the database immediately, and it returns a proxy instance in place of the target entity instance. Therefore, JPA is able to defer database queries related with the entity until the entity instance is really needed. As a consequence of not hitting the database immediately and returning a proxy in place of a real entity, this method may throw an exception if the record doesn't exist when the related SQL query is executed.

Another important feature of JPA or ORM in general is *transparent persistence*. JPA tracks changes performed on entity instances loaded with the `EntityManager` instance. Changed entities are marked as dirty. This process is also called *automatic dirty checking*. Changes performed on entities result in update statements, and JPA executes those update statements when the developer commits the transaction. Entities are tracked so long as they are connected with their `EntityManager` instance, and it is kept open. When it is closed, loaded entities become detached, and their state changes won't be tracked at all. You need to either reload or re-associate them with a new `EntityManager` instance using the `merge` operation.

`entityManager.remove(book2);` causes the `book2` entity to be deleted from the database. The important point here is that you can only delete already associated entities; you are not allowed to delete detached entities.

Querying with Object Query Language

JPA also offers an object query language whose structure is similar to SQL, but instead of using table column names, you are able to use entity names and properties in Java classes. It also transparently handles some joins that would need to be done between tables if you were using SQL directly to fetch data. The following Try It Out shows you how you can query the database using JPA Query Language (QL) with an example.

TRY IT OUT Querying a Database with JPA QL

You can find the source code within the project named `configuring-and-using-jdbctemplate` in the `spring-book-ch5.zip` file.

In this Try It Out, you create a JPA query and execute it via `EntityManager`. You can continue from the previous Try It Out. To begin, follow these steps:

1. Open an `EntityManager` within the `main` method:

    ```
    public static void main(String[] args) {
        EntityManagerFactory entityManagerFactory =
            Persistence.createEntityManagerFactory("test-jpa");
        EntityManager entityManager = entityManagerFactory.createEntityManager();
    ```

2. Create a query using `EntityManager` by giving the query string as follows:

    ```
    Query query = entityManager.createQuery(
        "select s from Student s where s.firstName like ?");
    ```

3. Provide the query with an input parameter:

    ```
    query.setParameter(1, "Jo%");
    ```

4. Run the query, and display the returned result via the console:

    ```
    List<Student> students = query.getResultList();
    Student s = students.get(0);
    System.out.println(students.size());
    System.out.println(s.getFirstName());
    ```

5. Close the `EntityManager`:

    ```
    entityManager.close();
    }
    ```

How It Works

You opened an `EntityManager` instance as usual. However, this time you didn't need to open a new `EntityTransaction` because JPA doesn't require having an active transaction while executing JPA queries only. `entityManager.createQuery(..);` expects a JPA QL and creates and returns a `Query` object. After setting any necessary parameters, a `Query` instance is executed either with the `getResultList()` method, which returns a list of entities, or with `getSingleResult()`, which returns a single entity.

For more information about JPA QL, you can visit `http://docs.oracle.com/javaee/7/tutorial/doc/persistence-querylanguage.htm`.

SPRING'S JPA SUPPORT

Spring adds significant enhancements to your application if you are using JPA. Following are several benefits of using Spring's JPA support in your data access layer:

➤ Easier and more powerful persistence unit configuration

➤ Automatic `EntityManager` management

➤ Easier testing

➤ Common data access exceptions

➤ Integrated transaction management

Persistence unit configuration with Spring—that is, the `EntityManagerFactory` configuration—is much easier, more powerful, and more flexible than configuring it without using Spring. With Spring ORM support, it is possible to configure JPA without a `META-INF/persistence.xml` file and it is easier to enable vendor-specific features. The `EntityManager` instance is managed automatically, and can be injected into data access object (DAO) beans; so you don't need to manage it manually in your application code. Testing JPA-related code becomes easier and is possible without an application server or deploying the application to the server. Exceptions specific to the JPA layer are automatically translated into Spring's data access exception hierarchy. That way, you can mix several different data access strategies in your DAO layer, and you won't have to bother dealing with each of their proprietary exception hierarchies in upper layers. Spring's JPA support is naturally integrated with its transaction management infrastructure. You can employ declarative and programmatic transaction management approaches without depending on a JPA-specific `EntityTransaction` API at all. You will also be able to mix up different data access strategies in the same transaction.

Setting Up JPA in Spring Container

Spring offers three different options to configure `EntityManagerFactory` in a project:

➤ `LocalEntityManagerFactoryBean`

➤ `EntityManagerFactory` lookup over JNDI

➤ `LocalContainerEntityManagerFactoryBean`

`LocalEntityManagerFactoryBean` is the most basic and limited one. It is mainly used for testing purposes and standalone environments. It reads JPA configuration from `/META-INF/persistence.xml`, doesn't allow you to use a Spring-managed `DataSource` instance, and doesn't support distributed transaction management.

Following is the Java-based JPA configuration. You need to create a Java instance from `LocalEntityManagerFactoryBean` and set the persistence unit name to it:

```
@Configuration
public class Ch5Configuration {
    @Bean
```

```
    public LocalEntityManagerFactoryBean entityManagerFactory() {
        LocalEntityManagerFactoryBean factoryBean =
            new LocalEntityManagerFactoryBean();
        factoryBean.setPersistenceUnitName("test-jpa");
        return factoryBean;
    }
}
```

The XML equivalent of the preceding configuration is as follows:

```xml
<?xml version="1.0" encoding="UTF-8"?>
<beans xmlns="http://www.springframework.org/schema/beans"
    xmlns:xsi="http://www.w3.org/2001/XMLSchema-instance"
    xsi:schemaLocation="http://www.springframework.org/schema/beans
    http://www.springframework.org/schema/beans/spring-beans.xsd">
    <bean id="FileName_entityManagerFactory"
        class="org.springframework.orm.jpa.LocalEntityManagerFactoryBean">
        <property name="persistenceUnitName" value="test-jpa" />
    </bean>
</beans>
```

Use `EntityManagerFactory` lookup over JNDI if the run time is Java EE 5 Server. A Java EE 5-compatible server autodetects the persistence unit across the application java archive (JAR) files and registers them to the appropriate JNDI location. The Spring `EntityManagerFactory` bean is merely a delegate to the persistence unit obtained from JNDI.

You need to activate the JEE namespace in your application context configuration file in order to perform `EntityManagerFactory` instance lookup over the JEE 5 container's JNDI repository:

```xml
<?xml version="1.0" encoding="UTF-8"?>
<beans xmlns="http://www.springframework.org/schema/beans"
    xmlns:xsi="http://www.w3.org/2001/XMLSchema-instance"
    xmlns:jee="http://www.springframework.org/schema/jee"
    xsi:schemaLocation="http://www.springframework.org/schema/jee
    http://www.springframework.org/schema/jee/spring-jee-4.0.xsd
        http://www.springframework.org/schema/beans
        http://www.springframework.org/schema/beans/spring-beans.xsd">

    <jee:jndi-lookup id="FileName_entityManagerFactory" jndi-name="persistence/test-jpa"/>

</beans>
```

It is possible to perform Java-based JNDI object lookup using Spring's `org.springframework.jndi.JndiObjectFactoryBean` class:

```java
@Configuration
public class Ch5Configuration {
    @Bean
    public JndiObjectFactoryBean entityManagerFactory() {
        JndiObjectFactoryBean factoryBean = new JndiObjectFactoryBean();
        factoryBean.setJndiName("persistence/test-jpa");
        return factoryBean;
    }
}
```

`LocalContainerEntityManagerFactoryBean` is the most powerful and flexible JPA configuration approach Spring offers. It gives full control over `EntityManagerFactory` configuration, and it's suitable for environments where fine-grained control is required. It enables you to work with a Spring-managed `DataSource`, lets you selectively load entity classes in your project's classpath, and so on. It works both in application servers and standalone environments. The following example shows you how to create an `EntityManagerFactory` bean using `LocalContainerEntityManagerFactoryBean` support.

| TRY IT OUT | Configuring and Using JPA with LocalContainerEntityManagerFactoryBean |

You can find the source code within the project named `configuring-and-using-jdbctemplate` in the `spring-book-ch5.zip` file.

In this Try It Out, you configure JPA using `LocalContainerEntityManagerFactoryBean`. You can continue from the previous Try It Out. To begin, follow these steps:

1. Create a `Configuration` class:

    ```
    @Configuration
    public class Ch5Configuration {
    ```

2. You are going to configure `EntityManagerFactory` without a `META-INF/persistence.xml` file and make it use a Spring-managed `DataSource` bean. Therefore, create a `DataSource` bean definition similar to the following:

    ```
    @Bean
    public DataSource dataSource() {
        DriverManagerDataSource dataSource = new DriverManagerDataSource();
        dataSource.setDriverClassName("org.h2.Driver");
        dataSource.setUrl("jdbc:h2:tcp://localhost/~/test");
        dataSource.setUsername("sa");
        dataSource.setPassword("");
        return dataSource;
    }
    ```

3. You may need to pass some JPA configuration properties, such as dialect class, schema generation mode, and so on. For this purpose, create a helper method that returns `Map`, putting your configuration properties as key/value pairs into that map:

    ```
    private Map<String,?> jpaProperties() {
        Map<String,String> jpaPropertiesMap = new HashMap<String,String>();
        jpaPropertiesMap.put("hibernate.dialect","org.hibernate.dialect.H2Dialect");
        jpaPropertiesMap.put("hibernate.hbm2ddl.auto", "update");
        return jpaPropertiesMap;
    }
    ```

4. Create a method in which you instantiate the `LocalContainerEntityFactoryBean` object and return it as follows:

    ```
    @Bean
    public LocalContainerEntityManagerFactoryBean entityManagerFactory() {
        LocalContainerEntityManagerFactoryBean factoryBean =
    ```

```
            new LocalContainerEntityManagerFactoryBean();
        factoryBean.setPersistenceProviderClass(HibernatePersistenceProvider.class);
        factoryBean.setDataSource(dataSource());
        factoryBean.setPackagesToScan("com.wiley.beginningspring.ch5");
        factoryBean.setJpaPropertyMap(jpaProperties());
        return factoryBean;
    }
}
```

5. Create a Spring `ApplicationContext` in the `main` method with the `Configuration` class you created previously:

```
public class Main {
    public static void main(String[] args) {
        ApplicationContext applicationContext =
            new AnnotationConfigApplicationContext(Ch5Configuration.class);
```

6. You can now get `EntityManagerFactory` instance from the container with bean lookup and use it to perform JPA operations as follows:

```
        EntityManagerFactory entityManagerFactory =
            applicationContext.getBean(EntityManagerFactory.class);
        EntityManager entityManager = entityManagerFactory.createEntityManager();
        EntityTransaction transaction = entityManager.getTransaction();
        transaction.begin();

        Student student = new Student();
        student.setFirstName("John");
        student.setLastName("Smith");

        entityManager.persist(student);

        transaction.commit();
        entityManager.close();
    }
}
```

How It Works

First, you created a `DataSource` bean definition. This bean will be used by `EntityManagerFactory` to obtain JDBC connections. The second auxiliary bean definition is called `jpaProperties`. It is of type `java.util.Map`, and its role is to provide JPA-specific configuration parameters. The example has two JPA vendor-specific properties in it. The first one is with a key named `hibernate.dialect`. It is required by Hibernate to generate correct SQL statements for the underlying database. Because the example uses the H2 database, its value here is given as `org.hibernate.dialect.H2Dialect`. Hibernate provides dialect implementations for every database vendor in the market. You can also implement your own dialect or extend from the available ones.

The second property is `hibernate.hbm2ddl.auto`, and it is an optional property. It tells Hibernate to perform a database schema update by employing ORMmetadata. Its values could be `create`, `update`, `create-drop`, `none`, and so on. The `update` value causes changes in entity mapping metadata that are not satisfied on the database side to be reflected onto. If you set its value to `create`, a database schema would be created, deleting all data in the database during the `EntityManagerFactory` bootstrap process. Although it is a very useful property for the development or testing phase, it could be dangerous for production environments. Its default value, if not specified, is `none`.

The main bean definition is made by using the `LocalContainerEntityManagerFactoryBean` class. The previously created `dataSource` and `jpaProperties` beans are injected into it. JPA in the Java EE environment automatically scans the classpath to find and load classes with JPA `@Entity` annotations. On the other hand, it is not a must for standalone or non-Java EE environments—for example, Tomcat. However, when used as a JPA vendor, Hibernate carries this automatic mapping metadata discovery process to these environments as well. By default, classes with mapping metadata will be sought starting from the root classpath. If you want to limit the search area, Spring provides an attribute to specify packages to scan for. The last property in the `FactoryBean` wire-up is the `HibernatePersistenceProvider` class. It is an implementation of the `javax.persistence.PersistenceProvider` interface of the JPA SPI. Its role is to create an actual `EntityManagerFactory` instance specific to the JPA vendor.

You created an `ApplicationContext` instance using the `Configuration` class in the `main` method. You then obtained the `EntityManagerFactory` bean using bean lookup and used it to create an `EntityManager`. The rest is the same as in the previously explained JPA operations.

You employed a Java-based configuration in this Try It Out. You could achieve the same result with an XML-based configuration as follows:

```xml
<?xml version="1.0" encoding="UTF-8"?>
<beans xmlns="http://www.springframework.org/schema/beans"
    xmlns:xsi="http://www.w3.org/2001/XMLSchema-instance"
    xsi:schemaLocation="http://www.springframework.org/schema/beans
    http://www.springframework.org/schema/beans/spring-beans.xsd">

    <bean id="FileName_entityManagerFactory"
class="org.springframework.orm.jpa.LocalContainerEntityManagerFactoryBean">
        <property name="dataSource" ref="dataSource"/>
        <property name="packagesToScan" value="com.wiley.beginningspring.ch5"/>
        <property name="persistenceProviderClass"
value="org.hibernate.jpa.HibernatePersistenceProvider"/>
        <property name="jpaPropertyMap">
            <map>
                <entry key="hibernate.dialect"
value="org.hibernate.dialect.H2Dialect"/>
                <entry key="hibernate.hbm2ddl.auto" value="update"/>
            </map>
        </property>
    </bean>

    <bean id="FileName_dataSource"
class="org.springframework.jdbc.datasource.DriverManagerDataSource">
        <property name="driverClassName" value="org.h2.Driver"/>
        <property name="url" value="jdbc:h2:tcp://localhost/~/test"/>
        <property name="username" value="sa"/>
        <property name="password" value=""/>
```

```
    </bean>
</beans>
```

Implementing DAOs Based on Plain JPA

Previous versions of Spring offered two support classes to help work with JPA or Hibernate. They are JpaTemplate and HibernateTemplate, respectively. They were similar to JdbcTemplate in functionality. However, with the improvements in Hibernate and JPA, they have become obsolete. At present, Spring discourages using them to perform ORM operations. Indeed, JpaTemplate has been removed from Spring completely, and HibernateTemplate is mainly kept for easy migration of older Hibernate projects.

With the current version of Spring, you can implement your DAO layer purely based on the plain persistence technology API and persistence annotations, while still benefiting from Spring's data access enrichments. You can obtain EntityManagerFactory or EntityManager from a container via dependency injection, and you can automatically participate in the current transaction. ORM vendor-specific exceptions are also converted into Spring's custom exception hierarchies. More about this exception translation is explained in the next section.

JPA has two annotations to obtain container-managed EntityManagerFactory or EntityManager instances within Java EE environments. The @PersistenceUnit annotation expresses a dependency on an EntityManagerFactory, and @PersistenceContext expresses a dependency on a container-managed EntityManager instance, too. Spring supports those two annotations as well.

You need to configure the PersistenceAnnotationBeanPostProcessor of Spring in order for those annotations to be processed. You can either define it as bean, or enable a context namespace and add <context:annotation-config/> or <context:component-scan/> elements into your XML bean configuration file. Those XML namespace elements actually configure a default PersistenceAnnotationBeanPostProcessor on your behalf.

Both @PersistenceContext and @PersistenceUnit annotations can be used at either the field or method level. Visibility of those fields and methods doesn't matter. In the following example, you obtain an EntityManagerFactory instance using the @PersistenceUnit annotation.

TRY IT OUT Using @PersistenceUnit to Obtain EntityManagerFactory

You can find the source code within the project named configuring-and-using-jdbctemplate in the spring-book-ch5.zip file.

In this Try It Out, you inject the EntityManagerFactory bean into your DAO bean using the @PersistenceUnit annotation, create an EntityManager from it, and use it to perform persistence operations in your DAO bean. You can continue from the preceding Try It Out. To begin, follow these steps:

1. Create a StudentDaoJpaImpl class:

```
public class StudentDaoJpaImpl {
```

2. Define an `EntityManagerFactory` field in the class and place an `@PersistenceUnit` annotation onto it:

    ```
    @PersistenceUnit
    private EntityManagerFactory entityManagerFactory;
    ```

3. Add a `save` method to the `StudentDaoJpaImpl` class; accepting a transient `Student` entity. Within the `save` method, create an `EntityManager` instance and start a new `EntityTransaction`:

    ```
    public void save(Student student) {
        EntityManager entityManager = entityManagerFactory
                .createEntityManager();
        EntityTransaction transaction = entityManager.getTransaction();
        transaction.begin();
    ```

4. Persist the transient student instance given by calling the `entityManager.persist(student)` method:

    ```
    entityManager.persist(student);
    ```

5. Commit the `transaction` and close the `entityManager` instance:

    ```
        transaction.commit();
        entityManager.close();
        }
    }
    ```

6. Define a bean for this DAO class in the Spring bean `Configuration` class:

    ```
    @Bean
    public StudentDaoJpaImpl studentDao() {
        StudentDaoJpaImpl dao = new StudentDaoJpaImpl();
        return dao;
    }
    ```

7. Perform a bean lookup in the `main` method and use it to persist a `Student` entity:

    ```
    public static void main(String[] args) {
        ApplicationContext applicationContext = new AnnotationConfigApplicationContext(
                Ch5Configuration.class);

        StudentDaoJpaImpl dao = applicationContext.getBean(StudentDaoJpaImpl.class);

        Student student = new Student();
        student.setFirstName("Joe");
        student.setLastName("Smith");

        dao.save(student);
    }
    ```

How It Works

The `@PersistenceUnit` annotation causes the `entityManagerFactory` bean defined in Spring Container to be injected. As stated earlier, you don't need to define a public setter method. You can place the annotation onto a private field, and Spring assigns a bean instance to that field via the

Reflection API. Because you need to have an active transaction in order to perform data manipulation operations using JPA, you created one and managed the transaction appropriately. Within the active transaction, you called `entityManager.persist(student)` to insert a new transient student instance. Finally, you committed the transaction and closed the `entityManager` at hand.

`@PersistenceUnit` has a `unitName` attribute. Its value is optional; however, it can be used to inject another `entityManagerFactory` bean defined in the container.

Similar to the preceding Try It Out, the following example shows you how to obtain an `EntityManager` instance managed by Spring Container using the `@PersistenceContext` annotation and use it to perform persistence operations within your DAO beans.

TRY IT OUT Using @PersistenceContext to Obtain EntityManager

To be able to use `@PersistenceContext` you need to have an active transaction managed either by Spring Container or EJB CMT. Chapter 6 covers transactions in detail.

You can find the source code within the project named `configuring-and-using-jdbctemplate` in the `spring-book-ch5.zip` file.

In this Try It Out, you obtain a transactional `EntityManager` instance using the `@PersistenceContext` annotation in your DAO bean, and use it to perform persistence operations. You can continue from the previous Try It Out. To begin, follow these steps:

1. For now, create the following `transactionManager` bean definition and enable the Spring Container-managed transaction by placing the `@EnableTansactionManagement` annotation on top of your bean configuration class:

```
@Configuration
@EnableTransactionManagement
public class Ch5Configuration {
    @Bean
    @Autowired
    public PlatformTransactionManager transactionManager(
            EntityManagerFactory entityManagerFactory) {
        JpaTransactionManager transactionManager = new JpaTransactionManager();
        transactionManager.setEntityManagerFactory(entityManagerFactory);
        return transactionManager;
    }
//...
}
```

2. Create a `BookDao` interface with the `save(Book book)` method in it, and create the `BookDaoJpaImpl` class that implements this interface:

```
public interface BookDao {
    public void save(Book book);
```

```
    }

public class BookDaoJpaImpl implements BookDao {
    @Override
    public void save(Book book) {
    }
}
```

3. Define an `EntityManager` field in the DAO class and place the `@PersistenceContext` annotation onto it:

    ```
    @PersistenceContext
    private EntityManager entityManager;
    ```

4. Persist the transient book instance given by calling the `entityManager.persist(book)` method within the `save(..)` method of `BookDaoJpaImpl`:

    ```
    @Override
    public void save(Book book) {
        entityManager.persist(book);
    }
    ```

5. Transaction management should be handled at the service layer. Therefore, first create a `BookService` interface with the `save(Book book)` method in it, and then create a `BookServiceImpl` class implementing the `BookService` interface and place the `@org`
    `.springframework.transaction.annotation.Transactional` annotation on top of it:

    ```
    public interface BookService {
        public void save(Book book);
    }

    @Transactional
    public class BookServiceImpl implements BookService {
        @Override
        public void save(Book book) {
        }
    }
    ```

6. Add a property with type `BookDao`, and using that DAO bean, perform a save operation within the service class:

    ```
    private BookDao bookDao;

    public void setBookDao(BookDao bookDao) {
        this.bookDao = bookDao;
    }

    @Override
    public void save(Book book) {
        bookDao.save(book);
    }
    ```

7. Define the `bookDao` and `bookService` beans, and inject the `bookDao` bean into the `bookService` bean in the `Configuration` class:

    ```
    @Bean
    public BookDao bookDao() {
    ```

```
        BookDaoJpaImpl bean = new BookDaoJpaImpl();
        return bean;
    }

    @Bean
    public BookService bookService() {
        BookServiceImpl bean = new BookServiceImpl();
        bean.setBookDao(bookDao());
        return bean;
    }
```

8. Perform a bean lookup to `bookService` in the `main` method, create a `Book` entity, and persist it as follows:

```
public class Main {
    public static void main(String[] args) {
        ApplicationContext applicationContext =
            new AnnotationConfigApplicationContext(Ch5Configuration.class);

        BookService bookService = applicationContext.getBean(BookService.class);

        Book book = new Book();
        book.setName("book1");
        bookService.save(book);
    }
}
```

How It Works

The first and second steps are required to enable Spring Container–managed transactions. The `transactionManager()` method creates a bean from the `JpaTransactionManager` class and sets the `EntityManagerFactory` instance taken with autowiring into it. `@EnableTansactionManagement` makes Spring recognize `@Transactional` annotations. Therefore in step 3, you put an `@Transactional` annotation on top of the `BookDao` class so that methods defined inside this class are transactional. As stated earlier, you look at this part in detail in Chapter 6. That's enough for you to have an active transaction and use a shared `EntityManager` instance managed by Spring Container.

`@PersistenceContext` is put onto the `private EntityManager entityManager;` field definition. At run time, Spring Container creates an `EntityManager` bound to the currently active transaction and injects that instance into this field.

After defining the `bookDao` and `bookService` beans within the `Configuration` class, in the last step you created a `Main` class, and loaded the `ApplicationContext` within its `main` method. Finally, the `Book` instance is persisted with the obtained `bookService` bean in the `main` method.

Note that if you try to call `entityManager.getTransaction();` through this shared *entityManager* instance, you get an `IllegalStateException` mentioning that you can only have an active transaction either via Spring or EJB CMT.

> ### TRANSACTIONAL VERSUS EXTENDED PERSISTENCE CONTEXT
>
> `@PersistenceContext` has a `type` attribute whose value can be
> `PersistenceContextType.TRANSACTION` or `PersistenceContextType.EXTENDED`.
> In stateless beans it is safe to use only the `PersistenceContextType.TRANSACTION`
> value for a shared `EntityManager` to be created and injected into for the current active
> transaction's scope. If the value were `EXTENDED`, the shared `EntityManager` instance
> wouldn't be bound to the active transaction and might span more than one transaction.
> `PersistenceContextType.EXTENDED` is purposefully designed to support beans, like
> stateful EJBs, session Spring beans, or request-scoped Spring beans. The default value
> of the `type` attribute in `@PersistenceContext` annotation is `TRANSACTION`.

Handling and Translating Exceptions

Each data access technology has its own exception types and hierarchy to express that errors or
misusages happened while performing data access operations. When using JPA, you have to specifically deal with `javax.persistence.PersistenceException` typed exceptions. You also need
to take care of JPA vendor-specific exceptions that may be thrown during run time, including
`IllegalArgumentException` and `IllegalStateException` exception types as well. What can be
more frustrating is that if you mix different data access technologies—for example, use JDBC and
JPA to perform some operations—you also have to deal with `java.sql.SQLException`, in addition
to `javax.persistence.PersistenceException`.

Spring eases life here by handling different types of data access exceptions thrown from the data-
access layer, and translates them into a standard data access exception hierarchy defined by Spring.
Therefore, you won't need to know which specific exceptions might be thrown while using a specific
method of your particular data access technology. The only exception hierarchy you need to
handle is Spring's `org.springframework.dao.DataAccessException`. It is of type `java.lang`
`.RuntimeException`. Thus, you use a `try...catch` block only when you need to handle those data
access exceptions. For example, the following code snippet shows how `DataAccessExceptions` can
be handled within the service layer:

```
@Transactional
public class BookServiceImpl implements BookService {

    private BookDao bookDao;

    public void setBookDao(BookDao bookDao) {
        this.bookDao = bookDao;
    }

    @Override
    public void save(Book book) {
        try {
            //perform some business logic here...
            bookDao.save(book);
        } catch(DataAccessException ex) {
            //handle the data access exception,
            //without depending on particular
```

```
        //data access technology used beneath...
      }
    }
  }
```

To use the exception handling and translation feature of Spring, you need to mark your DAO beans with the `@Repository` annotation as follows:

```
@Repository
public class BookDaoJpaImpl implements BookDao {
//...
}
```

Then, you need to create a bean definition from the `PersistenceExceptionTranslationPostProcessor` class, so that Spring advises your DAO beans, catches technology-specific data access exceptions, and translates them to its own `DataAccessException` hierarchy.

You can define this bean either using class-based configuration or XML-based configuration. If you prefer class-based configuration, you need to define the factory method as static:

```
@Configuration
public class Ch5Configuration {

    @Bean
    public static PersistenceExceptionTranslationPostProcessor
                persistenceExceptionTranslationPostProcessor() {
        PersistenceExceptionTranslationPostProcessor bean =
            new PersistenceExceptionTranslationPostProcessor();
        return bean;
    }

    //...

}

<bean class="org.springframework.dao.annotation.↵
    PersistenceExceptionTranslationPostProcessor
"/>
```

The `PersistenceExceptionTranslationPostProcessor` bean tries to identify all beans implementing the `PersistenceExceptionTranslator` interface in the application context and uses them during the exception translation phase. Several implementations of `PersistenceExceptionTranslator` are provided by Spring, and the `LocalEntityManagerFactoryBean` and `LocalContainerEntityManagerFactoryBean` classes are among them. Therefore, you don't need to perform any translator bean configuration by default.

Further JPA Configuration in Spring Environment

Spring provides some additional means to configure JPA within Spring Container. Those additional features help you enable some advanced features of JPA, usually in a vendor-specific manner. In this section, you examine those additional features of JPA configuration.

JpaDialect

Spring has the `JpaDialect` interface, which is used to enable some advanced features for the JPA environment, usually in a JPA vendor-specific manner. Those features are listed in Spring Reference Documentation as follows:

➤ Applying specific transaction semantics such as custom isolation level or transaction timeout

➤ Retrieving the transactional JDBC Connection for exposure to JDBC-based DAOs

➤ Advanced translation of PersistenceExceptions to Spring DataAccessExceptions

You can inject a custom `JpaDialect` instance into `JpaTransactionManager`, `LocalEntityManagerFactoryBean`, or `LocalContainerEntityManagerFactoryBean`. Default implementation of it is called `DefaultJpaDialect`, and it doesn't provide any of the listed special capabilities. If you need the features listed earlier, you have to specify the appropriate dialect. For example, because you are using Hibernate as the JPA provider, you can create an instance from the `HibernateJpaDialect` class and inject it into the `LocalContainerEntityManagerFactoryBean`.

JpaVendorAdapter

While configuring JPA, you may need to provide several different vendor-specific properties with Spring's `EntityManagerFactory` creators. For example, you have to set the `PersistenceProvider` implementation class, some vendor-specific properties within a `Map`, or a `JpaDialect` instance in order to activate some vendor-dependent advanced features. Instead of specifying them separately, it is also possible for you to configure and manage them from a single point. Spring offers the `JpaVendorAdapter` interface for this purpose. Several implementations of it exist that correspond to each different JPA vendor. Therefore, the following lines in the `entityManagerFactory` bean creation steps become useless and are reduced to one line as follows:

```java
@Bean
public LocalContainerEntityManagerFactoryBean entityManagerFactory() {
    LocalContainerEntityManagerFactoryBean factoryBean =
        new LocalContainerEntityManagerFactoryBean();
    factoryBean.setDataSource(dataSource());
    //factoryBean.setJpaPropertyMap(jpaProperties());
    //factoryBean.setPersistenceProviderClass(HibernatePersistenceProvider.class);
    //factoryBean.setJpaDialect(new HibernateJpaDialect());

    factoryBean.setJpaVendorAdapter(jpaVendorAdapter());
    return factoryBean;
}


@Bean
private JpaVendorAdapter jpaVendorAdapter() {
    HibernateJpaVendorAdapter jpaVendorAdapter = new HibernateJpaVendorAdapter();
    jpaVendorAdapter.setGenerateDdl(true);
    jpaVendorAdapter.setDatabase(Database.H2);
    return jpaVendorAdapter;
}
```

JPA and Load-Time Weaving

JPA specification defines some requirements about lazy loading of associations and monitoring of entities. However, the specification doesn't say anything about how these features will be implemented. Therefore, some JPA vendors employ proxy class generation, and some other byte code enhancement to handle lazy loading of object associations, and so on. OpenJPA, for example, prefers byte code enhancement. Hibernate, on the other hand, is not one of those JPA providers. It employs a class-based proxy mechanism instead. If a class-based proxy mechanism is used, you, as a developer, don't have to do anything at all. However, if your ORM vendor employs byte code enhancement, you need to modify domain classes either at compile time or at run time.

If you choose to modify domain classes during the class load process, you can usually achieve this using Java 5 javaagent support. You can specify Java agents using a virtual machine (VM) argument called -javaagent.

Spring tries to ease the class transformation at run time. It has a special interface called LoadTimeWeaver, and this interface has several distinct implementations for different platforms. Spring tries to detect the target application runtime platform, and defines the correct LoadTimeWeaver instance as a bean automatically. The following code snippet shows an XML-based configuration to enable load-time weaving:

```xml
<?xml version="1.0" encoding="UTF-8"?>
<beans xmlns="http://www.springframework.org/schema/beans"
    xmlns:xsi="http://www.w3.org/2001/XMLSchema-instance"
    xmlns:context="http://www.springframework.org/schema/context"
    xsi:schemaLocation="http://www.springframework.org/schema/beans
    http://www.springframework.org/schema/beans/spring-beans.xsd
        http://www.springframework.org/schema/context
        http://www.springframework.org/schema/context/spring-context-4.0.xsd">

    <context:load-time-weaver/>

</beans>
```

The following code snippet shows the Java-based configuration to enable load-time weaving:

```java
@Configuration
@EnableLoadTimeWeaving
public class Ch5Configuration {
}
```

After load-time weaving is enabled using either an XML-based or Java-based configuration as shown earlier, Spring identifies a target runtime platform and then registers the correct LoadTimeWeaver implementation as a bean in the container. From now on, you can apply byte code enhancement using this LoadTimeWeaver instance.

LocalContainerEntityManagerFactoryBean, for example, implements the LoadTimeWeaverAware interface, and Spring automatically injects the loadTimeWeaver bean into that bean. In that case, the entityManagerFactory bean uses loadTimeWeaver to perform byte code enhancement to domain classes.

> **WARNING** *Behind the scenes, actual work is done by*
> `ClassFileTransformers` *registered at* `ClassLoader` *via* `loadTimeWeaver`.
> *However, for* `ClassFileTransformers` *to be registered successfully,*
> `ClassLoader`, *in use, must support this feature. Unfortunately, this is not the*
> *case for all application runtime platforms. For instance, Tomcat and Resin web*
> *containers don't offer such a* `ClassLoader` *implementation. In such cases, you*
> *can use Spring's* `InstrumentationSavingAgent` *VM agent to enable load-time*
> *weaving. It will be just enough to add the following line to your VM arguments:*
>
> ```
> java -javaagent:/path/to/spring-instrument.jar ...
> ```
>
> `InstrumentationSavingAgent` *just saves the* `java.lang.instrument`
> `.Instrumentation` *instance during JVM startup. From Java 5 on, the*
> `Instrumentation` *interface is used to provide services to enhance Java*
> *byte codes. If your runtime application platform is either Tomcat or Resin*
> *Spring, it automatically detects the environment and decides on using*
> *the* `InstrumentationLoadTimeWeaver` *implementation. You can then use*
> *this instance to register related* `ClassFileTransformer` *instances via the*
> `Instrumentation` *interface.*

Dealing with Multiple Persistence Units

Sample applications may depend on several different persistent unit locations. Each of those persistence unit files may come from different jar files in the classpath. The discovery process of those persistence unit files is an expensive process. Spring provides a mechanism so that all those different persistence unit locations are discovered once during bootstrap and can be accessed via persistent unit names.

`PersistenceUnitManager` is the interface of that mechanism that acts as a central repository for those persistent unit locations. There is a default implementation called `DefaultPersistenceUnitManager`, and it allows access to those persistent units via their names. You need to define a bean as `persistenceUnitManager` and inject it into `entityManagerFactory` beans similar to the following code snippet:

```xml
<bean id="FileName_persistenceUnitManager"
  class="org.springframework.orm.jpa.persistenceunit.DefaultPersistenceUnitManager">
    <property name="persistenceXmlLocations">
        <list>
            <value>classpath:META-INF/persistence.xml</value>
            <value>classpath:/my/package/*/test-persistence.xml</value>
        </list>
    </property>
    <property name="dataSources">
        <map>
            <entry key="localDataSource" value-ref="h2DataSource" />
            <entry key="remoteDataSource" value-ref="oracleDataSource" />
        </map>
    </property>
```

```
            <property name="defaultDataSource" ref="remoteDataSource" />
    </bean>

    <bean id="FileName_entityManagerFactory1"
        class="org.springframework.orm.jpa.LocalContainerEntityManagerFactoryBean">
        <property name="persistenceUnitManager" ref="persistenceUnitManager" />
        <property name="persistenceUnitName" value="test-jpa" />
    </bean>

    <bean id="FileName_entityManagerFactory2"
        class="org.springframework.orm.jpa.LocalContainerEntityManagerFactoryBean">
        <property name="persistenceUnitManager" ref="persistenceUnitManager" />
        <property name="persistenceUnitName" value="prod-jpa" />
    </bean>
```

`DefaultPersistenceUnitManager` seeks `/META-INF/persistence.xml` files by default. The preceding example listed both `/META-INF/persistence.xml` and `classpath:/my/package/*/test-persistence.xml` files. It loads all the persistence units found within those files and makes them available to the `entityManagerFactory` beans. Actually, `LocalContainerEntityManagerFactoryBean` creates a `PersistenceUnitManager` unless a bean of this type has not been injected.

SUMMARY

This chapter first gave a brief introduction to ORM and JPA and explained the paradigm mismatch between the object world and the relational world. Then it continued with the fundamental building blocks of an ORM framework. You walked through OR mapping constructs used to map an object model to a relational model and saw how to define entities, map their attributes to columns, and create associations between entities. The chapter also exposed you to some details about mapping Java types to SQL data types.

Later, the chapter introduced persistence unit and persistence context concepts in JPA, and gave some examples to show how to configure and use JPA in a nutshell. The chapter explained several different persistence operations and queries that you can perform using `EntityManager`.

After this brief introduction to ORM and JPA, you saw different ways of handling `EntityManagerFactory` bean configuration, and learned about their pros and cons. After configuring a persistence unit in Spring Container, you saw how to implement DAOs using the JPA API directly. The chapter explained `@PersistenceUnit` and `@PersistenceContext` annotations and showed their usages. It also explained how Spring helps you when a persistence-related exception occurs, and how it tries to handle and convert those different types of persistence exceptions to its `DataAccessException` hierarchy.

The chapter concluded with some further information about how to configure JPA, such as using the `JpaDialect` and `JpaVendorAdapter` interfaces of Spring. You also learned about byte code enhancement and when it is necessary to perform byte code enhancement while using JPA; load-time weaving, which is a method to perform byte code enhancement; and how Spring tries to help you perform byte code enhancement using load-time weaving in different application runtime environments.

EXERCISES

You can find possible solutions to the following exercises in Appendix A.

1. Try to configure your environment so that it uses a different JPA vendor—for example, EclipseLink—to perform persistence operations.

2. Create `EntityManagerFactory` using the `LocalContainerEntityManagerFactoryBean`, which loads a `META-INF/my-persistence.xml` file as its only JPA configuration.

3. Try to perform a persistence operation using JPA outside of an active transaction and observe the exception thrown.

▶ WHAT YOU LEARNED IN THIS CHAPTER

TOPIC	KEY POINTS
`@Entity`	Annotation representing the persistent domain class that has a corresponding table in a database
`@Id`	Annotation representing the primary key attribute of the persistent class
`@OneToOne, @OneToMany, @ManyToOne, @ManyToMany`	Annotations used to map 1:1,1:M, M:1, and N:M associations in a database
`@JoinColumn, @JoinTable`	Annotations used to map foreign keys and association tables
`@Temporal, @Enumerated, @Lob`	Annotations used to map `Date`, `Time`, `Timestamp`, `Enum`, and `byte[]` Java types to corresponding SQL data types
`META-INF/persistence.xml`	Default JPA persistence unit configuration file
`javax.persistence.Persistence`	Class that is used to load persistence unit configurations and to create an `EntityManagerFactory`
persistence unit, `EntityManagerFactory`	Instance that represents persistence unit configuration used to obtain persistence context instances
persistence context, `EntityManager`	Bridge between the application and database that is used to perform persistence operations
`LocalContainerEntityManagerFactoryBean`	Spring's `FactoryBean` implementations to create an `EntityManagerFactory` bean in the `ApplicationContext`
`javax.persistence.PersistenceProvider`	Java SPI interface that is actually used to create an `EntityManagerFactory` instance
`@PersistenceUnit`	Annotation used to inject a managed `EntityManagerFactory` instance
`@PersistenceContext`	Annotation used to inject a managed `EntityManager` instance
`JpaTransactionManager`	Spring's `PlatformTransactionManager` implementation for JPA data access strategy used in local transactions
`PersistenceException, DataAccessException`	Base exceptions for JPA and Spring's DAO operations, respectively

TOPIC	KEY POINTS
`PersistenceExceptionTranslator`	Interface used to handle and translate data access strategy-specific exceptions into a generic `DataAccessException` hierarchy of Spring
`JpaDialect, JpaVendorAdapter`	Interfaces used to perform JPA vendor-specific configurations persistence unit creation
Byte code enhancement	Dynamically modifying class definitions either at compile time or at run time
Load-time weaving, `LoadTimeWeaver`	Modifying class definitions at run time and the Spring interface for this purpose
javaagent	Java 5 feature to perform JVM-related operations at run time
`java.lang.instrument.Instrumentation`	Java 5 class used to perform class definition modifications on `ClassLoader` instances
`InstrumentationSavingAgent`	Spring's Java agent implementation used to expose `Instrumentation` instances in JVM
`InstrumentationLoadTimeWeaver`	`LoadTimeWeaver` implementation that uses the `Instrumentation` interface to perform class definition modifications

6

Managing Transactions
with Spring

WHAT YOU WILL LEARN IN THIS CHAPTER:

➤ Understanding how transaction management works

➤ Advantages of Spring's transaction abstraction

➤ Performing declarative and programmatic transaction management with Spring

➤ Differences between local and global transactions

➤ Choosing among different transaction managers

➤ Differences between various transaction propagation rules

➤ Executing custom logic after transaction commits or rollbacks

Protecting the integrity of data in an enterprise application is probably the most important thing. After all, an application that corrupts balances of its customers during a money transfer operation is certainly unacceptable, despite how fast that application operates or how nice it looks to its users.

Database transactions protect the integrity of data that is operated on. They are managed by the application, and several data access operations performed within their boundaries are seen as a single atomic unit. They are either persisted or discarded altogether, according to the outcome of the business scenario. Atomicity is one of the several defining properties of transactions, along with consistency, isolation, and durability. Each characteristic plays an important role in protecting the integrity of application data.

This chapter first explains the fundamental features of transactions and how transactions are created and managed using JDBC. Later, the chapter focuses on Spring's transaction abstraction and how declarative and programmatic transaction demarcations are performed using Spring. You will see different propagation rules that can be used when several transactional methods call each other. You will also see some interesting features that Spring's transaction subsystem offers, such as executing custom business logic before or after transaction demarcations.

UNDERSTANDING TRANSACTION MANAGEMENT

Any system that deals with data must protect its integrity. A system that causes incorrect account balances, lost orders, missing entries in a document, or other errors will definitely be deemed unacceptable by its users. You need a way to protect data integrity, and transactions offer a mechanism for this purpose. Transactions define a boundary for data-related operations and group them together so that the final outcome of those operations never leaves the underlying data in an inconsistent state.

ACID (atomicity, consistency, isolation, and durability) is an old acronym that expresses how a reliable transaction management system should behave in order to protect data integrity across multiple concurrent user operations while not sacrificing performance requirements. Jim Gray defined these properties in the late 1970s, and he also developed technologies to demonstrate how to achieve them automatically. In 1983, Andreas Reuter and Theo Härder coined the acronym ACID to describe them. Let's look at them briefly:

➤ **Atomicity:** Several operations might be performed over data in any transaction. Those operations must all succeed or commit, or, if something goes wrong, none of them should be persisted; in other words, they all must be rolled back. Atomicity is also known as *unit of work*.

➤ **Consistency:** For a system to have consistency, at the end of an active transaction the underlying database can never be in an inconsistent state. For example, if order items cannot exist without an order, the system won't let you add order items without first adding an order.

➤ **Isolation:** Isolation defines how protected your uncommitted data is to other concurrent transactions. Isolation levels range from least protective, which offers access to uncommitted data, to most protective, at which no two transactions work at the same time. Isolation is closely related to concurrency and consistency. If you increase the level of isolation, you get more consistency but lose concurrency—that is, performance. On the other hand, if you decrease the level, your transaction performance increases, but you risk losing consistency.

➤ **Durability:** A system has durability when you receive a successful commit message, and you can be sure that your changes are reflected to the system and will survive any system failure that might occur after that time. Basically, when you commit, your changes are permanent and won't be lost.

Before going into details of transaction management using Spring's transaction support, it would be better to examine how a transaction is started and completed using JDBC API directly. This would help you understand what is actually brought by Spring's transaction support. In the following example, you see how a transaction can be managed using JDBC API.

TRY IT OUT Defining Transaction Boundary Using JDBC API

You can find the source code within the project named `defining-transaction-with-jdbc` in the `spring-book-ch6.zip` file.

In this Try It Out, you create a simple method that transfers some amount of money from a source account to a target account and make it transactional with pure JDBC API. To begin, follow these steps:

1. Create a Maven project with the following Maven command:

```
mvn archetype:generate -DarchetypeGroupId=org.apache.maven.archetypes
    -DgroupId= com.wiley.beginningspring -DartifactId=spring-book-ch6
```

2. Open the H2 database. Add the following `<dependency>` element into your `pom.xml` file:

```
<dependency>
    <groupId>com.h2database</groupId>
    <artifactId>h2</artifactId>
    <version>1.3.176</version>
</dependency>
```

3. Find the `org.h2.tools.Console` class of the H2 database from the project classpath, and run it as a Java application from your IDE. When it runs, the browser automatically appears in your screen with the database console. You can select Generic H2 Server and log in to it using "sa" as the username with an empty password.

4. Prepare your database schema. Create an ACCOUNT table with the following DDL statement (you can execute it from your database console):

```
CREATE TABLE ACCOUNT (
    ID BIGINT IDENTITY PRIMARY KEY,
    OWNER_NAME VARCHAR(255),
    BALANCE DOUBLE,
    ACCESS_TIME TIMESTAMP,
    LOCKED BOOLEAN
);
```

5. Insert two account entries into the ACCOUNT table:

```
INSERT INTO ACCOUNT(ID,OWNER_NAME,BALANCE, ACCESS_TIME , LOCKED )
    VALUES(100,'owner-1',10,'2014-01-01',false);
INSERT INTO ACCOUNT(ID,OWNER_NAME,BALANCE, ACCESS_TIME , LOCKED )
    VALUES(101,'owner-2',0,'2014-01-01',false);
```

6. Define an `AccountService` interface that has the `transferMoney(..)` method in which you transfer a specified amount from a source account to a target account:

```
public interface AccountService {
    public void transferMoney(
        long sourceAccountId, long targetAccountId, double amount);
}
```

7. Create an `AccountServiceJdbcTxImpl` class that implements the `AccountService` interface:

```
public class AccountServiceJdbcTxImpl implements AccountService {
    public void transferMoney(long sourceAccountId, long targetAccountId,
            double amount) {
        Connection connection = null;
        try {
            DriverManager.registerDriver(new Driver());
            connection = DriverManager.getConnection(
                    "jdbc:h2:tcp://localhost/~/test", "sa", "");
            connection.setAutoCommit(false);
```

The point at which you call `connection.setAutoCommit(false)` marks the beginning of your transaction boundary with JDBC API:

```
            Statement statement = connection.createStatement();
            statement.executeUpdate("update account set balance = balance - "
                    + amount + " where id = " + sourceAccountId);
            statement.executeUpdate("update account set balance = balance + "
                    + amount + " where id = " + targetAccountId);
            connection.commit();
        }
```

When your data manipulation operations are over, you need to call `connection.commit()`. This line indicates successful termination of your transaction demarcation, and the changes you've made so far are reflected to the database:

```
        catch (SQLException e) {
            try {
                connection.rollback();
            } catch (SQLException ex) {
                //you can ignore the exception thrown here
            }
            throw new RuntimeException(e);
        }
```

On the other hand, if something goes wrong during the course of data manipulation operations, you catch the resulting error and call `connection.rollback()`. This tells JDBC to discard any changes you made so far:

```
        finally {
            try {
                connection.close();
            } catch (SQLException e) {
                //you can ignore the exception thrown here
            }
        }
    }
}
```

8. Create a `Main` class with the `main` method as follows:

```
public class Main {
    public static void main(String[] args) {
        AccountService accountService = new AccountServiceJdbcTxImpl();
        accountService.transferMoney(100L,101L, 5.0d);
    }
}
```

When you run the test method and then look up the `ACCOUNT` table from within the H2 Console, you see that account balances have been changed.

How It Works

The `DriverManager.registerDriver(..)` method call is used to register the H2 JDBC Driver to `DriverManager`. It is also possible to load a JDBC Driver class using the `Class.forName("org .h2.Driver")` method as well. Even though, the `Class.forName(..)` approach is more common in Java projects, we chose to use `DriverManager.registerDriver(..)` in order to make the JDBC Driver registration step more explicit. You can use the one that best suits your needs.

You begin a transaction differently depending on the data access technology you use. In JPA, for example, you would use `entityManager.beginTransaction()`. Here, as you are using JDBC API directly, it is `connection.setAutoCommit(false)` that causes a new transaction to begin.

Normally, each data manipulation SQL operation is executed separately and is completely independent from the others. Therefore, unless you call `connection.setAutoCommit(false)`, two update statements will execute separately, and their changes will be reflected immediately to the database and become visible to other users. If something goes wrong—for example, while executing the second update statement—there will probably be no change caused by the second statement, but because the first one already executed successfully, its changes are permanent. The system will be in an inconsistent state from now on.

However, calling `connection.setAutoCommit(false)` makes the transaction active, and JDBC waits to reflect changes until the end of the transaction. At this point you decide how the transaction ends, either with success by issuing `connection.commit()` or with failure by issuing `connection.rollback()`. A commit reflects changes to the underlying database, changes are made permanent, and they become visible to other users. A rollback discards changes made so far, and data is left unchanged in the underlying database.

For example, if you had thrown an exception just before executing the second SQL update, nothing would be changed in the database. Alternatively, if you hadn't started the transaction here, the first account's balance would be updated but the second one would not, resulting in a data loss.

Almost every method call in JDBC API throws checked `java.sql.SQLException`. Therefore, you have to deal with those checked exceptions in your code by either handling them with a catch block or by adding a throws clause in your method definition. If you prefer to catch the checked exception, as was the case here with the `SQLException`, you should either try to recover from the error or rethrow it by wrapping a new exception, usually with an instance of `RuntimeException`. That way, upper layers in the application won't bother with those checked exceptions at all. Here, in the example code, we haven't defined a separate custom `RuntimeException` subclass; instead we instantiated a `RuntimeException`, wrapped the `SQLException` instance, and rethrew it in order to keep the example focused on how the transaction is demarcated using JDBC API.

SPRING'S TRANSACTION ABSTRACTION MODEL

Each data access technology has its own transaction mechanism. In other words, they provide different APIs to begin a new transaction, commit the transaction when data operations finish with success, or roll it back in case an error occurs. This is called *transaction demarcation*. Spring's role here is to abstract away those different transaction demarcation steps from your code and provide a standard API to demarcate transactions either programmatically or declaratively. That way, as your system becomes isolated from the underlying data access technology, it becomes easier to switch among them and even use more than one data access technology at the same time.

Spring's transaction abstraction model is based on the `PlatformTransactionManager` interface. Different concrete implementations of it exist, and each one corresponds to one particular data access technology. As a developer, your responsibility is to decide which `PlatformTransactionManager` implementation will be used by Spring Container. This decision results in a bean definition called `transactionManager`, by default.

By depending on Spring's `PlatformTransactionManager` API you secure your code from changes in data access technologies, even though you have the chance to mix different ones in the same transaction. That way, when you decide to change your data access strategy, you don't need to modify your transactional code. It is enough to just change the bean definition of `transactionManager`.

The following Try It Out shows you how to activate Spring's transaction mechanism while using JDBC as your data access strategy.

TRY IT OUT   Configuring the PlatformTransactionManager Bean in Spring Container

You can find the source code within the project named `configuring-platform-tx-manager` in the `spring-book-ch6.zip` file.

In this Try It Out, you activate Spring's transaction mechanism while using JDBC as the data access strategy beneath it. You can continue with the project you created for the previous Try It Out. To begin, follow these steps:

1. Add the following dependencies into your project's `pom.xml` file if they are not already available among your dependency list:

```
<dependency>
    <groupId>org.springframework</groupId>
    <artifactId>spring-tx</artifactId>
    <version>4.0.5.RELEASE</version>
```

```
</dependency>

<dependency>
    <groupId>org.springframework</groupId>
    <artifactId>spring-context</artifactId>
    <version>4.0.5.RELEASE</version>
</dependency>

<dependency>
    <groupId>org.springframework</groupId>
    <artifactId>spring-jdbc</artifactId>
    <version>4.0.5.RELEASE</version>
</dependency>
```

2. Create the following bean configuration class in your Spring Container:

```
@Configuration
public class Ch6Configuration {
```

3. Transaction management for JDBC operations are performed by Spring's org.springframework
.jdbc.datasource.DataSourceTransactionManager. It expects a bean with type javax.sql
.DataSource, so add the following into the bean configuration class:

```
@Bean
public DataSource dataSource() {
    DriverManagerDataSource dataSource = new DriverManagerDataSource();
    dataSource.setDriverClassName("org.h2.Driver");
    dataSource.setUrl("jdbc:h2:tcp://localhost/~/test");
    dataSource.setUsername("sa");
    dataSource.setPassword("");
    return dataSource;
}
```

4. Add the following transactionManager bean definition into the configuration class:.

```
@Bean
public PlatformTransactionManager transactionManager() {
    DataSourceTransactionManager transactionManager =
        new DataSourceTransactionManager();
    transactionManager.setDataSource(dataSource());
    return transactionManager;
}
}
```

5. Create a Spring Container within the main method to check that the bean configuration is valid and
ready to use to perform transaction management:

```
public class Main {
    public static void main(String[] args) {
        AnnotationConfigApplicationContext applicationContext =
        new AnnotationConfigApplicationContext(Ch6Configuration.class);
        PlatformTransactionManager transactionManager =
        applicationContext.getBean(PlatformTransactionManager.class);
        System.out.println(transactionManager != null);
    }
}
```

How It Works

As the Spring's `DataSourceTransactionManager` class expected a bean of type `javax.sql.DataSource`, you defined a `dataSource` bean. You used Spring's `DriverManagerDataSource` class to define it. It is an implementation of the `javax.sql.DataSource` type. Properties given during bean definition are the values that are required to connect to the underlying database. After that, you defined the `transactionManager` bean.

Applications need to obtain new JDBC `Connections` via Spring's `DataSourceUtils.getConnection(DataSource)` instead of directly calling `DataSource.getConnection()` or `DriverManager.getConnection()` methods. That way, `transactionManager` is able to operate on the same `Connection` instance you obtain to perform your JDBC operations. Spring's `JdbcTemplate` class also makes use of `DataSourceUtils.getConnection(DataSource)` behind the scenes.

The application, at this point, is ready to make use of Spring's transaction support. You will see how transaction management is performed using both programmatic and declarative methods in the following sections. In either way, behind the scenes the `transactionManager` bean changes the JDBC `Connection` instances' `autoCommit` mode to false so that transaction demarcation starts at appropriate positions.

Local versus Global Transactions

Local transaction means that your application works with a single database, and your transactions only control DML operations performed on that single database. Global transaction, on the other hand, means distributed transaction management. More than one database may be involved in a transaction. JEE offers JTA to deal with global transactions, and EJBs by default use JTA to perform transaction management. JTA causes considerable overhead to the system because of its two-phase commit (2PC) strategy. You also need to work with a full-featured JEE application server to have JTA capability. Although a few standalone JTA implementations are available, they are not so common.

On the other hand, many applications just don't work with multiple databases, or at least they don't need to in a single transaction. They just need to access a single database, and perform DML operations on that single database within their transactions. Therefore, it becomes unnecessary to pay the performance price of JTA's 2PC without actually needing it. Those applications are also usually servlet-based web applications, and they again don't need most of the other features of a full-featured JEE application server. All they need is a simple servlet container to work with.

As a result, it would be very nice to help those applications to just run on a lightweight web container, such as Tomcat or Jetty, and provide them with a transaction management mechanism that doesn't need JTA in the first place. Here, Spring comes to the rescue. With its abstract platform transaction model, it becomes possible to just start with local transactions and run on a lightweight web container until global transaction requirements arise. ·

PlatformTransactionManager Implementations

The most important part in configuring `transactionManager` is to choose the correct `PlatformTransactionManager` implementation according to your data access strategy.

Spring provides several implementations for different data access technologies, as shown in Table 6-1.

TABLE 6-1: PlatformTransactionManager Implementations Corresponding to Data Access Technologies

TRANSACTIONMANAGER CLASS	DATA ACCESS TECHNOLOGY
`DataSourceTransactionManager`	Suitable if you are only using JDBC.
`JpaTransactionManager`	Suitable if you are using JPA. It is also possible to use JDBC at the same time with this implementation.
`HibernateTransactionManager`	Suitable if you are using Hibernate without JPA. It is also possible to use JDBC at the same time with this implementation.
`JdoTransactionManager`	Suitable if you are using JDO. It is also possible to use JDBC at the same time with this implementation.
`JtaTransactionManager`	Suitable if you are using global transactions—that is, the distributed transaction management capability of your application server. You can use any data access technology.

Advantages of Spring's Abstract Transaction Model

Spring's abstract platform transaction model provides several benefits to the application. First, it enables you to use several data access technologies in the same application. It is possible to use both declarative and programmatic transaction models simultaneously.

If you need to change your application's data access technology, all you need to change is the `transactionManager` bean definition. It doesn't matter whether you use programmatic or declarative transactions. It is possible to change declarative rollback rules, and you can execute custom logic before and after transactions.

It is very easy to switch from local transactions to global ones, or vice versa. You only need to define the corresponding `transactionManager` suitable for the data access strategy, and the rest is handled by Spring itself. For example, you might be switching from local transactions using JDBC to global transactions using Hibernate. You just reconfigure your `transactionManager` bean definition in your bean configuration. As Spring's `PlatformTransactionManager` API isolates the underlying transaction management technology from your application, you don't need to touch your already-written application logic at all.

DECLARATIVE TRANSACTION MANAGEMENT WITH SPRING

As stated earlier in this chapter, transactions have boundaries. In other words, you need to define where a transaction starts, perform business logic that needs to execute inside the transaction, and finish it at some point either with a commit or a rollback. Here is a pseudo-code that represents the general structure of the transactional methods:

```
try
    begin transaction
    execute transactional code block
    commit transaction
```

```
    } catch(Exception e) {
        handle exception
        rollback transaction
    } finally {
        do resource clean up
    }
```

This pattern repeats itself in every method that needs transactional behavior around the system. Transaction management is a cross-cutting concern, and cross-cutting concerns are best handled with aspect-oriented programming (AOP). Spring employs aspect-oriented programming techniques to do transaction management as well.

For declarative transaction management, Spring only expects you to specify which methods of your Spring-managed beans will be transactional. You can do this via Java annotations or from within XML configuration files. Basically, when those specified methods are called, Spring begins a new transaction, and when the method returns without any exception it commits the transaction; otherwise, it rolls back. Hence, you don't have to write a single line of transaction demarcation code in your method bodies.

In the following example, you see how transactions are enabled declaratively using Spring's transaction support.

TRY IT OUT Enabling Declarative Transaction Management in Spring

You can find the source code within the project named enabling-declarative-tx-management in the spring-book-ch6.zip file.

In this Try It Out, you employ declarative transaction management to your transferMoney method. You can continue with the previous Try It Out. To begin, follow these steps:

1. Tell Spring you are going to use Java annotations to specify on which methods you apply declarative transaction management. You should place the @EnableTransactionManagement annotation on top of the configuration class for this purpose:

```
@Configuration
@EnableTransactionManagement
public class Ch6Configuration {
//...
}
```

2. Instead of replacing already written code in the AccountServiceJdbcTxImpl class, create a new class called AccountServiceJdbcTxImplWithSpring. Add a property with type javax.sql.DataSource into this class together with its setter method:

```
public class AccountServiceJdbcTxImplWithSpring implements AccountService {

    private DataSource dataSource;

    public void setDataSource(DataSource dataSource) {
        this.dataSource = dataSource;
    }

    @Override
    public void transferMoney(
```

```
            long sourceAccountId, long targetAccountId, double amount) {

    }

}
```

3. Mark your `transferMoney` with the `org.springframework.transaction.annotation` `.Transactional` annotation:

```
@Transactional
public void transferMoney(long sourceAccountId, long targetAccountId,
        double amount) {
    //...
}
```

4. Change the implementation of `transferMoney` so that it will employ Spring's `DataSourceUtils` `.getConnection(DataSource)` to obtain the JDBC connection, and execute SQL update statements:

```
@Override
@Transactional
public void transferMoney(long sourceAccountId, long targetAccountId, double amount) {
    Connection connection = DataSourceUtils.getConnection(dataSource);
    try {
        Statement statement = connection.createStatement();
        statement.executeUpdate("update account set balance = balance - "
                + amount + " where id = " + sourceAccountId);
        statement.executeUpdate("update account set balance = balance + "
                + amount + " where id = " + targetAccountId);
    } catch (SQLException e) {
        throw new RuntimeException(e);
    } finally {
        DataSourceUtils.releaseConnection(connection, dataSource);
    }
}
```

5. Define `AccountService` as a Spring-managed bean:

```
@Configuration
@EnableTransactionManagement
public class Ch6Configuration {

    //...
    @Bean
    public AccountService accountService() {
        AccountServiceJdbcTxImplWithSpring bean =
            new AccountServiceJdbcTxImplWithSpring();
        bean.setDataSource(dataSource());
        return bean;
    }
}
```

6. Access the `accountService` bean from within Spring Container, and call its `transferMoney` method within the `main` method as follows:

```
public class Main {
    public static void main(String[] args) {
        AnnotationConfigApplicationContext applicationContext =
            new AnnotationConfigApplicationContext(Ch6Configuration.class);
        AccountService accountService =
            applicationContext.getBean(AccountService.class);

        accountService.transferMoney(100L, 101L, 5.0d);
    }
}
```

How It Works

The `@EnableTransactionManagement` annotation activates annotation-based declarative transaction management. Spring Container scans managed beans' classes for the `@Transactional` annotation. When the annotation is found, it creates a proxy that wraps your actual bean instance. From now on, that proxy instance becomes your bean, and it's delivered from Spring Container when requested.

When you call the `accountService` bean's `transferMoney` method, first the proxy instance intercepts the call. It checks whether the transaction needs to be started, and if it does it begins the transaction. It then calls the real target bean's `transferMoney` method to execute business logic. When the target bean's method returns, the proxy commits the transaction, and it also returns.

On the other hand, when an exception is thrown from within the body of the transactional method, Spring checks the exception type in order to decide if the transaction will commit or rollback. By default, `java.lang.RuntimeException` and exceptions that inherit from it cause transaction rollback. Such exceptions are called as *system* or *unchecked* exceptions. However, `java.lang.Exception` and exceptions that inherit from it cause transaction commit. Such exceptions are called as *application* or *checked* exceptions. This behavior is the same as with the EJB specification and is preserved by Spring, as well. You can change this behavior so that application exceptions can also cause transaction rollback using rollback rules in the `@Transactional` annotation.

Isolating the Service Layer from Data Access Technology Details

In previous Try It Outs you performed JDBC data access operations within your service class. This was for illustrating how transaction management can be performed using JDBC directly, or by using Spring's transaction management support. You had transactional behavior, but your service layer was coupled with the implementation details of the data access technology you used. It would be better if you had encapsulated data access operations below another layer and let the service layer focus on its own tasks, such as coordinating business logic, demarcating transactions, applying security restrictions, doing validations, and so on. You can achieve this by adding another layer, called the data access layer, or DAO layer for short. The service layer individually requests data access operations from this layer, and data access-specific implementation details are completely hidden behind its interface. Service objects depend on one or several different data access objects through their interfaces, and they make use of those DAO objects while executing their business tasks at hand.

The biggest problem in achieving such isolation occurs when transferring transactional resources among several layers. For example, let's say you work with JDBC as the data access technology. Therefore, you start a transaction using the JDBC Connection object in your service layer and then need to pass this resource to the DAO layer below somehow, so that persistence operations performed using this resource will participate in the same transaction. You must develop a mechanism to share such resources among several layers while keeping each layer unaware of the implementation details of the layer beneath it. Spring, with its declarative transaction management mechanism, actually helps you define those layers and separates them from each other while each layer solely focuses on its own job without exposing technology-specific details to upper layers. The following example shows how this separation can be achieved easily with the help of Spring's declarative transactional mechanism.

TRY IT OUT   Separating the Service Layer from the Data Access Layer

You can find the source code within the project named `separating-service-layer` in the `spring-book-ch6.zip` file.

In this Try It Out, you use the `AccountDao` interface and implementation you created in Chapter 4 to perform JDBC operations within the transactional service layer so that they will automatically participate in the active transaction. You can continue from the previous Try It Out. To begin, follow these steps:

1. Copy the classes you created in Chapter 4's "Inserting, Updating, and Deleting Records Using JdbcTemplate" Try It Out example into this project. You can find the source code of the Chapter 4 Try It Out in the project named `inserting-updating-deleting-records` in the `spring-book-ch4.zip` file.

2. Create a service class called `AccountServiceImpl`, and create a property of type `AccountDao` within that class:

    ```
    public class AccountServiceImpl implements AccountService {

        private AccountDao accountDao;

        public void setAccountDao(AccountDao accountDao) {
            this.accountDao = accountDao;
        }

        @Override
        public void transferMoney(long sourceAccountId, long targetAccountId,
                double amount) {

        }

    }
    ```

3. Mark the `transferMoney(..)` method of the service class with the `@Transactional` annotation, and implement the `transferMoney(..)` method. Use the `AccountDao` `.find(long accountId)` method to find the source and target accounts from the database. Perform balance modifications, and then update the accounts using the `AccountDao` `.update(Account account)` method:

    ```
    @Override
    @Transactional
    ```

```
public void transferMoney(long sourceAccountId, long targetAccountId,
        double amount) {
    Account sourceAccount = accountDao.find(sourceAccountId);
    Account targetAccount = accountDao.find(targetAccountId);
    sourceAccount.setBalance(sourceAccount.getBalance() - amount);
    targetAccount.setBalance(targetAccount.getBalance() + amount);
    accountDao.update(sourceAccount);
    accountDao.update(targetAccount);
}
```

4. Change the `accountService` bean creation method so that it instantiates the service object from `AccountServiceImpl` and injects an `accountDao` bean into it. You can use the `Ch4Configuration` class instead of repeating DAO-specific bean definitions.

```
@Configuration
@EnableTransactionManagement
@Import(Ch4Configuration.class)
public class Ch6Configuration {

    //...

    @Bean
    @Autowired
    public AccountService accountService(AccountDao accountDao) {
        AccountServiceImpl bean = new AccountServiceImpl();
        bean.setAccountDao(accountDao);
        return bean;
    }

}
```

5. At this point you can test your new implementation within the `main` method:

```
public class Main {
    public static void main(String[] args) {
        AnnotationConfigApplicationContext applicationContext =
            new AnnotationConfigApplicationContext(Ch6Configuration.class);
        AccountService accountService =
            applicationContext.getBean(AccountService.class);

        accountService.transferMoney(100L, 101L, 5.0d);
    }
}
```

How It Works

Spring's declarative transaction management performs the hard part. When the service method is called, it begins the transaction if one doesn't exist. Then the transactional resource, here the `Connection` object, is stored in a `ThreadLocal` data structure, which can be accessible from any other location in the codebase. You don't need to know how to access this `ThreadLocal` data structure directly.

In `AccountDaoJdbcImpl`, you employed Spring's JDBC support, which is mainly based on the `JdbcTemplate` class. `JdbcTemplate` performs data access operations while being aware of any active transaction demarcation in the environment. Indeed, `JdbcTemplate` actually uses the same `DataSourceUtils` class previously used to illustrate how a `Connection` object, participating to the current transaction, can be obtained. The `DataSourceUtils` class deals with that thread's local data structure, and returns an open `Connection`.

In the end, the service class doesn't contain any technology-specific dependency in it. Everything is buried in the DAO implementation class. The service bean works as long as any DAO bean that satisfies the interface contract is provided.

During configuration you employed the `org.springframework.context.annotation.Import` annotation so that bean definitions in another `Configuration` class will be loaded when the current `Configuration` class is processed. The `accountDao` bean, for example, is defined within the `Ch4Configuration` class, but it is injected into the `accountService` bean with an autowire mechanism. The `org.springframework.beans.factory.annotation.Autowired` annotation on top of the bean creation method causes the `accountDao` bean to be passed as a method input parameter during the bean-creation method call.

Customizing Default Transactional Behavior

`@Transactional` annotation has the set of default attributes used during transaction demarcation. Developers can change this default transactional behavior according to their specific needs in their applications. The following are the default values of `@Transactional` annotation:

- ➤ `propagation`: REQUIRED
- ➤ `isolation`: DEFAULT
- ➤ `timeout`: TIMEOUT_DEFAULT
- ➤ `readOnly`: false
- ➤ `rollbackFor`: `java.lang.RuntimeException` or its subclasses
- ➤ `noRollbackFor`: `java.lang.Exception` or its subclasses

The `propagation` attribute defines the scope of the transaction, whether it spans multiple method invocations, and so on. Its values can be REQUIRED, REQUIRES_NEW, NESTED, SUPPORTS, NOT_SUPPORTED, MANDATORY, or NEVER. More information about how propagation works is given in the next section.

The `isolation` attribute specifies the underlying database system's isolation level. Possible values are READ_UNCOMMITTED, READ_COMMITTED, REPEATABLE_READ, and SERIALIZABLE. However, you must be aware that the underlying database system should have support for the given value to be active.

The `timeout` value specifies the transaction timeout period. It is directly passed into the underlying database system.

The `readOnly` attribute is actually a hint to the underlying transaction subsystem, and it tells the transaction subsystem that the method performs only read operations but the transaction should still be active. If the underlying subsystem doesn't understand, it causes no harm to the current transaction, and changes reflect to the database.

The `rollbackFor` and `noRollbackFor` attributes expect classes, and they specify what happens when an exception occurs while executing the transactional method.

If you need to customize any of these attributes, just add the corresponding attribute in your `@Transactional` annotation.

Using @Transactional on the Class Level

You can place an `@Transactional` annotation not only on methods but also on classes as well. If it is placed on the class level, all public methods of the class become transactional. Otherwise, only public methods with the `@Transactional` annotation become transactional. It is possible to override the transactional behavior defined on class level using the `@Transactional` annotation, by placing the `@Transactional` annotation on the method level as well. For example:

```
@Transactional
public class AccountServiceImpl implements AccountService {

    @Override
    public void transferMoney(
        long sourceAccountId, long targetAccountId, double amount) {
        //...
    }

    @Override
    @Transactional(rollbackFor=Exception.class)
    public void depositMoney(long accountId, double amount) throws Exception {
        //...
    }

    @Override
    @Transactional(readOnly=true)
    public Account getAccount(long accountId) {
        //...
    }
}
```

In the preceding example, the `AccountServiceImpl` class has an `@Transactional` attribute with its default values. This makes all of its public methods transactional. On the other hand, the `getAccount(..)` method's transaction is changed as `readOnly=true`. The `depositMoney(..)` method's default rollback rule has changed so that `java.lang.Exception` also causes rollback. `transferMoney(..)` has no annotation defined on it, so therefore, values from the class-level annotation will apply.

PROPERLY PLACE @TRANSACTIONAL ANNOTATIONS

It is good practice to put `@Transactional` annotations on a class and on its public methods. It is possible to place an `@Transactional` annotation on an interface and on its methods, too. However, doing so is discouraged because of Spring's proxy generation mechanism. Spring has interface-based and class-based proxy generation mechanisms. If class-based proxy generation is used, the generated proxy class inherits from your bean's class, and that proxy won't inherit annotations from its interface.

HOW TO PERFORM TRANSACTION ROLLBACK WITHOUT THROWING AN EXCEPTION

Spring's declarative transaction management subsystem commits the current transaction if the method returns without an exception. To roll back, first there must be an exception thrown by the method. Then Spring examines the type of the exception and decides on commit or rollback based on the type of exception and rollback rules of the current transaction.

Sometimes you may want to make a declarative transaction management subsystem roll back the current transaction without throwing an exception from within your service method. You can achieve this as follows:

```java
public class SomeService {
    @Transactional
    public void transactionalMethod() {
        try {
            //perform business logic which may cause exceptions...
        } catch(Exception e) {
            TransactionAspectSupport.currentTransactionStatus()
                .setRollbackOnly();
        }
    }
}
```

Here, you obtain the current transaction, which is represented by the `TransactionStatus` object via `TransactionAspectSupport`'s static `currentTransactionStatus()` method, and set its `rollbackOnly` attribute to true. As a result, the transaction management subsystem checks on this attribute at the end of the method call and rolls back if its value is true even though the method returns with success.

Understanding Transaction Propagation Rules

Propagation rules define transaction scope, when the transaction triggers, whether to suspend the existing transaction, or fail if there is no transaction when the method is called, and so on.

Propagation REQUIRED

Propagation REQUIRED starts a new transaction if there is no transaction when a method is called. If there is an active transaction started by another method call, that transaction is kept and the second method call is executed within the same transaction. Figure 6-1 shows the case that both methods have the Propagation REQUIRED attribute, so they share the same physical transaction.

If the second method throws an exception that causes rollback, the whole transaction rolls back. It doesn't matter if the first transaction handles that exception or not.

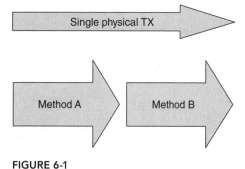

FIGURE 6-1

When an exception that causes rollback in the second method occurs and it crosses that method, the physical transaction is marked for rollback. If the first method handles the exception and returns with success, the transaction management subsystem tries to perform a commit on the current transaction. However, because those two methods share the same physical transaction, and it was marked for rollback previously, the transaction management subsystem will throw an `UnexpectedRollbackException`.

Propagation REQUIRES_NEW

Propagation REQUIRES_NEW always starts a new transaction regardless of whether there is already an active one. Figure 6-2 shows the case that the second method has the Propagation REQUIRES_NEW attribute, so it causes a new physical transaction to start.

Both methods have their own transactions. Therefore, if the second method throws an exception that causes rollback, only its transaction is affected. The first method still has a chance to commit if it handles that exception.

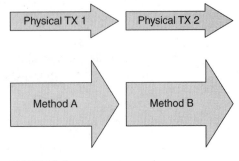

FIGURE 6-2

Propagation NESTED

Propagation NESTED is similar to the REQUIRES_NEW rule, but instead of having two separate transactions, there is only one active transaction that spans method calls. JDBC 3.0 support is required for this rule to work, and Propagation NESTED is only available if your persistence technology is JDBC. In other words, it won't work if you are using JPA or Hibernate. Figure 6-3 shows that the second method has the Propagation NESTED attribute, so it causes a savepoint to be created at the point that the second method is invoked.

JDBC *savepoints* are used to mark new method calls. When an exception occurs in the second method, the transaction until the last savepoint is rolled back.

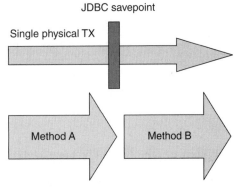

FIGURE 6-3

Propagation SUPPORTS

This rule makes the current method work in a transaction if one already exists. Otherwise, the method will work without any transaction.

Propagation NOT_SUPPORTED

If there is an active transaction when the method is called, the active transaction is suspended until the end of the method call.

Propagation NEVER

An error occurs if there is an active transaction in the system when the method is called. You have to call the method without any active transaction in the system.

Propagation MANDATORY

An error occurs if there is not an active transaction in the system when the method is called. You have to make sure that there is already a transaction created before accessing this method.

Table 6-2 summarizes what happens when the currently invoked method has the specific propagation rule in case there is and is not an active transaction at the run time.

TABLE 6-2: Transaction Propagation Rule Behaviors

PROPAGATION RULE	NO ACTIVE TX, SO STARTS A NEW TX?	WORKS WITH THE ACTIVE TX?
REQUIRED	Yes	Yes
REQUIRES_NEW	Yes	No, suspends the active TX, and always creates a new TX
NESTED	Yes	Yes, but creates a savepoint at the new method call
SUPPORTS	No	Yes
NOT_SUPPORTED	No	No, and suspends the active TX
NEVER	No	No, and throws an exception if there is an active TX
MANDATORY	No	No, and throws an exception if there isn't any active TX

INVOKING TRANSACTIONAL METHODS FROM ANOTHER TRANSACTIONAL METHOD IN THE SAME BEAN

Spring performs declarative transaction management using proxies. Client code is not aware that it is actually calling methods of a proxy instance that handles transaction logic. The proxy instance handles the transaction logic, before delegating the method invocation to the actual target bean. When the actual bean method invocation completes, the proxy decides whether to commit or roll back the transaction according to the outcome of the method call . Proxy instances are generated during bean instantiation, wrap the target bean, and are injected into client beans in place of an actual target bean.

continues

continued

However, sometimes an actual bean instance may need to invoke its own transactional methods with different transaction attributes from within some other transactional method that is called from the client. In that case, the second method call isn't able to trigger a new transaction

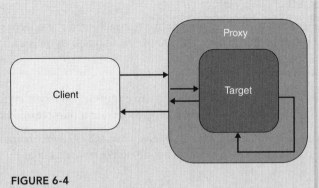

FIGURE 6-4

behavior because that call happens inside the target bean, and it won't pass through the proxy bean. Figure 6-4 illustrates this case.

To solve this problem, you can allow the target bean to access its current proxy instance inside its first method's body and perform the second method call over that proxy instance. This time, the second method call also passes through the proxy instance, and the transaction demarcation occurs properly:

```
public class SomeService {

    @Transactional
    public void transactionalMethod() {
      //do some business operation...
        ((SomeService)AopContext.currentProxy())
            .anotherTransactionalMethod();
    }

    @Transactional(propagation=Propagation.REQUIRES_NEW)
    public void anotherTransactionalMethod() {
        //do some other business operation...
    }
}
```

The `AopContext.currentProxy()` static method call returns the currently active proxy object. After casting it to the specific type, you can invoke the second method appropriately. However, the Spring Framework doesn't expose proxies by default because there is a performance cost of doing so. If you need this feature, you need to enable it via an `<aop:aspectj-autoproxy expose-proxy="true"/>` element in your Spring bean configuration file.

Currently, as of Spring 4.0.5.RELEASE, the `@EnableAspectJAutoProxy` annotation, which is the Java-based configuration counterpart of the `<aop:aspectj-autoproxy/>` XML element, doesn't support this attribute.

Using <tx:advice> for Declarative Transaction Management

Besides the annotation-driven declarative transaction management Spring provides, there is also an XML-based alternative that you can use. Actually, it was the primary way to make beans transactional before Java 5. After the introduction of annotations into Java 5, Spring also introduced the @Transactional annotation, and it became more popular. However, it is still possible to make use of an XML-based approach as well, especially if you want to apply transactional behavior to some beans whose classes you cannot change, or you don't want to depend on Spring's API at all. In that case, XML is the way to go. The following Try It Out demonstrates how it is applied.

TRY IT OUT Using <tx:advice> for Declarative Transaction Management

You can find the source code within the project named using-txadvice-for-declarative-tx in the spring-book-ch6.zip file.

In this Try It Out, you use the <tx:advice> XML element to enable transactional behavior in your service methods. You can continue from the previous Try It Out. To begin, follow these steps:

1. Add the following <dependency> element into your pom.xml file:

```
<dependency>
    <groupId>org.aspectj</groupId>
    <artifactId>aspectjweaver</artifactId>
    <version>1.6.11</version>
</dependency>
```

2. Create a Spring bean configuration file—for example, named beans-tx.xml—in the project classpath, and then enable tx and aop namespaces as follows:

```
<?xml version="1.0" encoding="UTF-8"?>
<beans xmlns="http://www.springframework.org/schema/beans"
    xmlns:xsi="http://www.w3.org/2001/XMLSchema-instance"
    xmlns:tx="http://www.springframework.org/schema/tx"
    xmlns:aop="http://www.springframework.org/schema/aop"
    xsi:schemaLocation="http://www.springframework.org/schema/aop
    http://www.springframework.org/schema/aop/spring-aop.xsd
        http://www.springframework.org/schema/beans
    http://www.springframework.org/schema/beans/spring-beans.xsd
        http://www.springframework.org/schema/tx
    http://www.springframework.org/schema/tx/spring-tx.xsd">
```

3. Add <tx:advice> to configure transaction attributes:

```
<tx:advice id="FileName_txAdvice" transaction-manager="transactionManager">
    <tx:attributes>
        <tx:method name="*" propagation="REQUIRED"/>
    </tx:attributes>
</tx:advice>
```

4. Specify on which public methods of Spring beans they will be applied using `<aop:config>`:

```
<aop:config>
    <aop:advisor advice-ref="txAdvice" pointcut="bean(accountService)"/>
</aop:config>

</beans>
```

5. Comment out or remove the `@Transactional` annotation in your `AccountServiceImpl` class:

```
public class AccountServiceImpl implements AccountService {

    private AccountDao accountDao;

    public void setAccountDao(AccountDao accountDao) {
        this.accountDao = accountDao;
    }

    @Override
    //@Transactional
    public void transferMoney(long sourceAccountId, long targetAccountId,
            double amount) {
        Account sourceAccount = accountDao.find(sourceAccountId);
        Account targetAccount = accountDao.find(targetAccountId);
        sourceAccount.setBalance(sourceAccount.getBalance() - amount);
        targetAccount.setBalance(targetAccount.getBalance() + amount);
        accountDao.update(sourceAccount);
        accountDao.update(targetAccount);
    }
}
```

6. Configure your `Configuration` class so that it also loads your previously created XML bean configuration file during container startup using the `@ImportResource` annotation. You can also remove `@EnableTransactionManagement` because transactional behavior is not specified with the `@Transactional` annotation:

```
@Configuration
@Import(Ch4Configuration.class)
@ImportResource("classpath:/beans-tx.xml")
public class Ch6Configuration {

    @Bean
    public PlatformTransactionManager transactionManager() {
        DataSourceTransactionManager transactionManager =
            new DataSourceTransactionManager();
        transactionManager.setDataSource(dataSource());
        return transactionManager;
    }

    @Bean
    public DataSource dataSource() {
        DriverManagerDataSource dataSource = new DriverManagerDataSource();
        dataSource.setDriverClassName("org.h2.Driver");
        dataSource.setUrl("jdbc:h2:tcp://localhost/~/test");
```

```
            dataSource.setUsername("sa");
            dataSource.setPassword("");
            return dataSource;
    }


    @Bean
    @Autowired
    public AccountService accountService(AccountDao accountDao) {
        AccountServiceImpl bean = new AccountServiceImpl();
        bean.setAccountDao(accountDao);
        return bean;
    }

}
```

7. You can now run the `main` method and see that `accountService` bean works as expected.

How It Works

`<tx:advice>` is used to define transaction attributes for public methods of specific Spring beans. Spring beans are specified with the `pointcut` attribute of the `<aop:advisor>` element. Those public methods will be intercepted during run time, and transaction behavior will be applied to them. Default attributes of `<tx:advice>` are the same as the default attributes of the `@Transactional` annotation, and you can change values of those attributes by using the `name` attribute of the `<tx:method>` element. You can use the wildcard character (*) in the `name` attribute of the `<tx:method>` element so that you can specify methods with patterns. If you name your transaction manager bean `transactionManager`, you don't need to add the `transactionManager` attribute of `<tx:advice>`.

The second important step was to tie up that `<tx:advice>` part with the Spring bean so that public methods of the Spring bean are intercepted and a `tx` proxy is generated around the target bean using `<aop:advisor>` in the `<aop:config>` element. Advisors are Spring-specific constructs that bring a reusable advice with a pointcut together. More information about advisors and advices are provided in Chapter 8.This example uses the `bean()` pointcut construct, which is only available in Spring AOP.

Finally, you load `beans-tx.xml` with the help of the `@ImportResource` annotation. `@ImportResource` is used to load Spring Container configuration files in which you perform some bean configuration that cannot go into Java-based configuration.

PROGRAMMATIC TRANSACTION MANAGEMENT WITH SPRING

Spring also provides a mechanism to control transactions programmatically. That way, you can decide where a transaction begins and ends. For example, there might be a big method, and you may want only some part of that method to be transactional.

Following are two approaches to programmatic transaction management:

➤ Using `TransactionTemplate`, which is recommended by Spring

➤ Using `PlatformTransactionManager` directly, which is low level, and it is similar to how you managed the transaction boundary using JDBC API in the beginning of the chapter

The following Try It Out shows how to use the `TransactionTemplate` approach.

TRY IT OUT Using Programmatic Transaction Management with TransactionTemplate

You can find the source code within the project named `using-transaction-template` in the `spring-book-ch6.zip` file.

In this Try It Out, you use `TransactionTemplate` to perform programmatic transaction management in your service methods. You can continue from the previous Try It Out. To begin, follow these steps:

1. Add a `TransactionTemplate` property together with its setter into the `AccountServiceImpl` class:

```
public class AccountServiceImpl implements AccountService {

    private AccountDao accountDao;
    private TransactionTemplate transactionTemplate;

    public void setAccountDao(AccountDao accountDao) {
        this.accountDao = accountDao;
    }

    public void setTransactionTemplate(TransactionTemplate transactionTemplate) {
        this.transactionTemplate = transactionTemplate;
    }
```

2. Call the `TransactionTemplate.execute(TransactionCallback)` method within the `transferMoney(..)` method, while creating an anonymous class from the `TransactionCallbackWithoutResult` class and giving it as an input parameter to the `execute(..)` method:

```
@Override
public void transferMoney(final long sourceAccountId,
        final long targetAccountId, final double amount) {
    transactionTemplate.execute(new TransactionCallbackWithoutResult() {

        @Override
        protected void doInTransactionWithoutResult(TransactionStatus status) {
            Account sourceAccount = accountDao.find(sourceAccountId);
            Account targetAccount = accountDao.find(targetAccountId);
            sourceAccount.setBalance(sourceAccount.getBalance() - amount);
            targetAccount.setBalance(targetAccount.getBalance() + amount);
            accountDao.update(sourceAccount);
            accountDao.update(targetAccount);
        }
    });
}
}
```

Notice that there is no `@Transactional` annotation on either the class or method level.

3. Define the `transactionTemplate` bean by injecting `transactionManager` into its constructor in your `Configuration` class:

```
@Configuration
@Import(Ch4Configuration.class)
public class Ch6Configuration {
    @Bean
    public TransactionTemplate transactionTemplate() {
        TransactionTemplate transactionTemplate = new TransactionTemplate();
        transactionTemplate.setTransactionManager(transactionManager());
        return transactionTemplate;
    }
}
```

Notice that you haven't used the `@EnableTransactionManagement` or `@ImportResource("classpath:/beans-tx.xml")` annotations in the `Configuration` class. You don't need them because you manage the transaction boundary by yourself in the service method. However, you keep defining `transactionManager` and `dataSource` beans as before:

```
@Bean
public PlatformTransactionManager transactionManager() {
    DataSourceTransactionManager transactionManager =
        new DataSourceTransactionManager();
    transactionManager.setDataSource(dataSource());
    return transactionManager;
}

@Bean
public DataSource dataSource() {
    DriverManagerDataSource dataSource = new DriverManagerDataSource();
    dataSource.setDriverClassName("org.h2.Driver");
    dataSource.setUrl("jdbc:h2:tcp://localhost/~/test");
    dataSource.setUsername("sa");
    dataSource.setPassword("");
    return dataSource;
}
```

4. Inject `transactionTemplate` into the `accountService` bean in which you use it to execute transactions:

```
@Bean
@Autowired
public AccountService accountService(AccountDao accountDao) {
    AccountServiceImple bean = new AccountServiceImpl ();
    bean.setAccountDao(accountDao);
    bean.setTransactionTemplate(transactionTemplate());
    return bean;
}
}
```

5. At this point you can test your new implementation by running the `main` method in the `Main` class:

```
public class Main {
    public static void main(String[] args) {
        AnnotationConfigApplicationContext applicationContext =
            new AnnotationConfigApplicationContext(Ch6Configuration.class);
        AccountService accountService =
            applicationContext.getBean(AccountService.class);

        accountService.transferMoney(100L, 101L, 5.0d);
    }
}
```

How It Works

`TransactionTemplate` is actually based on the Template Method pattern. This pattern is useful when the main flow of an algorithmic process is predefined and fixed. You just need to add changing parts into it via callbacks so that they can be executed within that flow of logic at the right time. `TransactionTemplate` forms a flow of logic similar to the following:

```
try
    begin transaction
    execute transactional code block
    commit transaction
} catch(Exception e) {
    handle exception
    rollback transaction
} finally {
    do resource clean up
}
```

You only need to provide the highlighted part as a callback instance. That callback instance should implement the `TransactionCallback` interface. `TransactionCallbackWithoutResult` also extends the `TransactionCallback` interface, and it can be used if the transactional code block doesn't need to return anything.

You can change default transaction attribute values of `TransactionTemplate` as follows:

```
transactionTemplate.setTimeout(60);
transactionTemplate.setPropagationBehavior↵
    (TransactionDefinition.PROPAGATION_REQUIRES_NEW);
transactionTemplate.setIsolationLevel(TransactionDefinition.ISOLATION_↵
    REPEATABLE_READ);
```

ROLLBACK BEHAVIOR OF TRANSACTIONTEMPLATE

The default attributes of `TransactionTemplate` are the same as those of the `@Transactional` annotation, except for the rollback rules when an exception occurs. Although it is possible to change rollback and no-rollback rules for an `@Transactional` annotation, `TransactionTemplate` doesn't provide a mechanism for this purpose, and it treats all exceptions as equal. In other words, it performs rollback both on unchecked and checked exceptions.

Using the PlatformTransactionManager Approach

You can also perform programmatic transaction management by accessing
PlatformTransactionManager directly. This is called the low-level approach. Transaction demarcation begins and ends via your calls to the PlatformTransactionManager API.

The following Try It Out shows how to use the PlatformTransactionManager approach.

TRY IT OUT Using Programmatic Transaction Management with the
PlatformTransactionManager API

You can find the source code within the project named using-platform-tx-manager in the
spring-book-ch6.zip file.

In this Try It Out, you use the PlatformTransactionManager API to perform programmatic transaction management in your service methods. You can continue from the previous Try It Out. To begin, follow these steps:

1. Add a PlatformTransactionManager property together with its setter method into the
   AccountServiceImpl class:

   ```java
   public class AccountServiceImpl implements AccountService {

       private AccountDao accountDao;
       private PlatformTransactionManager transactionManager;

       public void setAccountDao(AccountDao accountDao) {
           this.accountDao = accountDao;
       }

       public void setTransactionManager(
               PlatformTransactionManager transactionManager) {
           this.transactionManager = transactionManager;
       }
   ```

2. Create a new TransactionDefinition object to obtain a TransactionStatus in the
   transferMoney(..) method using PlatformTransactionManager:

   ```java
   @Override
   public void transferMoney(long sourceAccountId, long targetAccountId,
           double amount) {
       TransactionDefinition definition = new DefaultTransactionDefinition();
       TransactionStatus status = transactionManager.getTransaction(definition);
   ```

3. Perform data access operations using AccountDao methods, which need to be executed within an
   active transaction:

   ```java
   try {
       Account sourceAccount = accountDao.find(sourceAccountId);
       Account targetAccount = accountDao.find(targetAccountId);
       sourceAccount.setBalance(sourceAccount.getBalance() - amount);
       targetAccount.setBalance(targetAccount.getBalance() + amount);
       accountDao.update(sourceAccount);
       accountDao.update(targetAccount);
   ```

4. If everything goes well, commit via a `transactionManager` bean:

```
            transactionManager.commit(status);
        } catch (Exception e) {
```

5. Otherwise, handle the exception and decide whether to roll back again using the `transactionManager` bean:

```
            transactionManager.rollback(status);
            throw new RuntimeException(e);
        }
    }
}
```

6. Inject `transactionManager` into an `accountService` bean in which you will use it to execute transactions:

```java
@Configuration
@Import(Ch4Configuration.class)
public class Ch6Configuration {
    @Bean
    public PlatformTransactionManager transactionManager() {
        DataSourceTransactionManager transactionManager =
            new DataSourceTransactionManager();
        transactionManager.setDataSource(dataSource());
        return transactionManager;
    }

    @Bean
    public DataSource dataSource() {
        DriverManagerDataSource dataSource = new DriverManagerDataSource();
        dataSource.setDriverClassName("org.h2.Driver");
        dataSource.setUrl("jdbc:h2:tcp://localhost/~/test");
        dataSource.setUsername("sa");
        dataSource.setPassword("");
        return dataSource;
    }

    @Bean
    @Autowired
    public AccountService accountService(AccountDao accountDao) {
        AccountServiceImpl bean = new AccountServiceImpl ();
        bean.setAccountDao(accountDao);
        bean.setTransactionManager(transactionManager());
        return bean;
    }
}
```

7. At this point you can test your new implementation by running the `main` method in the `Main` class:

```java
public class Main {
    public static void main(String[] args) {
        AnnotationConfigApplicationContext applicationContext =
            new AnnotationConfigApplicationContext(Ch6Configuration.class);
```

```
          AccountService accountService =
              applicationContext.getBean(AccountService.class);

          accountService.transferMoney(100L, 101L, 5.0d);
      }
  }
```

How It Works

The `TransactionDefinition` instance represents your current transaction configuration, which is valid during service method execution. You can set its propagation behavior, `readOnly` status, and so on. Default values are the same as for the `@Transactional` annotation.

Using this definition object, you obtain an actual transaction instance by calling `transactionManager` `.getTransaction(definition)`. At this point you can assume that your transaction has been started. After executing business logic you come to the point at which you commit the transaction by calling `transactionManager.commit(status)`. If there is an exception, you handle it within the `catch` block and roll back the transaction again, giving `TransactionStatus` as the input parameter to the `trans-actionManager.rollback(status)` method. Notice that `TransactionStatus` roughly corresponds to the underlying transaction instance of the system, and you end the transaction by using it.

EXECUTING CUSTOM LOGIC BEFORE OR AFTER TRANSACTIONS

One of the distinguishing features of Spring's transaction management abstraction compared to EJB's is its ability to allow application developers to register a custom business logic that will be executed before or after current transaction demarcations. You can achieve such requirements in two ways. One is using the AOP features of Spring, and the other is to register a callback instance that is executed at the end of the current transaction. They are explained in the following two sections.

Advising Transactional Operations

As stated earlier, Spring's transaction infrastructure is built up on top of the Spring AOP module. However, for the most part you don't need to understand the details of Spring AOP to have transactional ability.

Spring actually handles the transaction functionality as an AOP advice, and in that respect it is no different than any other Spring AOP advice. For example, you may also need to execute some profiling logic to monitor execution times of current methods and want that logic also to count on the time spent during transaction demarcation as well. Therefore, you may want that logic to start before your transaction starts and end right after your transaction completes. You can create a profiling advice to monitor method executions. The following code block illustrates how such advice can be implemented using the `org.aopalliance.intercept.MethodInterceptor` interface:

```
public class Profiler implements MethodInterceptor {
    @Override
    public Object invoke(MethodInvocation invocation) throws Throwable {
```

```
            Long start = System.currentTimeMillis();
            try {
                return invocation.proceed();
            } finally {
                Long end = System.currentTimeMillis();
                System.out.println("Execution time of method " +
                invocation.getMethod().getName() + " :" + (end - start) + " msec");
            }
        }
    }
}
```

Note that `MethodInterceptor` interface is included in the `aopallience.jar` dependency, and it normally comes automatically with the `spring-aop.jar` dependency. Basically, `MethodInterceptor` is used to intercept a method invocation, and it lets you perform extra operations before or after the invocation. After implementing your profiling logic, you need to register it as an advice and define at which methods it is triggered. You do this using `<aop:advisor>` inside the `<aop:config>` element inside a bean configuration XML file, similar to the `<tx:advice>` configuration shown earlier in the section "Using <tx:advice> for Declarative Transaction Management":

```
<bean id="profiler" class="com.wiley.beginningspring.ch6.Profiler"/>

<aop:config>
    <aop:advisor advice-ref="profiler" pointcut="bean(accountService)" order="1"/>
    <aop:advisor advice-ref="txAdvice" pointcut="bean(accountService)" order="2"/>
</aop:config>
```

As you can see, you need to define `Profiler` as a bean and then refer to it from `<aop:advisor>` and give a pointcut value to specify the points to which it will be applied. The more important thing here is the `order` attribute given to both advisors. That attribute specifies the order of advices that will be applied to the `accountService` bean methods.

Executing Logic after Transactions Using TransactionSynchronization

In this method, you employ a callback mechanism to specify a custom code block that needs to be executed at the end of the current transaction. Custom business logic that is executed at the specified points of the current transaction is represented as a `TransactionSynchronization` object. It is an interface provided by Spring, and it has several methods to be implemented. We are more interested in the following methods right at the moment:

```
public interface TransactionSynchronization extends Flushable {
    int STATUS_COMMITTED = 0;

    int STATUS_ROLLED_BACK = 1;

    int STATUS_UNKNOWN = 2;

    void beforeCommit(boolean readOnly);
```

```
        void afterCommit();

        void afterCompletion(int status);
}
```

The `beforeCommit(readOnly)` method is called before the current transaction commits. However, it is not certain that the current transaction will commit after this point. Here is the excerpt taken from the Spring Javadoc comments of this method:

> *This callback does not mean that the transaction will actually be committed. A rollback decision can still occur after this method has been called. This callback is rather meant to perform work that's only relevant if a commit still has a chance to happen, such as flushing SQL statements to the database.*

It is also important to note that any exceptions thrown from this method are passed to the caller, and they also affect the outcome of the current transaction according to rollback rules. `afterCommit()` is executed right after the current transaction has successfully committed. `afterCompletion(status)` is called after the current transaction has either committed or rolled back. You can check the status input parameter to identify the outcome of current transaction demarcation.

Spring also offers the `TransactionSynchronizationAdapter` class, which implements `TransactionSynchronization` with empty methods. Therefore, you can extend from that class instead and only override the necessary method or methods for your purpose instead of implementing all of them.

After you implement your custom business logic that needs to be executed after a current transaction, you need to register it to the transaction infrastructure. You do this using the `TransactionSynchronizationManager` class. It has a static `registerSynchronization(TransactionSynchronization synchronization)` method to register your synchronization instance. It is important to perform registration within an active transaction. Otherwise, you get an `IllegalStateException`.

You can register more than one `TransactionSynchronization` instance to the current transaction. If you need to apply an order among those instances, you also need to implement Spring's `Ordered` interface and give an order to your implementation. Spring orders instances by looking at their order numbers if they implement this interface; otherwise, the `TransactionSynchronization` instance is put at the end of the queue. The `TransactionSynchronizationAdapter` class also implements the `Ordered` interface.

SUMMARY

In this chapter, you learned what transaction means, and its fundamental properties—atomicity, consistency, isolation, and durability (ACID). You learned Spring's `PlatformTransactionManager`, different implementations that correspond to different data access technologies, and how to specify the correct implementation among them in Spring Container. You configured Spring Container to perform declarative transactions both with annotation and XML-based configurations. You learned how to configure transaction attributes of methods using the `@Transactional` annotation and

<tx:advice>. You looked closely at different propagation rules, and how method calls affect each other's transaction context by using propagation rules.

In addition, you performed programmatic transaction management with two different approaches: one using TransactionTemplate and the other using PlatformTransactionManager directly. Finally, you saw how custom business logic could be executed before or after transaction demarcations. You used MethodInterceptor and advisors to execute custom logic before transaction demarcation, and the TransactionSynchronization interface of Spring after transaction demarcation.

EXERCISES

You can find possible solutions to these exercises in Appendix A.

1. Configure your system using JpaTransactionManager and implement the depositMoney(long accountId, double amount) method of the AccountServiceImpl class using JPA. The AccountServiceImpl class is written in the "Using @Transactional on Class Level" section of Chapter 6.

2. What needs to be done to switch from local transactions to JTA—that is, global transactions?

3. Implement a TransactionSyncronization class containing a logic that will be executed after a transaction rolls back. This logic can be a simple System.out.println() statement that prints the current transaction status to the console.

▶ WHAT YOU LEARNED IN THIS CHAPTER

TOPIC	KEY POINTS
ACID	Fundamental features of transactions: atomicity, consistency, isolation, durability
Transaction boundary	Where to start and end a transaction
`@EnableTransactionManagement`	Enables annotation-based declarative transaction management
`@Transactional`	Marks methods as transactional
`PlatformTransactionManager`	Spring's transaction manager abstraction
`TransactionTemplate`	Template method to perform transactional operations
`TransactionCallback`	Callback interface to pass transactional logic
Propagation rules	Defines transaction scope
Local versus global transactions	Transactions that access a single database or transactions accessing and coordinating multiple databases
`<aop:aspectj-autoproxy expose-proxy="true"/>`	Exposes current proxy via `threadlocal`
`AopContext.currentProxy()`	Enables you to obtain the current proxy instance
`setRollbackOnly`	`TransactionStatus` rollback status flag
`<tx:advice>`	Transaction attribute definition for XML-based configuration
`<aop:config>`	AOP config element to configure `tx:advices`
`<aop:advisor>`	Combines `tx:advice` with pointcut
`MethodInterceptor`	Interface to intercept actual method calls and execute custom logic before or after those method calls
`TransactionSynchronization`	Callback interface that is used to execute custom business logic after a transaction
`TransactionSynchronizationAdapter`	Adapter class for the `TransactionSynchronization` interface
`TransactionSynchronizationManager`	Used to register synchronization instances to the currently active transaction

7

Test-Driven Development with Spring

WHAT YOU WILL LEARN IN THIS CHAPTER:

➤ Configuring and caching ApplicationContext

➤ Injecting dependencies of test fixtures

➤ Working with transaction management in tests

➤ Testing web applications

➤ Using mock objects and other utilities for testing

> **CODE DOWNLOADS** *The wrox.com code downloads for this chapter are found at* `www.wrox.com/go/beginningspring` *on the Download Code tab. The code is in the Chapter 7 download and individually named according to the names throughout the chapter.*

Applying the Inversion of Control (IoC) pattern alone in an application makes the codebase suitable for unit testing. You can easily create mock dependencies and set them into the object that is being tested. For unit testing, the central unit under focus is the class or the method under test. There should be no environmental dependency—such as a database, a network, or even an IoC container—during unit testing. However, it is not enough to test units separately. Testing units separately is like testing the tires, engine, and doors of a car separately under the assumption that everything will work as expected when you assemble those parts and build the car.

You need to bring some parts of the whole system together to see if they will work. Those parts in a software system usually include objects from several layers, such as existing transactional context and database, network interaction, security context, or IoC container. It would be great if integration testing could be performed without deploying and running the whole application onto an application server.

Spring provides first-class integration testing support to help developers write integration tests without deploying and running the whole system. Called the *Spring TestContext Framework*, it is completely independent of the actual test framework, and you can employ it while running tests in a standalone environment. Therefore, you can use either JUnit or TestNG to run your tests.

The main goal of the Spring TestContext Framework is to ease configuration and creation of the Spring Container, while injecting dependencies into beans as well as test suites. It also aims to help test database interactions and object-relational mapping (ORM) codes within an existing transactional context so that developers can be sure that their ORM mappings are done correctly, queries are valid and returning expected results, and so on. It is also very easy to test web functionality without deploying the application code into a web container.

This chapter focuses on these features of the Spring Application Framework that help you test your code in a standalone environment. You first find out how context management and dependency injection are handled for test classes. Later, the chapter discusses transaction demarcation provided in test methods and how web applications can be tested out of a web container or application server environment. The chapter ends with an overview of mock objects and other utilities provided by the framework.

CONFIGURING AND CACHING APPLICATIONCONTEXT

Spring enables automatic creation and management of `ApplicationContext` while running your tests. You can use different formats of configuration metadata: XML based, annotation based, or Java based. Moreover, you can use more than one configuration metadata format in any application. The Spring TestContext Framework supports loading of all those different formats of configuration metadata while running integration tests.

Using XML- and Java-Based Context Configuration in Tests

The first Try It Out activity shows you how you can create an integration test with the expectation that `ApplicationContext` will be created and made available during testing.

TRY IT OUT   Configuring ApplicationContext within the Test Using JUnit

You can find the source code within the project named `context-configuration-and-caching` in the `spring-book-ch7.zip` file.

Use the following steps to create and configure an integration test case using the Spring TestContext Framework, and then run it with JUnit.

1.   Create a Maven project with the following Maven command:

```
mvn archetype:generate -DarchetypeGroupId=org.apache.maven.archetypes
    -DgroupId=com.wiley.beginningspring -DartifactId=spring-book-ch7
```

2. Add the following Spring dependencies to your pom.xml file if they are not already available there:

```
<dependency>
    <groupId>org.springframework</groupId>
    <artifactId>spring-context</artifactId>
    <version>4.0.5.RELEASE</version>
</dependency>

<dependency>
    <groupId>org.springframework</groupId>
    <artifactId>spring-test</artifactId>
    <version>4.0.5.RELEASE</version>
</dependency>

<dependency>
    <groupId>junit</groupId>
    <artifactId>junit</artifactId>
    <version>4.11</version>
</dependency>
```

3. Create a package called com.wiley.beginningspring.ch7 in the src/main/java source folder.

4. Create the classes already listed in step 3 of the "Creating and Using the Spring Container in a Standalone Environment with Java-Based Configuration" Try It Out activity in Chapter 2. They should be created in the package from step 3.

5. Create the applicationContext.xml bean configuration file in src/main/resources with the following content:

```
<?xml version="1.0" encoding="UTF-8"?>
<beans xmlns="http://www.springframework.org/schema/beans"
    xmlns:xsi="http://www.w3.org/2001/XMLSchema-instance"
    xsi:schemaLocation="http://www.springframework.org/schema/beans
    http://www.springframework.org/schema/beans/spring-beans.xsd">

    <bean id="accountService"
            class="com.wiley.beginningspring.ch7.AccountServiceImpl">
        <property name="accountDao" ref="accountDao" />
    </bean>

    <bean id="accountDao"
        class="com.wiley.beginningspring.ch7.AccountDaoInMemoryImpl"/>

</beans>
```

6. Create a package called com.wiley.beginningspring.ch7 in the src/test/java source folder.

7. Create a class called AccountIntegrationTests with the following content in that package:

```
@RunWith(SpringJUnit4ClassRunner.class)
@ContextConfiguration("/applicationContext.xml")
public class AccountIntegrationTests {

    @Autowired
```

```
    private AccountService accountService;

    @Test
    public void accountServiceShouldBeInjected() {
        Assert.assertNotNull(accountService);
    }
}
```

8. Run the test with JUnit.

How It Works

The Spring TestContext Framework is configured using several annotations. First you had to specify a JUnit runner class with which this test class will be run. The `org.junit.runner.RunWith` annotation is used for this purpose. You provided it with the `org.springframework.test.context` `.junit4.SpringJUnit4ClassRunner` class. The `SpringJUnit4ClassRunner` class is used to create and manage `ApplicationContext` and also to perform dependency injections into the test suite. The second annotation is the `org.springframework.test.context.ContextConfiguration` class. It is used to specify which configuration metadata sources will be used to create the Spring Container while running tests. The example uses `"/applicationContext.xml"` as the input argument. It will be loaded from the root classpath and used to create the `ApplicationContext` instance. More than one file can be given with the `locations` attribute. If nothing is provided, Spring tries to load a file with a name pattern `<TestClassName>-context.xml` in the same package as the test class.

Within the test class you defined a variable with the `AccountService` type and annotated it with `org.springframework.beans.factory.annotation.Autowired`. Spring automatically injects that dependency into the test class before running test methods. It is also possible to inject that dependency by creating a setter method for the variable and putting the `@Autowired` annotation on top of that setter, but field-level autowiring is more convenient for integration tests. The next section discusses more about injecting dependencies into test suites.

`org.junit.Test` is placed on top of the test method. When the test method is run, `ApplicationContext` is created, and any dependencies are injected into the test instance. Test methods within the test instance are then run with the injected dependencies by the JUnit.

The core of the Spring TestContext Framework consists of the `TestContext`, `TestContextManager`, `TestExecutionListener`, `ContextLoader`, and `SmartContextLoader` classes in the `org` `.springframework.test.context` package. Although you don't interact with those classes while using the framework, it is still beneficial to know what is going on behind the scenes. When tests are run, a `TestContextManager` is created for the execution of each test method. One of its roles is to manage the `TestContext` object that holds the context of the current test. `ContextLoader` or `SmartContextLoader` is responsible for loading `ApplicationContext` for the test class. Actual test execution is preprocessed by various `TestExecutionListener` objects that provide dependency injection, transaction management, and so on. `TestExecutionListener` actually defines an application programming interface (API) for reacting to test execution events published by `TestContextManager`. By default, the framework registers four listeners: `ServletTestExecutionListener`, `DependencyInjectionTestExecutionListener`, `DirtiesContextTestExecutionListener`, and `TransactionalTestExecutionListener`. It is also possible to disable default listeners or register custom versions using the `org.springframework.test` `.context.TestExecutionListeners` annotation on the test class level.

Instead of XML-based configuration metadata, you can use Java-based configuration metadata in the test configuration. The `@ContextConfiguration` annotation has the `classes` attribute, with which you can specify Java-based configuration classes as follows:

```
@RunWith(SpringJUnit4ClassRunner.class)
@ContextConfiguration(classes={Ch7Configuration.class})
public class AccountIntegrationTestsWithJavaConfig {
//...
}
```

In the preceding code snippet, the `Ch7Configuration` class contains bean definitions. It is listed in the `classes` attribute of the `@ContextConfiguration` annotation.

In some cases you need to provide both XML- and Java-based configuration metadata in the same test class as well. However, `@ContextConfiguration` accepts either XML- or Java-based configurations, but not both in the same test class. You can easily overcome this limitation by using the `org` `.springframework.context.annotation.ImportResource` annotation in configuration classes to load XML-based configuration metadata:

```
@RunWith(SpringJUnit4ClassRunner.class)
@ContextConfiguration(classes={Ch7Configuration.class,Config.class})
public class AccountIntegrationTestsWithMixedConfig {

    @Configuration
    @ImportResource("classpath:/applicationContext.xml")
    static class Config {
    }
//...
}
```

The preceding code snippet created a static inner class with the `@Configuration` annotation. It is also marked with the `@ImportResource` annotation, which specifies `"classpath:/applicationContext.xml"` as the configuration metadata. Then the `Config` class together with the `Ch7Configuration` class is listed in `@ContextConfiguration` on top of the test class.

> **TIP** *You may have created some bean configurations that are expected to be enabled when their corresponding profiles are enabled in the environment. To load and test such bean definition configurations in the test environment, the Spring TestContext Framework provides the* `org.springframework.test` `.context.ActiveProfiles` *annotation:*
>
> ```
> @RunWith(SpringJUnit4ClassRunner.class)
> @ContextConfiguration("classpath:/applicationContext.xml")
> @ActiveProfiles(profiles={"test","c3p0"})
> public class IntegrationTests {
>
> }
> ```
> *continues*

> *continued*
>
> You can use the `@ActiveProfile` annotation on the test-class level to specify which profiles should be activated when Spring `ApplicationContext` is loaded by the TestContext Framework. For example, in the preceding test class, `test` and `c3p0` profiles are activated with the annotation.

Configuring Context with ApplicationContextInitializer

There is also a fourth way to configure `ApplicationContext` instances while executing integration tests. Spring has the `org.springframework.context.ApplicationContextInitializer` interface, which enables you to configure `ApplicationContext` instances prior to their initialization:

```
public interface ApplicationContextInitializer<C extends
  ConfigurableApplicationContext> {
    void initialize(C applicationContext);
}
```

You can specify configuration metadata sources in addition to other environmental initializations on the `ApplicationContext` instance during this pre-initialization phase. The important thing is that the generic parameter for the initializer class must be of type `GenericApplicationContext` from which `ApplicationContext` is instantiated by the test infrastructure. The following code snippet shows this:

```
public class TestInitializer implements
ApplicationContextInitializer<GenericApplicationContext> {

    @Override
    public void initialize(GenericApplicationContext applicationContext) {
        XmlBeanDefinitionReader reader =
            new XmlBeanDefinitionReader(applicationContext);
        reader.loadBeanDefinitions("classpath:/applicationContext.xml");
    }

}

@RunWith(SpringJUnit4ClassRunner.class)
@ContextConfiguration(initializers={TestInitializer.class})
public class AccountIntegrationTestsWithInitializer {
//...
}
```

In the preceding code snippet, an XML-based configuration metadata file is loaded by the initializer. The `@ContextConfiguration` annotation has the `initializers` attribute, which accepts a list of `ApplicationContextInitializer` classes.

Inheriting Context Configuration

In a big project there exist lots of test classes. Those test classes may share some code and other configurations with other classes. Therefore, there might be some base or intermediate classes from which other test classes inherit. The Spring TestContext Framework supports inheriting configuration from base test classes, as demonstrated by the next Try It Out activity.

TRY IT OUT   Inheriting Context Configuration

You can find the source code within the project named `context-config-inheritance` in the `spring-book-ch7.zip` file.

Use the following steps to create two test classes that have an inheritance relationship between them so that subclass inherits the test configuration from its parent. You can continue from the place you left off in the previous Try It Out.

1.   Create the following two classes in the `com.wiley.beginningspring.ch7` package:

```
public class Foo {

}

public class Bar {

}
```

2.   Create an XML-based configuration file named `baseContext.xml` in the `src/main/resources` source folder:

```
<?xml version="1.0" encoding="UTF-8"?>
<beans xmlns="http://www.springframework.org/schema/beans"
    xmlns:xsi="http://www.w3.org/2001/XMLSchema-instance"
    xsi:schemaLocation="http://www.springframework.org/schema/beans
    http://www.springframework.org/schema/beans/spring-beans.xsd">

    <bean id="foo" class="com.wiley.beginningspring.ch7.Foo"/>

</beans>
```

3.   Create an XML-based configuration file named `subContext.xml` in the `src/main/resources` source folder:

```
<?xml version="1.0" encoding="UTF-8"?>
<beans xmlns="http://www.springframework.org/schema/beans"
    xmlns:xsi="http://www.w3.org/2001/XMLSchema-instance"
    xsi:schemaLocation="http://www.springframework.org/schema/beans
    http://www.springframework.org/schema/beans/spring-beans.xsd">

    <bean id="bar" class="com.wiley.beginningspring.ch7.Bar"/>

</beans>
```

4.   Create the `BaseTest` class with the following content in the `com.wiley.beginningspring.ch7` package:

```
@RunWith(SpringJUnit4ClassRunner.class)
@ContextConfiguration("classpath:/baseContext.xml")
public class BaseTest {
```

```
    @Autowired
    protected Foo foo;
}
```

5. Create the `ChildTest` class with the following content in the `com.wiley.beginningspring.ch7` package:

```java
@ContextConfiguration("classpath:/subContext.xml")
public class ChildTest extends BaseTest {
    @Autowired
    private Bar bar;

    @Test
    public void dependenciesShouldBeAvailable() {
        Assert.assertNotNull(foo);
        Assert.assertNotNull(bar);
    }
}
```

6. Run the test method in the `ChildTest` class with JUnit. Note that the `BaseTest` class cannot be run as a test case because it doesn't contain a unit test method. However, it is possible that it can contain test methods, too. In that case, `BaseTest` also becomes runnable by JUnit as well.

How It Works

By default, the configuration of the `ChildTest` class inherits XML-based configuration metadata locations, Java-based configuration classes, and any initializers available in the `@ContextConfiguration` annotation of its superclass `BaseTest`. Consequently, when the Spring TestContext Framework creates the `ApplicationContext` for the `ChildTest` class, it loads both the `baseContext.xml` and `subContext.xml` files.

The `@ContextConfiguration` annotation has the `inheritLocations` and `inheritInitializers` attributes, whose default values are true. If you need to disable this feature, you can set their values to false in child test classes so that the child tests will no longer inherit any configuration information from their superclass.

ApplicationContext Caching

If the exact same XML locations and configuration classes are specified by several test classes, the Spring TestContext Framework creates the `ApplicationContext` instance only once and shares it among those test classes at run time:

```java
@RunWith(SpringJUnit4ClassRunner.class)
@ContextConfiguration("/applicationContext.xml")
public class FooTests {
    @Test
    public void testFoo1() {

    }
```

```
    @Test
    public void testFoo2() {

    }
}

@RunWith(SpringJUnit4ClassRunner.class)
@ContextConfiguration("/applicationContext.xml")
public class BarTests {
    @Test
    public void testBar() {

    }
}
```

In the preceding code snippet, two test classes each specified the same XML configuration location file, "/applicationContext.xml", in their @ContextConfiguration annotation. In that case, when you run those two tests together within the IDE, Spring creates ApplicationContext only once, caches it, and reuses it while running test methods within each test class.

The cache is kept in a static variable. Therefore, test suites need to be run in the same process. If, for example, you run tests using a build tool such as Ant, Maven, or Gradle, you need to be sure that the build tool won't fork between tests.

In some cases, the cached ApplicationContext instance needs to be discarded after a test method or test suite is run. Spring provides the org.springframework.test.annotation.DirtiesContext annotation for this purpose. You can use it on the test-method or test-class level, and it tells the Spring TestContext Framework that it should discard the current ApplicationContext instance just after running that test method or test class and reload ApplicationContext for the next test method.

INJECTING DEPENDENCIES OF TEST FIXTURES

The Spring TestContext Framework can inject beans resolved from the configured ApplicationContext into properties of test instances. To indicate which property to inject as a dependency, you can use the @Autowired annotation as well as the @Resource and @Inject annotations, as shown in the following Try It Out activity. You can choose setter or field-level injection.

TRY IT OUT   Injecting Dependencies of Test Fixtures

You can find the source code within the project named dependency-injection-in-tests in the spring-book-ch7.zip file.

Use the following steps to perform dependency injection into the test class. You can continue from the place you left off in the previous Try It Out.

1. Create the following two classes:

```
public class Foo {

}

public class Bar {

}
```

2. Create the following Java-based configuration class:

```
@Configuration
public class Ch7ConfigurationForDependencyInjection {
    @Bean
    public Foo foo1() {
        return new Foo();
    }

    @Bean
    public Foo foo2() {
        return new Foo();
    }

    @Bean
    public Bar bar1() {
        return new Bar();
    }
}
```

3. Create a test class:

```
@RunWith(SpringJUnit4ClassRunner.class)
@ContextConfiguration(classes=Ch7ConfigurationForDependencyInjection.class)
public class DependencyInjectionTests {

}
```

4. Add the following properties into the test class:

```
@Autowired
@Qualifier("foo1")
private Foo foo1;

@Resource
private Foo foo2;

@Resource
private Bar bar;
```

5. Create a test method that has assertions to check whether dependencies are injected as expected:

```
@Test
public void testInjections() {
    Assert.assertNotNull(foo1);
```

```
        Assert.assertNotNull(foo2);
        Assert.assertNotNull(bar);
   }
```

6.   Run the test method using JUnit.

How It Works

By default, `@Autowired` performs dependency injection by type. Because you have two bean definitions of the `Foo` class, you used the `@Qualifier` annotation to specify which bean will be injected into which property in the test. The `@Resource` annotation, on the other hand, can be used to perform dependency injection based on the name of the property. If there is only one bean available in the container, `@Resource` behaves the same as `@Autowired` by type.

The `@Inject` and `@Named` annotations were introduced with the JSR-330 Dependency Injection for Java specification. They correspond to the `@Autowired` and `@Qualifier` annotations, respectively. You need to add the necessary javax.inject.jar library to your classpath so that you can use those annotations in your tests for dependency injection.

As shown in the following code snippet, it is also possible to inject `ApplicationContext` into the test instance and do explicit bean lookup by yourself via the `ApplicationContext.getBean()` method:

```
@RunWith(SpringJUnit4ClassRunner.class)
@ContextConfiguration
public class DependencyInjectionTests {
    @Autowired
    private ApplicationContext applicationContext;
    //...
}
```

USING TRANSACTION MANAGEMENT IN TESTS

The Spring TestContext Framework provides support to execute tests within an active transactional context. You find out how transaction management is configured and used in Chapter 6. The TestContext Framework needs an active `transactionManager` bean of type `PlatformTransactionManager` defined in the container for that feature. You also need to place the `@Transactional` annotation either on the test-class level or on individual test methods.

In the following code snippet, the `@Transactional` annotation is used on the class level. Therefore, all test methods in that class are executed within an active transaction. Each test method is run within a separate transaction. It is assumed that the `transactionManager` bean is properly configured in the `applicationContext.xml` file:

```
@RunWith(SpringJUnit4ClassRunner.class)
@ContextConfiguration("classpath:/applicationContext.xml")
@Transactional
```

```
public class TransactionalTests {

    @Test
    public void transactionalTestMethod1() {
        //...
    }

    @Test
    public void transactionalTestMethod2() {
        //...
    }
}
```

In the next code snippet, we instead placed the @Transactional annotation on the method level. In this case, only that method with the @Transactional annotation is run within the active transaction:

```
@RunWith(SpringJUnit4ClassRunner.class)
@ContextConfiguration("classpath:/applicationContext.xml")
public class IntegrationTests {

    @Test
    public void nonTransactionalTestMethod() {
        //...
    }

    @Test
    @Transactional
    public void transactionalTestMethod() {
        //...
    }
}
```

The main philosophy of unit tests is "expect a clean environment before you run, and leave that environment clean after you finish execution." In accordance with this philosophy, the Spring TestContext Framework's transaction supports rollbacks at the end of test methods instead of committing. That way, changes in the database don't cause any side effects in later tests that interact with the database as well. In some cases, you may want the transaction to commit, though. For that purpose, you can use the @Rollback(false) annotation on the test-method or test-class level, as shown in the following code:

```
@Test
@Transactional
@Rollback(false)
public void transactionalTestMethod() {
    //...
}
```

JUnit provides @Before and @After annotations to run code snippets before and after the execution of each test method. They are called *setup* and *teardown* methods. However, those methods will execute within an active transaction if the test method is configured to run so. Occasionally you may want to execute some setup and teardown code outside the current transaction. The `org.springframework.test.context.transaction.BeforeTransaction` and `org.springframework.test.context.transaction.AfterTransaction` annotations are provided for this purpose:

```
@RunWith(SpringJUnit4ClassRunner.class)
@ContextConfiguration("classpath:/applicationContext.xml")
public class TransactionalTests {

    @BeforeTransaction
    public void setUp() {
        //setup code that will run before transaction initiation...
    }

    @AfterTransaction
    public void tearDown() {
        //cleanup code that will run after transaction completion...
    }

    @Test
    public void nonTransactionalTestMethod() {
        //...
    }

    @Test
    @Transactional
    public void transactionalTestMethod() {
        //...
    }
}
```

> **WARNING** *If the method is not running within an active transaction, methods marked with* `@BeforeTransaction` *and* `@AfterTransaction` *won't work before and after execution of that test method either. For example, in the preceding code snippet, the* `setUp()` *and* `tearDown()` *methods only run for* `transactionalTestMethod()`.

The default configuration of the TestContext Framework is to look for a bean with the exact name `transactionManager` in the container and perform rollbacks at the end of the test methods. However, you can change this behavior using the `org.springframework.test.context` `.transaction.TransactionConfiguration` annotation. It is used to define class-level metadata to specify which bean name should be used during look up, and what to perform (either commit or rollback) at the end of the test methods.

In the following code snippet, the bean responsible for the transaction management is specified as `myTxManager`. Therefore, the TestContext Framework looks for a bean with that name in the container, and it commits transactions because `defaultRollback` is set to false in `@TransactionConfiguration`:

```
@RunWith(SpringJUnit4ClassRunner.class)
@ContextConfiguration("classpath:/applicationContext.xml")
@Transactional
@TransactionConfiguration(transactionManager="myTxMgr",defaultRollback=false)
public class TransactionalTests {

    //...

}
```

When working with any ORM framework, such as Hibernate or JPA, you need to flush the current Hibernate `Session` or JPA `EntityManager` at the end of the test method. This is because ORM frameworks accumulate persistence operations in their internal states—in Hibernate `Session` or in JPA `EntityManager`. They execute those accumulated operations at some specific point of time, creating, updating, or deleting records in the database, usually at transaction commit time. However, the Spring TestContext Framework performs rollback instead of commit at the end of the test method. Because of this, unless you manually perform a flush in your current Hibernate `Session` or JPA `EntityManager`, your persistence operations executed within the test method aren't translated into the corresponding SQL instructions, and there isn't any interaction with the database. Hence, some tests that would fail if there were a database interaction—for example, because of constraint violations—pass in the test environment, and this causes you to incorrectly assume that your application will run in production as expected. However, your application will most probably fail in production instead.

In the next code snippet, `SessionFactory` is injected into the test class, and it is used to obtain the current `Session` to perform a manual flush at the end of the test method. That way, SQL operations are executed in the database, although no change persists because the current transaction is rolled back by the TestContext Framework:

```
@RunWith(SpringJUnit4ClassRunner.class)
@ContextConfiguration("classpath:/applicationContext.xml")
@Transactional
@TransactionConfiguration(transactionManager="myTxMgr",defaultRollback=false)
public class TransactionalTests {

    @Autowired
    private SessionFactory sessionFactory;

    @Test
    public void testMethod() {
        //persistence operations...
        sessionFactory.getCurrentSession().flush();
    }
}
```

TESTING WEB APPLICATIONS

One of the nicest features of the Spring TestContext Framework is that it enables you to load `WebApplicationContext` in integration tests, as shown in the following Try It Out activity.

TRY IT OUT | Loading WebApplicationContext

You can find the source code within the project named `loading-webapplicationcontext` in the `spring-book-ch7.zip` file.

In this Try It Out, you configure the test class so that Spring creates a `WebApplicationContext` in the standalone environment. To begin, follow these steps:

1. Create a Maven webapp project with the following Maven command:

```
mvn archetype:maven-archetype-webapp -DarchetypeGroupId=org.apache.maven.archetypes
    -DgroupId=com.wiley.beginningspring -DartifactId=spring-book-ch7-webapp
```

2. Add the following Spring dependencies to your `pom.xml` file if they are not already available there:

```
<dependency>
    <groupId>org.springframework</groupId>
    <artifactId>spring-context</artifactId>
    <version>4.0.5.RELEASE</version>
</dependency>

<dependency>
    <groupId>org.springframework</groupId>
    <artifactId>spring-test</artifactId>
    <version>4.0.5.RELEASE</version>
</dependency>

<dependency>
    <groupId>org.springframework</groupId>
    <artifactId>spring-web</artifactId>
    <version>4.0.5.RELEASE</version>
</dependency>

<dependency>
    <groupId>junit</groupId>
    <artifactId>junit</artifactId>
    <version>4.11</version>
</dependency>

<dependency>
    <groupId>javax.servlet</groupId>
    <artifactId>javax.servlet-api</artifactId>
    <version>3.1.0</version>
</dependency>
```

3. Create an empty XML configuration metadata file named `applicationContext.xml` in the `src/main/resources` folder:

```
<?xml version="1.0" encoding="UTF-8"?>
<beans xmlns="http://www.springframework.org/schema/beans"
    xmlns:xsi="http://www.w3.org/2001/XMLSchema-instance"
    xsi:schemaLocation="http://www.springframework.org/schema/beans
    http://www.springframework.org/schema/beans/spring-beans.xsd">
</beans>
```

4. Create the `src/test/java` source folder and put the `com.wiley.beginningspring.ch7` package in it.

5. Create the following test class in that package:

```
@RunWith(SpringJUnit4ClassRunner.class)
@ContextConfiguration("/applicationContext.xml")
public class WebApplicationTests {


}
```

6. Place the `org.springframework.test.context.web.WebAppConfiguration` annotation on top of the test class:

```
@WebAppConfiguration
public class WebApplicationTests {


}
```

7. Create two variables from the `org.springframework.web.context.WebApplicationContext` and `org.springframework.mock.web.MockServletContext` types and annotate them with `@Autowired` in the test class:

```
@Autowired
private WebApplicationContext applicationContext;

@Autowired
private MockServletContext servletContext;
```

8. Create a test method and assert that both of those fields are injected at run time:

```
@Test
public void testWebApp() {
    Assert.assertNotNull(applicationContext);
    Assert.assertNotNull(servletContext);
}
```

9. Run the test with JUnit.

How It Works

Spring provides the `org.springframework.test.context.web.WebAppConfiguration` annotation to enable loading `WebApplicationContext` in standalone integration tests. It is used on the test-class level. Behind the scenes, a `ServletContext` instance from `org.springframework.mock.web.MockServletContext` is created and made available to tests. By default, `ServletContext`'s base resource path is assumed to be the `src/main/webapp` folder. You can always override this by simply providing an alternative path to `@WebApplicationConfiguration`. For example, `@WebApplicationConfiguration("classpath:/com/wiley/beginningspring/ch7")` changes the root context path to the `/com/wiley/beginningspring/ch7` package in your classpath.

The Spring TestContext Framework also creates the `HttpServletRequest` and `HttpServletResponse` instances from the `org.springframework.mock.web` `.MockHttpServletRequest` and `org.springframework.mock.web.MockHttpServletResponse` classes. They are created per the test method in a test suite and put into Spring Web's thread local `RequestContextHolder` at the beginning of the test method. After the test method is complete, the thread local variable is cleared.

Context Hierarchies in Tests

Chapter 3 discusses more about context hierarchies and Spring Web MVC. However, to understand context hierarchy support of the TestContext Framework, it is enough to know here that in a typical web application developed using the Spring Framework, a `WebApplicationContext` is usually created using `ContextLoaderListener`. This `WebApplicationContext` usually becomes the root `ApplicationContext` of your web application. If you also employ Spring Web MVC in your web application, you also have a `DispatcherServlet` configuration that has its own `WebApplicationContext` instance. This second one becomes the child `ApplicationContext` of the previous one, which is created by `ContextLoaderListener`.

By default, the Spring TestContext Framework creates a single `ApplicationContext` or `WebApplicationContext` instance that is made available to the tests. Most of the time it is sufficient to test against a single context, but sometimes you need to create the exact context hierarchy that will exist at run time. It is possible to write integration tests that use context hierarchies by declaring the context configuration via the `org.springframework.test.context.ContextHierarchy` annotation.

In the following code snippet, we declare two `@ContextConfiguration` annotations, each loading a different Java-based configuration class within the `@ContextHierarchy` annotation. In this case, Spring creates a parent `WebApplicationContext` using `ParentConfig.class` and a child `WebApplicationContext` using `ChildConfig.class`. If we define a `WebApplicationContext` property and mark it with `@Autowired`, the child `WebApplicationContext` will be injected into the test instance at run time. It will always be the lowest one in the defined hierarchy.

```
@RunWith(SpringJUnit4ClassRunner.class)
@WebAppConfiguration
@ContextHierarchy({
    @ContextConfiguration(classes = ParentConfig.class),
    @ContextConfiguration(classes = ChildConfig.class)
})
public class WebAppTests {

    @Autowired
    private WebApplicationContext applicationContext;

    // ...
}
```

Testing Request- and Session-Scoped Beans

Although request- and session-scoped beans are supported for a long time, testing those beans in standalone integration tests becomes much easier after introduction of `@WebAppConfiguration`. To test request- and session-scoped beans you first need to enable creation of `WebApplicationContext` by placing `@WebAppConfiguration` on top of the test class. Then you can inject `MockHttpServletRequest` and `MockHttpSession` instances into your test so that you can prepare the current request or session object for the use of scoped beans.

In the following code snippet, XML-based configuration has the `loginAction` bean, which is request-scoped, and its `username` and `password` properties are resolved with Spring Expression Language (SpEL) from the current request. The other scoped bean is `userPreferences`. It is defined as session-scoped, and its `theme` property is resolved from the current session.

> **NOTE** *You can read more about SpEL in Chapter 9.*

```xml
<bean id="loginAction" class="com.wiley.beginningspring.ch7.LoginAction"
        scope="request">
    <property name="username" value="#{request.getParameter('username')}"/>
    <property name="password" value="#{request.getParameter('password')}"/>
    <aop:scoped-proxy/>
</bean>

<bean id="userPreferences" class="com.wiley.beginningspring.ch7.UserPreferences"
    scope="session">
    <property name="theme" value="#{session.getAttribute('theme')}"/>
    <aop:scoped-proxy/>
</bean>

<bean id="userService" class="com.wiley.beginningspring.ch7.UserService">
    <property name="loginAction" ref="loginAction"/>
    <property name="userPreferences" ref="userPreferences"/>
</bean>
```

Before accessing any of the properties of those scoped beans, you need to populate current web objects with necessary parameters and attributes. For that purpose, within the test class in the following snippet, we injected current request and session instances that are mock objects managed by the TestContext Framework. That way, we are able to access those properties of scoped beans whose values are resolved from current `HttpServletRequest` and `HttpSession` objects at run time:

```java
@RunWith(SpringJUnit4ClassRunner.class)
@WebAppConfiguration
@ContextConfiguration("classpath:/applicationContext.xml")
public class ScopedBeanTests {
    @Autowired
    private UserService userService;

    @Autowired
    private MockHttpServletRequest httpServletRequest;

    @Autowired
    private MockHttpSession httpSession;

    @Test
    public void testScopedBeans() {
```

```
            httpServletRequest.setParameter("username", "jdoe");
            httpServletRequest.setParameter("password", "secret");

            httpSession.setAttribute("theme", "blue");

            Assert.assertEquals("jdoe",userService.getLoginAction().getUsername());
            Assert.assertEquals("secret", userService.getLoginAction().getPassword());
            Assert.assertEquals("blue", httpSession.getAttribute("theme"));
    }
}
```

Testing Spring MVC Projects

Spring offers extensive testing features out of the box, and for Spring MVC it's no different. With version 3.2, it brought new testing features that ease a web application developer's life. It enables you to do testing by invoking `DispatcherServlet` for requests made by the test code. You can say that it's similar to integration tests that run without the servlet container.

If you encounter `ClassNotFoundException` for the `ServletContext` class while running the tests, you need to add the `servlet-api` dependency to your project, as shown in the next snippet. For the version of the dependency, we used 3.1 because Spring 4 is solely focused on Java EE7. But if you are running Java EE6, you can use version 3.0.1. Note that `scope` is set to `provided`:

```
<dependency>
    <groupId>javax.servlet</groupId>
    <artifactId>javax.servlet-api</artifactId>
    <version>3.1.0</version>
    <scope>provided</scope>
</dependency>
```

Testing Controllers

As stated earlier in this chapter, Spring TestContext Framework provides mock implementations of the Servlet API, and with the builders provided it's possible to set values of these mock instances.

To do the integration tests, first you create an abstract base class that integrates with JUnit and loads the application context from the test configuration file. All of your test classes will extend from it:

```
@RunWith(SpringJUnit4ClassRunner.class)
@WebAppConfiguration
@ContextConfiguration("file:src/main/webapp/WEB-INF/springmvc-servlet.xml")
public abstract class BaseControllerTests {
}
```

The `@WebAppConfiguration` annotation defines that the application context will be a web application context, which will be loaded by the `@ContextConfiguration`.

A simple controller test for the first controller example, which is given in the "Your First Spring MVC Application" section of Chapter 3, is shown here:

```
public class HelloReaderControllerTests extends BaseControllerTests {

    @Autowired
```

```
    private WebApplicationContext wac;

    private MockMvc mockMvc;

    @Before
    public void setup() {
        this.mockMvc = MockMvcBuilders.webAppContextSetup(this.wac).build();
    }

    @Test
    public void helloReaderControllerWorksOk() throws Exception {
        mockMvc.perform(get("/hello"))
                .andExpect(status().isOk())
                .andExpect(model().attribute("message", "Hello Reader!"))
                .andExpect(view().name("helloReader"));
    }
}
```

HelloReaderControllerTests extends the base class that you defined. Because you created
WebApplicationContext by annotation, you can easily inject it because you have the component-
scan definition in the configuration file. The @Before annotation of JUnit creates an instance of the
MockMvc class with the help of the builders. MockMvc is the main class that you will be using for the
controller tests.

In the helloReaderControllerWorksOk method annotated with @Test, you are first sending an
HTTP request to "/hello"—which is a mapped URL in the controller. This HTTP request is specified as a GET method by calling the perform method of the mockMvc instance and then setting expecta-
tions stating that the HTTP response status should be 200 (ok). The model should have the message
attribute with the value "Hello Reader!" and the response view name should be helloReader.

MockMvcRequestBuilders and MockMvcResultMatchers are the two main static factory classes that
are used to build the request and then assert the result with matching outputs. With the fluent API
provided with these classes, it's easy to read the code and understand what the test method is all about.

Testing Form Submit

Submitting form data to a controller method is an everyday job for developers working on Spring
MVC projects, so with no exception you should test those controller methods in detail. Spring
TestContext Framework supports the HTTP POST method for perform(), and you can also set the
parameters of the form with param(). You will test the UserController class that is provided in
the "Validating User Input" section of Chapter 3:

```
public class UserControllerTests extends BaseControllerTests {

    @Autowired
    private WebApplicationContext wac;

    private MockMvc mockMvc;

    @Before
    public void setup() {
        this.mockMvc = MockMvcBuilders.webAppContextSetup(this.wac).build();
```

```
        }

            @Test
    public void formSubmittedSuccessfully() throws Exception {
        this.mockMvc.perform(
                post("/result")
                        .param("username", "johndoe")
                        .param("email", "john@doe.com")
                        .param("ccNumber", "5245771326014172")
                        .param("password", "TestR0ck"))
                .andExpect(status().isOk())
                .andExpect(view().name("userResult"))
                .andExpect(model().hasNoErrors())
                .andExpect(model().attribute("u",
                        hasProperty("username", is("johndoe"))))
                .andExpect(model().attribute("u",
                        hasProperty("email", is("john@doe.com"))))
                .andExpect(model().attribute("u",
                        hasProperty("ccNumber", is("5245771326014172"))))
                .andExpect(model().attribute("u",
                        hasProperty("password", is("TestR0ck"))));
        }
    }
```

In the preceding code you set the `username`, `email`, `ccNumber`, and `password` input parameters of the form and expect them to be set to the properties of the `User` model class. The `hasProperty()` method is a static import from the `org.hamcrest.Matchers` class, and it does not exist in the `hamcrest-core` library. To use it, you need you add the `hamcrest-all` dependency to the project.

But this is a happy path for the form submit, and everything works smoothly. What if a validation error occurs with an input field, such as the length of the characters for the username is not met? You can also test these behaviors in the controller tests. The following snippet shows an example test case. Here you're submitting just `"ok"` for the username, and it doesn't meet the validation criteria:

```
@Test
public void formSubmittedSuccessfullyButContainsValidationErrors()
            throws Exception {
    this.mockMvc.perform(
            post("/result")
                    .param("username", "ok"))
            .andDo(print())
            .andExpect(status().isOk())
            .andExpect(view().name("userForm"))
            .andExpect(model().hasErrors());
}
```

With the `model().hasErrors()` method, you're asserting that the model has the validation error with the input data submitted.

While running the tests of your project, if you encounter an exception in your console like this:

```
Caused by: javax.validation.ValidationException: HV000183: Unable to load
'javax.el.ExpressionFactory'. Check that you have the EL dependencies
on the classpath
```

it means that you need to add the `el-api` and `el-ri` dependencies to your project's test classpath along with a provided dependency to `servlet-api`. The reference implementation that you used for this Expression Language 3.0 API is from Glassfish:

```
<dependency>
    <groupId>javax.el</groupId>
    <artifactId>javax.el-api</artifactId>
    <version>3.0.0</version>
    <scope>test</scope>
</dependency>

<dependency>
    <groupId>org.glassfish</groupId>
    <artifactId>javax.el</artifactId>
    <version>3.0.0</version>
    <scope>test</scope>
</dependency>

<dependency>
    <groupId>javax.servlet</groupId>
    <artifactId>javax.servlet-api</artifactId>
    <version>3.1.0</version>
    <scope>provided</scope>
</dependency>
```

Testing Exception Handlers

It's also possible to test the exception handlers within test cases. The next example tests the `UserController` class from the "Handling Exceptions" section in Chapter 3. The test method submits the form with username `johndoe` to raise the exception in the controller. For the assertion, you check for the `errorMessage` attribute in the model with an exception message as its value:

```
public class UserControllerTests extends BaseControllerTests {

    @Autowired
    private WebApplicationContext wac;

    private MockMvc mockMvc;

    @Before
    public void setup() {
        this.mockMvc = MockMvcBuilders.webAppContextSetup(this.wac).build();
    }

    @Test
    public void userNotFoundExceptionHandledSuccessfully() throws Exception {
        this.mockMvc.perform(get("/findUser").param("name", "johndoe"))
                .andExpect(status().isOk())
                .andExpect(view().name("errorUser"))
                .andExpect(model().attribute("errorMessage",
                        "User not found with name: johndoe"));
    }
}
```

Printing Mock Request and Response

While executing the test code, it's possible to print the content of the `MockHttpServletRequest` and `MockHttpServletResponse` with the `print()` method. The usage of the method is highlighted for the `helloReaderControllerWorksOk()` method in the following snippet:

```
@Test
public void helloReaderControllerWorksOk() throws Exception {
    mockMvc.perform(get("/hello"))
            .andExpect(status().isOk())
            .andDo(print())
            .andExpect(model().attribute("message", "Hello Reader!"))
            .andExpect(view().name("helloReader"));
}
```

USING MOCK OBJECTS AND OTHER UTILITIES FOR TESTING

No useful objects exist alone. They need other objects in their environments to operate. They collaborate with each other and form more complex object networks within the application. Those objects that an object needs for its expected behavior are called its dependencies. There might be several dependencies of an object that are needed during execution of an operation. Some of those dependent objects may interact with a database; some may interact with the filesystem; or some may involve network communication.

On the other hand, unit tests need to focus on only the object that is under the test. The operation that is being tested should work without any other dependency. It should be enough for the test scenario to provide only the necessary input to the method under test, then call it, and check the returned value—if any exists—against the expected results. If the object under the test were wired with all of its dependent objects, it would also be required that all those dependent objects need to be wired with their dependencies and so on. However, the operation under the test may need to connect to the database or establish a network connection via another dependent object to fulfill the request.

Therefore, the unit test wires up the object under test with its expected dependencies so that the object can operate without any problem. However, those dependent objects injected into the object under test are just substitutes for their real counterparts. They actually don't connect to the database or establish a network connection, but they act as if they are doing so. Such objects are called *mock objects*. Mock objects can be trained to behave according to the scenario that is being tested. Therefore, when the object under test interacts with those mock objects, mock objects just return the expected values so that the object can continue to operate for the specific scenario to complete. After the method under test completes, the state of the mock objects can also be queried in order to check that the object under test interacted with them as expected.

Spring Provided Mock Objects for Testing

The `org.springframework.mock` package contains several different sub-packages that contain different mock object implementations for various kinds of API and service provider interface (SPI) dependencies. They help you to write unit and integration tests for code that depends on those APIs or SPIs.

The `org.springframework.mock.env` package contains mock implementations of Spring's `org.springframework.core.env.Environment` and `org.springframework.core.env` `.PropertySource` abstractions. You can use the `MockEnvironment` and `MockPropertySource` classes for developing out-of-container tests to test code that depends on those abstractions.

Spring helps you to set up a simple Java Naming and Directory Interface (JNDI) environment for testing purposes or standalone applications. There is a mock implementation of the JNDI SPI in the `org.springframework.mock.jndi` package. You can use the mock JNDI SPI implementation to bind objects into the JNDI registry and obtain them later in your application through `javax` `.naming.InitialContext`. The following code snippet shows how an object can be bound to the JNDI registry:

```
SimpleNamingContextBuilder builder = new SimpleNamingContextBuilder();
DataSource ds = new DriverManagerDataSource(
    "jdbc:h2:tcp://localhost/~/test","sa","");
builder.bind("java:comp/env/jdbc/myds", ds);
builder.activate();
```

Spring provides a comprehensive set of mock objects for the Servlet API. They are located in the `org.springframework.mock.web` package. You can use them to test your Spring MVC controllers in a standalone environment. They are usually more convenient to use than creating dynamic mock objects for `HttpServletRequest`, `HttpServletResponse`, `HttpSession`, and so on. `@WebAppConfiguration` also enables injection of web objects of those mock types into integration tests.

Other Utilities and Test Annotations

The `org.springframework.test.util.ReflectionTestUtils` class has a collection of reflection-based utility methods to access and set nonpublic fields or to invoke nonpublic setter methods when testing application code. Such code usually appears when working with ORM frameworks, such as JPA and Hibernate, or when dependency injection annotations such as `@Autowired`, `@Inject`, and `@Resource` are used on private fields or nonpublic setter methods.

`org.springframework.test.jdbc.JdbcTestUtils` contains JDBC-related utility methods to simplify JDBC-related testing scenarios.

The Spring TestContext Framework offers several other annotations to help out unit and integration testing scenarios. You can use the `org.springframework.test.annotation.Timed` annotation to set a time limit for tests to execute. Unless the tests execute within that time limit, they fail. You can use the `org.springframework.test.annotation.Repeat` annotation to run a test method a specified number of times. With the `org.springframework.test.annotation.IfProfileValue` annotation you can enable or disable tests according to some property value. Tests only run if a property value obtained from the environment equals the value or values specified in the `@IfProfileValue` annotation.

In the following code snippet, `@IfProfileValue` is defined with the `runTest` property expecting the value "true". The test only runs if it is run with the `-DrunTest=true` JVM argument. By default, profile values are searched from system properties. However, it can be customized with the `org` `.springframework.test.annotation.ProfileValueSourceConfiguration` annotation. You can use the `@IfProfileValue` annotation both on the test-class and test-method levels:

```
@RunWith(SpringJUnit4ClassRunner.class)
@ContextConfiguration("classpath:/applicationContext.xml")
@IfProfileValue(name="runTest",value="true")
public class IntegrationTests {
    @Test
    public void testMethod() {
        //...
    }
}
```

SUMMARY

From this chapter, you have learned that Spring provides first-class integration testing support for applications. It is very easy to create and manage ApplicationContext for test classes. Dependency injection is automatically performed by the TestContext Framework. For performance reasons, ApplicationContext is cached and reused among several test classes. Testing database- and persistence-related code had always been problematic due to data modifications that cause side effects to other tests. However, Spring provides automatic transaction demarcation for tests, and it solves this side-effect problem with transaction rollback at the end of the test method so that no data modification will remain when test execution finishes.

This chapter discussed how you can configure and customize transaction demarcation features according to the specific needs of your application. It also examined how WebApplicationContext can be bootstrapped in a standalone environment using the TestContext Framework, and how web functionality can be tested by accessing mock web objects such as HTTP request, response, session, and so on.

The chapter finished with a short overview of mock objects provided for testing application code, which depends on various APIs and SPIs, and some other utility annotations available in the TestContext Framework.

EXERCISES

You can find possible solutions to these exercises in Appendix A.

1. How can you disable TestExecutionListeners configured by default and see that no dependency injection is performed at all?

2. Create a test class that loads both XML-based and Java-based bean configurations.

3. Register a Java object into JNDI Context using SimpleNamingContextBuilder, and then look it up using javax.naming.InitialContext in your test class.

▶ **WHAT YOU LEARNED IN THIS CHAPTER**

TOPIC	KEY POINTS
`@RunWith`	JUnit annotation to specify a custom JUnit Runner class with which to execute test classes
`SpringJUnit4ClassRunner`	JUnit Runner implementation of the Spring TestContext Framework that executes tests
`@ContextConfiguration`	Annotation used to specify configuration metadata to create `ApplicationContext` specific for test fixtures
`@ActiveProfiles`	Annotation to specify what profile values will be active while creating `ApplicationContext`
`@DirtiesContext`	Annotation to tell the TestContext Framework that it should discard `ApplicationContext` before executing the next test
`@Autowired, @Inject, @Resource`	Dependency injection annotations that can be used to inject test fixtures into test classes
`ApplicationContextInitializer`	API to configure `ApplicationContext` during its initialization
`@TransactionConfiguration`	Annotation to configure and customize transaction management configuration of the framework
`@Rollback`	Annotation to control the outcome of current transaction demarcation at the end of test methods
`@BeforeTransaction,` `@AfterTransaction`	Setup and teardown annotations that indicate that such code should be executed outside the current transaction demarcation
`@WebAppConfiguration`	Annotation to bootstrap `WebApplicationContext` in a standalone test environment
`@ContextHierarchy`	Annotation to create parent-child `ApplicationContext` hierarchies in the test environment

`MockHttpServletRequest,`
`MockHttpServletResponse,`
`MockHttpSession,`
`MockServletContext,`
`MockServletConfig`
	Servlet API mock objects provided by the Spring TestContext Framework to help test web functionality

`@IfProfileValue`	Annotation to run the test conditionally

TOPIC	KEY POINTS
`@Timed`	Annotation to run the test within a time limit
`@Repeat`	Annotation to run the test several times consecutively
`MockMvc`	Main implementation class that is used in tests. It's built up with a `WebApplicationContext` and performs the mock HTTP request operations.

8

Aspect-Oriented Programming with Spring

WHAT YOU WILL LEARN IN THIS CHAPTER:

➤ Getting started with AOP with Spring

➤ Becoming familiar with types of advices

➤ Defining point-cut designators

➤ Capitalizing on the power of annotations

➤ Blending AspectJ with Spring

➤ Configuring Spring AOP with annotations

With the dawn of object-oriented programming (OOP), software systems started to be represented as a collection of discrete classes with each class defined with a clearly stated task. This paradigm had replaced the procedural approach of programming, but it also introduced shortages on parts like cross-cutting abilities where a feature can affect most parts of a system. The most prominent example of this might be a logging facility where detailed information for each method execution is logged for auditing, or you can think of exception handling where errors that occur across the layers of the application are handled at a single point and applicable measures are immediately taken to address the issues. One last example that we can give is the *Declarative Transaction Management*, which allows us to make the transaction configuration in a non-obtrusive way without doing any coding for each code part that has an access to the database. Of course, there are lots of similar cases and features—such as logging facility, exception handling, or declarative transaction management—that could be implemented across each class that needs to be applied, but doing so would violate the good old principle that each class should have a well-defined responsibility.

This is where *Aspect-Oriented Programming* (AOP) kicks in. In OOP the unit of modularity is the *class,* and in AOP the unit of modularity is an *aspect.* You can think of an aspect as the common feature that implements the cross-cutting parts of a software system in separate entities. The aim here is to increase the modularity by separating these cross-cutting concerns. Also it conforms to the *Don't Repeat Yourself* (DRY) principle for avoiding the code duplication.

> **NOTE** *The premise of the DRY principle is to reduce multiple occurrences of any code blocks, especially within a multilayered architecture.*

In addition to *aspect,* AOP terminology introduces some other new keywords that explain what's going on under the hood. The following list briefly defines the semantics of AOP with these words, and sections later in the chapter cover the concepts in detail and provide examples:

➤ **Join-point:** The point within the actual code where the aspect gets executed to insert additional logic into the application.

➤ **Advice:** The action—or the chunk of code—that is executed by the aspect at a specific join-point.

➤ **Point-cut:** An expression that selects one or more join-points for execution. You can think of a point-cut as a group of join-points.

➤ **Target:** The object where its execution flow is modified by an aspect so it is meant to be the actual business logic.

➤ **Weaving:** The process of wiring aspects to the target objects, which can be done at three different levels: compile time, load time, or run time:

   ➤ Compile-time weaving is the simplest method. The compiler passes through the source code of the application and creates woven classes.

   ➤ Load-time weaving is the process where the specific class loaders weave the class while loading it.

   ➤ Runtime weaving is a more dynamic approach compared to the compile-time and load-time weaving processes. Spring AOP uses this method by utilizing the Proxy pattern, which is covered in the next section.

GETTING STARTED WITH AOP IN SPRING

Spring provides a subproject, the Spring AOP, which offers a pure Java solution for defining method execution join points on the target object—the Spring beans—by employing the *Proxy pattern*. You can think of the *proxy objects* as the wrappers around the actual objects, so the features can be introduced *before*, *after,* or *around* the method calls of the originator objects. Figure 8-1 briefly describes the Proxy pattern. The client makes call to a proxy object, which delegates the actual job to another one.

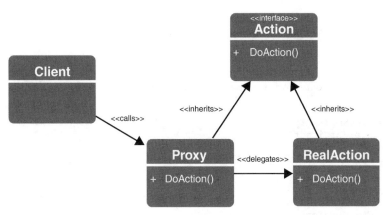

FIGURE 8-1

Spring AOP only applies runtime weaving while creating the proxy object mentioned, so there is no need to do any processing at the compilation time of the classes. Configuration of the AOP within the Spring framework could either be done in XML or with the help of annotations. Upcoming sections of this chapter cover both of these methods. Spring AOP is the second most important part of the Spring framework; only dependency injection, which is covered Chapter 2, is more important.

Under the hood, Spring AOP leverages the use of *AspectJ*, which is one of the most popular AOP frameworks that became a de facto standard in the industry. It provides an easy approach for defining aspects with AspectJ annotations easily with the help of the weaver integration mechanism. Despite Spring AOP's dynamic, runtime weaving, AspectJ provides static, compile-time, and load-time weaving on the target objects. But most of the popular Java AOP frameworks offer creating the proxy classes at run time as Spring AOP does.

With Spring AOP, either JDK dynamic proxy mechanism or CGLIB proxy mechanism is used to create the proxy classes. If a Spring bean implements an interface, all the implementation of that interface will be proxied by the JDK, and if the bean does not implement any interface, CGLIB proxying is applied to the concrete class objects. It's also possible to use the CGLIB proxy mechanism at all times with the configuration. This feature is mentioned in the "Blending AspectJ with Spring" section at the end of this chapter. Unlike AspectJ, Spring AOP only provides method execution point-cuts that reside inside the Spring beans, so it's not possible to apply aspects to your domain object classes.

To better understand how an aspect is defined in Spring AOP along with the point-cut and advisor definitions; check out the sample implementation in the next Try It Out.

TRY IT OUT Logging Method Execution Times

This example logs the method execution times with an aspect for any public method defined within an application. You can find the source code of the project in the executiontimelogging file in the code downloads.

1. Create an empty Maven web application project from the archetype, maven-archetype-quickstart. Add spring-aop dependency to your pom.xml file. At the time of writing, the latest version of Spring subprojects was the 4.0.5.RELEASE.

    ```
    <dependency>
        <groupId>org.springframework</groupId>
        <artifactId>spring-aop</artifactId>
        <version>4.0.5.RELEASE</version>
    </dependency>
    ```

2. spring-aop depends on spring-core and spring-beans subprojects, so you need to add them.

    ```
    <dependency>
        <groupId>org.springframework</groupId>
        <artifactId>spring-core</artifactId>
        <version>4.0.5.RELEASE</version>
    </dependency>
    <dependency>
        <groupId>org.springframework</groupId>
        <artifactId>spring-beans</artifactId>
        <version>4.0.5.RELEASE</version>
    </dependency>
    ```

3. Add spring-context as a dependency to your project.

    ```
    <dependency>
        <groupId>org.springframework</groupId>
        <artifactId>spring-context</artifactId>
        <version>4.0.5.RELEASE</version>
    </dependency>
    ```

4. Add aspectjweaver as a dependency to your project.

    ```
    <dependency>
        <groupId>org.aspectj</groupId>
        <artifactId>aspectjweaver</artifactId>
        <version>1.8.1</version>
    </dependency>
    ```

5. Implement the executionTimeLoggingSpringAop advice bean under package com.wiley .beginningspring.ch8, which is the actual implementation that calculates the time spent for each method execution.

    ```
    public class ExecutionTimeLoggingSpringAOP
        implements MethodBeforeAdvice, AfterReturningAdvice {

        long startTime = 0;

        @Override
        public void before(Method method, Object[] args, Object target)
    ```

```
        throws Throwable {
        startTime = System.nanoTime();
    }

    @Override
    public void afterReturning(Object returnValue, Method method,
                               Object[] args, Object target) throws Throwable {
        long elapsedTime = System.nanoTime() - startTime;
        String className = target.getClass().getCanonicalName();
        String methodName = method.getName();
        System.out.println("Execution of " + className + "#" + methodName
+ " ended in " + new BigDecimal(elapsedTime).divide(
new BigDecimal(1000000)) + " milliseconds");
    }
}
```

6. Create an application context configuration file that provides advice and point-cut definitions, under the classpath with the folder `/src/main/resources`.

```xml
<?xml version="1.0" encoding="UTF-8"?>
<beans xmlns="http://www.springframework.org/schema/beans"
       xmlns:xsi="http://www.w3.org/2001/XMLSchema-instance"
       xmlns:context="http://www.springframework.org/schema/context"
       xmlns:aop="http://www.springframework.org/schema/aop"
       xsi:schemaLocation="http://www.springframework.org/schema/beans
    http://www.springframework.org/schema/beans/spring-beans-4.0.xsd
    http://www.springframework.org/schema/context
    http://www.springframework.org/schema/context/spring-context-4.0.xsd
    http://www.springframework.org/schema/aop
    http://www.springframework.org/schema/aop/spring-aop-4.0.xsd">

    <context:component-scan base-package="com.wiley.beginningspring.ch8" />
    <context:annotation-config />

    <bean id="executionTimeLoggingSpringAop"
    class="com.wiley.beginningspring.ch8.aspect.ExecutionTimeLoggingSpringAOP" />

     <aop:config>
         <aop:pointcut id="executionTimeLoggingPointcut"
                     expression="execution(public * *(..))" />

         <aop:advisor id="executionTimeLoggingAdvisor"
                     advice-ref="executionTimeLoggingSpringAop"
                     pointcut-ref="executionTimeLoggingPointcut" />
     </aop:config>

</beans>
```

7. Create the `MyBean` and `MyOtherBean` spring beans under package `com.wiley.beginningspring.ch8`.

```java
@Component
public class MyBean {

    public void sayHello() {
        System.out.println("Hello..!");
```

```
        }
    }

    @Component
    public class MyOtherBean {

        public void sayHelloDelayed() throws InterruptedException {
            Thread.sleep(1000);
            System.out.println("Hello..!");
        }
    }
```

8. Create the `Main` class for invoking the beans' methods.

```
    public class Main {

        public static void main(String... args) throws InterruptedException {
            ApplicationContext context = new ClassPathXmlApplicationContext(
                    "/applicationContext.xml", Main.class);
            MyBean myBean = context.getBean(MyBean.class);
            myBean.sayHello();

            MyOtherBean myOtherBean = context.getBean(MyOtherBean.class);
            myOtherBean.sayHelloDelayed();
        }
    }
```

9. The final output of the application will be the following:

```
    Hello..!
    Execution of com.wiley.beginningspring.ch8.bean.MyBean#sayHello ended
    in 15.656 milliseconds
    Hello..!
    Execution of com.wiley.beginningspring.ch8.bean.MyOtherBean#sayHelloDelayed ended
    in 1010.071 milliseconds
```

How It Works

First you created an empty Java project with the *quick-start* Maven archetype. Then you added the dependencies for `spring-aop` along with the `spring-core` and `spring-beans` projects because `spring-aop` transitively depends on them. You also added `spring-context` as a dependency because you used the `@Component` annotation to create your sample beans in the project. Finally you added the `aspectjweaver` dependency because Spring AOP reuses some of the classes from this project; the dependency was needed to overcome any type of `java.lang.ClassNotFoundException`. At the time of writing, the latest available version of project `aspectjweaver` was `1.8.1`.

After configuring the dependencies, you implemented the spring bean of ID `executionTimeLoggingSpringAop`. This bean implemented two advice interfaces—the `MethodBeforeAdvice` and `AfterReturningAdvice`—with the following signatures:

```
    public interface MethodBeforeAdvice extends BeforeAdvice {
        void before(Method method, Object[] args, Object target) throws Throwable;
```

```
    }

    public interface AfterReturningAdvice extends AfterAdvice {
        void afterReturning(Object returnValue, Method method, Object[] args,
                            Object target) throws Throwable;
    }
```

The `MethodBeforeAdvice` advice is invoked before the actual method is invoked, and `AfterReturningAdvice` advice is invoked on return of the actual method if no exception is thrown from the method. So these two advices give you the ability to log the start and finish execution times of any public method that matches with the pattern `public * *(..)`. The method signatures given in the interfaces also take an argument of type `java.lang.reflect.Method` to access the information about the actual method, such as its name, declared annotations, and so on. Another important parameter is the `target` object that is an instance of `java.lang.Object` to access the weaved Spring bean. After collecting the timings in the `before()` and `afterReturning()` methods, you calculated the difference in between to print out the actual method execution times in milliseconds along with the class and method names.

The application context configuration file contains the `executionTimeLoggingSpringAop` bean definition. The AOP configurations—which reside inside the `<aop:config>` tag that provides a section for defining aspects, point-cuts, and so on—contains the point-cut definition of ID `executionTimeLoggingPointcut` with the expression `execution(public * *(..))`. Here the keyword `execution` is used to filter the methods that match the method signature given. In your sample definition, it's stated that any public scoped method with any return type, class name, and parameters will be advised. The use of the point-cut expressions is explained further in the "Defining Point-Cut Designators" section later in this chapter. Finally you define `executionTimeLoggingAdvisor` that references to the `executionTimeLoggingSpringAop` advice and `executionTimeLoggingPointcut` point-cut definitions. Its job is to match the advice with a given point-cut.

You created two different Spring beans—`MyBean` and `MyOtherBean`—which have two public methods, `sayHello()` and `sayHelloDelayed()`, respectively. The method named with the `Delayed` suffix pauses the current thread for one second to make the elapsed time longer when compared to the other method. You also create a `Main` class that creates the application context from the given configuration file and then accesses these two beans to call their public methods. The aspect intercepts these public method calls and collects the elapsed time for their executions as stated in the preceding steps.

> **NOTE** *It should be noted that the advice wouldn't get applied for the methods that are being invoked from an advice-applied method if all reside in the same class.*

BECOMING FAMILIAR WITH TYPES OF ADVICES

In the Try It Out activity in the preceding section, the usage of `MethodBeforeAdvice` and `AfterReturningAdvice` interfaces are demonstrated by logging the method execution times. Spring AOP also provides other types of advices, and you can find the full list of them in Table 8-1 along with the execution point they have. There are working examples of each one later in this section.

TABLE 8-1: The List of Advices

TYPE	INTERFACE	EXECUTION POINT
Before	MethodBeforeAdvice	The advice gets executed before the join-point.
After Returning	AfterReturningAdvice	The advice gets executed after the execution of the join-point finishes.
After Throwing	ThrowsAdvice	The advice gets executed if any exception is thrown from the join-point.
After (Finally)	N/A	The advice gets executed after the execution of the join-point whether it throws an exception or not.
Around	N/A	The advice gets executed around the join-point, which means that it is invoked before the join-point and after the execution of the join-point.

Figure 8-2 shows a sketch of the execution flow for the advice types.

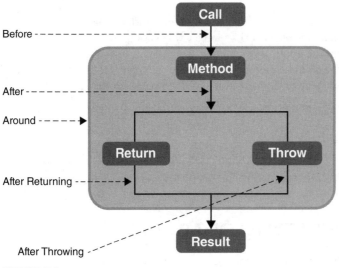

FIGURE 8-2

Before

The Before advice is invoked before the actual method call. To get it working, the aspect should implement the `MethodBeforeAdvice` interface shown here:

```
public interface MethodBeforeAdvice extends BeforeAdvice {
    void before(Method method, Object[] args, Object target) throws Throwable;
}
```

Refer to the Try It Out activity in the preceding section for a detailed example of this advice.

After Returning

The After Returning advice is invoked after the execution of the actual method. If an exception is thrown from the advised method, the advice is not executed. To get it working, the aspect should implement the `AfterReturningAdvice` interface as shown here:

```
public interface AfterReturningAdvice extends AfterAdvice {
    void afterReturning(Object returnValue, Method method,
                        Object[] args, Object target) throws Throwable;
}
```

The Try It Out activity in the "Getting Started with AOP Programming in Spring" section demonstrates a detailed example of this advice.

After Throwing

You can use the After Throwing advice to define any specific business logic for execution when an exception is thrown and right before it is caught in the invoker method. You need to implement the `ThrowsAdvice` interface to use this advice, but the interface does not contain any method signature because it's just a marker interface. So while implementing the interface, one of the following methods should also be implemented in the advice, and that very method will be invoked by reflection:

```
public void afterThrowing(Exception ex);
public void afterThrowing(RemoteException);
public void afterThrowing(Method method, Object[] args,
                          Object target, Exception ex);
public void afterThrowing(Method method, Object[] args,
                          Object target, ServletException ex);
```

We selected the third method signature, and the implementation of the advice that contains this method is shown here:

```
public class ExecutionTimeLoggingThrowsAdvice implements ThrowsAdvice {

    public void afterThrowing(Method method, Object[] args,
                              Object target, Exception ex) {
```

```
            String className = target.getClass().getCanonicalName();
            String methodName = method.getName();
            System.out.println("Execution of " + className + "#" + methodName
+ " ended with exception: " + ex.getMessage());
        }
}
```

With the preceding code, we're accessing the message of the exception easily. The configuration for the advice, point-cut, and advisor is the following:

```
<bean id="executionTimeLoggingThrowsAdvice"
class="com.wiley.beginningspring.ch8.aspect.ExecutionTimeLoggingThrowsAdvice" />

<aop:config>
    <aop:pointcut id="executionTimeLoggingPointcut"
                    expression="execution(public * *(..))" />

    <aop:advisor id="executionTimeLoggingAdvisor"
                    advice-ref="executionTimeLoggingThrowsAdvice"
                    pointcut-ref="executionTimeLoggingPointcut" />
</aop:config>
```

> **WARNING** Keep in mind that if an exception gets thrown within one of the methods of `ThrowsAdvice`, it overrides the original exception.

After (Finally)

The After (Finally) advice is executed regardless of the execution of the join-point. It could either return normally or throw an exception, but the advice code is executed no matter what.

The following code snippet shows the implementation of the advice with its configuration. Here we're passing an instance of `JoinPoint` to the advice method:

```
public class ExecutionTimeLoggingWithAfterAdvice {

    public void executiontimeLogging(JoinPoint jp) throws Throwable {
        String className = jp.getTarget().getClass().getCanonicalName();
        String methodName = jp.getSignature().getName();

        System.out.println("Execution of " + className + "#" + methodName
+ " ended");
    }
}
```

The definition of the advice with the XML configuration is a little bit different compared to others. Within the `<aop:config>` we used the aspect tag and defined `point-cut` and `after` tags inside it. Notice that the `method` attribute of the `<aop:after>` matches the method name defined in the advice.

```xml
<bean id="executionTimeLoggingWithAfterAdvice"
class="com.wiley.beginningspring.ch8.aspect.ExecutionTimeLoggingWithAfterAdvice" />

<aop:config>
    <aop:aspect ref="executionTimeLoggingWithAfterAdvice">
        <aop:pointcut id="logPointCut" expression="execution(public * *(..))" />
        <aop:after pointcut-ref="logPointCut" method="executiontimeLogging" />
    </aop:aspect>
</aop:config>
```

Around

The Around advice is a more popular approach used in the AOP programming where it is executed *before* and *after* the join-point, which is practically *around* the join-point by surrounding it.

The following is the implementation of logging method execution times with the Around advice instead of the Before and After Returning advice types.

```java
public class ExecutionTimeLoggingWithAroundAdvice {

    public void executiontimeLogging(ProceedingJoinPoint jp) throws Throwable {
        long startTime = System.nanoTime();
        String className = jp.getTarget().getClass().getCanonicalName();
        String methodName = jp.getSignature().getName();

        jp.proceed();

        long elapsedTime = System.nanoTime() - startTime;
        System.out.println("Execution of " + className + "#" + methodName
+ " ended in " + new BigDecimal(elapsedTime).divide(
new BigDecimal(1000000)) + " milliseconds");
    }
}
```

The advice does not implement any interface as was done in the examples before with the `MethodBeforeAdvice` and `AfterReturningAdvice`. Instead it takes an instance of `ProceedingJoinPoint` that is used to execute the actual method. `ProceedingJoinPoint` extends the `JoinPoint` interface, and it is passed as an argument to the Around advice. From a join-point we can access the target object with `getTarget()`, the method signature with `getSignature()`, and the arguments of the method with the `getArgs()` methods.

The definition of the advice with the XML configuration is a little bit different compared to others. Within the `<aop:config>` we used the `aspect` tag and defined `point-cut` and `around` tags inside it. Notice that the `method` attribute of the `<aop:around>` matches the method name defined in the advice.

```xml
<bean id="executionTimeLoggingWithAroundAdvice"
class="com.wiley.beginningspring.ch8. ↵
    aspect.ExecutionTimeLoggingWithAroundAdvice" />
<aop:config>
```

```
    <aop:aspect ref="executionTimeLoggingWithAroundAdvice">
        <aop:pointcut id="logPointCut" expression="execution(public * *(..))" />
        <aop:around pointcut-ref="logPointCut" method="executiontimeLogging" />
    </aop:aspect>
</aop:config>
```

> **NOTE** Keep in mind that `ProceedingJoinPoint` is only supported for Around advices, and you cannot use it for the other ones, say, After (Finally) advices.

> **NOTE** When multiple advices of type Before, After Returning, After (Finally), and Around are applied on the same join-point, the execution order can be defined according to their precedence. To provide the priority, aspects can implement the `org.springframework.core.Ordered` interface, and the order can be specified by the `getOrder()` method. The lowest value returned by this method has the highest precedence for the Before advices and the lowest precedence for the After advices. For AspectJ advice annotations, the order of the advices can also be set with the `@Order` annotation.

DEFINING POINT-CUT DESIGNATORS

Spring AOP provides various matcher expressions in order to filter methods for applying the advices to Spring beans. These are also called point-cut designators. We've already used the execution expression in our previous examples. In this section we try to cover the rest by starting with the type signature expressions that could be used for package name– or class name–based filtering; method signature expressions that could be used for filtering methods based on their actual signatures; and bean name expressions that could be used for filtering methods, which reside in a bean given with a name pattern. It's also possible to blend the expressions with grammatical operators: and, or, and not (or with &&, ||, and !). So the sky is the limit in the designator world!

The Type Signature Expressions

For filtering methods according to its types—like interfaces, class names, or package names—Spring AOP provides the `within` keyword. The type signature pattern is as follows, and *type name* could be replaced with *package name* or *class name*.

```
within(<type name>)
```

Here are some examples for the type signature usages:

➤   `within(com.wiley..*)`: This advice will match for all the methods in all classes of the `com.wiley` package and all of its subpackages.

➤ `within(com.wiley.spring.ch8.MyService)`: This advice will match for all the methods in the `MyService` class.

➤ `within(MyServiceInterface+)`: This advice will match for all the methods of classes that implement the `MyServiceInterface`.

➤ `within(com.wiley.spring.ch8.MyBaseService+)`: This advice will match for `MyBaseService` class and for all of its subclasses.

The Method Signature Expressions

For filtering according to the method signatures, the `execution` keyword can be used. Its pattern is stated as follows:

```
execution(<scope> <return-type> <fully-qualified-class-name>.*(parameters))
```

Here the methods that match with the given scope, return type, fully qualified class name, and parameter will have the specified advice applied. The scope of the methods could either be public, protected, or private. To bypass the parameter filtering, you can specify two dots `..`, as we did for the advice definition in the earlier Try It Out activity, to say that the method could have any number and type of parameters. The following are descriptions of the sample method signatures:

➤ `execution(* com.wiley.spring.ch8.MyBean.*(..))`: This advice will match for all the methods of `MyBean`.

➤ `execution(public * com.wiley.spring.ch8.MyBean.*(..))`: This advice will match for all the public methods of `MyBean`.

➤ `execution(public String com.wiley.spring.ch8.MyBean.*(..))`: This advice will match for all the public methods of `MyBean` that return a `String`.

➤ `execution(public * com.wiley.spring.ch8.MyBean.*(long, ..))`: This advice will match for all the public methods of `MyBean` with the first parameter defined as `long`.

Other Alternative Point-Cut Designators

This part lists the designators that are supported by the Spring AOP. AOP only supports a subset of the designators that are available in the other AOP projects.

➤ `bean(*Service)`: It's possible to filter beans according to their names with the `bean` keyword. The point-cut expression given above will match for the beans that have the suffix `Service` in their names.

➤ `@annotation(com.wiley.spring.ch8.MarkerMethodAnnotation)`: It's possible to filter the methods according to an annotation applied on. The point-cut expression here states that the methods that have the `MarkerMethodAnnotation` annotation will be advised.

➤ `@within(com.wiley.spring.ch8.MarkerAnnotation)`: While point-cut expressions with the `within` keyword match a package, class, or an interface, it's also possible to restrict filtering of the classes according to an annotation that the class would have. Here, the classes with the `MarkerAnnotation` will be advised by the `@within` keyword.

➤ `this(com.wiley.spring.ch8.MarkerInterface)`: This point-cut expression will filter the methods of any proxy object that implements the `MarkerInterface`.

Wildcards

While defining expressions we have used wildcards like, *, . ., or +. Table 8-2 describes these wildcards.

TABLE 8-2: The List of Wildcards

WILDCARD	DEFINITION
. .	This wildcard matches any number of arguments within method definitions, and it matches any number of packages within the class definitions.
+	This wildcard matches any subclasses of a given class.
*	This wildcard matches any number of characters.

CAPITALIZING ON THE POWER OF ANNOTATIONS

Doing aspect-oriented development becomes an easy job with the help of Spring AOP and AspectJ cooperation. To define an aspect, advice, or a point-cut, we did some XML configuration in our examples, but because Spring AOP also employs the annotations provided by AspectJ, the definition of the aspects can be done with pure Java code instead of the bloated XML. This section covers the annotations that you can use to implement AOP.

@Before

With this annotation, the annotated advice methods are invoked *before* the actual method call according to the expression given.

```
@Before("execution(public * *(..))")
public void before(JoinPoint joinPoint) {
}
```

Here, advice intercepts the public methods of the Spring beans. You can also access the information such as the advised method signature, the intercepted target object, and so on, from the instance of the `JoinPoint` passed as a parameter.

Within the advice, it's also possible to access a parameter that is passed to the actual method. To achieve this you need to bind the method argument name into the filter expression with the `args()` keyword. The following is an example definition of the target object:

```
@Component
public class MyBean {
    public void sayHello(String param) {
        System.out.println("Actual method execution with param: " + param);
    }
}
```

The next snippet shows the definition of the advice. Here we're defining a string method argument with the name `param`, and it's defined in the filter expression as `args(param)`. So we can access the parameter passed to the actual method within our advice definition.

```
@Component
@Aspect
public class ExecutionOrderBefore {

    @Before(value = "execution(public * *(..)) and args(param)")
    public void before(JoinPoint joinPoint, String param) {
        System.out.println("Before Advice. Argument: " + param);
    }
}
```

> **NOTE** If the first argument of the method is a type of `JoinPoint` or `ProceedingJoinPoint`, there is no need to define the name of that argument in the `args()` description of the filter expression.

@Pointcut

Point-cuts can be defined with this annotation by providing a method declaration. The return type of the method should be `void` and the parameters of the method should match the parameters of the point-cut. There is no need to define the method body because it will be omitted. In the following snippet, the sample given for the `@Before` annotation with the `@Pointcut` has been rewritten:

```
@Pointcut("execution(public * *(..))")
public void anyPublicMethod()  {
}

@Before("anyPublicMethod()")
public void beforeWithPointcut(JoinPoint joinPoint) {
}
```

The point-cut defined here applies on any public method with any return type, method name, and parameters. Because the name of the method declared with the annotation is given as `anyPublicMethod()`, this method name is directly used within the `@Before` annotation definition, and that's how we're binding the point-cut definition with the advice that we have.

Point-cuts can also be combined with the `boolean` operators to create one large point-cut. We stated two point-cut definitions with two different expressions; one applies for any public method with any return type, method name, and parameters, and the other one applies for the methods annotated with the `@MarkerAnnotation`.

```
@Pointcut("execution(public * *(..))")
public void anyPublicMethod()  {
}

@Pointcut("@annotation(com.wiley.beginningspring.ch8.MarkerAnnotation)")
public void annotatedWithMarkerAnnotation()  {
}
```

So these point-cut definitions can be used on an advice as shown in the following code. The &, |, &&, and || operators can be used to join the point-cuts.

```
@After(value = "anyPublicMethod() && annotatedWithMarkerAnnotation()")
public void afterWithMultiplePointcut(JoinPoint joinPoint) {
}
```

The `@annotation` used within the point-cut definition here is called a *point-cut designator*, which is covered in detail in the "Defining Point-Cut Designators" section.

@After

With this annotation, the annotated advice methods are invoked *after* the actual method call, and they will be called either when the method is returned successfully or if an exception is thrown from the method. The following is an example for the advice definition:

```
@After("execution(public * *(..))")
public void after(JoinPoint joinPoint) {
}
```

Here, any public method that resides in a Spring bean will be intercepted. From the instance of `JoinPoint` you can access information such as the advised method signature and the intercepted target object.

@AfterReturning

This annotation defines an advice that will be executed after the execution of the join-point finishes. If an exception is thrown from the advised method, the advice is not executed. The following example defines an advice that is applied to any public method declared in a spring bean.

```
@AfterReturning(value = "execution(public * *(..))")
public void after(JoinPoint joinPoint) {
    System.out.println("After Returning Advice.");
}
```

It's also possible to access the value returned by the join-point by defining the `returning` attribute of the `@AfterReturning` advice. Here's an example:

```
@Component
@Aspect
public class ExecutionOrderAfterReturning {

    @AfterReturning(value = "execution(public * *(..))", returning = "result")
    public void after(String result) {
        System.out.println("After Returning Advice with result: " + result);
    }
}
```

Here the value of the `returning` attribute is set to `result`. This matches with the name of the advice method argument, which is also set as `result`.

@AfterThrowing

With this annotation it's possible to intercept an exception after it's thrown and right before it's caught in the invoker method. The `AfterThrowing` advice definition will only intercept the methods of `MyBean` class as shown here:

```
@AfterThrowing(value = "within(com.wiley.beginningspring.ch8.bean.MyBean)",
               throwing = "t")
public void afterThrowing(JoinPoint joinPoint, Throwable t) {
}
```

Here you can also access the exception as an instance of Throwable with the advice configuration parameter throwing. The name of the parameter should match with the method argument's name, which is set as t in the example.

@Aspect

This is the annotation that declares the aspect. It should be applied on the class level of a Spring bean, which should also be annotated with @Component or with derivatives of it. Following is an example of an aspect definition along with a Before advice:

```
@Component
@Aspect
public class ExecutionOrderBefore {

    @Before(value = "execution(public * *(..))")
    public void before(JoinPoint joinPoint) {
    }
}
```

By default, there will be only one instance of each aspect declared within the application context that conforms to the singleton instantiation model.

> **NOTE** Keep in mind that implementing business logic with aspects introduces an overhead on the method execution times. Thus, they should be applied carefully.

@Around

This annotation enables the execution of the advice method both before and after the execution of the target method, which means literally around the join-point. Here's an example for the advice definition:

```
@Around("execution(public * *(..))")
public void around(ProceedingJoinPoint jp) throws Throwable {
    System.out.println("Before proceeding part of the Around advice.");
    jp.proceed();
    System.out.println("After proceeding part of the Around advice.");
}
```

As you can see in the method signature, an instance of ProceedingJoinPoint is passed to the method. ProceedingJoinPoint extends the JoinPoint interface, and it can only be used in the Around type of advices.

@DeclareParents

In Spring AOP, it's possible to make the target objects implement an interface dynamically by also providing a concrete class of that interface. This is called *Introduction*, and it enables the path to do "multiple inheritance" in Java, as described in this section.

Figure 8-3 defines a domain model with three classes to demonstrate the feature.

In Figure 8-3 we have the `Pegasus` class that extends the `Horse` and the `Bird` classes. Pegasus is a creature from the Greek mythology, which can be described as a winged stallion, so it has both the ability to walk and the ability to fly. Here, we will make an implementation so that the `Pegasus` class extends the `Horse` and `Bird` classes at the same time, which is not possible in Java.

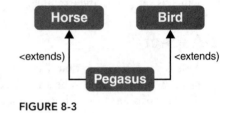

FIGURE 8-3

Let's first define our `Pegasus` Spring bean with the `@Component`.

```
@Component
public class Pegasus extends Horse {
}
```

The `Horse` class that the `Pegasus` class extends from is shown in the following snippet. It contains the implementation of the `ride()` method.

```
public class Horse {
    public void ride() {
        System.out.println("Pegasus is wandering..!");
    }
}
```

The next snippet shows you the implementation of the `Bird` class with its interface definition `IBird`. The `Bird` class contains the implementation of the `fly()` method.

```
public interface IBird {
    void fly();
}

public class Bird implements IBird {

    @Override
    public void fly() {
        System.out.println("Pegasus is flying..!");
    }
}
```

Because `Pegasus` class knows nothing about the `IBird` interface and `Bird` class, we introduce them by defining them in an aspect, class `GreekMythologyIntroducer`, which contains the `@DeclareParents` annotation on top of a static interface definition.

```
@Component
@Aspect
public class GreekMythologyIntroducer {
    @DeclareParents(
```

```
                value = "com.wiley.beginningspring.ch8.bean.Pegasus+",
                defaultImpl = Bird.class)
        public static IBird iBird;
}
```

Here with the value of the `@DeclareParents` annotation we're stating that for the `Pegasus` class and all of its subclasses the aspect will apply the interface `IBird` along with the concrete implementation, `Bird`.

Now we can retrieve the `Pegasus` Spring bean from the application context, cast it to the `Horse` class and `IBird` interface, and then invoke the `ride()` and `fly()` methods respectively.

```
public class Main {

    public static void main(String... args) {
        ApplicationContext context = new ClassPathXmlApplicationContext(
"/applicationContext.xml", Main.class);
        Object pegasus = context.getBean("pegasus");

        ((Horse) pegasus).ride();
        ((IBird) pegasus).fly();
    }
}
```

So our bean became an instance of `Horse` and `Bird` at the same time and started to behave like that. The following is the output of the application:

```
Pegasus is wandering..!
Pegasus is flying..!
```

BLENDING ASPECTJ WITH SPRING

AspectJ framework offers an easy way for handling the implementation of AOP programming with the help of annotations. Spring AOP provides the feature for using AspectJ annotations, such as `@Aspect`, `@Pointcut`, and `@Around`, `@Before`, `@After` and so on, within the Spring container run time, and the next Try It Out activity shows you an example of logging method execution times with AspectJ.

TRY IT OUT   Logging Method Execution Times with AspectJ

In this Try It Out, you re-implement the example given in the earlier activity that logs the method execution times in a pure annotation-based configuration to demonstrate the AspectJ approach. You can find the source code of the project in the `executiontimeloggingaspectj` file of the code downloads.

1. Add a `spring-aop` dependency to your `pom.xml` file. At the time of writing this book the latest version of Spring subprojects was the `4.0.5.RELEASE`.

```
<dependency>
    <groupId>org.springframework</groupId>
    <artifactId>spring-aop</artifactId>
    <version>4.0.5.RELEASE</version>
</dependency>
```

2. spring-aop depends on the spring-core and spring-beans subprojects, so you need to add them.

```
<dependency>
    <groupId>org.springframework</groupId>
    <artifactId>spring-core</artifactId>
    <version>4.0.5.RELEASE</version>
</dependency>
<dependency>
    <groupId>org.springframework</groupId>
    <artifactId>spring-beans</artifactId>
    <version>4.0.5.RELEASE</version>
</dependency>
```

3. Also add spring-context as a dependency to your project.

```
<dependency>
    <groupId>org.springframework</groupId>
    <artifactId>spring-context</artifactId>
    <version>4.0.5.RELEASE</version>
</dependency>
```

4. Finally add the aspectjweaver dependency to your project.

```
<dependency>
    <groupId>org.aspectj</groupId>
    <artifactId>aspectjweaver</artifactId>
    <version>1.8.1</version>
</dependency>
```

5. Implement the ExecutionTimeLoggingAspectJ advice bean under package com.wiley .beginningspring.ch8, which is the actual implementation that calculates the time spent for each method execution.

```
@Component
@Aspect
public class ExecutionTimeLoggingAspectJ {

    @Around("execution(public * *(..))")
    public Object profile(ProceedingJoinPoint pjp) throws Throwable {
        long startTime = System.nanoTime();

        String className = pjp.getTarget().getClass().getCanonicalName();
        String methodName = pjp.getSignature().getName();

        Object output = pjp.proceed();
        long elapsedTime = System.nanoTime() - startTime;
        System.out.println("Execution of " + className + "#" + methodName
+ " ended in " + new BigDecimal(elapsedTime).divide(
new BigDecimal(1000000)) + " milliseconds");

        return output;
    }
}
```

6. Create the application context configuration file that provides aspect auto-proxy configuration, under the classpath with the folder `/src/main/resources`.

```xml
<?xml version="1.0" encoding="UTF-8"?>
<beans xmlns="http://www.springframework.org/schema/beans"
        xmlns:xsi="http://www.w3.org/2001/XMLSchema-instance"
        xmlns:context="http://www.springframework.org/schema/context"
        xmlns:aop="http://www.springframework.org/schema/aop"
        xsi:schemaLocation="http://www.springframework.org/schema/beans
    http://www.springframework.org/schema/beans/spring-beans-4.0.xsd
    http://www.springframework.org/schema/context
    http://www.springframework.org/schema/context/spring-context-4.0.xsd
    http://www.springframework.org/schema/aop
    http://www.springframework.org/schema/aop/spring-aop-4.0.xsd">

    <context:component-scan base-package="com.wiley.beginningspring.ch8"/>
    <context:annotation-config/>

    <aop:aspectj-autoproxy/>

</beans>
```

7. Create the `MyBean` and `MyOtherBean` Spring beans under the package `com.wiley.beginning-spring.ch8`.

```java
@Component
public class MyBean {

    public void sayHello() {
        System.out.println("Hello..!");
    }
}

@Component
public class MyOtherBean {

    public void sayHelloDelayed() throws InterruptedException {
        Thread.sleep(1000);
        System.out.println("Hello..!");
    }
}
```

8. Create the `Main` class for demonstration purposes.

```java
public class Main {

    public static void main(String... args) throws InterruptedException {
        ApplicationContext context = new ClassPathXmlApplicationContext(
                "/applicationContext.xml", Main.class);
        MyBean myBean = context.getBean(MyBean.class);
        myBean.sayHello();

        MyOtherBean myOtherBean = context.getBean(MyOtherBean.class);
        myOtherBean.sayHelloDelayed();
    }
}
```

How It Works

First you created an empty Java project with the `quick-start` Maven archetype. Then you added the dependencies for `spring-aop` along with `spring-core` and `spring-beans` projects because `spring-aop` transitively depends on them. You also added `spring-context` as a dependency because you used the `@Component` annotation to create sample beans in the project. Finally you added the `aspectjweaver` dependency to the project.

Then you implemented the advice bean, `ExecutionTimeLoggingAspectJ` with the `@Component`. The bean also annotated with `@Aspect` to define it as an aspect. Both of these annotations are required, but `@Component` can be omitted by reconfiguring the `component-scan` tag in the application context configuration as

```
<context:component-scan base-package="com.wiley.beginningspring.ch8">
    <context:include-filter type="annotation"
        expression="org.aspectj.lang.annotation.Aspect"/>
</context:component-scan>
```

The aspect contains a method annotated with `@Around`, which contains the point-cut expression for weaving the public methods. The method takes an instance of `ProceedingJoinPoint` that is used to execute the actual method. You can find the details of this advice in the "Becoming Familiar with Types of Advices" section.

The `@Aspect` and `@Around` annotations are coming from the AspectJ implementation. You can find the list of all the possible annotations in the "Capitalizing on the Power of Annotations" section.

For the application context configuration, you only added one new tag definition: `<aop:aspectj-autoproxy/>`. This enabled the usage of annotations and created the Spring AOP proxies. It just allows the use of annotations and does not involve any usage of the AspectJ run time.

The `<aop:aspectj-autoproxy/>` tag contains the attribute `proxy-target-class` that forces the CGLIB proxies to be created instead of dynamic JDK proxies by setting the attribute value to `true`. As of Spring 4, CGLIB-based proxy classes do not require a default constructor with the help of the `objenesis` library.

> **NOTE** The classes of `objenesis` and `CGLIB` projects were repackaged into the `org.springframework.objenesis` and `org.springframework.cglib` packages, respectively, under the `spring-core` project. So there is no need for third-party dependencies to include for creating `CGLIB` based proxy classes.
>
> You created two different spring beans: `MyBean` and `MyOtherBean`. To demonstrate the usage you also created a `Main` class that creates the application context and then accesses these two beans to call their public methods. The implementations of all these three classes are the same as given in the previous Try It Out activity. The final output of the application is the following:
>
> ```
> Hello..!
> Execution of com.wiley.beginningspring.ch8.bean.MyBean#sayHello
> ended in 15.889 milliseconds
> Hello..!
> Execution of com.wiley.beginningspring.ch8.bean. ↵
> MyOtherBean#sayHelloDelayed
> ended in 1008.861 milliseconds
> ```

CONFIGURING SPRING AOP WITH ANNOTATIONS

It's also possible to do the application context configuration with annotations instead of an XML file. To demonstrate it, we convert the XML configuration that is given in the Try It Out activity from the preceding section into an annotation-based one.

First we need to create a configurator class. The class will have the `@Configuration` annotation, stating that it could contain one or more methods annotated with `@Bean`. For scanning components starting with a given base package, we use the `@ComponentScan` annotation that does the same job with the XML configuration `<context:component-scan>` tag.

The `@EnableAspectJAutoProxy` does the same job with the `<aop:aspectj-autoproxy>` tag, which enables the usage of AspectJ annotations. The whole definition of the configurator class will be as follows:

```
@Configuration
@ComponentScan(basePackages = {"com.wiley.beginningspring.ch8"})
@EnableAspectJAutoProxy
public class ApplicationConfig {
}
```

Now we need to load this configuration in the `Main` class and access the methods of the beans as

```
public class Main {

    public static void main(String... args) throws InterruptedException {
        ApplicationContext context =
          new AnnotationConfigApplicationContext(ApplicationConfig.class);
        MyBean myBean = context.getBean(MyBean.class);
        myBean.sayHello();

        MyOtherBean myOtherBean = context.getBean(MyOtherBean.class);
        myOtherBean.sayHelloDelayed();
    }
}
```

To define the aspects and advices, we can use the annotations shipping with the AspectJ framework. The "Capitalizing on the Power of Annotations" section explains the use of these annotations.

SUMMARY

This chapter briefly defined what Aspect-Oriented Programming is and how it's different from object-oriented programming. You were introduced to the concept of the AOP and its terminology. The chapter explained what Spring AOP offers with its runtime weaving by utilizing the Proxy Pattern, and the first Try It Out activity gave a self-contained example that logs the public method execution times for all defined Spring beans.

The chapter described the types of advices supported with Spring AOP: Before, After Returning, After Throwing, After (Finally), and Around. You saw samples of their uses with the implementation of interfaces and the XML configuration needed to make them run.

Later, you were introduced to the details of the filter expressions that can be used for the point-cuts.

Because Spring AOP employs AspectJ annotations to define aspects, point-cuts, and advices, the chapter detailed them in a separate section with sample codes. The second Try It Out activity showed you how to convert the earlier example into an annotation-based configuration.

Finally, the chapter explained how you can configure the Spring AOP with a pure annotation–based approach and remove the entire XML configuration.

EXERCISES

You can find possible solutions to these exercises in Appendix A.

1. Create a new application that employs the Around advice for logging method execution times.

2. Define an aspect that point-cuts before the methods that are annotated with `@MyAnnotation`.

▶ WHAT YOU LEARNED IN THIS CHAPTER

TOPIC	KEY POINTS
AOP	It stands for Aspect-Oriented Programming, which increases the modularity of an application by employing aspects to meet the cross-cutting concerns across the application.
aspect	It's the common feature that implements the cross-cutting parts of a software system in separate entities. It's the unit of modularity in AOP as compared to the class in OOP.
advice	It is the action, or the chunk of code, that is executed by the aspect at a specific join-point.
join-point	It's point within the actual code where the aspect gets executed to insert additional logic into the application.
point-cut	Point-cut is an expression that selects one or more join-points for execution. It can be thought of as a group of join-points.
target	It's the object where its execution flow is modified by an aspect, so it is meant to be the actual business logic in your application.
weaving	It can be defined as the process of wiring aspects to the target objects, and it can be done at three different levels: compile time, run time, or load time.
AspectJ	It's one of the most popular AOP frameworks that became a de facto standard in the industry. Spring AOP provides integration with AspectJ and its annotations so that they can be used to define aspects, advices, join-points, and so on within the application.
Before	It's the advice that is executed before the join-point.
After Returning	It's the advice that is executed after the execution of the join-point finishes.
After Throwing	It's the advice that is executed if any exception is thrown from the join-point.
After (Finally)	It's the advice that is executed after the execution of a join-point whether it throws an exception or not.
Around	It's the advice that is executed around the join-point, which means it is invoked before the join-point and after the execution of the join-point.
within	It's the keyword that can be used for filtering methods according to its types: interfaces, class names, or package names.
execution	It's the keyword that can be used for filtering methods according to their method signatures.

continues

(continued)

TOPIC	KEY POINTS
bean	It's the keyword for filtering Spring beans according to their names.
@Aspect	This is the annotation that declares the aspect. It should be applied on the class level of a Spring bean.
@Pointcut	This is the annotation that defines the point-cut with the filter expression. A method declaration with a void return type can be annotated with it so that it can be used by an advice.
@DeclareParents	It's the annotation that makes the target objects implement an interface dynamically by also providing the concrete class of that interface.
@EnableAspectJAutoProxy	This is the annotation that makes the usage of AspectJ annotations in an application that employs an annotation-based Spring configuration.

9

Spring Expression Language

WHAT YOU WILL LEARN IN THIS CHAPTER:

➤ Configuring applications with SpEL

➤ Creating a parser

➤ Invoking methods

➤ Working with variables and functions

➤ Understanding SpEL operators

➤ Using utilities in SpEL

> **CODE DOWNLOAD** *The wrox.com code downloads for this chapter are found at* www.wrox.com/go/beginningspring *on the Download Code tab. The code is in the Chapter 9 download and individually named according to the names throughout the chapter.*

An *expression language* (EL) is a special type of programming language that provides for the compilation and evaluation of expressions. With its simple syntax it offers an extensive set of features, including various operators, functions, and variables. The EL is also commonly used in web application frameworks, where these expressions help link the presentation layer with the application data. The first versions of EL derived from other languages like ECMAScript and XPath, but they didn't meet the requirements of enterprise development, so each framework brought its own implementation of EL into the field.

In the history of Java web development, EL was first introduced with JSTL version 1.0, which helped to bridge the application data with the view layer. Nowadays the Enterprise Java ecosystem offers a good deal of options when it comes to the EL. Presentation layer frameworks such as JSF and JSP adopted the *Unified Expression Language* (UEL); other frameworks such as Struts and Tapestry used *Object Graph Navigation Language* (OGNL) under the hood. JBoss EL, MVEL, and JEXL are other alternatives that are available, and they can be also used for dynamic expression evaluation.

Spring Expression Language, or SpEL, is also an expression language that provides an extensive set of features to interact with objects within the run time of a Spring-based application. It provides functionalities similar to UEL and OGNL, and it's based on a technology-agnostic API; thus, other EL implementations can also be integrated. For all the subprojects in the Spring portfolio, SpEL offers the use of expression languages for features such as accessing the nested beans, system properties, and so on, with its dynamic expression syntax. Because of this, it can be seen as a cross-cutting subproject that provides utility features.

With Java EE7, UEL version 3.0.0 was also introduced with a solid overhaul of its features, and it is one of the closest matches to what SpEL offers to its developers. UEL is a union of the expression languages from JSP and JSF. Unlike the previous versions, it supports new features such as method invocation. But because SpEL is tightly integrated with the Spring subprojects, it's very convenient to use it in a Spring-based application instead of dealing with the integration of UEL.

You can use SpEL both within the XML configuration and within the programmatic Java code. In the next section you see demonstrations of the features of SpEL that use these two approaches.

CONFIGURING APPLICATIONS WITH SpEL

While writing an XML configuration or doing annotation-based configuration for an application context, things could get complicated, and you might need a more powerful way to wire the beans or set their property values. SpEL offers a more dynamic approach here in which you can do arithmetic calculations or invoke methods to set values to beans' properties.

This section shows you the simplest SpEL usage with both XML- and annotation-based configuration. The rest of the features that are introduced in this chapter can be applied to both of these configurations, which means that you can use the same pattern of SpEL in your configuration easily. In the following Try It Out, you use SpEL to create a simple XML-based application to inject a system property into a bean's field.

TRY IT OUT   System Property Injection via SpEL

Follow these steps to create a simple application that has XML-based configuration using SpEL to inject a system property into a bean's field. You can find the source code of the project in the `xmlconfig` file of the code downloads.

1. Create an empty Maven application project from the archetype `maven-archetype-quickstart`. Add a `spring-expression` dependency to your `pom.xml` file. At the time of writing this book the latest version of Spring subprojects was the `4.0.5.RELEASE`:

```xml
<dependency>
    <groupId>org.springframework</groupId>
    <artifactId>spring-expression</artifactId>
    <version>4.0.5.RELEASE</version>
</dependency>
```

2. `spring-expression` depends on the `spring-core` subproject, so you need to add it:

```xml
<dependency>
    <groupId>org.springframework</groupId>
    <artifactId>spring-core</artifactId>
    <version>4.0.5.RELEASE</version>
</dependency>
```

3. Add the `spring-context` dependency to the project:

```xml
<dependency>
    <groupId>org.springframework</groupId>
    <artifactId>spring-context</artifactId>
    <version>4.0.5.RELEASE</version>
</dependency>
```

4. Create the `applicationContext.xml` context configuration file under the `src/main/resources` folder:

```xml
<?xml version="1.0" encoding="UTF-8"?>
<beans xmlns="http://www.springframework.org/schema/beans"
       xmlns:xsi="http://www.w3.org/2001/XMLSchema-instance"
       xsi:schemaLocation="http://www.springframework.org/schema/beans
    http://www.springframework.org/schema/beans/spring-beans-4.0.xsd">

    <bean id="show1" class="com.wiley.beginningspring.ch9.MyBean">
        <property name="message" value="#{systemProperties['user.language']}" />
    </bean>
</beans>
```

5. Create the `MyBean` class under the `com.wiley.beginningspring.ch9` package:

```java
public class MyBean {
    private String message;

    public String getMessage() {
        return message;
    }

    public void setMessage(String message) {
        this.message = message;
    }
}
```

6. Create the `Main` class under the `com.wiley.beginningspring.ch9` package and execute the `main` method:

```java
public clas Main {

    public static void main(String... args) {
```

```
ApplicationContext context =
    new ClassPathXmlApplicationContext("applicationContext.xml");
MyBean myBean = context.getBean(MyBean.class);
System.out.println(myBean.getMessage());
    }
}
```

How It Works

First you created an empty Java project with the quick-start maven archetype. Then you added the dependencies for spring-expression along with spring-core and spring-context. spring-expression transitively depends on the core, and you used the ClassPathXmlApplicationContext class, which resides under spring-context, to initialize the application context from the configuration file.

You defined one bean, named myBean. The message field of the bean is set by an expression, and its literal is wrapped with #{...} in order to be evaluated. Here you're getting the user.language system property and setting the value to the message field via setter injection. systemProperties is a reserved word and is used to retrieve the properties of the system with a key value (such as a property name). You can find more information on reserved words later in the chapter in the "Working with Variables and Functions" section.

The output of the application would probably be as follows (depending on your machine's locale):

```
en
```

You can create the same configuration given in the preceding Try It Out using only annotations. Following is the application configuration class:

```
@Configuration
@ComponentScan(basePackages = {"com.wiley.beginningspring.ch9"})
public class ApplicationConfig {
}
```

The MyBean class is defined as a Spring bean with @Component. Here you are using the @Value annotation on the message field that is used to set a default value when the bean is instantiated. The same expression that you used to retrieve the user language system property, #{systemProperties['user.language']}, is used again here to set the value:

```
@Component
public class MyBean {

    @Value("#{systemProperties['user.language']}")
    private String message;

    public String getMessage() {
        return message;
    }
}
```

> **NOTE** It is possible to use the @Value annotation on a field of a class or on arguments of constructors and methods of it.

CREATING A PARSER

We've defined the bits of SpEL and stated a simple scenario for both XML-based and annotation-based configurations for a Spring application. This section gives you a look at the foundational features that SpEL offers, starting with the parsing.

Every expression defined within the context of SpEL gets parsed and then evaluated. The parsing process is handled by the parsers, which implement the `ExpressionParser` interface. `SpelExpressionParser` is an implementation of `ExpressionParser` provided by the SpEL, and it parses the string expressions into compiled `Expression` objects. The instance of a parser becomes thread-safe when created so it can be reused in many places without a problem.

You can easily create a parser for yourself as shown here:

```
ExpressionParser parser = new SpelExpressionParser();
```

After creating the parser, an expression can be parsed with the `parseExpression` method provided by the `ExpressionParser` interface. The expression that will be parsed is treated as an *expression template*, and the template is used to define an *evaluation block*. An evaluation block is determined when a literal is delimited by a prefix and a suffix. By default in SpEL, the prefix is `'#{'` and the suffix is `'}'`. If no prefix and suffix are provided, the expression string is treated as a plaintext literal. (This is valid only for an XML configuration. Programmatic parsing does not require a prefix and suffix unless the default values have been overridden.) As shown in the XML configuration part of the "Configuring Applications with SpEL" section, the evaluation block definition should be done carefully. After creating the parser, the expression can be parsed as in the following:

```
Expression expression = parser.parseExpression("'Hello World!'");
```

With the expression instance created, you can invoke the `getValue()` method to evaluate the expression in the standard evaluation context. (You find out about the purpose of the context in a bit.) The `getValue()` method contains numerous overloaded versions, and one of them is the `getValue(Class<T> desiredResultType)`, which takes a `java.lang.Class` argument in order to set the return type. For the string that you parsed you can set the return type to `String` like this:

```
String value = expression.getValue(String.class);
```

The `Expression` class also contains the `setValue()` method, so it's also possible to set the property of an object that exists in the evaluation context.

The parser can handle the parsing of the literal expressions with different types, such as strings, dates, or numeric values. An instance of the `org.springframework.core.convert.ConversionService` is employed by SpEL to handle these conversion operations:

```
assertThat(parser.parseExpression("'2001/01/01'").
        getValue(Date.class), is(getTime()));
assertThat(parser.parseExpression("0xABCDEF").
        getValue(Integer.class), is(11259375));
assertThat(parser.parseExpression("false").getValue(Boolean.class), is(false));
assertThat(parser.parseExpression("null").getValue(), nullValue());
```

The parser optionally takes a second argument—an instance of the `ParserContext`. This context can also identify the prefix and the suffix that denotes the start and end of an expression. So by providing the context, it's possible to change the default values for the prefix and suffix. The following test method defines _ as prefix and suffix and the expression is parsed according to that:

```
@Test
public void helloWorldParsedWithDifferentPrefixAndSuffix() {
    Expression exp = parser.parseExpression(
            "_'Hello World!'_", new TemplateParserContext("_", "_"));
    String value = exp.getValue(String.class);
    assertThat(value, is("Hello World!"));
}
```

> **NOTE** While doing XML coding for the application context configuration, you have probably come across two syntaxes: #{...} and ${...}. Both of these definitions are valid and defined for different purposes, and they do not cancel each other.
>
> You can use ${...} to define property placeholders, like reading values from a property file and replacing the occurrences with the defined values.
>
> Use #{...} to define a Spring expression that will be evaluated dynamically.

Previously we referred to the evaluation context and its usage while evaluating the expressions. While evaluating an expression, any references that exist within the expression are resolved through a context, which is an instance of the EvaluationContext interface. The default implementation that is provided by the SpEL is an instance of the StandardEvaluationContext. The fields and methods are resolved by the reflection from this context. Variables can also be set to the evaluation context, and they can be accessed while parsing the expression. You can read about examples of this in the "Working with Variables and Functions" section later in the chapter.

In the next Try It Out you create your first programmatic parsing application from scratch.

TRY IT OUT Parsing Hello World with SpEL

Follow these steps to create a programmatic parsing application that evaluates the most fashionable string literal: Hello World. You can find the source code of the project in the helloworld file in the code downloads.

1. Create an empty maven application project from the archetype maven-archetype-quickstart. Add a spring-expression dependency to your pom.xml file. At the time of writing this book the latest version of Spring subprojects was the 4.0.5.RELEASE:

```
<dependency>
    <groupId>org.springframework</groupId>
    <artifactId>spring-expression</artifactId>
    <version>4.0.5.RELEASE</version>
</dependency>
```

2. spring-expression depends on the spring-core subproject, so add it as shown here:

```
<dependency>
    <groupId>org.springframework</groupId>
```

```
    <artifactId>spring-core</artifactId>
    <version>4.0.5.RELEASE</version>
</dependency>
```

3. Add a `junit` dependency in `test` scope to the project:

```xml
<dependency>
    <groupId>junit</groupId>
    <artifactId>junit</artifactId>
    <version>4.11</version>
    <scope>test</scope>
</dependency>
```

4. Create a `src/test/java` folder if it does not already exist in the project.

5. Create the test class underneath it, `HelloWorldTest`:

```java
public class HelloWorldTest {

    ExpressionParser parser;

    @Before
    public void setup() {
        parser = new SpelExpressionParser();
    }

    @Test
    public void helloWorldParsedOK() {
        Expression exp = parser.parseExpression("'Hello World!'");
        String value = exp.getValue(String.class);
        assertThat(value, is("Hello World!"));
    }
}
```

6. Run a test class within your IDE to see the test status bar go green.

How It Works

First you created an empty Java project with the quick-start maven archetype. Then you added the dependencies for `spring-expression` along with the `spring-core` project because `spring-expression` transitively depends on the core. You also added the `junit` dependency to your project because you'll be showing the features of the SpEL within a test class. At the time of writing this book the latest version of the JUnit framework was 4.11.

Then you created the test class to create a parser in the setup method of the test and then parse the `'Hello World!'` string. Because you are parsing a string literal you wrapped the expression with single quotes.

After parsing the literal and getting an instance of `Expression`, you evaluated the value with the `getValue` method by providing a `String` class type. If any problem occurs during the evaluation, an evaluation exception will be thrown by the method. For instance, if you try to evaluate the value as an integer like this:

```java
Integer value = exp.getValue(Integer.class);
```

you get a `SpelEvaluationException` stating the following:

```
Type conversion problem, cannot convert from java.lang.String to java.lang.Integer
```

The final statement in the test method is the assertion that states the value evaluated is equal to `Hello World!`.

INVOKING METHODS

SpEL provides ways to invoke the constructors, methods, or the static methods of classes by evaluating expressions. The following Try It Out activity demonstrates this by invoking a method on a Spring bean and setting the returned value into a property of the same bean.

TRY IT OUT Invoking a Spring Bean's Method via SpEL

Follow these steps to create two beans and set the property of one of them by invoking a method with a given expression. You can find the source code for the project in the `methodinvocation` file in the code downloads.

1. Create an empty maven application project from the archetype, `maven-archetype-quickstart`. Add a `spring-expression` dependency to your `pom.xml` file. At the time this book was written, the latest version of Spring subprojects was the `4.0.5.RELEASE`:

```
<dependency>
    <groupId>org.springframework</groupId>
    <artifactId>spring-expression</artifactId>
    <version>4.0.5.RELEASE</version>
</dependency>
```

2. `spring-expression` depends on the `spring-core` subproject, so add its definition:

```
<dependency>
    <groupId>org.springframework</groupId>
    <artifactId>spring-core</artifactId>
    <version>4.0.5.RELEASE</version>
</dependency>
```

3. Add a `spring-context` dependency to the project:

```
<dependency>
    <groupId>org.springframework</groupId>
    <artifactId>spring-context</artifactId>
    <version>4.0.5.RELEASE</version>
</dependency>
```

4. Create the `applicationContext.xml` context configuration file under the `src/main/resources` folder:

```
<?xml version="1.0" encoding="UTF-8"?>
<beans xmlns="http://www.springframework.org/schema/beans"
       xmlns:xsi="http://www.w3.org/2001/XMLSchema-instance"
       xsi:schemaLocation="http://www.springframework.org/schema/beans
```

```
http://www.springframework.org/schema/beans/spring-beans-4.0.xsd">

<bean id="show1" class="com.wiley.beginningspring.ch9.Show">
    <property name="instrument" value="Piano" />
    <property name="song" value="Turning Tables" />
</bean>

<bean id="show2" class="com.wiley.beginningspring.ch9.Show">
    <property name="instrument" value="Guitar" />
    <property name="song" value="#{show2.guitarSong()}" />
</bean>
</beans>
```

5. Create the Show class under the com.wiley.beginningspring.ch9 package:

```
public class Show {

    private String instrument;
    private String song;

    public void setInstrument(String instrument) {
        this.instrument = instrument;
    }

    public void setSong(String song) {
        this.song = song;
    }

    public String guitarSong() {
        return "More Than Words";
    }

    public void present() {
        System.out.println("Playing " + song + " with instrument " + instrument);
    }
}
```

6. Create the Main class under the com.wiley.beginningspring.ch9 package and execute the main method:

```
public class Main {

    public static void main(String... args) {
        ApplicationContext context =
                new ClassPathXmlApplicationContext("applicationContext.xml");
        Show show1 = (Show) context.getBean("show1");
        show1.present();
        Show show2 = (Show) context.getBean("show2");
        show2.present();
    }
}
```

How It Works

You created an empty Java project with the quick-start maven archetype. Then you added the dependencies for spring-expression along with spring-core and spring-context. spring-expression transitively depends on the core, and you used the `ClassPathXmlApplicationContext` class, which resides under `spring-context`, to initialize the application context from the configuration file.

You defined two beans—`show1` and `show2`—which are the instances of the `Show` class. The bean definitions take values for `instrument` and `song` as properties. Here, the value for `show1` is hard-coded, and the `song` property definition for `show2` refers to an expression string. For the instrument Guitar, you are setting the value for the song by invoking the `guitarSong` method on the bean `show2`. You're dynamically setting the value of the property by getting the returned value of the method. The expression is wrapped with #{...} in order to be evaluated.

The `Main` class creates the application context, accesses the `show1` and `show2` beans, and then invokes the `present` method on both. The output will be as follows:

```
Playing Turning Tables with instrument Piano
Playing More Than Words with instrument Guitar
```

It's also possible to invoke a method on the string literal. The following snippet concatenates two strings and then does an assertion to match the string result, `Hello World!`:

```
@Test
public void helloParsedAndConcatenatedWithWorld() {
    Expression exp = parser.parseExpression("'Hello'.concat(' World!')");
    String value = exp.getValue(String.class);
    assertThat(value, is("Hello World!"));
}
```

You can also chain invocations to access nested methods or properties. The following test method demonstrates the invocation of the `length` method after the `concat` method that is also invoked:

```
@Test
public void helloParsedAndConcatenatedWithWorldAndThenLengthMethodInvoked() {
    Expression exp = parser.parseExpression("'Hello'.concat(' World!').length()");
    Integer value = exp.getValue(Integer.class);
    assertThat(value, is(12));
}
```

Calling Constructors

Within an expression, you can create an object by calling its constructor and providing an argument. The following code creates an expression that creates a `Double` object with the value of pi given as an argument:

```
Expression exp = parser.parseExpression("new Double(3.141592)");
```

Calling Static Methods

With the `T()` operator, SpEL offers a simple way to invoke a static method. By wrapping the fully qualified class name with `T`, you can define the expression as in the following snippet. But the class types that reside under the `java.lang` package do not need to be fully qualified for giving a reference:

```
Expression exp = parser.parseExpression("T(java.lang.Math).random()");
Double value = exp.getValue(Double.class);
```

The preceding example invoked the `random` method of the `Math` class, which returns a double value. It's also possible to access a static constant field on a given class as shown here:

```
Expression exp = parser.parseExpression("T(java.lang.Math).PI");
Double value = exp.getValue(Double.class);
```

> **NOTE** *If you would like to access a nested class that resides in a class, you can concatenate the simple name with $ like so:*
>
> ```
> Expression exp = parser.parseExpression(
>     "T(com.wiley.beginningspring.ch9.
>         domain.MyClass$MyNestedClass).VALUE");
> ```

WORKING WITH VARIABLES AND FUNCTIONS

SpEL uses a context, `StandardEvaluationContext`, to look up any variables that exist within an expression. In an expression, you can reference the registered variables by placing a hashtag prefix (#) in front of the variable name. The test method in the following snippet registers a variable with the `message` keyword to the context, and then an expression is parsed that contains a reference to the variable:

```
@Test
public void variableRegisteredOK() {
    StandardEvaluationContext context = new StandardEvaluationContext();
    context.setVariable("message", "Hello World!");
    String value = parser.parseExpression("#message").
            getValue(context, String.class);
    assertThat(value, is("Hello World!"));
}
```

#root

You can also set a root object in the evaluation context, which will be used by the framework to look up when an unknown method or a property is encountered within an expression. You can access the root object with the #root notation, and it does not change while evaluating the expression. The test method in the following snippet sets a root object to the context with the `setRootObject()` method:

```
@Test
public void rootVariableRegisteredOK() {
    StandardEvaluationContext context = new StandardEvaluationContext();
    context.setRootObject(new MyBean());
    assertTrue(parser.parseExpression("#root").
            getValue(context) instanceof MyBean);
}
```

#this

While iterating through a collection in an expression, the #this variable offers access to the current evaluation. It can be changed during this evaluation, unlike the #root object. The use of #this is explained in the "Collection Selection and Projection" section later in this chapter.

Accessing System Properties and Environment

For accessing system properties or environment variables, SpEL offers built-in predefined variables: systemProperties and systemEnvironment. Actually they are two beans implicitly defined in the AbstractApplicationContext, so in the programmatic approach they need to be accessed with the @ prefix, but in XML definitions you can access them directly by wrapping the expression with #{...}.

Use the following code to access the java.version system property:

```
parser.parseExpression("@systemProperties['java.version']").getValue(context);
```

To access the JAVA_HOME system environment variable, use this:

```
parser.parseExpression("@systemEnvironment[JAVA_HOME]").getValue(context);
```

Note that JAVA_HOME does not need to be defined as a string literal.

Inline Lists

{} represents a list in an expression. {1,2,3} defines a list of integers. It's also possible to create a list of lists as {{1,2},{3,4},{5,6}}. The test methods that demonstrate the creation of lists and the inline lists are shown here:

```
@Test
public void inlineListCreatedOK() {
    List<Integer> value = parser.parseExpression("{1,2,3}").getValue(List.class);
    assertThat(value, hasItems(1, 2, 3));
}

@Test
public void inlineListOfListsCreatedOK() {
    List<List<Integer>> value = parser.parseExpression("{{1,2},{3,4},{5,6}}").
            getValue(List.class);
    assertThat(value, hasItems(Arrays.asList(1,2), Arrays.asList(3,4),
            Arrays.asList(5,6)));
}
```

Registering Functions

SpEL enables registering user-defined methods into the evaluation context with the registerFunction(String name, Method method). The following snippet demonstrates this feature by registering the capitalize method that exists in the org.springframework .util.StringUtils class. You can invoke the registered function by prefixing its name with the hashtag (#):

```
@Test
public void functionRegisteredOK() throws NoSuchMethodException {
    StandardEvaluationContext context = new StandardEvaluationContext();
    context.registerFunction("capitalize",
            StringUtils.class.getDeclaredMethod("capitalize",
                    new Class[] { String.class }));

    String value = parser.parseExpression("#capitalize('hello')").getValue(context,
            String.class);
    assertThat(value, is("Hello"));
}
```

UNDERSTANDING SpEL OPERATORS

SpEL provides a wide range of operators from arithmetic and logical operators to relational and conditional ones, such as ternary or elvis. Table 9-1 lists all the operators that can be used in an expression. The operators defined with symbols can also be determined with a corresponding textual representation if applicable; they are listed after the symbols. The text options are case-insensitive, which means you can blend upper- and lowercase characters together.

TABLE 9-1: Expression Language Operator List

TYPE	OPERATORS
Relational	<, >, <=, >=, ==, !=, lt, gt, le, ge, eq, ne
Arithmetic	+, -, *, /, %, ^
Logical	&&, ||, !, and, or, not, between, instanceof
Conditional	? : (ternary), ?: (elvis)
Regular Expression	matches
Other Types	?. (safe navigation), ?[...] (selection), ![...] (projection), ^[...] (first element), $[...] (last element)

> **NOTE** The textual representations of the operators are reserved words, so try to avoid using them in package names in your project. You may face exceptions while parsing an expression that contains the textual representation of an operation in a fully qualified class name. For example, the following snippet contains the eq operator:
>
> ```
> Expression exp = parser.parseExpression(
> "T(com.wiley.beginningspring.ch9.eq.MyClass).HI");
> ```

Relational Operators

Expressions that use the relational operators always evaluate to a boolean result. The following test method details the relational operators in action with assertions:

```
@Test
public void relationalOperatorsWorkOK() {
    assertThat(p.parseExpression("1<2").getValue(Boolean.class), is(true));
    assertThat(p.parseExpression("2>1").getValue(Boolean.class), is(true));
    assertThat(p.parseExpression("3<=3").getValue(Boolean.class), is(true));
    assertThat(p.parseExpression("3>=3").getValue(Boolean.class), is(true));
    assertThat(p.parseExpression("3==3").getValue(Boolean.class), is(true));
    assertThat(p.parseExpression("3!=4").getValue(Boolean.class), is(true));

    assertThat(p.parseExpression("1 lt 2").getValue(Boolean.class), is(true));
    assertThat(p.parseExpression("2 gt 1").getValue(Boolean.class), is(true));
    assertThat(p.parseExpression("3 le 3").getValue(Boolean.class), is(true));
    assertThat(p.parseExpression("3 ge 3").getValue(Boolean.class), is(true));
    assertThat(p.parseExpression("3 eq 3").getValue(Boolean.class), is(true));
    assertThat(p.parseExpression("3 ne 4").getValue(Boolean.class), is(true));
}
```

Arithmetic Operators

The arithmetic operators are shown in the following test method. Only the modulus operator (`%`) has a corresponding textual representation (`mod`):

```
@Test
public void arithmeticOperatorsWorkOK() {
    assertThat(p.parseExpression("1+1").getValue(Integer.class), is(2));
    assertThat(p.parseExpression("1-1").getValue(Integer.class), is(0));
    assertThat(p.parseExpression("2*2").getValue(Integer.class), is(4));
    assertThat(p.parseExpression("2/2").getValue(Integer.class), is(1));
    assertThat(p.parseExpression("5%2").getValue(Integer.class), is(1));
    assertThat(p.parseExpression("2^3").getValue(Integer.class), is(8));

    assertThat(p.parseExpression("5 mod 2").getValue(Integer.class), is(1));
}
```

Logical Operators

The next test method lists the logical operators:

```
@Test
public void logicalOperatorsWorkOK() {
    assertThat(p.parseExpression("true && false").getValue(Boolean.class),
            is(false));
    assertThat(p.parseExpression("true || false").getValue(Boolean.class),
            is(true));
    assertThat(p.parseExpression("!false").getValue(Boolean.class),
            is(true));

    assertThat(p.parseExpression("true and false").getValue(Boolean.class),
            is(false));
```

```
        assertThat(p.parseExpression("true or false").getValue(Boolean.class),
                is(true));
        assertThat(p.parseExpression("not false").getValue(Boolean.class),
                is(true));

        assertThat(p.parseExpression("3 between {2,5}").getValue(Boolean.class),
                is(true));
    }
```

The `between` and `instanceof` operators are different from the other logical operators. The `between` operator compares the left-hand operator with the list given as the right-hand operator. The list should be a two-element list and can be defined with the curly braces.

SpEL provides `instanceof` to check as it is done in Java, with the keyword `instanceof`. In the following test method, `T()` operator checks for the given string literal to see whether it is an instance of the `java.lang.String` class. The `T()` operator should wrap the class given on the right side of the expression:

```
    @Test
    public void instanceOfCheckWorksOK() {
        Expression exp = parser.parseExpression("'Hello' instanceof T(String)");
        Boolean value = exp.getValue(Boolean.class);
        assertThat(value, is(true));
    }
```

Conditional Operators

SpEL supports both the ternary and elvis operators. The elvis operator is a simplified form of the ternary operator that eliminates the necessity of recurrence of the variable. For the following test methods, a `User` class is defined with a property called `name`. With the ternary operator definition, if the `name` field of a user object is not `null`, the name is set to `Mert`, and if it's `null` it's set to `Funda`. The same rule applies for the elvis operator, and it has a more simplified usage compared to the ternary operator. When the `name` field of the user object is not `null`, the name of the user object is used as the return value of the expression, which is also `Mert` in this example. And if the `name` field is set to `null`, the value `Funda` is used as the return value:

```
    public class User {

        private String name;

        public User() {}

        public User(String name) {
            this.name = name;
        }

        public String getName() {
            return name;
        }
    }

    @Test
    public void ternaryOperatorWorksOK() {
```

```
        User user1 = new User();
        StandardEvaluationContext context1 = new StandardEvaluationContext(user1);
        assertThat(p.parseExpression("Name != null ? 'Mert' : 'Funda'").
            getValue(context1, String.class), is("Funda"));

        User user2 = new User("Mert");
        StandardEvaluationContext context2 = new StandardEvaluationContext(user2);
        assertThat(p.parseExpression("Name != null ? 'Mert' : 'Funda'").
            getValue(context2, String.class), is("Mert"));
    }

    @Test
    public void elvisOperatorWorksOK() {
        User user1 = new User();
        StandardEvaluationContext context1 = new StandardEvaluationContext(user1);
        assertThat(p.parseExpression("Name ?: 'Funda'").
            getValue(context1, String.class), is("Funda"));

        User user2 = new User("Mert");
        StandardEvaluationContext context2 = new StandardEvaluationContext(user2);
        assertThat(p.parseExpression("Name ?: 'Funda'").
            getValue(context2, String.class), is("Mert"));
    }
```

Regular Expression Operator

The matches operator uses java.util.regex.Matcher to match a given operand with a regular expression. The following is a test method that matches the number 35 with regex [0-9]+ and the string literal John with regex [A-Za-z]+:

```
    @Test
    public void relationalOperatorsWorkOK() {
        assertThat(p.parseExpression("35 matches '[0-9]+'").
            getValue(Boolean.class), is(true));
        assertThat(p.parseExpression("'John' matches '[A-Za-z]+'").
            getValue(Boolean.class), is(true));
    }
```

Safe Navigation Operator

The safe navigation operator (?.) provides navigation on the nested properties without getting any exception when a null value is evaluated from any of the properties iterated. Suppose that you have two domain classes named Employee and Address with a one-to-one reference in between that states that the employee has an address. The test for the operator creates an employee with a name but no address value. With the help of the operator, the evaluation of the Address?.Name expression that tries to navigate to the name field of a null address object returns a null value instead of throwing the SpelEvaluationException.

```
    @Test
    public void safeNavigationOperatorsWorkOK() {
        Employee employee = new Employee("Mert");
        StandardEvaluationContext context = new
```

```
StandardEvaluationContext(employee);

    assertThat(p.parseExpression("Address?.Name").
        getValue(context, String.class), is(nullValue()));
}
```

Collection Selection and Projection

With SpEL, it's possible to iterate through a collection in an expression and select some of its elements or transform the collection into another one by doing projection on it. The #this predefined variable is the essence of these operations where you can access the current evaluation.

For doing a selection on the even numbers that exist in the collection {1, 2, 3, 4, 5, 6, 7, 8, 9}, we defined the expression as #root.?[#this%2 == 0 ?: false]. It also uses the elvis operator to simplify the conditional matching because the expression that resides inside the brackets should evaluate to a boolean value:

```
@Test
public void collectionSelectedOK() {
    StandardEvaluationContext context = new StandardEvaluationContext();
    context.setRootObject(Arrays.asList(1,2,3,4,5,6,7,8,9));
    List<Integer> evenNumbers = parser.parseExpression(
        "#root.?[#this%2 == 0 ?: false]").getValue(context, List.class);
    assertThat(evenNumbers, hasItems(2, 4, 6, 8));
}
```

By using ![...],you can project a collection into a new one. For the following User class we fetch the countries of the users' birthplaces and create a new list:

```
public class User {

    private String name;
    private Country birthPlace;

    public User(String name, Country birthPlace) {
        this.name = name;
        this.birthPlace = birthPlace;
    }

    public String getName() {
        return name;
    }

    public Country getBirthPlace() {
        return birthPlace;
    }
}

public enum Country {
    TR,
    USA,
    DE
}
```

```
@Test
public void collectionProjectedOK() {
    StandardEvaluationContext context = new StandardEvaluationContext();
    context.setRootObject(Arrays.asList(
            new Worker("Mert", Country.DE),
            new Worker("Funda", Country.TR),
            new Worker("Tugce", Country.USA)));
    List<Country> birthPlaces = parser.parseExpression(
            "#root.![#this.birthPlace]").getValue(context, List.class);
    assertThat(birthPlaces, hasItems(Country.TR, Country.USA, Country.DE));
}
```

Selecting the First and Last Element of a Collection

SpEL also provides operators for selecting the first and the last element of a collection according to a given selection criterion. To select the first element, use the ^[...] operator; use the $[...] operator to select the last element of the collection. The following test methods filter the first and the last elements, which are 4 and 9, respectively:

```
@Test
public void collectionFirstElementAccessOK() {
    StandardEvaluationContext context = new StandardEvaluationContext();
    context.setRootObject(Arrays.asList(1,2,3,4,5,6,7,8,9));
    Integer element = parser.parseExpression("#root.^[#this>3]").
            getValue(context, Integer.class);
    assertThat(element, is(4));
}

@Test
public void collectionLastElementAccessOK() {
    StandardEvaluationContext context = new StandardEvaluationContext();
    context.setRootObject(Arrays.asList(1,2,3,4,5,6,7,8,9));
    Integer element = parser.parseExpression("#root.$[#this>3]").
            getValue(context, Integer.class);
    assertThat(element, is(9));
}
```

USING UTILITIES IN SpEL

This section covers the utility features that SpEL offers to access Spring beans and to evaluate expressions within JSP pages.

Accessing Spring Beans

While programmatically resolving expressions, it's possible to access Spring beans by putting the @ prefix before the bean name. To resolve the bean you need to register a bean resolver to the evaluation context first. The bean resolver gets a bean factory as a constructor argument, so with the following test method we instantiated an application context with the annotation-based configuration and passed it as a parameter to the bean resolver:

```
@Configuration
@ComponentScan(basePackages = {"com.wiley.beginningspring.ch9"})
```

```
public class ApplicationConfig {
}

@Test
public void instanceOfCheckWorksOK() {
    StandardEvaluationContext context = new StandardEvaluationContext();
    context.setBeanResolver(new BeanFactoryResolver(
        new AnnotationConfigApplicationContext(ApplicationConfig.class)));
    Expression exp = parser.parseExpression("@myBean.sayHello()");
    String value = exp.getValue(context, String.class);
    assertThat(value, is("Hello!"));
}
```

<spring:eval>

With the `<spring:eval>` tag that resides under the `spring.tld` tag library definition, it's possible to render an evaluated value to a JSP page or to assign the value to a variable. The following snippet is the definition of the `myBean` bean that contains the `sayHi()` method and the corresponding JSP page that uses the eval tag:

```
@Component
public class MyBean {
    public String sayHi() {
        return "hello";
    }
}

<%@ page contentType="text/html;charset=ISO-8859-9" %>
<%@ taglib prefix="spring" uri="http://www.springframework.org/tags"%>
<html>
<body>
    <spring:eval expression="@myBean.sayHi()" />
</body>
</html>
```

Expressions in Caching

For the `key` attribute of the `@Cacheable` annotation, it's also possible to use SpEL expressions to evaluate the value dynamically. SpEL usage also applies for the `condition` attribute. Here's a sample definition:

```
@Cacheable(key="#user.name", condition="#user.name.length = 30")
```

SUMMARY

This chapter explained the aim of the expression languages and how Spring Expression Language (SpEL) provides features to meet the enterprise demands. First you saw XML-based and annotation-based configurations that demonstrated the use of a simple expression in a Spring-based project.

Then you created a parser and evaluated your first expression. The chapter mentioned the evaluation context and how it's used to resolve references that exist in an expression. It also explained the difference between ${ } and #{ }. Because SpEL has the capability to invoke methods, you were introduced to the ways to invoke methods, constructors, and static methods.

The chapter explained how a variable can be defined in an expression, covered what #this and #root are about, and listed the predefined variables systemProperties and systemEnvironment. It also detailed the function registration feature that is provided by SpEL.

You were introduced to the extensive set of operators provided by SpEL—from arithmetic and logical operators to relational and conditional ones—and you saw examples of operators for doing safe navigation, collection selection, and projection.

Keep in mind that SpEL expressions are just string literals, so there is no type safety or compile-time check while doing development.

EXERCISES

You can find possible solutions to these exercises in Appendix A.

1. Inject system property 'user.country' via annotation into a property of the bean.

2. Implement a method that reverses a given string and registers it as an EL function. Demonstrate the code within a test method by providing a string to it.

▶ WHAT YOU LEARNED IN THIS CHAPTER

TOPIC	KEY POINTS
Expression language (EL)	A special type of programming language that provides the compilation and evaluation of expressions based on string literals.
Unified Expression Language (UEL)	An expression language that is featured in the Java Enterprise Edition Specification. JSF and JSP adopted UEL and have been using it under the hood. Version 3.0.0 was introduced with Java EE7.
Spring Expression Language (SpEL)	An expression language that provides an extensive set of ways to interact with objects within the run time of a Spring-based application.
@Value	An annotation that can be used on a field of a class or on arguments of constructors and methods of it. It's possible to provide Spring expressions by this annotation in order to set default values into the fields.
SpelExpressionParser	Default parser implementation provided by SpEL that parses the string expressions into compiled Expression objects.
Expression	Interface class that encapsulates the details of the parsed expression string literal.
getValue(Class<T> desiredResultType)	Parser method that evaluates the value from the Expression object. It takes a java.lang.Class argument in order to set the return type.
${...}	Symbol that defines static expressions like the property place-holders in the XML configuration.
#{...}	Symbol that defines dynamic expressions like the Spring expressions in an XML configuration, which will be evaluated dynamically at run time.
StandardEvaluationContext	The context from where references that exist within the expression are resolved.
T()	Operator that gets an instance of java.lang.Class as an argument and it can be used to invoke static methods on the given classes.
#root	Variable that refers to the root object where any references for an unknown method or property is looked up.
#this	Variable that refers to the current evaluation while iterating through a collection in an expression.

continues

(continued)

TOPIC	KEY POINTS
systemProperties	A predefined variable to access system properties with a key value.
systemEnvironment	A predefined variable to access system environment variables with a key value.
registerFunction(String name, Method method)	Method of the StandardEvaluationContext class that can be used to register a user-defined function to be used within an expression string.
lt	Less than operator.
gt	Greater than operator.
le	Less than or equal to operator.
ge	Greater than or equal to operator.
eq	Equal to operator.
ne	Not equal to operator.
<spring:eval>	A JSP tag that renders an evaluated value to a JSP page or assigns the value to a variable.

10

Caching

WHAT YOU WILL LEARN IN THIS CHAPTER:

➤ Building your first caching application

➤ Working with cache annotations

➤ Implementing cache managers

➤ Casting your SpEL on caches

➤ Initializing your caches programmatically

➤ Finding alternative cache providers

> **CODE DOWNLOAD** *The wrox.com code downloads for this chapter are found at* www.wrox.com/go/beginningspring *on the Download Code tab. The code is in the Chapter 10 download and individually named according to the names throughout the chapter.*

We can define *cache* as a storage mechanism that holds the data in one place to be served for future requests in a faster way. One of the common use cases of employing cache mechanisms in an application is avoiding multiple executions of the methods to overcome the performance drawbacks. You can achieve this by caching the outcome data of methods according to the input values given. Of course, you can apply this process to deterministic methods that produce the same output every time, for the exact input given regardless of the numerous executions. If any of the methods contain any implementation of a random calculation computing, for instance, caching will lead to drastic problems, and caching these randomized methods should be avoided.

To boost performance in the enterprise applications, Spring also provides a caching abstraction that offers method-level caching. By employing aspect-oriented programming (AOP) principles, methods are weaved, and if they have already been executed for the supplied arguments, cached results are returned without execution of actual methods. To enable the weaving, proxy classes are generated for all the classes of the application that have the methods marked with the caching annotations.

Spring caching just provides an abstraction and does not involve providing any implementation for the caching infrastructure. A vast number of caching frameworks are available in the Enterprise Java land. This chapter focuses on the features of Spring caching, demonstrates them with examples, and also gives details for integrating third-party caching frameworks such as Ehcache, Guava, and Hazelcast. So stay tuned to boost your applications' performance!

BUILDING YOUR FIRST CACHING APPLICATION

The Try It Out in this section demonstrates caching ability with a simple application. You utilize the Java Development Kit's (JDK) caching under the hood by employing its `ConcurrentMap` class.

TRY IT OUT Caching Service Layer Methods

Use the following steps to create your first application with a Maven archetype and then apply caching on the service layer with Spring caching annotations. You can find the source code for the project in the `simplecachemanager` file in the code downloads.

1. Create an empty Maven application project from the archetype `maven-archetype-quickstart`. Add `spring-core` and `spring-context` dependencies to your `pom.xml` file. At the time of writing the latest version of Spring subprojects was the `4.0.5.RELEASE`:

```
<dependency>
    <groupId>org.springframework</groupId>
    <artifactId>spring-core</artifactId>
    <version>4.0.5.RELEASE</version>
</dependency>
<dependency>
    <groupId>org.springframework</groupId>
    <artifactId>spring-context</artifactId>
    <version>4.0.5.RELEASE</version>
</dependency>
```

2. Create the `User` domain class under package `com.wiley.beginningspring.ch10`:

```
public class User {

    private int id;
    private String name;

    public User(int id, String name) {
        this.id = id;
        this.name = name;
    }

    @Override
    public String toString() {
        return "User{" + "id=" + id +", name='" + name + '\'' + '}';
    }
}
```

3. Create the `UserService` class under the package `com.wiley.beginningspring.ch10`:

```java
public class UserService {

    private Map<Integer, User> users = new HashMap<>();
    {
        users.put(1, new User(1, "Kenan"));
        users.put(2, new User(2, "Mert"));
    }

    @Cacheable(value = "users")
    public User getUser(int id) {
        System.out.println("User with id " + id + " requested.");
        return users.get(id);
    }
}
```

4. Create the `applicationContext.xml` configuration file under the `src/main/resources` folder:

```xml
<?xml version="1.0" encoding="UTF-8"?>
<beans xmlns="http://www.springframework.org/schema/beans"
        xmlns:xsi="http://www.w3.org/2001/XMLSchema-instance"
        xmlns:cache="http://www.springframework.org/schema/cache"
        xsi:schemaLocation="http://www.springframework.org/schema/beans
    http://www.springframework.org/schema/beans/spring-beans-4.0.xsd
    http://www.springframework.org/schema/cache
    http://www.springframework.org/schema/cache/spring-cache-4.0.xsd">

    <cache:annotation-driven />

    <bean id="userService" class="com.wiley.beginningspring.ch10.UserService" />

    <bean id="cacheManager"
          class="org.springframework.cache.support.SimpleCacheManager">
        <property name="caches">
            <set>
                <bean id="users"
    class="org.springframework.cache.concurrent.ConcurrentMapCacheFactoryBean" />
            </set>
        </property>
    </bean>
</beans>
```

5. Create the `Main` class and execute the `main` method:

```java
public class Main {
    public static void main(String… args) {
        ApplicationContext context =
                new ClassPathXmlApplicationContext("applicationContext.xml");
        UserService userService = context.getBean(UserService.class);
        User userFetch1 = userService.getUser(1);
```

```
            System.out.println(userFetch1);

            User userFetch2 = userService.getUser(1);
            System.out.println(userFetch2);
        }
    }
```

How It Works

First you created an empty Java project with the quick-start Maven archetype. Then you added the dependencies for spring-core and spring-context. Spring caching abstraction is not bundled in a separate JAR artifact. The classes—such as the cache annotations—reside under the spring-context JAR bundle.

You created a simple domain class named User, which consists of the id and name fields. You created a service class, UserService, with one method, getUser(int id), for retrieving a user with its ID. The class initializes a user hash map with two elements in an initializer block during its creation. The getUser method is marked with the @Cacheable annotation, which states that the return value of the method will be cached according to its argument.

While defining the application configuration file, you first declared the <cache:annotation-driven> tag, which states that the cache configuration will be done with annotations applied on the bean classes or on their methods. This configuration enables the use of the @Cacheable, @CacheEvict, @CachePut, and @Caching annotations. Because caching abstraction employs AOP principles, the proxy classes will be created automatically when aforementioned annotations are encountered on the beans. You then declared the userService bean as a singleton in the configuration file. Finally, you declared the cacheManager bean as an instance of SimpleCacheManager. The "Implementing Cache Managers" section gives variations of the managers.

> **NOTE** If you forget to declare the cacheManager bean, you will encounter a NoSuchBeanDefinitionException such as:
>
> ```
> org.springframework.beans.factory.NoSuchBeanDefinitionException:
> No bean named 'cacheManager' is defined
> ```

So the cache manager should always be defined if you are using caching annotations in your application. And it should be defined with the name cacheManager unless you've defined it with a different name explicitly using the <cache:annotation-driven> tag.

cacheManager contains the definition of the cache regions determined with the caches attribute. Here, you set an inner bean into caches with the ID users. This is an instance of the class ConcurrentMapCacheFactoryBean. The cacheManager uses ConcurrentMap from the JDK as its backing storage. Out of the box, Spring caching supports JDK's ConcurrentMap with its factory bean approach. The tricky part here is the ID of the inner bean (users) should match the value attribute of the @Cacheable annotation that is used (users). So with this naming convention, you are binding the cache region to the annotation used.

You defined the userService bean in the configuration file, and its corresponding class is the UserService class. UserService contains the getUser method, which is annotated with @Cacheable. Beware that the getUser method is defined with public visibility.

In the `Main` class, you are retrieving the `userService` bean from the context and then invoking the `getUser(1)` method two times. The method prints out a message with the template `"User with id " + id + " requested."` to specify which user is requested with a given identifier. The output of the execution is shown here:

```
User with id 1 requested.
User{id=1, name='Kenan'}
User{id=1, name='Kenan'}
```

As shown in the output, the `getUser` method is executed only once because you're seeing the message from the method just once. At first invocation, the method return value is cached, and when you invoked the method with the same argument a second time, the result was returned from the `users` cache.

Configuring the Cache Manager with a Different Name

When you define the cache manager bean with the ID/name `cacheManager`, the caching abstraction automatically picks it up. It's also possible to explicitly specify the cache manager with a different ID/name. You can do this with the `cache-manager` attribute of the configuration tag as follows:

```
<cache:annotation-driven cache-manager="myCacheManager" />
<bean id="myCacheManager"
      class="org.springframework.cache.support.SimpleCacheManager">
    ...
</bean>
```

Configuring the Caching Abstraction with Annotations

Instead of the XML configuration that you used in the previous section, you can also use annotations to enable the caching mechanism for the `getUser` method. To achieve this you need to create a configuration class first, which contains the annotations needed. The `@EnableCaching` annotation does the same job as the `<cache:annotation-driven>` tag, which states that the cache configuration will be done with annotations applied on the bean classes or on their methods:

```
@Configuration
@ComponentScan(basePackages = {"com.wiley.beginningspring.ch10"})
@EnableCaching
public class ApplicationConfig {

    @Bean
    public CacheManager cacheManager() {
        SimpleCacheManager cacheManager = new SimpleCacheManager();
        cacheManager.setCaches(Arrays.asList(new ConcurrentMapCache("users")));
        return cacheManager;
    }
}
```

You still need to declare the `cacheManager` bean inside the configuration class as you did in the application configuration file, so you used the `@Bean` annotation on a public method that creates a `SimpleCacheManager` and sets a new `ConcurrentMapCache` with the name `users` in it.

By doing this you match the caching storage definition given in the earlier Try It Out activity. After configuring the `ApplicationConfig` class, you can easily create the application context and invoke the `userService` twice as shown here:

```
public class Main {

    public static void main(String… args) {
        ApplicationContext context =
      new AnnotationConfigApplicationContext(ApplicationConfig.class);
        UserService userService = context.getBean(UserService.class);
        User userFetch1 = userService.getUser(1);
        System.out.println(userFetch1);
        User userFetch2 = userService.getUser(1);
        System.out.println(userFetch2);
    }
```

> **NOTE** *The Spring caching abstraction employs AOP principles, so proxy classes are created for the classes that contain caching annotations. Invocation of the cached methods from the methods that reside in the same proxy class does not lead to the caching interception even if the invoked method is marked with* `@Cacheable`.

WORKING WITH CACHE ANNOTATIONS

Caching provides four essential annotations that can be used on either the method level or the class level. Annotations define the methods whose return values are going to be cached to or evicted from the cache storage. The method must be defined with `public` visibility to be cached. `private` methods, `protected` methods, or methods with the `default` modifier are not cached. When annotations are applied on a class, every public method of that class is cached to/evicted from the storage given. This section gives details about the four annotations with their usage and supported properties.

@Cacheable

`@Cacheable` is the main annotation, and it defines that the result of an executed method is cached in a given cache storage. The name of the storage is a required value, and it must be given with the declaration of the annotation. The name could either be defined by its own quotation marks or with the `value` attribute. The following definitions show you the declaration of the `users` cache storage along with the annotation:

```
@Cacheable("users")
@Cacheable(value = "users")
```

It's also possible to provide multiple cache storages as a list with their names separated with commas and wrapped by curly braces. The definition of two storages in an `@Cacheable` annotation with the names `cache1` and `cache2` are given here:

```
@Cacheable(value = {"cache", "cache2"})
```

A proper definition of how the @Cacheable annotation is applied on a method is given in the following code snippet. The getUser method is given and caches the users into the users storage with their id, which is also the parameter of the method. It's also possible to provide custom keys for getting your data stored in a region. The details about the key generation are covered in the "Key Generator" section.

```
@Cacheable(value = "users")
public User getUser(int id) {
    return users.get(id);
}
```

Key Generator

When you look at it from another perspective, you can also call a cache a collection of key/value pairs. By default, the caching abstraction uses the method signature and arguments' values as a key value and stores the key by pairing it with the result of the method invocation. It's possible to customize the key value because the @Cacheable annotation provides the key attribute for this feature where you can specify your custom keys with the Spring Expression Language (SpEL). Following is an example of caching users according to their national identification values. The details of SpEL features are given in the "Casting Your SpEL on Caches" section.

```
@Cacheable(value = "users", key = "#user.nationalId")
public User getUser(User user) {
    return users.get(user.getId());
}
```

Conditional Caching

With the condition attribute of the @Cacheable annotation, it's possible to apply caching to a method according to a given condition. condition makes use of SpEL expressions so it's possible to refer to the method's arguments to evaluate the conditions dynamically. Read the "Casting Your SpEL on Caches" section for information about the SpEL evaluation context.

For the getUser method that was declared by @Cacheable, you are going to apply a condition to enable the caching for users whose age is less than 35:

```
@Cacheable(value = "users", condition = "#user.age < 35")
public User getUser(User user) {
    System.out.println("User with id " + user.getId() + " requested.");
    return users.get(user.getId());
}
```

In the definition, the hash tag (#) defines the variable user, which has the same name as the method's argument. After accessing the argument, you are accessing the age property by navigating to it with a dot. The condition declared for an annotation gets evaluated before the invocation of the method, so there is no redundant execution if the condition is not met.

Like condition, you can use the unless attribute to veto the caching process according to a given SpEL expression. The following example rejects caching the users whose age is more than or equal to 35:

```
@Cacheable(value = "users", unless = "#user.age >= 35")
public User getUser(User user) {
```

```
        System.out.println("User with id " + user.getId() + " requested.");
        return users.get(user.getId());
    }
```

@CacheEvict

The `@CacheEvict` annotation defines that the method is responsible for evicting a value from a given cache storage. Most of the caching frameworks offer the expiration of the cache data in a timely manner, but with this annotation it's possible to explicitly remove stale data from the cache storage immediately. This annotation is often used where the user manipulates the existing data with the update or delete operations. The following method definition removes a user from a map, and the `@CacheEvict` annotation does the same job by removing the cached user from the users storage:

```
@CacheEvict("users")
public void removeUser(int id) {
    users.remove(id);
}
```

As with `@Cacheable`, `@CacheEvict` provides `key` and `condition` attributes where you can specify your custom key and condition with SpEL expressions. The `condition` attribute is not provided with `@CacheEvict`.

Two different attributes are specific to `@CacheEvict`. The `allEntries` attribute defines whether all entries from the cache are evicted. The default behavior is not to evict them. The `beforeInvocation` attribute defines whether eviction is done before the invocation of the method or after. By default, the `@CacheEvict` process runs after the invocation of the method, unlike what happens with `@Cacheable`.

> **NOTE** *Using the `@Cacheable` and `@CacheEvict` annotations on the same method and pointing them to the same cache storage will not make any sense because the data is cached and evicted immediately afterward, so try to avoid using them together.*

@CachePut

The `@CachePut` annotation does the same job as `@Cacheable`, but it always gets the method executed first and then puts the return value into the cache. This is a feasible approach when you always want to update your cache storage with the method return value, as shown here:

```
@CachePut(value = "users")
public User getUser(int id) {
    System.out.println("User with id " + id + " requested.");
    return users.get(id);
}
```

The `getUser` method in the preceding snippet is executed first, and then the outcome value is put into the `users` cache. `@CachePut` also offers `key`, `condition`, and `unless` attributes, like the `@Cacheable` annotation.

@Caching

@Caching is a group annotation where you can provide arrays of @Cacheable, @CacheEvict, or @CachePut for one method definition. To demonstrate this, let's define a domain graph with the Person, Teacher, and Studentclasses. There is a simple hierarchy in between where Person is an abstract class, and the Teacher and Student classes are extending it.

The ClassroomService class in the following snippet is a Spring service bean, and it contains the getPerson method. We declare two @Cacheable annotations and point them to two different cache storages: students and teachers. The method's argument is checked against the conditions of the two @Cacheable definitions to see if it's an instance of the Teacher or the Student class. So according to the instance type of the parameter, the object is either stored in the teachers region or students region:

```
public class ClassroomService {

    @Caching(cacheable = {
        @Cacheable(value = "students",
condition = "#obj instanceof T(com.wiley.beginningspring.ch10.Student)"),
        @Cacheable(value = "teachers",
condition = "#obj instanceof T(com.wiley.beginningspring.ch10.Teacher)")
    })
    public Person getPerson(Person obj) {
        return ppl.get(obj.getId());
    }
}
```

IMPLEMENTING CACHE MANAGERS

CacheManager is the Service Provider Interface (SPI) that provides methods for accessing the cache names and the cache object itself by its name. It's the managing implementation behind the scenes where handling the caching and the eviction take place. This section lists the cache manager implementations that are offered by the caching framework.

SimpleCacheManager

SimpleCacheManager is the cache manager implementation that provides a way to set a list of caches and utilize them for caching operations. Because it's the simple version of a cache manager, we used this implementation in our examples throughout this chapter. The following code snippet is a sample configuration example for the cache manager. For the cache definition here, we use the ConcurrentMapCacheFactoryBean class, which instantiates an instance of ConcurrentMapCache. Under the hood this instance employs JDK's ConcurrentMap implementation for storage:

```
<bean id="cacheManager"
class="org.springframework.cache.support.SimpleCacheManager">
    <property name="caches">
        <set>
            <bean id="storage"
class="org.springframework.cache.concurrent.ConcurrentMapCacheFactoryBean" />
```

```
            </set>
        </property>
    </bean>
```

NoOpCacheManager

NoOpCacheManager is an implementation that is mostly used for testing purposes where it actually doesn't cache any items in the storage. The configuration definition of the cache manager is given in the following code. As shown, there is also no cache list provided for the manager:

```
<bean id="cacheManager"
      class="org.springframework.cache.support.NoOpCacheManager" />
```

ConcurrentMapCacheManager

ConcurrentMapCacheManager is the cache manager implementation that offers the use of JDK's ConcurrentMap under the hood. It offers the same ability with the SimpleCacheManager configuration described earlier, but here we don't need to define the cache storages as we did before. The cache manager definition is shown here:

```
<bean id="cacheManager"
    class="org.springframework.cache.concurrent.ConcurrentMapCacheManager" />
```

CompositeCacheManager

CompositeCacheManager enables us to define multiple cache managers with a single cache manager definition. While declaring the <cache:annotation-driven> tag within the context of an application, it's only possible to provide one cache manager. The composite cache manager definition makes it possible to extend this ability by grouping the cache manager definitions in one place. CompositeCacheManager also provides a mechanism for falling back to the NoOpCacheManager if needed with the fallbackToNoOpCache boolean property. The definition in the following snippet is a composite cache manager definition that bundles a simple cache manager with the Hazelcast cache manager. The simple cache manager defines the teachers cache storage, and the Hazelcast cache manager defines the cache storage for students. The details of configuring the Hazelcast cache manager are in the "Alternative Cache Providers" section later in this chapter. The following example shows that you can store different types of objects in different cache storages, which are also managed by different cache managers:

```
<bean id="cacheManager"
  class="org.springframework.cache.support.CompositeCacheManager">
    <property name="cacheManagers">
        <list>
            <bean class="org.springframework.cache.support.SimpleCacheManager">
                <property name="caches">
                    <set>
                        <bean id="teachers"
class="org.springframework.cache.concurrent.ConcurrentMapCacheFactoryBean" />
                    </set>
                </property>
            </bean>
```

```
                      <bean class="com.hazelcast.spring.cache.HazelcastCacheManager">
                          <constructor-arg ref="hazelcast" />
                      </bean>
                  </list>
              </property>
          </bean>
```

CASTING YOUR SPEL ON CACHES

Spring's caching abstraction leverages the use of SpEL in annotations' attributes such as `key`, `condition`, and `unless`. This provides dynamic generation of the values for the attributes and provides flexibility. The method in the following code caches users according to their national identification number. For the `key` attribute, the expression is used for custom key generation.

```
@Cacheable(value = "users", key = "#user.nationalId")
public User getUser(User user) {
    return users.get(user.getId());
}
```

We can also apply a condition in the following code snippet to enable the caching for users whose age is lower than 35:

```
@Cacheable(value = "users", condition = "#user.age < 35")
public User getUser(User user) {
    System.out.println("User with id " + user.getId() + " requested.");
    return users.get(user.getId());
}
```

SpEL evaluates the expressions in a context, and with caching abstraction it provides cache-specific built-in parameters that are relative to the `root` object. Table 10-1 describes the expressions.

TABLE 10-1: List of Possible Expressions on #root

EXPRESSION	DETAIL
`#root.methodName`	The name of the method being invoked.
`#root.method`	The method itself being invoked. The *method* part of the expression will be an instance of `java.lang.reflect.Method`. The name of the return type of the method can be accessed as `#root.method.returnType.name`.
`#root.target`	The target object instance that contains the method being invoked.
`#root.targetClass`	The class of the target object that contains the method being invoked.
`#root.args`	The arguments array passed to the method being invoked.
`#root.caches`	The collection of caches that is mapped by the method being invoked via annotations.

continues

TABLE 10-1: *(continued)*

EXPRESSION	DETAIL
`#result`	The result of the method being invoked. It can be used with ➤ The `unless` attribute of `@Cacheable` ➤ The `@CachePut` annotation ➤ `@CacheEvict` with `beforeInvocation` set to `false`
`#p<argIndex>`	The argument of the method being invoked. `argIndex` refers to the argument index, and it starts from 0.
`#<argument name>`	Name of the argument passed to the method being invoked. Example usages would be ➤ `#id` ➤ `#name` ➤ `#user` ➤ `#address`

You can read more about the features of SpEL in Chapter 9.

INITIALIZING YOUR CACHES PROGRAMMATICALLY

Sometimes you might need to fill up the cache storages before hitting them with requests. A prominent example of this is loading your data into the caches while getting your application up and running. It's possible to implement this approach by accessing the cache manager first and then manually putting the data into cache storages that are differentiated with names. In the following Try It Out, you load a list of users into a cache region while initializing the context of the application.

TRY IT OUT Bootstrapping Cache Storages

Use the following steps to create an application with the Maven archetype that initializes the `users` cache storage in an `@PostConstruct` annotated method of a Spring bean. The bean also contains the `getUser` method that is annotated for caching. You can find the source code for the project in the `initialisecache` file in the code downloads.

1. Create an empty Maven application project from the archetype `maven-archetype-quickstart`. Add the `spring-core` and `spring-context` dependencies to your `pom.xml` file. At the time of writing, the latest version of Spring subprojects was the `4.0.5.RELEASE`:

```
<dependency>
    <groupId>org.springframework</groupId>
    <artifactId>spring-core</artifactId>
    <version>4.0.5.RELEASE</version>
</dependency>
```

```xml
<dependency>
    <groupId>org.springframework</groupId>
    <artifactId>spring-context</artifactId>
    <version>4.0.5.RELEASE</version>
</dependency>
```

2. Create the `User` domain class under the package `com.wiley.beginningspring.ch10`:

```java
public class User {

    private int id;
    private String name;

    public User(int id, String name) {
        this.id = id;
        this.name = name;
    }

    @Override
    public String toString() {
        return "User{" + "id=" + id +", name='" + name + '\'' + '}';
    }
}
```

3. Create the `UserService` class under the package `com.wiley.beginningspring.ch10`:

```java
@Service
public class UserService {

    private Map<Integer, User> users = new HashMap<>();
    {
        users.put(1, new User(1, "Kenan"));
        users.put(2, new User(2, "Mert"));
    }

    @Autowired
    private CacheManager cacheManager;

    @PostConstruct
    public void setup() {
        Cache usersCache = cacheManager.getCache("users");
        for (Integer key : users.keySet()) {
            usersCache.put(key, users.get(key));
        }
    }

    @Cacheable(value = "users")
    public User getUser(int id) {
        System.out.println("User with id " + id + " requested.");
        return users.get(id);
    }
}
```

4. Create the `ApplicationConfig` class:

```java
@Configuration
```

```
@ComponentScan(basePackages = {"com.wiley.beginningspring.ch10"})
@EnableCaching
public class ApplicationConfig {
    @Bean
    public CacheManager cacheManager() {
        SimpleCacheManager cacheManager = new SimpleCacheManager();
        cacheManager.setCaches(Arrays.asList(new ConcurrentMapCache("users")));
        return cacheManager;
    }
}
```

5. Create the `Main` class and execute the `main` method:

```
public class Main {

    public static void main(String… args) {
        ApplicationContext context =
            new AnnotationConfigApplicationContext(ApplicationConfig.class);
        UserService userService = context.getBean(UserService.class);

        User userFetch1 = userService.getUser(1);
        System.out.println(userFetch1);
        User userFetch2 = userService.getUser(2);
        System.out.println(userFetch2);
    }
}
```

How It Works

First you created an empty Java project with the quick-start Maven archetype. Then you added the dependencies for `spring-core` and `spring-context`. You created the `User` class as a domain object and the `UserService` class as a Spring service bean. `UserService` auto-wires `CacheManager` into itself, and in an `@PostConstruct` method, it puts all the data into the cache with the key value that will be used for retrieval. You can think of this sample scenario like loading a list of users from the database on application startup and putting them into the cache before waiting for the users to log in to the system to get cached.

In the `Main` class, you retrieved the `userService` bean from the context and then invoked `getUser(1)` and `getUser(2)` consecutively. The method will not print out the messages given here because all users exist in the cache:

```
User with id 1 requested.
User with id 2 requested.
```

FINDING ALTERNATIVE CACHE PROVIDERS

Because an enterprise application demands enterprise features, using a cache provider other than `SimpleCacheManager` is what most developers do. Spring caching offers integration with various Cache frameworks in the land of Enterprise Java.

Ehcache

Ehcache is one of the widely used Java caching libraries. The following Try It Out shows ways of integrating with it by employing Spring's caching abstraction.

TRY IT OUT Integrating with Ehcache Cache Manager

Use the following steps to create an application with a Maven archetype that integrates with the Ehcache for the creation of the `users` cache storage. You can find the source code for the project in the `ehcacheintegration` file in the code downloads.

1. Create an empty Maven application project from the archetype `maven-archetype-quickstart`. Add the `spring-core`, `spring-context`, and `spring-context-support` dependencies to your `pom.xml` file. At the time of writing this book, the latest version of Spring subprojects was the `4.0.5.RELEASE`:

```
<dependency>
    <groupId>org.springframework</groupId>
    <artifactId>spring-core</artifactId>
    <version>4.0.5.RELEASE</version>
</dependency>
<dependency>
    <groupId>org.springframework</groupId>
    <artifactId>spring-context</artifactId>
    <version>4.0.5.RELEASE</version>
</dependency>
<dependency>
    <groupId>org.springframework</groupId>
    <artifactId>spring-context-support</artifactId>
    <version>4.0.5.RELEASE</version>
</dependency>
```

2. Add the Ehcache dependency to your project. The latest version available at the time of writing was `2.8.3`:

```
<dependency>
    <groupId>net.sf.ehcache</groupId>
    <artifactId>ehcache</artifactId>
    <version>2.8.3</version>
</dependency>
```

3. Create the `User` domain class under the package `com.wiley.beginningspring.ch10`:

```
public class User {

    private int id;
    private String name;
    private String phoneNumber;
    private int age;

    public User(int id, String name, String phoneNumber, int age) {
```

```
            this.id = id;
            this.name = name;
            this.phoneNumber = phoneNumber;
            this.age = age;
        }

        public int getId() {
            return id;
        }

        public int getAge() {
            return age;
        }
    }
```

4. Create the `UserService` class under the package `com.wiley.beginningspring.ch10`:

```
public class UserService {

    private Map<Integer, User> users = new HashMap<Integer, User>();
    {
        users.put(1, new User(1, "Kenan", "5554332088", 37));
        users.put(2, new User(2, "Mert", "5552345060", 34));
    }

    @Cacheable(value = "users", condition = "#user.age < 35")
    public User getUser(User user) {
        System.out.println("User with id " + user.getId() + " requested.");
        return users.get(user.getId());
    }
}
```

5. Create the `applicationContext.xml` configuration file under the `src/main/resources` folder:

```
<?xml version="1.0" encoding="UTF-8"?>
<beans xmlns="http://www.springframework.org/schema/beans"
       xmlns:xsi="http://www.w3.org/2001/XMLSchema-instance"
       xmlns:cache="http://www.springframework.org/schema/cache"
       xsi:schemaLocation="http://www.springframework.org/schema/beans
http://www.springframework.org/schema/beans/spring-beans-4.0.xsd
http://www.springframework.org/schema/cache
http://www.springframework.org/schema/cache/spring-cache-4.0.xsd">

    <cache:annotation-driven />

    <bean id="userService" class="com.wiley.beginningspring.ch10.UserService" />

    <bean id="cacheManager"
          class="org.springframework.cache.ehcache.EhCacheCacheManager">
        <property name="cacheManager" ref="ehcache" />
    </bean>
    <bean id="ehcache"
          class="org.springframework.cache.ehcache.EhCacheManagerFactoryBean">
```

```xml
                    <property name="configLocation" value="classpath:ehcache.xml"/>
        </bean>
</beans>
```

6. Create the `ehcache.xml` configuration file under the `src/main/resources` folder:

```xml
<ehcache>
    <cache name="users" maxElementsInMemory="1000" />
</ehcache>
```

7. Create the `Main` class and execute the `main` method:

```java
public class Main {

    public static void main(String... args) {
        ApplicationContext context =
            new ClassPathXmlApplicationContext("applicationContext.xml");
        UserService userService = context.getBean(UserService.class);

        User user1 = new User(2, "Mert", "5552345060", 34);
        User userFetch1 = userService.getUser(user1);
        System.out.println(userFetch1);
        User userFetch2 = userService.getUser(user1);
        System.out.println(userFetch2);

        User user2 = new User(1, "Kenan", "5554332088", 37);
        User userFetch3 = userService.getUser(user2);
        System.out.println(userFetch3);
        User userFetch4 = userService.getUser(user2);
        System.out.println(userFetch4);

    }
}
```

How It Works

First you created an empty Java project with the quick-start Maven archetype. Then you added the dependencies for `spring-core`, `spring-context`, and `spring-context-support`. With the `spring-context-support` artifact, Spring ships with the Ehcache cache manager for out-of-the-box integration.

You created a simple domain class named `User` and a service class named `UserService` that contains one method, `getUser(int id)`, for retrieving a user with its ID. The class initializes a user hash map with two elements during its creation. The `getUser` method is marked with the `@Cacheable` annotation stating that the return value of the method will be cached according to its argument. The annotation also contains the condition attribute stating that only users who are younger than 35 will be cached.

You declared the `userService` bean as a singleton in the configuration file and also declared the `cacheManager` bean. With Ehcache, defining `cacheManager` is simple and straightforward. It just wraps another bean named `ehcache` that configures itself with the `ehcache.xml` configuration file.

The simplest `ehcache.xml` configuration file given contains the definition for the `users` cache storage.

> **NOTE** *Ehcache also provides features like TTL or Eviction Policy, which you can configure. The configuration should be done directly by the cache provider because the caching abstraction does not provide any configuration for these features (they might not be supported with different providers, such as JDK's* `ConcurrentMap`*). Please refer to the documentation of Ehcache for further configuration.*

Guava

With Spring version 4.0, Guava is a supported framework with its own cache manager. Guava is an open source common library set that also provides caching features under the hood. The Maven dependency for Guava is shown in the following snippet. The latest version available at the time of writing was 18.0:

```
<dependency>
    <groupId>com.google.guava</groupId>
    <artifactId>guava</artifactId>
    <version>18.0</version>
</dependency>
```

Configuring `GuavaCacheManager` is pretty straightforward. Defining the `cacheManager` bean is enough for getting the configuration up and running. There is no need for defining cache storages because they will be created on demand:

```
<bean id="cacheManager"
      class="org.springframework.cache.guava.GuavaCacheManager" />
```

Hazelcast

Hazelcast is one of the most popular in-memory data grid solutions available in the industry. Like other frameworks, Hazelcast also provides its own cache manager based on Spring's caching abstraction. The Maven dependency for Hazelcast is given in the following snippet. At the time of writing, the latest version available was 3.3:

```
<dependency>
    <groupId>com.hazelcast</groupId>
    <artifactId>hazelcast-all</artifactId>
    <version>3.3</version>
</dependency>
```

Currently `HazelcastCacheManager` resides under the `hazelcast-all` artifact and is not included inside the `spring-context-support`. As shown in the following code, the `HazelcastCacheManager` refers to another bean as its wrapped `cacheManager`:

```
<bean id="cacheManager" class="com.hazelcast.spring.cache.HazelcastCacheManager">
    <constructor-arg ref="hazelcast" />
</bean>
```

With the `hazelcast` bean, you are doing the configuration for Hazelcast by creating your usual users cache storage:

```
<hz:hazelcast id="hazelcast">
    <hz:config>
        <hz:map name="users">
            <hz:map-store enabled="true"
                class-name="com.wiley.beginningspring.ch10.User"
                write-delay-seconds="0"/>
        </hz:map>
    </hz:config>
</hz:hazelcast>
```

The `hz` namespace can be defined with its schema location, as shown here:

```
xmlns:hz=http://www.hazelcast.com/schema/spring
...
xsi:schemaLocation="http://www.hazelcast.com/schema/spring
    http://www.hazelcast.com/schema/spring/hazelcast-spring-3.3.xsd">
```

> **NOTE** Hazelcast expects your domain classes to implement the `Serializable` interface and to contain the default constructor if it's not implemented in your class.

SUMMARY

This chapter explained what Spring offers with its Caching Abstraction. You created an application that defines a simple cache manager, which employs JDK's `ConcurrentMap` under the hood. The chapter explained how to configure the cache manager with a different name and also showed you a full-blown annotation-based configuration that corresponds with the XML configuration.

The chapter detailed the four essential annotations (`@Cacheable`, `@CacheEvict`, `@CachePut`, and `@Caching`) that can be used to cache the data or evict it from the storage. It listed the cache managers you can use with the abstraction and emphasized the importance of expressions in defining the cache regions by giving examples from Spring Expression Language. You also saw how to initialize the cache storages automatically in the application startup, which is a common use case among enterprise applications. The final section listed alternative cache providers—such as Ehcache, Guava, and Hazelcast—and detailed their integrations with Spring's Caching Abstraction.

EXERCISES

You can find possible solutions to these exercises in Appendix A.

1. Create domain class `Course` with properties `id` and `name`. Create a cache manager in Spring configuration and use Hazelcast as your cache provider. Create a `CourseService` bean and implement the `findById` service that returns the course for a given ID. Within the service, cache all the courses that have the name starting with the `BBM` keyword.

2. What's the main difference between the `@Cacheable` and `@CachePut` annotations? Will it be possible to use either of these annotations on methods with `void` return types?

▶ WHAT YOU LEARNED IN THIS CHAPTER

TOPIC	KEY POINTS
cache	A storage mechanism that holds the data in one place to be served for future requests in a faster way.
`<cache:annotation-driven>`	Configuration tag that defines that the cache configuration will be done with annotations applied on the bean classes or on their methods.
`@Cacheable`	Annotation that defines the result of an executed method will be cached in a given cache storage.
`@CachePut`	Annotation that does the same job as `@Cacheable`, but it always gets the method executed first and then puts the return value into the cache.
`@CacheEvict`	Annotation that defines the method that will be responsible for evicting a value from a given cache storage.
`@Caching`	A group annotation where arrays of `@Cacheable`, `@CacheEvict`, or `@CachePut` can be provided for one method definition.
SpEL	Spring Expression Language
`@EnableCaching`	Does the same job as the `<cache:annotation-driven>` tag, which states that cache configuration will be done with annotations applied on the bean classes or on their methods.
`SimpleCacheManager`	Cache manager implementation that provides a way to set a list of caches and utilize them for caching operations.
`NoOpCacheManager`	Cache manager implementation that is mostly used for testing purposes where it actually doesn't cache any items in the storage.
`ConcurrentMapCacheManager`	Cache manager implementation that offers the use of JDK's `ConcurrentMap` under the hood.
`CompositeCacheManager`	Cache manager implementation that allows defining multiple cache managers with a single cache manager definition.

11

RESTful Web Services
with Spring

WHAT YOU WILL LEARN IN THIS CHAPTER:

- ➤ Creating your first REST web service
- ➤ Returning Different HTTP Status Codes from REST Web Service
- ➤ Learning an annotation-based configuration alternative
- ➤ Using REST web services with XML
- ➤ Using the exception handling mechanism
- ➤ Unit testing RESTful services

CODE DOWNLOAD *The wrox.com code downloads for this chapter are found at* www.wrox.com/go/beginningspring *on the Download Code tab. The code is in the Chapter 11 download and individually named according to the names throughout the chapter.*

REST stands for *REpresentational State Transfer*. It is an architectural principle based on top of HTTP to represent resources by doing operations on them. You can definitely say that it's neither a specification nor a standard. It's a way of representing data and manipulating a resource that resides on the server. REST web services solely depend on the HTTP methods. For each method, respective operations on a resource take place.

The GET method is used to retrieve a resource or a collection of resources. The POST method is used to create. The PUT method is used to update, and the DELETE method is used to remove the resource from the system.

Providing REST web services within a web application is one of the most popular approaches for offering your application programming interface (API) to third-party applications. Popular sites such as Facebook, Twitter, and LinkedIn offer REST web services for accessing stored data. Consuming REST web services is also a widely adopted approach in mobile applications for connecting the server-side components with the mobile applications.

Since version 3.0, Spring MVC also offers the creation of RESTful services with the help of data validation, serialization, and de-serialization. In the context of Spring, all requests go through the *Dispatcher Servlet*, which is the main servlet that handles all requests and dispatches to the appropriate channels. The Dispatcher Servlet follows the Front Controller pattern that provides an entry point for handling all requests. You can find more details of the Dispatcher Servlet in Chapter 3.

This chapter shows you how easy it is to create RESTful web services with Spring MVC. So sit up and enjoy the REST in peace!

CREATING YOUR FIRST REST WEB SERVICE

With the Try It Out in this section you create a simple web application that contains one REST web service. You are going to create a domain class and construct service operations to interact with the domain through the REST approach. Figure 11-1 shows a diagram of the service. In the diagram, you see the URLs requested along with the HTTP methods right next to them, and these requests point out the corresponding methods of the REST controller class.

You use *SoapUI* for testing these service methods. It's one of the leading tools available for functional API testing. The Try It Out explains the details of installing and using the SoapUI.

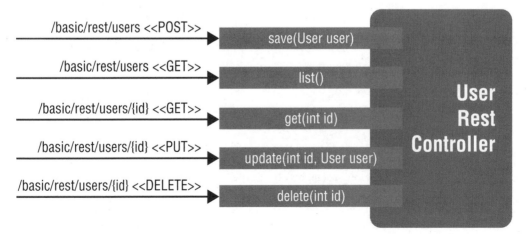

FIGURE 11-1

TRY IT OUT CRUD Operations with REST Web Services

Use the following steps to create a web application that contains a REST web service and to consume service via SoapUI. You can find the source code of the project in the basic file in the code downloads.

1. Create an empty Maven web application project from the archetype maven-archetype-webapp. Add the spring-webmvc dependency to your pom.xml file. At the time of writing, the latest version of Spring subprojects is the 4.0.5.RELEASE:

```
<dependency>
    <groupId>org.springframework</groupId>
    <artifactId>spring-webmvc</artifactId>
    <version>4.0.5.RELEASE</version>
</dependency>
```

2. spring-webmvc depends on the spring-core, spring-beans, spring-context, and spring-web subprojects, so you need to add them as dependencies to the project:

```
<dependency>
    <groupId>org.springframework</groupId>
    <artifactId>spring-core</artifactId>
    <version>4.0.5.RELEASE</version>
</dependency>

<dependency>
    <groupId>org.springframework</groupId>
    <artifactId>spring-beans</artifactId>
    <version>4.0.5.RELEASE</version>
</dependency>

<dependency>
    <groupId>org.springframework</groupId>
    <artifactId>spring-context</artifactId>
    <version>4.0.5.RELEASE</version>
</dependency>

<dependency>
    <groupId>org.springframework</groupId>
    <artifactId>spring-web</artifactId>
    <version>4.0.5.RELEASE</version>
</dependency>
```

3. Add the jackson-core and jackson-databind dependencies to your pom.xml file. At the time of writing, the latest version of the Jackson projects is 2.4.0:

```
<dependency>
    <groupId>com.fasterxml.jackson.core</groupId>
    <artifactId>jackson-core</artifactId>
    <version>2.4.0</version>
</dependency>

<dependency>
    <groupId>com.fasterxml.jackson.core</groupId>
    <artifactId>jackson-databind</artifactId>
```

```
    <version>2.4.0</version>
</dependency>
```

4. Create the `User` domain class under the `com.wiley.beginningspring.ch11` package:

```java
public class User {

    private int id;
    private String name;

    public User() {}

    public User(int id, String name) {
        this.id = id;
        this.name = name;
    }

    public int getId() {
        return id;
    }

    public String getName() {
        return name;
    }
}
```

5. Create the `UserRepository` class under the `com.wiley.beginningspring.ch11` package:

```java
@Repository
public class UserRepository {

    private Map<Integer, User> users = new HashMap<Integer, User>();

    @PostConstruct
    public void setup() {
        users.put(1, new User(1, "Mert Caliskan"));
        users.put(2, new User(2, "Kenan Sevindik"));
    }

    public void save(User user) {
        users.put(user.getId(), user);
    }

    public List<User> findAll() {
        return new ArrayList<User>(users.values());
    }

    public User find(int id) {
        return users.get(id);
    }

    public void update(int id, User user) {
        users.put(id, user);
    }
```

```
        public void delete(int id) {
            users.remove(id);
        }
    }
```

6. Create the `UserRestController` class under the `com.wiley.beginningspring.ch11` package:

```
@RestController
@RequestMapping("/rest")
public class UserRestController {

    @Autowired
    private UserRepository userRepository;

    @RequestMapping(value = "/users", method=RequestMethod.POST)
    public void save(@RequestBody User user) {
        userRepository.save(user);
    }

    @RequestMapping(value = "/users", method=RequestMethod.GET)
    public List<User> list() {
        return userRepository.findAll();
    }

    @RequestMapping(value="/users/{id}", method=RequestMethod.GET)
    public User get(@PathVariable("id") int id) {
        return userRepository.find(id);
    }

    @RequestMapping(value="/users/{id}", method=RequestMethod.PUT)
    public void update(@PathVariable("id") int id, @RequestBody User user) {
        userRepository.update(id, user);
    }

    @RequestMapping(value="/users/{id}", method=RequestMethod.DELETE)
    public ResponseEntity<Boolean> delete(@PathVariable("id") int id) {
        userRepository.delete(id);
        return new ResponseEntity<Boolean>(Boolean.TRUE, HttpStatus.OK);
    }
}
```

7. Create the `springmvc-servlet.xml` configuration file under the `src/main/webapp/WEB-INF` folder:

```
<?xml version="1.0" encoding="UTF-8"?>
<beans xmlns="http://www.springframework.org/schema/beans"
       xmlns:xsi="http://www.w3.org/2001/XMLSchema-instance"
       xmlns:context"http://www.springframework.org/schema/context"
       xmlns:mvc="http://www.springframework.org/schema/mvc"
       xsi:schemaLocation="http://www.springframework.org/schema/beans
    http://www.springframework.org/schema/beans/spring-beans-4.0.xsd
    http://www.springframework.org/schema/context
    http://www.springframework.org/schema/context/spring-context-4.0.xsd
    http://www.springframework.org/schema/mvc
```

```
http://www.springframework.org/schema/mvc/spring-mvc-4.0.xsd">

<context:component-scan base-package="com.wiley.beginningspring.ch11" />
<context:annotation-config />

<mvc:annotation-driven />
</beans>
```

8. Define the Dispatcher Servlet with its URL mapping in your web.xml file:

```
<web-app xmlns="http://xmlns.jcp.org/xml/ns/javaee"
    xmlns:xsi="http://www.w3.org/2001/XMLSchema-instance"
    xsi:schemaLocation="http://xmlns.jcp.org/xml/ns/javaee
http://xmlns.jcp.org/xml/ns/javaee/web-app_3_1.xsd"
    version="3.1">

<servlet>
<servlet-name>springmvc</servlet-name>
    <servlet-class>
        org.springframework.web.servlet.DispatcherServlet
    </servlet-class>
    <load-on-startup>1</load-on-startup>
</servlet>

<servlet-mapping>
    <servlet-name>springmvc</servlet-name>
    <url-pattern>/*</url-pattern>
</servlet-mapping>
</web-app>
```

We defined the web.xml compatible with Servlet 3.1 as shown in the namespace definitions. If you are not using a Java EE7 container then you can define the web.xml file compatible with Servlet 3.0 as shown here:

```
<web-app xmlns="http://java.sun.com/xml/ns/javaee"
    xmlns:xsi="http://www.w3.org/2001/XMLSchema-instance"
    xsi:schemaLocation="http://java.sun.com/xml/ns/javaee
http://java.sun.com/xml/ns/javaee/web-app_3_0.xsd"
    version="3.0">
...
</web-app>
```

9. Deploy the application on a web container. You can use Tomcat 8.0.12 or Jetty 9.2.3 as a container for deploying the application. After deploying, simply run the container.

10. Install SoapUI by downloading it from http://sourceforge.net/projects/soapui/files/soapui/5.0.0. At the time of writing, the latest version of SoapUI is 5.0.0.

11. From the File menu of SoapUI, select New REST Project. You see the screen shown in Figure 11-2. Enter **http://localhost:8080/basic/rest/users** into the URI field.

12. After clicking OK, REST Project 1 is added to the list of Projects on the left side of the SoapUI as shown in Figure 11-3.

13. Open Request 1 as shown in Figure 11-4. Make sure that you're at the JSON tab on the right for the output.

New REST Project
New REST Project
Creates a new REST Project in this workspace
URI: http://localhost:8080/basic/rest/users
OK
Cancel
Import WADL...

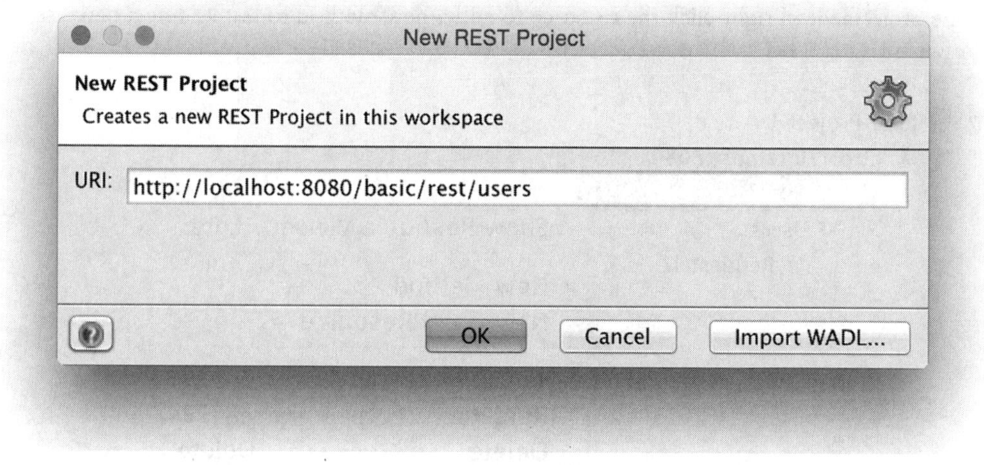

FIGURE 11-2

REST Project 1
http://localhost:8080
Users [/basic/rest/users]
GET Users
Request 1

FIGURE 11-3

Request 1
Method
GET
Endpoint
http://localhost:8080
Resource
/basic/rest/users
Parameters
Name
Value
Style
Level
Request
Raw
Required:
Sets if pa
XML
JSON
HTML
Raw
[
{
"id" : 1,
"name" : "Mert Caliskan"
},
{
"id" : 2,
"name" : "Kenan Sevindik"
}
]
response time: 69ms (66 bytes)
1 : 1

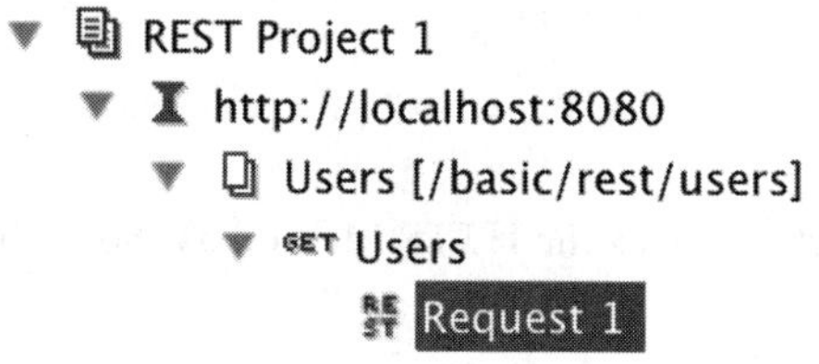

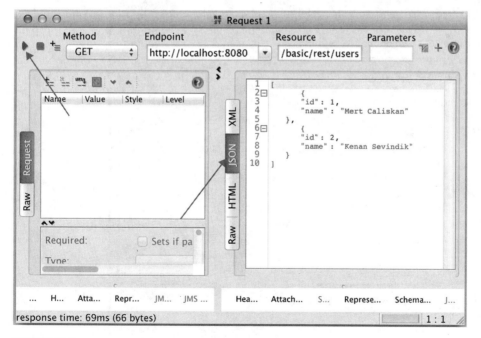

FIGURE 11-4

14. In the projects view, right-click the resource to add a new method to test adding a new user, as shown in Figure 11-5.

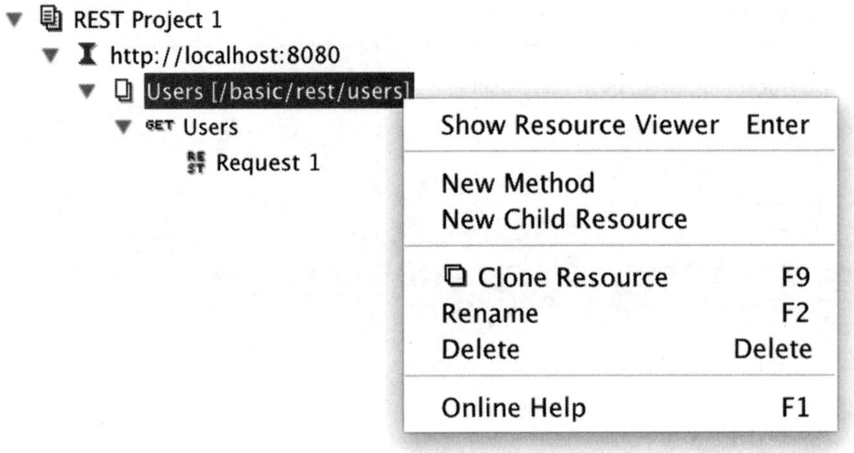

FIGURE 11-5

15. In the Method Name field, enter **New User** and select POST as the HTTP Method as shown in Figure 11-6.

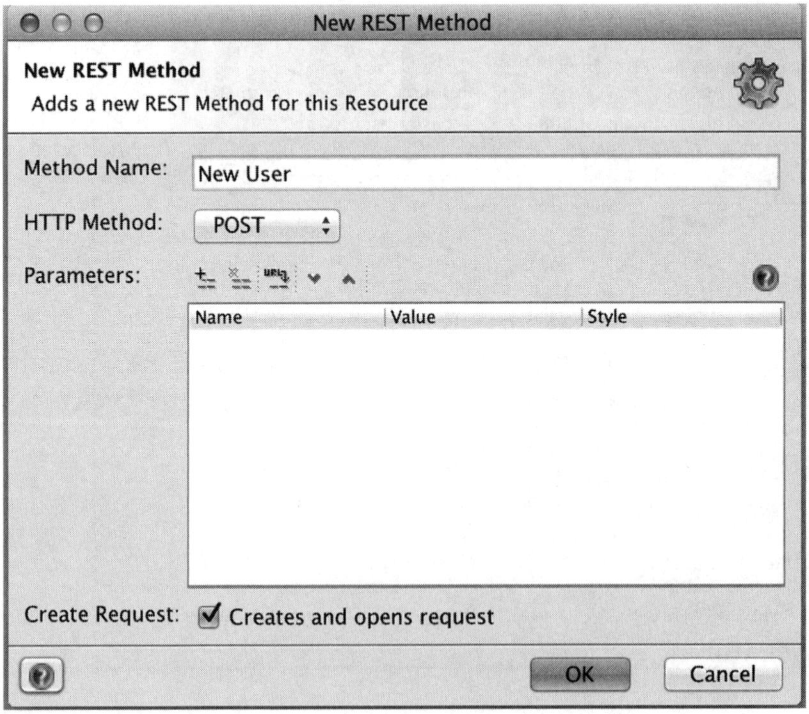

FIGURE 11-6

16. For the request, select application/json as the media type and enter **{"id":3,"name":"Funda Bayulu"}** into the text area. When you click the Run button you won't get any response as JSON. Just check for response time at the bottom of the screen as indicated in Figure 11-7.

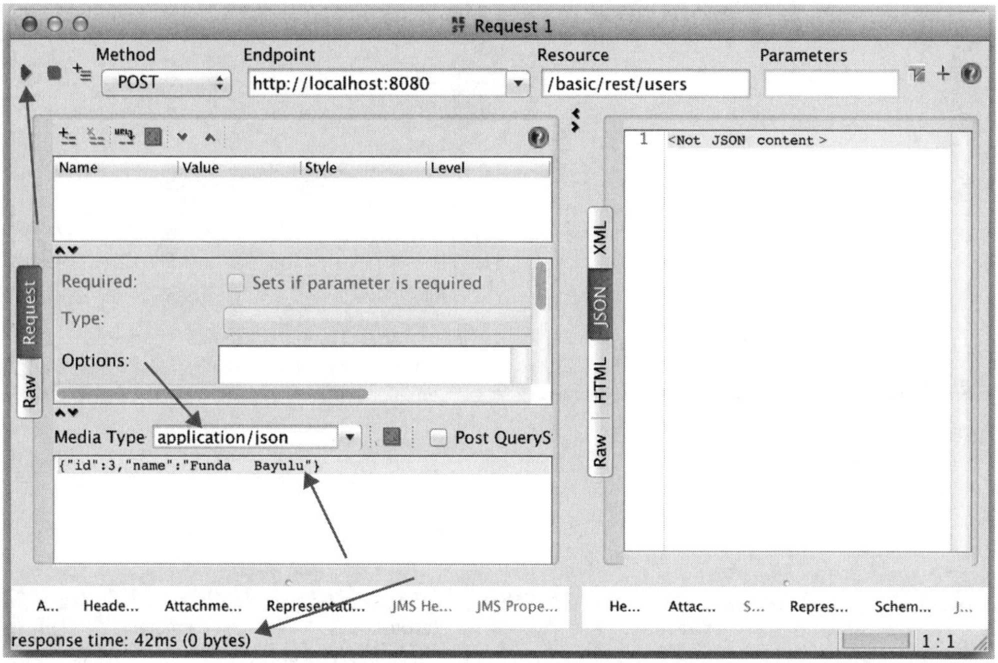

FIGURE 11-7

17. Execute the previous request of the Users method to see the newly added user in the JSON response, as shown in Figure 11-8.

18. Add a new method with the name **Update User** and select PUT as the HTTP Method.

19. Enter **/basic/rest/users/3** as the Resource, select application/json as the Media Type, and enter **{"id":3,"name":"Funda Caliskan"}** into the text area as shown in Figure 11-9. Click the Run button. Again, you won't get any response as JSON. Just check the response time at the bottom of the screen.

20. Execute the first GET method request to see the updated user with ID 3. You should see the JSON output as shown here:

```
[
    {
    "id": 1,
    "name": "Mert Caliskan"
    },
    {
```

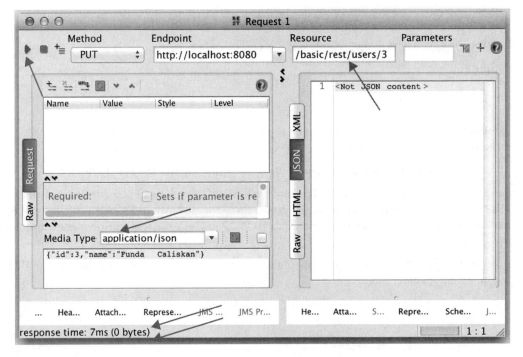

FIGURE 11-8

FIGURE 11-9

```
      "id": 2,
      "name": "Kenan Sevindik"
   },
      {
      "id": 3,
      "name": "Funda Caliskan"
   }
]
```

21. Add a new method with the name `Delete User` and select `DELETE` as the HTTP Method.

22. Enter `/basic/rest/users/3` as the Resource and click the Run button as shown in Figure 11-10. You should see `true` as the JSON response.

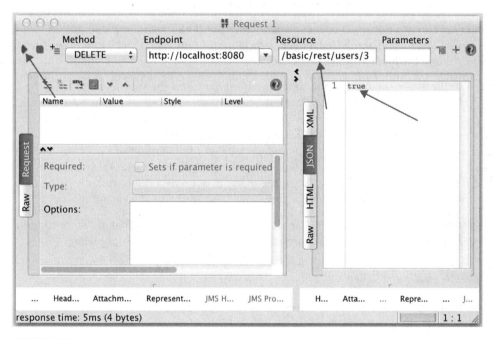

FIGURE 11-10

How It Works

First you created an empty Java project with the quick-start Maven archetype. Then you added the dependency for the `spring-webmvc`. Because the `spring-webmvc` artifact depends on `spring-core`, `spring-beans`, `spring-context`, and `spring-web`, you also added them as dependencies.

You then added the Jackson dependencies, which is the framework for handling serialization/ deserialization and mapping of the objects to JSON. Jackson provides two branches: one tagged for 1.x, and the other for the 2.x versions. At the time of writing this book, 2.x is the active development track, and with Spring 4 this branch is currently being supported. Dropping the Jackson artifacts on the class path automatically enables the use of the message converters for serializing/deserializing to JSON. You can state that this integration demands zero configurations. Spring offers two different converters per branch: MappingJackson2HttpMessageConverter and MappingJacksonHttpMessageConverter. The converter class with 2 in its name supports the 2.x branch.

You created a simple domain class named User, which consists of the id and name fields. You implemented a repository class, UserRepository, which acts as a data access layer object. It stores two users in a map; the users are instantiated within the @PostConstruct method. UserRepository offers four methods:

➤   void save(User user): Saves a user within the map by using its ID as the key

➤   List<User> findAll(): Returns the list of all users from the map

➤   User find(int id): Returns a specific user from the map given by its ID

➤   void delete(int id): Removes a specific user from the map given by its ID

The third and final class was UserRestController, which is a REST web service controller that exposes the service methods. It autowires the repository instance into itself and again offers four methods that correspond to the methods of the repository.

With Spring 4.0, the @ResponseBody annotation has been moved to the type level, so it can be added to interfaces, classes, or other annotations. With the help of @ResponseBody, Spring 4.0 introduced @RestController, a convenience annotation that composes the @Controller and @ResponseBody annotations together in one place. Our REST controller class contains this annotation on its class level so we did not need to define the @ResponseBody on each method of the controller. @ResponseBody is responsible for automatic conversion of the response to a JSON string literal by applying the serialization on the return value of the method. @Controller is an annotation that inherits from @Component, which provides the creation of the Spring beans via annotations.

As previously stated, the UserRestController class contains four methods that are mapped with the @RequestMapping annotations. Their signatures are given in the following code snippet:

```
@RequestMapping(value = "/users", method=RequestMethod.POST
void save(@RequestBody User user);

@RequestMapping(value = "/users", method=RequestMethod.GET)
List<User> list();

@RequestMapping(value="/users/{id}", method=RequestMethod.GET)
User get(@PathVariable("id") int id);

@RequestMapping(value="/users/{id}", method=RequestMethod.PUT)
void update(@PathVariable("id") int id, @RequestBody User user);

@RequestMapping(value="/users/{id}", method=RequestMethod.DELETE)
ResponseEntity<Boolean> delete(@PathVariable("id") int id);
```

@RequestMapping enables the mapping of web requests onto these handler methods. The class itself also contains the @RequestMapping annotation, which enables a base mapping URI for all the methods that reside inside the class. So the template URI for the requests would be like this:

```
http://<server-name>:<server-port>/<servlet-context>/<base-mapping>/<handler-method-mapping>
```

If you want to invoke the `list()` method, you need to request a URI with an HTTP POST method as shown here:

```
http://localhost:8080/basic/rest/users
```

Of course, doing these test requests with web browsers might not be suitable for all cases. Thus you used SoapUI for testing the REST web services. SoapUI has become a de facto functional testing tool in the industry, and it eases doing the requests with different HTTP methods because of its friendly user interface. You can read more about the usage scenarios of the SoapUI later in this Try It Out and also in the following Try It Out sections of this chapter. You can also use `curl` if you want; it's a command-line tool for doing HTTP requests. The `curl` version of retrieving the user list is the following:

```
curl -i -X GET -H "Content-Type:application/json" ↵
    http://localhost:8080/basic/rest/users
```

You created the `springmvc-servlet.xml` file under the `WEB-INF` folder of the web application, and it configures the Spring application context. It's being picked up with the naming convention `{servletname}-servlet.xml`. Within the configuration file, the `<context:component-scan>` tag states that all the beans that reside under the package `com.wiley.beginningspring.ch11` will be registered to the application context automatically. The `<context:annotation-config/>` tag activates the annotations that are defined in the beans, which are already registered within the context of the application. The `<mvc:annotation-driven />` tag configures the annotation-driven Spring MVC Controller programming model. In this case, by default, it enables features such as the registration of message converters that were mentioned earlier for the Jackson framework.

In the `web.xml` file, you defined the Dispatcher Servlet with the URL mapping as /*. So all the requests go through the Dispatcher Servlet. It handles the incoming request and decides which controller should handle the request with the help of the Handler Mappings.

After deploying the application on a web container you tested it with the SoapUI tool. The following is a list of tested URLs with the corresponding HTTP methods:

➤ **URI:** `http://localhost:8080/basic/rest/users`

  ➤ **HTTP Method:** GET

  ➤ **Activity:** Returns the list of all users

➤ **URI:** `http://localhost:8080/basic/rest/users`

  ➤ **HTTP Method:** POST

  ➤ **Activity:** Adds a new user

➤ **URI:** `http://localhost:8080/basic/rest/users/3`

  ➤ **HTTP Method:** PUT

  ➤ **Activity:** Updates the user specified with its id

➤ **URI:** `http://localhost:8080/basic/rest/users/3`

   ➤ **HTTP Method:** `DELETE`

   ➤ **Activity:** Deletes the user specified with its id

The test methods given in the steps of the Try It Out are self-explanatory. Note the URI syntax for the `PUT` and `DELETE` methods where you specify the URI template `{id}` to pass the parameter to the method with `@PathVariable` annotated method argument. With the test cases you are setting the value 3 for the ID value to update and delete a user.

> **NOTE** *REST web services provided by Spring MVC are not compliant with the JAX-RS specification. So annotations like* `@Path`*,* `@GET`*,* `@POST`*, and many others that come with the JAX-RS specification are not supported by Spring MVC.*

RETURNING DIFFERENT HTTP STATUS CODES FROM REST WEB SERVICE

Spring MVC offers the `HttpStatus` enumeration class that conforms to the HTTP status codes, from 1xx to 5xx, which is from 100 to 500. In the earlier Try It Out you returned `HTTP code 200 (OK)` in the `delete` method to inform the user about the action result. Table 11-1 lists the categories of the status codes. The codes fall into one of these five different categories.

TABLE 11-1: The List of HTTP Status Codes

CODE	DETAIL
1xx	Informational
2xx	Success
3xx	Redirection
4xx	Client error
5xx	Server error

LEARNING AN ANNOTATION-BASED CONFIGURATION ALTERNATIVE

It's also possible to do the application context configuration only with annotations instead of using any XML. The Try It Out in this section is a redo of the earlier Try It Out. It uses a pure annotation-based configuration.

TRY IT OUT REST Web Services with Annotation Configuration

Use the following steps to create an application that contains REST web services, which are configured by annotations. You can find the source code for the project in the basicwithannotations file in the code downloads.

1. Follow steps 1 through 6 of the first Try It Out.

2. Instead of defining the XML configuration given in step 7 of the earlier Try It Out, create the AppConfig class given in the following snippet under the package com.wiley.beginningspring.ch11:

```
@Configuration
@ComponentScan(basePackages = {"com.wiley.beginningspring.ch11"})
@EnableWebMvc
public class AppConfig {
}
```

3. Define the Dispatcher Servlet with its URL mapping in your web.xml file. The servlet also refers to the AppConfig class that does the actual context configuration:

```
<web-app xmlns="http://xmlns.jcp.org/xml/ns/javaee"
         xmlns:xsi="http://www.w3.org/2001/XMLSchema-instance"
         xsi:schemaLocation="http://xmlns.jcp.org/xml/ns/javaee
    http://xmlns.jcp.org/xml/ns/javaee/web-app_3_1.xsd"
    version="3.1">

    <servlet>
        <servlet-name>springmvc</servlet-name>
        <servlet-class>
            org.springframework.web.servlet.DispatcherServlet
        </servlet-class>
        <init-param>
            <param-name>contextClass</param-name>
            <param-value>
    org.springframework.web.context.support.AnnotationConfigWebApplicationContext
            </param-value>
        </init-param>
        <init-param>
             <param-name>contextConfigLocation</param-name>
             <param-value>
                 com.wiley.beginningspring.ch11.config.AppConfig
             </param-value>
         </init-param>
         <load-on-startup>1</load-on-startup>
    </servlet>

    <servlet-mapping>
        <servlet-name>springmvc</servlet-name>
        <url-pattern>/*</url-pattern>
    </servlet-mapping>
 </web-app>
```

4. Follow steps 9 to 22 of the earlier Try It Out. Throughout the steps specified, the servlet context path will be basicwithannotations instead of basic.

How It Works

To configure the application with annotations you first created the `AppConfig` class that is marked with `@Configuration`. This class is provided as a parameter in `web.xml`; you read more about that later in this section. For scanning components starting with a given base package you also used the `@ComponentScan` annotation that does the same job with XML's `<context:component-scan>` tag. One final annotation used on the configurator class is `@EnableWebMvc`, which does the same job as XML's `<mvc:annotation-driven>` tag for enabling MVC-centric features.

You also reconfigured the definition of the Dispatcher Servlet to load the application context via a class definition. With this approach the `contextClass` parameter refers to the `org.springframework.web`
`.context.support.AnnotationConfigWebApplicationContext` class, which is an implementation of `ApplicationContext`. This class uses the `contextConfigLocation` parameter to get the class annotated with `@Configuration`; in the example, it is the fully qualified name of the `AppConfig` class.

USING REST WEB SERVICES WITH XML

JSON stands for JavaScript Object Notation, which is a language-independent text format that enables you to represent objects as name/value pairs in an easily readable format. It's widely adopted in the industry, and many API providers have shifted from XML to JSON. XML is another option for formatted messaging between systems, and it provides features such as extensible architecture with name spacing, verbosity with its opening and closing tags, and validation of its content with predefined rules. Compared to JSON, it's our opinion that XML is harder to read with human eyes and slower to parse by computers. Because XML provides a more structured representation of the data, both of these message mechanisms offer usage scenarios with different pros and cons.

One misconception for REST web services is that they can only generate JSON responses. On the contrary—Spring MVC offers the architecture for enabling message converters that handle XML requests/responses with REST web services. In the following Try It Out you modify the first Try It Out to provide XML output instead of JSON.

TRY IT OUT   REST Web Services with XML Response

Use the following steps to create an application to produce an XML response out of a REST web service. You can find the source code for the project in the `basicwithxml` file in the code downloads.

1. Follow steps 1 and 2 of the "CRUD Operations with REST Web Services" Try It Out.

2. Create the following `User` class under the `com.wiley.beginningspring.ch11` package:

```
@XmlRootElement
public class User {

    @XmlElement
    private int id;
    @XmlElement
    private String name;

    public User() {}

    public User(int id, String name) {
```

```
            this.id = id;
            this.name = name;
        }

        public int getId() {
            return id;
        }

        public String getName() {
            return name;
        }
    }
```

3. Follow steps 5 through 10 of the first Try It Out.

4. From the File menu of SoapUI, select New REST Project. You see the screen shown in Figure 11-11. Enter **http://localhost:8080/basicwithxml/rest/users/1** into the URI field.

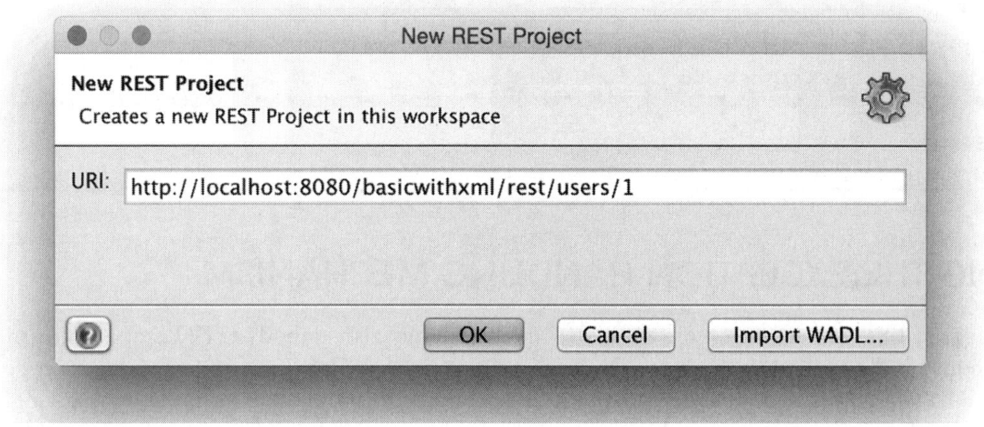

FIGURE 11-11

5. Enter **/basicwithxml/rest/users/1** in the Resource field and click the Run button. You should see XML output for the user as shown in Figure 11-12.

How It Works

Because you won't be generating any JSON output you omitted defining the Jackson project dependencies. You defined your User class annotated with the JAXB annotations such as @XmlRootElement and @XmlElement. You haven't added any dependencies for using these annotations because they come out of the box with the JDK.

With SoapUI, you made a request similar to the one you made with JSON. JAXB automatically created the XML tags for you with the User class name and the name of the properties that reside in the class.

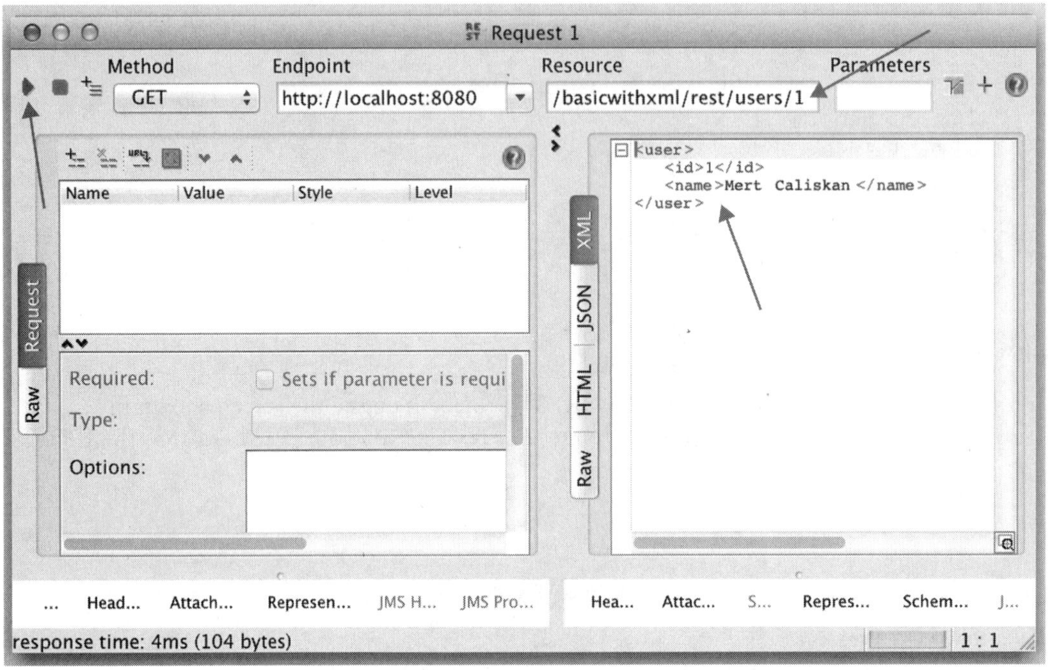

FIGURE 11-12

USING THE EXCEPTION HANDLING MECHANISM

Because REST web services work on HTTP methods, they also embody HTTP status codes in the response to the state of the result of the request. It is one of the best practices to use these codes in the RESTful API design, but they provide more generic data about an error rather than giving a detailed description on a particular problem. It's vital to give as much information as possible to API consumers because the easier it is to consume an API, the more likely it will be widely adopted and used.

With the Try It Out in this section you modify the `get` method that exists in the "CRUD Operations with REST Web Services" Try It Out to throw an exception when the requested user cannot be found. This exception is globally handled, and a custom JSON response is generated in order to return a response.

TRY IT OUT   Exception Handling in REST Web Services

Use the following steps to create an application that handles an exception that occurred in a REST web service. You can find the source code for the project in the `exceptionhandling` file in the code downloads.

1. Follow the steps 1 through 5 of the "CRUD Operations with REST Web Services" Try It Out earlier in this chapter.

2. Create the `UserRestController` class that contains the modified `get` method under the `com .wiley.beginningspring.ch11` package:

```java
@RestController
@RequestMapping("/rest")
public class UserRestController {

    @Autowired
    private UserRepository userRepository;

    @RequestMapping(value = "/users", method=RequestMethod.POST)
    public void save(@RequestBody User user) {
        userRepository.save(user);
    }

    @RequestMapping(value = "/users", method=RequestMethod.GET)
    public List<User> list() {
        return userRepository.findAll();
    }

    @RequestMapping(value="/users/{id}", method=RequestMethod.GET)
    public User get(@PathVariable("id") int id) {
        User user = userRepository.find(id);
        if (user == null) {
            throw new RestException(1, "User not found!",
                "User with id: " + id + " not found in the system");
        }
        return user;
    }

    @RequestMapping(value="/users/{id}", method=RequestMethod.PUT)
    public void update(@PathVariable("id") int id, @RequestBody User user) {
        userRepository.save(user);
    }

    @RequestMapping(value="/users/{id}", method=RequestMethod.DELETE)
    public ResponseEntity<Boolean> delete(@PathVariable("id") int id) {
        userRepository.delete(id);
        return new ResponseEntity<Boolean>(Boolean.TRUE, HttpStatus.OK);
    }
}
```

3. Create the `RestErrorMessage` class under the `com.wiley.beginningspring.ch11` package:

```java
public class RestErrorMessage {

    private HttpStatus status;
    private int code;
    private String message;
    private String detailedMessage;
    private String exceptionMessage;

    public RestErrorMessage(HttpStatus status, int code, String message,
                            String detailedMessage, String exceptionMessage) {
        this.status = status;
```

```
            this.code = code;
            this.message = message;
            this.detailedMessage = detailedMessage;
            this.exceptionMessage = exceptionMessage;
        }

        public HttpStatus getStatus() {
            return status;
        }

        public int getCode() {
            return code;
        }

        public String getMessage() {
            return message;
        }

        public String getDetailedMessage() {
            return detailedMessage;
        }

        public String getExceptionMessage() {
            return exceptionMessage;
        }
    }
}
```

4. Create the `RestException` class under the `com.wiley.beginningspring.ch11` package:

```
public class RestException extends RuntimeException {

    private int code;
    private String message;
    private String detailedMessage;

    public RestException(int code, String message, String detailedMessage) {
        this.code = code;
        this.message = message;
        this.detailedMessage = detailedMessage;
    }

    public int getCode() {
        return code;
    }

    public String getMessage() {
        return message;
    }

    public String getDetailedMessage() {
        return detailedMessage;
    }
}
```

5. Create the `RestExceptionHandler` class under the `com.wiley.beginningspring.ch11` package:

```
@ControllerAdvice
public class RestExceptionHandler extends ResponseEntityExceptionHandler {

    @ExceptionHandler(Exception.class)
    protected ResponseEntity<Object> handleInvalidRequest(RestException e,
        ServletWebRequest request) {
        RestErrorMessage error =
        new RestErrorMessage(HttpStatus.valueOf(request.getResponse().getStatus()),
                e.getCode(),
                e.getMessage(),
                e.getDetailedMessage(),
                e.toString());

        HttpHeaders headers = new HttpHeaders();
        headers.setContentType(MediaType.APPLICATION_JSON);

        return handleExceptionInternal(e, error, headers, HttpStatus.OK, request);
    }
}
```

6. Follow steps 7 through 9 of the "CRUD Operations with REST Web Services" Try It Out.

    Request the URL `http://localhost:8080/exceptionhandling/rest/users/3`.

7. See the output in the browser as shown here:

```
{
    "status":"OK",
    "code":1,
    "message":"User not found!",
    "detailedMessage":"User with id: 3 not found in the system",
    "exceptionMessage":"com.wiley.beginningspring.ch11.exception.RestException: ↵
        User not found!"
}
```

How It Works

Within the `UserRestController` class you modified the `get` method in order to throw an exception when the repository does not contain the requested user. The type of this exception is `RestException`, which extends the `RuntimeException`. Within the constructor of the exception, you provided `code`, `message`, and `detailedMessage` to give details about the exception to the requester. These values were converted with `RestExceptionHandler` into an instance of `RestErrorMessage`. The `RestExceptionHandler` extends the class `ResponseEntityExceptionHandler`, which is a base class that offers common methods for handling exceptions to return the instance of a `ResponseEntity`. The `RestExceptionHandler` class is annotated with `@ControllerAdvice`, and it enables you to centralize the code in one place and share it across the controllers. Thus, the `handleInvalidRequest` method annotated with `@ExceptionHandler` is invoked for all the exceptions thrown from all controllers. For the detailed usage of the annotation, read "Exploiting the power of annotations" section in Chapter 3.

The `handleExceptionInternal` method is defined in the `ResponseEntityExceptionHandler` class, and it offers a single entry point to construct the response body for all exception types.

After doing the request through the browser, the result will be rendered with HTTP code 200, depicting a meaningful response by containing all the details about the exception.

UNIT TESTING RESTFUL SERVICES

Spring provides a template class, named `RestTemplate`, for accessing a REST web service through client code. `RestTemplate` provides methods for making HTTP requests with types like GET, POST, PUT, DELETE, and so on. The names of these methods are defined according to a convention—the first word of the method maps to the name of the HTTP method that is being invoked—as described in Table 11-2.

TABLE 11-2: RestTemplate Methods Mapped to HTTP Methods

HTTP METHOD	`RestTemplate` METHOD
GET	`getForObject(String, Class, String...)`
PUT	`put(String, Object, String...)`
POST	`postForLocation(String, Object, String...)`
DELETE	`delete(String, String...)`
HEAD	`headForHeaders(String, String...)`
OPTIONS	`optionsForAllow(String, String...)`

In this section's Try It Out you implement test methods for the controller methods given in the "CRUD Operations with REST Web Services" Try It Out.

TRY IT OUT Unit Testing of REST Web Services

Use the following steps to create test classes that test listing, adding, updating, and deleting of users through a live web application URL, which is deployed on a container. You can find the source code for the project in the `testing` file in the code downloads.

1. Follow the steps 1 through 9 of the "CRUD Operations with REST Web Services" Try It Out earlier in the chapter.

2. Add the JUnit dependency to your `pom.xml` file. At the time of writing, the latest version of the JUnit project is `4.11`:

```xml
<dependency>
    <groupId>junit</groupId>
    <artifactId>junit</artifactId>
    <version>4.11</version>
    <scope>test</scope>
</dependency>
```

3. Create the `UserRestControllerTestSuite` test suite class and the `ListUsersTest`,
`AddUserTest`, `UpdateUserTest`, `DeleteUserTest` test classes under the `com.wiley`
`.beginningspring.ch11` package in the folder `src/test/java`:

```
@RunWith(Suite.class)
@Suite.SuiteClasses({
        ListUsersTest.class,
        AddUserTest.class,
        UpdateUserTest.class,
        DeleteUserTest.class
})
public class UserRestControllerTestSuite {
}

public class ListUsersTest {

    @Test
    public void listUsersWorksOK() {
        RestTemplate template = new RestTemplate();
        ResponseEntity<List> result =
      template.getForEntity("http://localhost:8080/basic/rest/users", List.class);
        assertNotNull(result);
        assertNotNull(result.getBody());
        assertThat(result.getBody().size(), is(2));
    }
}

public class AddUserTest {

    @Test
    public void addUserWorksOK() {
        RestTemplate template = new RestTemplate();
        User user = new User(3, "Funda Bayulu");
        ResponseEntity<Void> resultSave = template.postForEntity ⏎
           ("http://localhost:8080/basic/rest/users", user, Void.class);
        assertNotNull(resultSave);
    }
}

public class UpdateUserTest {

    @Test
    public void updateUserWorksOK() {
        RestTemplate template = new RestTemplate();
        User user = new User(3, "Funda Caliskan");
        template.put("http://localhost:8080/basic/rest/users/3", user);
    }
}

public class DeleteUserTest {

    @Test
    public void deleteUserWorksOK() {
        RestTemplate template = new RestTemplate();
```

```
            template.delete("http://localhost:8080/basic/rest/users/3");

            ResponseEntity<List> resultList =
        template.getForEntity("http://localhost:8080/basic/rest/users", List.class);
            assertNotNull(resultList);
            assertNotNull(resultList.getBody());
            assertThat(resultList.getBody().size(), is(2));
        }
    }
```

4. Run the test suite as a unit test within your integrated development environment (IDE) and expect all test methods to pass. The Servlet container should be up and running while running the unit tests.

How It Works

After configuring the project and adding the JUnit dependency, you created your four test classes to list, add, update, and delete users. Each test class employs RestTemplate, and you did GET, POST, PUT, and DELETE requests, respectively. You defined the test suite in order to execute the test classes in a specified order.

SUMMARY

This chapter showed you what Spring MVC offers for creating REST-based web services. You first created a REST web service for exposing CRUD operations on a domain object. You used SoapUI for testing the REST web services because using the browser directly wouldn't be enough for testing operations such as POST. You also did an annotation-based configuration for the application context to get your REST web services up and running.

To dispel the myth that REST is all about JSON notation, you saw an example for converting your REST web service to provide XML output instead of JSON. The chapter detailed the ways for handling exceptions in REST web services by also providing meaningful JSON output data to the requester.

Unit testing is a robust way to improve the code quality so you went through the RestTemplate class and worked through examples for doing HTTP method calls like GET, POST, PUT, and DELETE.

EXERCISES

You can find possible solutions to these exercises in Appendix A.

1. Is it possible to produce XML output with REST web services?

2. Create the User domain class with properties id, name, and address. Create a REST web service that outputs a User domain object list as JSON. While doing JSON conversion, omit the address field from the output.

▶ **WHAT YOU LEARNED IN THIS CHAPTER**

TOPIC	KEY POINTS
REST	REpresentational State Transfer
JSON	JavaScript Object Notation
SoapUI	Functional API testing tool that can be used for testing SOAP-based and REST-based web services
`MappingJackson2HttpMessageConverter`	Jackson 2.x converter class that provides serializing/deserializing of the object graph to JSON
`@RestController`	A convenience annotation that composes the `@Controller` and `@ResponseBody` annotations together in one place
`@RequestMapping`	Annotation that enables the mapping of web requests onto these handler methods
`curl`	A command-line tool for doing HTTP requests
`@EnableWebMvc`	`<mvc:annotation-driven>` tag that enables MVC-centric features
`RestTemplate`	Base class that provides methods for handling HTTP methods in REST client code

12

Securing Web Applications with Spring Security

WHAT YOU WILL LEARN IN THIS CHAPTER:

➤   Examining the features Spring Security provides

➤   Configuring and using Spring Security

➤   Authenticating users

➤   Authorizing web requests

> **CODE DOWNLOAD** *The wrox.com code downloads for this chapter are found at* www.wrox.com/go/beginningspring *on the Download Code tab. The code is in the Chapter 12 download and individually named according to the names throughout the chapter.*

Most applications today are multiuser, and they are usually accessed over insecure networks, such as the Internet. Therefore, security requirements for applications must be carefully thought out, and they must be implemented starting at day zero of the project development process. Unfortunately, many people mistakenly think that security features could be added at later steps of the project development, and teams delay working on them until a considerable amount of time has been spent on project development. As a result, applications lack some of the most fundamental security features, which causes some architectural changes and rework when developers attempt to cover those features gradually. One of the reasons for such delays is that teams usually don't have enough understanding of security concepts of multiuser enterprise web applications, and they usually choose to implement those security requirements by themselves as they discover and learn them over time.

Such an approach, however, results in legacy in-house security solutions that are lacking some fundamental security enforcements that must exist in any typical multiuser web application and that have not been thoroughly tested against attacks. It is much wiser to employ a prebuilt security framework that is specialized to handle all those security requirements and has extension points so that application-specific customizations can easily be added onto it. Such an off-the-shelf security solution is also much more robust compared to a legacy solution because it is used by hundreds of thousands of different projects. All those different projects probably run over various target platforms, which become natural test and verification environments of that security framework. This same level of testing and verification is definitely hard, though not impossible, to achieve with any legacy in-house solution.

This chapter examines one of those ready-to-use security frameworks. Spring Security Framework is specialized for providing multiuser web applications that employ Spring as their backbone with their security requirements.

WHY SPRING SECURITY?

Spring Security is a very popular and widely used security framework in Spring-enabled enterprise web applications. The Java and Java EE platforms have offered some standards-based solutions, namely Java Authentication and Authorization Service (JAAS) and web.xml security, to handle security requirements of those applications. However, they have failed at satisfying some of the most fundamental needs of those kinds of applications.

Security requirements can be divided into two main feature sets: *authentication* and *authorization*. Authentication means letting users present their identities to the target application and validating those presented identities against trusted credentials information available on the system. Authorization deals with what operations authenticated users are allowed or not allowed to perform in the target application.

JAAS is the standard security application programming interface (API) of the Java platform. However, it depends heavily on policy file configuration in the target Java Runtime Environment (JRE) onto which the web application is deployed. This means that when you want to deploy a target web application to several different JREs, you have to arrange policies of each of those JREs, which creates a very inconvenient and unportable deployment environment. The authentication part of JAAS is based on the pluggable authentication module (PAM) concept, and various authentication mechanisms can be used even in the same application. However, you need to implement your module so that it will obtain user credentials both from the user request and the user repository by itself. There is no ready-to-use module implementation for various authentication methods, and there is no code available to access different user repositories. The authorization part of JAAS is also based on fine-grained permissions that are defined in policy files and checked against the codebase. Unfortunately, it doesn't provide a high-level authorization API to protect against various kinds of resources, such as URL, method invocation, or domain objects.

Web.xml security has a similar story. It is defined by the Servlet Specification and implemented by any Java EE–compliant web container by default. However, the specification has left open how user information will be obtained from user repositories, and the result is that different application servers have different APIs to provide access to user repositories during the authentication process. You may either need to create an application server–specific configuration or code against a server-specific API to integrate your application with the web.xml security part of the target web container. Consequently, it is not possible to create a ready-to-use web artifact bundle that can be dropped into the web container and be run without any modification in the target environment.

The authorization part of web.xml security is also missing some critical features. It only has a protection mechanism against URL resources, which completely leaves out method-level and domain object–level authorization requirements, which are features that many applications need in addition to having protection for URL resources. URL resource protection is based on request path pattern matching; however, it is not very advanced in handling various kinds of request paths that have different parameters at run time. As a result, developers usually develop their own authentication and authorization subsystems that partly depend on web.xml security.

Since its early days, the aim of the Spring Security Framework has been to enable developers to create a portable web artifact that can easily be deployed over several different target web containers without any modification to the artifact or application server. It provides lots of authentication and authorization features that can be used out of the box, or you can easily customize or extend them through pluggable extension points in the framework. All those customizations and extensions can be bundled into a WAR file and deployed into different application servers.

FEATURES OF SPRING SECURITY

Spring Security Framework offers the following features:

➤ It supports several different authentication methods, such as classical login form–based authentication, authentication with X509 user certificates, LDAP authentication, Windows authentication over legacy NTLM or Kerberos methods, and basic and digest authentications. You can employ several different authentication methods in the same application as well. For example, a group of secure web resources could be available for access after form-based authentication, and some other group of secure web resources could be accessed after basic authentication.

➤ Authentication methods and access to user repositories are completely independent from each other. You can perform login form–based authentication while retrieving your user information from the active directory or relational database. It is also possible and very easy to implement your own user repository access logic and configure it in the framework.

➤ It is very well integrated with several different single sign-on (SSO) solutions, such as Central Authentication Service (CAS), OpenID, Siteminder, and OAuth. Authentication can be delegated completely to those SSO systems, whereas Spring Security handles the authorization parts by itself.

➤ It provides anonymous authentication or guest login. That way, a valid authentication token is always available in the security context, and configuration of secure methods is more consistent looking.

➤ It has built-in remember-me support so that you can close your browser and reopen it to be automatically logged in to your application. Spring Security can also differentiate among different kinds of authentications so that users who are automatically logged in using remember-me support could be prevented from accessing some of the more secure parts of the system. Access to such areas could be enforced with interactive authentication only.

➤ It has integration support with `javax.servlet.request.HttpServletRequest` so that the `getRemoteUser()` and `isUserInRole(String)` methods will work with the underlying

Spring Security–provided authentication information. It is also possible to delegate authentication to web.xml security or JAAS so that Spring Security deals exclusively with the authorization part.

➤ You can enforce your users to access your web application using secure HTTP only. It is also possible to make this enforcement partly in the application so that some resources are accessible without SSL and some others are accessible only using HTTPS.

➤ It has built-in support for keeping passwords encrypted in user repositories. That way, your users' passwords aren't exposed to your developers or database admins. It also has a passport to prevent dictionary attacks using system-wide or user property–specific salt mechanisms.

➤ It provides built-in protection against session fixation attacks by changing the HTTP session used during the login process. It also tracks logged-in users' sessions and provides concurrent user session management so that you can restrict your users' maximum concurrent access counts from different locations.

➤ It is possible to separately control access to URL resources, service method calls, and domain objects. You can also add roles to logged-in users temporarily at run time so that they can access some restricted areas with those additional roles.

CONFIGURING AND USING SPRING SECURITY

Spring Security is based heavily on servlet filters for proper functioning. Servlet filters are used to intercept and transform requests to web resources. There might be several different filters that may intercept requests to the same web resource. They can completely change the response, or even redirect the request to a different location. You can find more information about them at http://docs .oracle.com/javaee/6/tutorial/doc/bnagb.html.

Each different security filter has a specific role in the framework. Some filters depend on other filters to function properly. Therefore, you need to configure them in a specific order. This section examines the filters one by one and describes what roles they perform in the framework. Figure 12-1 shows security filters and their roles in the framework.

When a web request arrives, it flows through the security filters. First, it hits ChannelProcessingFilter. This filter checks the web request's HTTP scheme, and if the request is asked to be HTTPS and the arriving request's scheme is HTTP, the request is redirected to HTTPS.

ConcurrentSessionFilter performs concurrent user session management.

SecurityContextPersistenceFilter stores the authentication token in HttpSession in between requests, and puts it into SecurityContextHolder at the beginning of the next request so that the authentication token becomes available to the application during the request processing.

If the request URL matches the logout URL (the default is /j_spring_security_logout), LogoutFilter performs the logout, clears the authentication token, invalidates HttpSession, and redirects the user to the logout success URL.

Authentication is performed by UsernamePasswordAuthenticationFilter, which is one of the concrete subclasses of AbstractAuthenticationProcessingFilter. There can be one of its different implementations in that place according to the authentication method. If a login form–based authentication method is preferred, UsernamePasswordAuthenticationFilter is configured so that it grabs the username and password information from the URL when the request path is /j_spring_security_check, and it performs authentication.

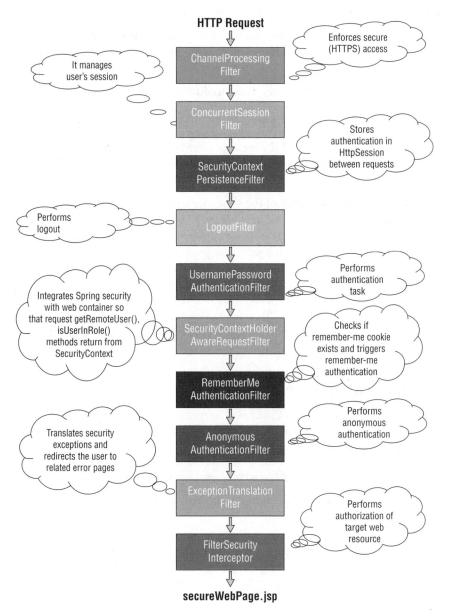

FIGURE 12-1

SecurityContextHolderAwareRequestFilter wraps the current HttpServletRequest object so that its getRemoteUser() and isUserInRole(String) method invocations could return information available in Spring Security Context. That way, application code that depends on the Servlet API security check method will continue to function properly without noticing Spring Security beneath.

`RememberMeAuthenticationFilter` checks cookies sent from the client. If a remember-me cookie exists and if it is valid, the remember-me authentication is performed.

`AnonymousAuthenticationFilter` creates a guest authentication token, unless there is a valid authentication token at that point, and places it into `org.springframework.security.core` `.context.SecurityContext`.

`ExceptionTranslationFilter` maps security exceptions to different URLs so that the user request is redirected to a target web page if a specific security exception occurs during the request processing.

`FilterSecurityInterceptor` is the last one in the security filter chain, and it performs authorization of web resources so that only allowed users will be able to access a secure web resource that is requested.

Some other filters may come and go, but most of the time any web request flows through the previously described filters. Actually, those filters create a layer above the core features of Spring Security Framework. For example, `UsernamePasswordAuthenticationFilter` doesn't perform whole authentication, but it delegates the work to `AuthenticationManager` at some point. Similarly, `FilterSecurityInterceptor` delegates the authorization to `AccessDecisionManager`. The configuration of the framework consists of configuring those filters with all their dependencies. Because of all those dependencies and the necessity to configure those filters in a very specific order, Spring Security Framework provides some conventions and facilities so that you can easily and correctly configure security features in applications, as shown in the next Try It Out.

TRY IT OUT Configuring and Using Spring Security

In this Try It Out, you create a web application and configure Spring Security in that web application. You can find the source code within the project named `configuring-and-using-spring-security` in the code downloads. To begin follow these steps:

1. Create a Maven web application project using the `maven-archetype-webapp` archetype.

2. Add the following Spring Security dependencies into the `pom.xml` of the project:

```
<dependency>
    <groupId>org.springframework.security</groupId>
    <artifactId>spring-security-web</artifactId>
    <version>3.2.5.RELEASE</version>
</dependency>

<dependency>
    <groupId>org.springframework.security</groupId>
    <artifactId>spring-security-config</artifactId>
    <version>3.2.5.RELEASE</version>
</dependency>
```

3. Add the `org.springframework.web.context.ContextLoaderListener` listener element into the `web.xml` file of the project:

```
<listener>
    <listener-class>
        org.springframework.web.context.ContextLoaderListener
    </listener-class>
</listener>
```

4. Create an `applicationContext.xml` file in the `WEB-INF` folder of the project.

5. Add the following namespace element into the `<beans>` element of the `applicationContext.xml` file to enable the Spring Security namespace:

```
<?xml version="1.0" encoding="UTF-8"?>
<beans xmlns="http://www.springframework.org/schema/beans"
    xmlns:xsi="http://www.w3.org/2001/XMLSchema-instance"
    xmlns:security="http://www.springframework.org/schema/security"
    xsi:schemaLocation="http://www.springframework.org/schema/security
    http://www.springframework.org/schema/security/spring-security-3.2.xsd
        http://www.springframework.org/schema/beans
        http://www.springframework.org/schema/beans/spring-beans.xsd">

</beans>
```

6. Add the following Spring Security namespace elements to configure Spring Security with minimal configuration settings:

```
<security:user-service id="userService">
 <security:user name="user1" password="secret" authorities="ROLE_USER"/>
 <security:user name="user2" password="secret" authorities="ROLE_USER,ROLE_EDITOR"/>
</security:user-service>

<security:authentication-manager>
    <security:authentication-provider user-service-ref="userService"/>
</security:authentication-manager>

<security:http pattern="/favicon.ico" security="none"/>

<security:http auto-config="true">
    <security:intercept-url pattern="/**" access="ROLE_USER"/>
</security:http>
```

7. Add the following filter configuration into the `web.xml` file of the project:

```
<filter>
    <filter-name>springSecurityFilterChain</filter-name>
    <filter-class>org.springframework.web.filter.DelegatingFilterProxy</filter-class>
</filter>

<filter-mapping>
    <filter-name>springSecurityFilterChain</filter-name>
    <url-pattern>/*</url-pattern>
</filter-mapping>
```

8. You can easily run and test your web application's security features by running it within a Jetty server. Jetty can be run using Maven. Add the following Jetty plug-in configuration into the `<build><plugins>...</plugins></build>` part of the `pom.xml` file:

```
<plugin>
    <groupId>org.eclipse.jetty</groupId>
    <artifactId>jetty-maven-plugin</artifactId>
    <version>9.2.1.v20140609</version>
    <configuration>
        <scanIntervalSeconds>2</scanIntervalSeconds>
        <webApp>
            <contextPath>/</contextPath>
        </webApp>
    </configuration>
</plugin>
```

9. Start Jetty with the `jetty:run` Maven goal.

10. Try to access the web application from your favorite browser using `http://localhost:8080` as the address.

11. Enter username **user1** and password **secret** into the login form and click the Login button to log in to the application. You should see the `"Hello World!"` message.

How It Works

First you created a web application project using the Maven archetype `maven-archetype-webapp`, and you added the minimum necessary Spring Security dependencies into the `pom.xml` file so that it runs with a login form–based authentication mechanism.

In the second step you needed to configure Spring and bootstrap it in the web application. To achieve this you added the `ContextLoaderListener` element into the `web.xml` file. `ContextLoaderListener` creates Spring `WebApplicationContext` by loading `applicationContext.xml`, which is located in the `WEB-INF` folder during web container startup.

Spring Security Filters don't need to be defined directly in the `web.xml` file. Indeed, it would be too impractical to do so because of their dependencies to other beans and their various configuration options. Instead, you will define those filters and other security-related beans in a Spring-bean configuration file. However, it would still be very difficult and error prone to try to define all those filters and their various dependencies one by one. To ease all those security-related bean configuration issues, Spring Security offers security namespace support. You enabled that security namespace by adding a related XSD schema location configuration into the `<beans>` element of the `applicationContext.xml` file.

The first element, `<security:user-service>`, creates a user repository bean named `userService` of type `org.springframework.security.core.userdetails.UserDetailsService`. It actually contains two sample users so that your configuration will work without needing any relational database or Active Directory integration to provide user information. The job of the `userService` bean is to return the `org.springframework.security.core.userdetails.UserDetails` object given its username.

The second element of security configuration is `<security:authentication-manager>`. It defines a bean of type `AuthenticationManager`, which coordinates the actual authentication process. It contains a child element of `<security:authentication-provider/>`, which also refers to the `userService` bean you previously defined. This element adds a bean of type `org.springframework.security` `.authentication.AuthenticationProvider`, which compares the given password of a user against the password property of the `UserDetails` object obtained via the `userService` bean.

The third and last element is `<security:http/>`. It creates a Spring Security Filter chain bean in Spring `ApplicationContext`. Its `auto-config="true"` element by default enables several security-related features, such as login form–based authentication, autogenerated login form, logout, guest authentication, and so on. The `<security:http>` element has a child element of `<security:intercept-url/>`. It configures the `FilterSecurityInterceptor` filter bean in the security filter chain by defining what URL resources could be accessible with which roles owned by the current authenticated user.

The `<security:http pattern="/favicon.ico" security="none"/>` element is added to make Spring Security discard web requests coming for `favicon.ico`. Without this, the Firefox browser throws a 404 not found error.

At this point you'd finished the security-related bean configuration. However, you needed a hook-up mechanism so that web requests coming into the web container will first pass through your Spring Security filter chain. For this purpose, Spring provides a special `javax.servlet.Filter` implementation of type `org.springframework.web.filter.DelegatingFilterProxy`. This filter actually acts as a proxy in front and delegates web requests to the Spring Security Filter chain bean defined by the `<security:http>` element. Figure 12-2 illustrates this flow.

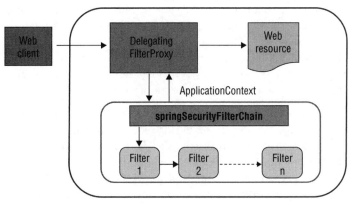

FIGURE 12-2

Its name must be defined exactly as `springSecurityFilterChain` in the `web.xml` file because that same name is also used by Spring Security while defining a filter chain as a bean in the `ApplicationContext` via the `<security:http>` element. When the request arrives in the `springSecurityFilterChain` bean, it passes it into Spring Security Filters enabled within the element. At the end of the chain, the `FilterSecurityInterceptor` filter bean is located, and its job is to perform access control of URL resources. You added only one `<security:intercept-url/>` element whose pattern is `/**` and access attribute is `ROLE_USER`. This means that when a request arrives into `FilterSecurityInterceptor`, it should first be matched against a given pattern. Here, any web request matches against pattern `/**`. When the match occurs, the request is allowed to access the URL resource if the current user's assigned roles contain `ROLE_USER`.

To test your security configuration, you added `jetty-maven-plugin` and configured it so that the `contextPath` of the application will be / when Jetty is run. You issued the `jetty:run` Maven goal to run Jetty and entered `http://localhost:8080/` as the URL to your browser to access the welcome page of the web application. Because the `<security:intercept-url/>` element disallows unauthorized access, you were presented with a login page generated by Spring Security Framework. Spring Security generates a login form to help you rapidly configure and start using the framework in applications. In the "Customizing the Login Page" section later in this chapter, you find out how to replace this autogenerated login form with a custom login form. When you enter `user1` as the username and `secret` as the password, you are able to log in to the application to see the welcome page message in the browser.

UNDERSTANDING THE FUNDAMENTAL BUILDING BLOCKS OF SPRING SECURITY

Before going into detail about how authentication and authorization work, you should have some more information about some fundamental pieces in Spring Security Framework.

Figure 12-3 shows some basic elements of the Spring Security domain model and their relationships between the elements. The `UserDetailsService` interface was previously mentioned. This interface abstracts access to the user repository from which user data can be obtained in the form of the `UserDetails` interface. Its default implementation class is `org.springframework.security.core.userdetails.User`. `User` class represents user-specific data in the system. This data is used during the authentication process and can later be accessed through the `org.springframework.security.core.Authentication` object available in the system. The `org.springframework.security.core.GrantedAuthority` interface abstracts roles assigned to users to represent their grants to secure resources. A simple implementation of `GrantedAuthority` is the `org.springframework.security.core.authority.SimpleGrantedAuthority` class in the framework.

Authentication information is represented by the `Authentication` interface. It is created during the authentication process and kept within a `SecurityContext` object during request handling. Several different `Authentication` implementations exist, and each corresponds to the authentication method available in the framework. For example, the `org.springframework.security.authentication.UsernamePasswordAuthenticationToken` implementation is used during login form authentication. That token is created by `UsernamePasswordAuthenticationFilter`, and is authenticated by `org.springframework.security.authentication.dao.DaoAuthenticationProvider`. The `Authentication` object contains current user information in the form of `UserDetails`, user credentials, and access rights in the form of `GrantedAuthority` objects.

`SecurityContext` abstracts a simple data holder in which `Authentication` data is kept during request handling. It is stored in `HttpSession` in between two different requests. When a request arrives, `SecurityContextPersistenceFilter` checks whether `HttpSession` contains a `SecurityContext`. If the `SecurityContext` exists within `HttpSession`, then that `SecurityContext` is put into `SecurityContextHolder`. `SecurityContextHolder` keeps `SecurityContext` in a `java.lang.ThreadLocal` variable within itself. That way, any code block can easily access the current authentication token without passing it as method parameters through several method invocations if one is available during the current request. At the end of the current request, `SecurityContextPersistenceFilter` clears out `SecurityContextHolder` after storing the current `SecurityContext` in `HttpSession` until the next request arrives from the current user.

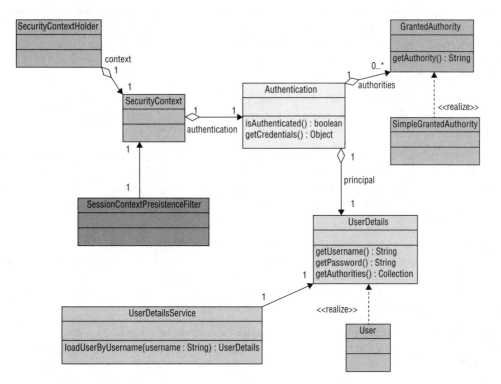

FIGURE 12-3

SECURITYCONTEXT WITH A VALID AUTHENTICATION TOKEN

For the Spring Security Framework, it is enough to see that there is a valid `Authentication` token within the `SecurityContext` that is accessible from `SecurityContextHolder` during request processing. Spring Security doesn't deal with how this valid `Authentication` token is placed into that `SecurityContext` object.

AUTHENTICATING USERS

The authentication process is triggered by a concrete implementation of `AbstractAuthentication ProcessingFilter` in the chain, and it's coordinated by the `AuthenticationManager` object behind the scenes. The following sections explain what is going on during this process by describing unsuccessful and successful login flows.

Unsuccessful Login Flow

When a request comes to a secure resource, `FilterSecurityInterceptor` at the end of the filter chain intercepts the request and delegates access control to `AccessDecisionManager`. `AccessDecisionManager` is actually a coordinator for authorization. You find out what is going on during the authorization process in detail later in this chapter in the "Authorizing Web Requests" section. At this point, it is enough to know that `AccessDecisionManager` throws `org` `.springframework.security.access.AccessDeniedException` when the access control check fails.

`ExceptionTranslationFilter` catches the `AccessDeniedException` exception thrown and decides to redirect the request to the authentication entry point, which by default is `/spring_security_login`.

When the request is redirected to the authentication entry point, a login form is displayed. The user is asked to provide his username and password. The form is submitted to a special URL `/j_spring_security_check`. When a request comes with that URL path, `UsernamePasswordAuthenticationFilter` intercepts the request, creates a `UsernamePasswordAuthenticationToken`, and delegates the authentication process to `AuthenticationManager`.

`AuthenticationManager` is actually a coordinator for the authentication process. There might be several `AuthenticationProvider` objects registered to handle different kinds of authentication tokens. `AuthenticationManager` asks each `AuthenticationProvider` if it can authenticate the current token. If the `AuthenticationProvider` doesn't recognize the token, it returns null so that the next provider is asked for.

`DaoAuthenticationProvider`, which is registered by default when the `<security:` `authentication-provider/>` element is put into `<security:authentication-manager>`, recognizes `UsernamePasswordAuthenticationToken`. It fetches `UserDetails` using the `UserDetailsService` object and compares credentials of `UserDetails` to those that the user entered. If the password comparison fails, it throws `org.springframework.security.core.AuthenticationException`. When that exception is thrown, `UsernamePasswordAuthenticationFilter` forwards the request to the authentication failure URL, which is `/spring_security_login?login_error` by default.

Figure 12-4 depicts the unsuccessful login flow.

Successful Login Flow

The scenario for a successful login flow is the same as the one described in the preceding section until it reaches the point of password check-in with `DaoAuthenticationProvider`. If two passwords match, `DaoAuthenticationProvider` creates a new valid `UsernamePasswordAuthenticationToken` and returns it. `UsernamePasswordAuthenticationFilter` notices that authentication is successful, places a valid authentication token into `SecurityContext` via `SecurityContextHolder`, and redirects the request to the target URL, which is asked for before the authentication flow begins. Sometimes, the target URL might not be available. For example, the user might have logged in by directly accessing the login page or the security configuration doesn't allow storing the target URL in `HttpSession`. In such a case, `UsernamePasswordAuthenticationProcessingFilter` redirects to the default target URL.

Figure 12-5 depicts the successful login flow.

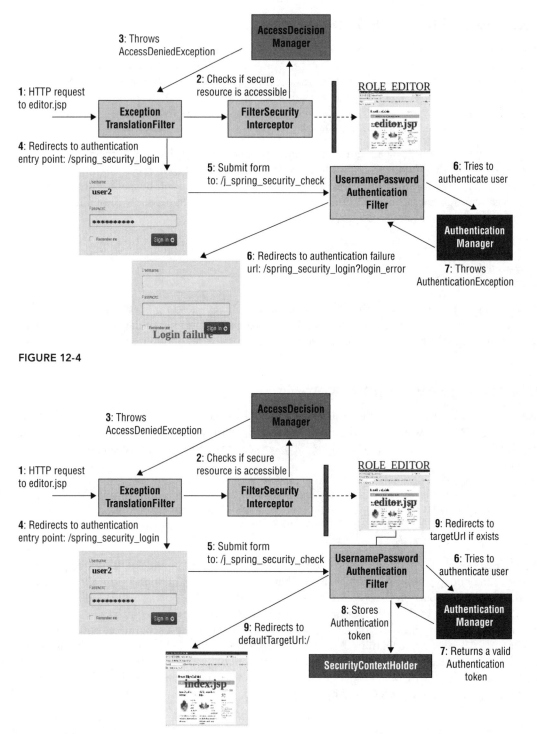

FIGURE 12-4

FIGURE 12-5

Anonymous Authentication

An anonymous authentication mechanism creates an `org.springframework.security`
`.authentication.AnonymousAuthenticationToken` and validates it automatically. The default
principal user and granted authority that are accessible from this token are `anonymous` String,
and the `GrantedAuthority` object with the `ROLE_ANONYMOUS` name. Anonymous authentication is
triggered by `AnonymousAuthenticationFilter` unless there is an `Authentication` token in the
`SecurityContext` when the request arrives.

Conceptually, authenticating a request anonymously is no different than not authenticating it at all,
but it guarantees that there will always be an `Authentication` token in the `SecurityContext`, and
the `<security:intercept-url>` definitions for some public URLs will be made more easily and
in a consistent manner in the configuration. The following code snippet shows how the anonymous
authentication mechanism is configured:

```
<security:http>
    <security:anonymous/>
</security:http>
```

Anonymous authentication is enabled by adding the `<security:authentication/>` element in
`<security:http>`. You can change the default principal and role names of the anonymous authentication token using the `username` and `granted-authority` attributes of the `<security:anonymous/>`
element.

Customizing the Login Page

You have already seen that Spring Security automatically generates a login page for quick bootstrap
of the framework. However, you will probably replace it with your custom login page, which is quite
easy. First you have to create an HTML or JSP page that has a form similar to the following:

```
<form action="j_spring_security_check" method="post">
    Username:<input name="j_username" type="text" /><br />
    Password:<input name="j_password" type="password" /><br />
    <input type="submit" value="Login">
</form>
```

As you can see, the form should be posted to `/j_spring_security_check` URL with the
`j_username` and `j_password` input elements that carry username and password values entered
by the user. It is important that the form method should be POST. Spring Security does accept
GET requests made to that URL. Spring Security also expects a URL to which the user will
be forwarded when authentication fails. People usually don't create a separate page for this;
instead, they use the same login page during authentication failure. After creating a login form
page and a page that will be used when authentication fails, you need to add the following
`<security:form-login/>` namespace element into `<security:http>` as follows so that the
custom login page can be recognized by the framework:

```
<security:http>
    <security:form-login login-page="/login.jsp"
```

```
            authentication-failure-url="/login.js?login_error"/>
    </security:http>
```

You can also customize the login form processing URL, username, and password input elements' names as well via the `<security:form-login>` element's related attributes.

The important point during form login page customization is that the login page and authentication failure URLs should be publicly accessible. This is because the login page and the authentication failure URLs will also be checked by `FilterSecurityInterceptor` for access control, and an `intercept-url` pattern like `/**` will definitely match with those two URLs as well, resulting in an `AccessDeniedException` with a redirect to the login page. At some point, you will come up with a message such as `Page is not redirecting properly` in your browser.

You have two solutions for this problem, and you can employ either one. The first option is to enable anonymous authentication and add an `intercept-url` with the `ROLE_ANONYMOUS` value in its `access` attribute for the login page. This makes the login page accessible for unauthenticated requests as well:

```
<security:http>
    <security:form-login login-page="/login.jsp"
            authentication-failure-url="/login.js?login_error"/>
    <security:anonymous/>
    <security:intercept-url pattern="/login.jsp" access="ROLE_ANONYMOUS"/>
    <security:intercept-url pattern="/**" access="ROLE_USER"/>
</security:http>
```

You can also define this `intercept-url` with the access attribute value `IS_AUTHENTICATED_ANONYMOUSLY` as shown here:

```
<security:intercept-url pattern="/login.jsp"
        access="IS_AUTHENTICATED_ANONYMOUSLY"/>
```

The important thing here is that the order among `intercept-url` elements is important, and they must be ordered from the most specific pattern to the most general one.

The second solution is to disable security for requests that try to access the login page. You can add several different `<security:http>` elements with different pattern attributes. The following example shows this:

```
<security:http pattern="/login.jsp" security="none"/>

<security:http>
    <security:form-login login-page="/login.jsp"
            authentication-failure-url="/login.js?login_error"/>
    <security:intercept-url pattern="/**" access="ROLE_USER"/>
</security:http>
```

Similar to the `intercept-url` elements, the order of the `<security:http>` elements is also important. They must also be ordered from the most specific pattern to the most general one. If you don't use the pattern attribute, the `<security:http>` element matches with any URL.

Logout Process

`LogoutFilter` manages the logout process, and you can configure it by adding the `<security:logout/>` element in `<security:http>` as follows:

```
<security:http>
    <security:logout/>
</security:http>
```

By default, logout is triggered with `/j_spring_security_logout` URL, and the application is redirected to `/` after logout. However, both of them can be customized using the `logout-url` and `logout-success-url` attributes of the element.

When `logout-url` is requested, `LogoutFilter` intercepts it and starts the logout process. It invokes a sequence of registered `LogoutHandler` beans and delegates them to an implementation of `LogoutSuccessHandler` at the end.

The `<security:logout>` element registers `SecurityContextLogoutHandler` and `SimpleUrlLogoutSuccessHandler` instances to the `LogoutFilter` instance. `SecurityContextLogoutHandler` clears `Authentication` in `SecurityContext` and also invalidates `HttpSession`. `SimpleUrlLogoutSuccessHandler` is called after processing `LogoutHandlers`, and it redirects to a URL specified with `logout-success-url`.

Accessing UserDetails Using JDBC

Spring Security accesses `UserDetails` information via the `UserDetailsService` interface. Therefore, user information can be fetched from any location, such as the Active Directory or a relational database. Spring Security provides built-in support for keeping user information in a relational database. The following Try It Out shows how `UserDetails` information can be accessed using JDBC API.

TRY IT OUT   Accessing UserDetails Using JDBC

In this Try It Out, you configure Spring Security so that it will access `UserDetails` information via JDBC. You can continue from where you left off in the preceding Try It Out, and you can find the source code within the project named `accessing-user-details-using-jdbc` in the code downloads. To begin follow these steps:

1. Add the following dependencies to the `pom.xml` file:

```
<dependency>
    <groupId>com.h2database</groupId>
    <artifactId>h2</artifactId>
    <version>1.3.175</version>
</dependency>

<dependency>
    <groupId>org.springframework</groupId>
    <artifactId>spring-jdbc</artifactId>
    <version>4.0.5.RELEASE</version>
</dependency>
```

2. Enable the JDBC namespace by adding the following parts into the `<beans>` element of the `applicationContext.xml` file:

```xml
<?xml version="1.0" encoding="UTF-8"?>
<beans xmlns="http://www.springframework.org/schema/beans"
    xmlns:xsi="http://www.w3.org/2001/XMLSchema-instance"
    xmlns:security="http://www.springframework.org/schema/security"
    xmlns:jdbc="http://www.springframework.org/schema/jdbc"
    xsi:schemaLocation="http://www.springframework.org/schema/jdbc
        http://www.springframework.org/schema/jdbc/spring-jdbc-4.0.xsd
            http://www.springframework.org/schema/security
        http://www.springframework.org/schema/security/spring-security-3.2.xsd
            http://www.springframework.org/schema/beans
        http://www.springframework.org/schema/beans/spring-beans.xsd">


</beans>
```

3. Create a `security.sql` script file in the classpath with the following content:

```sql
create table users(
username varchar_ignorecase(128) not null primary key,
password varchar_ignorecase(512) not null,
enabled boolean not null);

create table authorities (
username varchar_ignorecase(128) not null,
authority varchar_ignorecase(128) not null);

create unique index idx_auth_username on authorities (username,authority);

create table groups (
id bigint not null,
group_name varchar_ignorecase(128) not null);

alter table groups add constraint pk_groups primary key(id);

create table group_authorities (
group_id bigint not null,
authority varchar_ignorecase(128) not null,
constraint fk_group_authorities_group foreign key(group_id) references groups(id));

create table group_members (
id bigint not null,
username varchar_ignorecase(128) not null,
group_id bigint not null,
constraint fk_group_members_group foreign key(group_id) references groups(id));

alter table group_members add constraint pk_group_members primary key(id);

insert into users(username,password,enabled) values ('user1','secret',true);
insert into users(username,password,enabled) values ('user2','secret',true);

insert into authorities(username,authority) values ('user1','ROLE_USER');
```

```
insert into authorities(username,authority) values ('user2','ROLE_USER');
insert into authorities(username,authority) values ('user2','ROLE_EDITOR');
```

4. Define a `javax.sql.DataSource` bean with a `<jdbc:embedded-database>` element in the `applicationContext.xml` file as follows:

```
<jdbc:embedded-database id="dataSource" type="H2">
    <jdbc:script execution="INIT" location="classpath:security.sql"/>
</jdbc:embedded-database>
```

5. Remove the `<security:user-service>` element and add the `<security:jdbc-user-service>` element in the `applicationContext.xml` file as follows:

```
<security:jdbc-user-service data-source-ref="dataSource" id="userService"/>
```

6. Start Jetty with the `jetty:run` Maven goal.

7. Try to access the web application from your favorite browser using the `http://localhost:8080` address.

8. Enter the username **user1** and the password **secret** into the login form and click the Login button to log in to the application. You should see the `Hello World!` message.

How It Works

First you defined a `dataSource` bean with the `<jdbc:embedded-database/>` element of Spring JDBC namespace support. It creates an in-memory H2 database for demonstration purposes. You also created an SQL script file called `security.sql` and placed it into the project classpath. During initialization, the script is loaded by the database. The SQL script creates the tables shown in Figure 12-6, and it populates the `users` and `authorities` tables with two sample users.

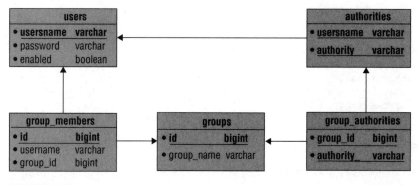

FIGURE 12-6

Instead of creating a `UserDetailsService` bean that looks up users from memory, you defined one using the `<security:jdbc-user-service/>` element. You also injected the `dataSource` bean so that it can connect to the database.

The security schema you just created represents what is expected by the JDBC implementation of the `UserDetailsService` bean as a minimum. It is always possible to have different tables in your application. In such a case, it is enough to customize related queries of the `userService` bean. `<security:jdbc-user-service>` has three attributes for this purpose: `users-by-username-query`, `authorities-by-username-query`, and `group-authorities-by-username-query`.

Spring Security expects `users-by-username-query` to return the `username`, `password`, and `enabled` properties of `UserDetails` given `username` as a query parameter. It expects `authorities-by-username-query` to return `username` and `authority` given `username` as a query parameter, and finally `group-authorities-by-username` query is expected to return `group_id`, `group_name`, and `authority` given `username` as the input parameter.

However, only authority names are used from the second and third queries. Therefore, as long as you return `authority` as the second element from the second query and as the third property in the third query, you can return whatever you want in place of other properties in those queries.

By default, the authority group feature is disabled. If you want to enable it you need to provide a query string with the `group-authorities-by-username` attribute of the `<security:jdbc-user-service>` element even if the query is the same as the default one.

Encrypting Passwords

One of the most common security weaknesses observed in applications is that user passwords are kept in clear text in user repositories, such as relational databases. Anyone who has access rights to the repositories can read the passwords. This definitely disrupts the privacy of users. No passwords should be kept in clear-text format.

Luckily, Spring Security provides an easy mechanism to keep passwords encrypted in user repositories. The main interface for this purpose is `org.springframework.security.crypto.password` `.PasswordEncoder`. It provides an encode method that accepts a clear-text password with a randomly generated salt value and returns an encrypted password. The salt value is used as a safeguard against dictionary attacks. If an attacker steals encrypted passwords, he might iterate over words in a dictionary to try to match their encrypted forms against the stolen encrypted passwords. To complicate this process, you can add a secret salt value during encryption. Spring Security provides the `org.springframework.security.authentication.dao.SaltSource` interface for this purpose.

Spring provides two different implementations of the salt source interface: `org.springframework` `.security.authentication.dao.SystemWideSaltSource` and `org.springframework.security` `.authentication.dao.ReflectionSaltSource`. `SystemWideSaltSource` uses the same secret value for all passwords; `ReflectionSaltSource` obtains the salt value from a specific property of the current `UserDetails` object. That way, each user's password is encrypted with a different salt value.

You can enable the password-encoding feature by adding the `<security:password-encoder>` element in `<security:authentication-provider>` as follows:

```
<security:authentication-provider user-service-ref="userService">
    <security:password-encoder hash="sha-256">
        <security:salt-source system-wide="keep it secret"/>
    </security:password-encoder>
</security:authentication-provider>
```

`<security:password-encoder>` has the `hash` attribute, which accepts different encoding algorithms available in the framework. You can also implement your own encoding scheme and use it by defining it as a bean in the `ApplicationContext` and referring to it from the `<security:password-encoder>` element with the `ref` attribute.

The important point to note is that the password entered by the user is encrypted on the server side before the authentication check. Therefore, it is transferred over the network in clear-text format, such as during login form submission. Hence, authentication methods in which the user enters the password should only be used over a secure transport layer, such as HTTPS.

Remember-Me Support

A very common security feature is to let the user close his browser without logging out from the system; when he opens his browser again, he is automatically logged in to the application. This function is performed by Spring Security with remember-me authentication. You enable it by adding the `<security:remember-me>` element into `<security:http>` as follows:

```
<security:http >
    <security:remember-me/>
</security:http>
```

Remember-me support is based on a cookie mechanism. A cookie containing the username is installed from the server to the client during the login process. When the user closes his browser and then opens it again, this cookie stored in the client machine is sent to the server. If no valid `Authentication` token exists in `SecurityContext`, `RememberMeAuthenticationFilter` extracts the username from the cookie and creates a `RememberMeAuthenticationToken`. `RememberMeAuthenticationProvider` registered to `AuthenticationManager` is responsible for automatically validating this `Authentication` token, and the user is logged in without being asked for a password. Remember-me cookies are valid for a set period of time, and they are invalidated when explicit logout is triggered via `LogoutFilter`.

The remember-me cookie installed in the client will be active for two weeks by default. You can customize it via the `token-validity-seconds` attribute as follows:

```
<security:http >
    <security:remember-me token-validity-seconds="1209600"/>
</security:http>
```

Storing the username in the client within a cookie can be considered a security weakness because an attacker may steal cookies stored in the client machine, decode them, and learn the username. Learning one of the usernames existing in the target system might be a starting point for the attack, even though that cookie had expired long before the attempted attack. Spring Security has a solution against this threat, too. It creates a token and replaces this token with the username in the remember-me cookie. The token and username pair is stored in the relational database table so that when the next request arrives with the cookie available, it extracts a token and obtains the corresponding username from the database table used for storing the token. This table is called `persistent_logins`, and you can create it with the following DDL SQL statement:

```
create table persistent_logins (
  username varchar(128) not null,
  series varchar(64) primary key,
```

```
    token varchar(64) not null,
    last_used timestamp not null);
```

To configure the remember-me mechanism to use the persistent token mechanism, you need to inject the `javax.sql.DataSource` bean into `RememberMeAuthenticationFilter`. You can do this via the `<security:remember-me>` element's `data-source-ref` attribute:

```
<security:http>
    <security:remember-me data-source-ref="dataSource"/>
</security:http>
```

The persistent token is changed during every request so that any theft of the remember-me cookie isn't useful for the attacker if another request by the user is performed just after the theft, because the stolen token expires and becomes useless when the user makes the new request.

User Session Management

Spring Security provides two separate session management features for web applications. The first one is support for invalidating `HttpSession` used during login, either with creating or changing its ID just after the login process. This is a protection against session fixation attacks. With session fixation attacks, a malicious user causes an `HttpSession` in the web application to be created. He then obtains the session ID and sends a legitimate user a URL containing this ID. When the legitimate user logs in using that URL, the malicious user also gains access to the system through that `HttpSession`. Web applications should never allow the `HttpSession` that is used during the login phase to be used after the login step. Web applications should either create a new `HttpSession` or change the session ID after login. You configure session fixation prevention by placing the `<security:session-management>` element in `<security:http>` as follows:

```
<security:http>
    <security:session-management/>
</security:http>
```

The `<security:session-management>` element has a `session-fixation-protection` attribute, which can accept one of the following values: `none`, `newSession`, `migrateSession`, or `changeSessionId`. The default value is `none`; it doesn't touch the current `HttpSession` that was created before the login process. When `newSession` is used, a new `HttpSession` is created after login. If `migrateSession` is used, a new `HttpSession` is created, and attributes in the old one are moved into the new one. The last value, `changeSessionId`, has been introduced recently. It is based on Servlet API 3.1. `HttpServletRequest` has the `changeSessionId()` method, and it just replaces the old session ID with a new one in the current `HttpSession` object.

The second feature is managing the number of concurrent sessions opened by the same user. Spring Security can track how many open sessions belong to a user, and you can limit the number. You enable the mechanism by adding the `<security:concurrency-control>` element in `<security:session-management>`. It provides two different behaviors. One behavior terminates the oldest session of the user when the maximum allowed session limit is exceeded. The following code snippet shows how you can enable this behavior:

```
<security:session-management>
    <security:concurrency-control
        error-if-maximum-exceeded="false"
        expired-url="/sessionExpired.jsp" max-sessions="1" />
</security:session-management>
```

When the `error-if-maximum-exceeded` attribute is set to `false`, Spring Security expires the oldest session of the user who opened up a new login session from somewhere else. When the user of that expired session tries to access the application the next time, she will be redirected to the specified `expired-url`.

The other behavior prevents a new login from occurring if the limit has been exceeded. Spring Security tracks session information using a bean of type `org.springframework.security.core.session.SessionRegistry`. The following code snippet shows how you can enable this behavior:

```
<security:session-management>
    <security:concurrency-control
        error-if-maximum-exceeded="true" max-sessions="1" />
</security:session-management>
```

For the second behavior to operate successfully, you need to add the following listener element into the `web.xml` file of the application:

```
<listener>
    <listener-class>
        org.springframework.security.web.session.HttpSessionEventPublisher
    </listener-class>
</listener>
```

`HttpSessionEventPublisher` is an implementation of `javax.servlet.HttpSessionListener`, and it's invoked at `HttpSession` creation and destruction times. It publishes `HttpSessionCreatedEvent` and `HttpSessionDestroyedEvent` in instances in the `ApplicationContext`. The `SessionRegistryImpl` class, which is an implementation of `SessionRegistry`, is also an `ApplicationListener` that listens for `HttpSessionDestroyedEvent` instances published in the `ApplicationContext`. When such an event is received, the corresponding session information is removed from the registry, and an open session count is managed accordingly. Unless `HttpSessionEventPublisher` is defined in the `web.xml` file and users leave their applications by just closing their browser windows, Spring Security won't be notified of expired `HttpSessions`. As a result, when the maximum allowed session limit is exceeded by a user, new logins won't be permitted at all.

Basic Authentication

Basic authentication is a very popular authentication mechanism used for authenticating stateless web services. It is quite common to use it with login form authentication where the application is used through a browser and its services are accessed over the web, such as through a RESTful API.

Basic authentication is defined by RFC 1945, and the Spring Security implementation conforms to it. Its popularity comes from its broad acceptance among user agents and from its very simple implementation. User credentials are encoded with Base64 encoding, and they are carried in an

HTTP header. This simplicity also becomes its weakness because users' passwords can easily be obtained by a third party who observes network traffic. Therefore, it should only be used over a secure transport layer, such as HTTPS.

Basic authentication is configured with the `<security:http-basic>` element in `<security:http>` as follows:

```
<security:http>
    <security:http-basic/>
</security:http>
```

When basic authentication is required, `org.springframework.security.web.authentication` `.www.BasicAuthenticationEntryPoint` just places the following headers in the HTTP response:

```
HTTP/1.1 401 Full authentication is required to access this resource
WWW-Authenticate: Basic realm="Spring Security Application"
```

This response header causes the browser to display its own login dialog box. When the user enters his username and password and submits the information, the request is sent with the following header:

```
Authorization: Basic dXNlcjE6c2VjcmV0
```

The encoded part is a Base64-encoded form of *username:password* entered by the user. If you try to access a web service resource via an HTTP client other than the web browser, you need to encode *username:password* with a Base64 encoder and place it into an HTTP request using your client's facilities.

On the server side, `BasicAuthenticationFilter` is responsible for processing credentials presented in the request header. It extracts the username and password to create a `UsernamePasswordAuthenticationToken`, and it delegates the task to the `AuthenticationManager` bean. The rest of the process is the same as login form authentication. `BasicAuthenticationFilter` only triggers authentication if the `Authorization` request header is present with a value starting with a "`Basic`" string.

AUTHORIZING WEB REQUESTS AND SERVICE METHOD CALLS

Authorization checks whether the currently authenticated user has the appropriate rights to perform operations on a secure resource. A secure resource can be any of the URL resources, a service method call, or a domain object. Operations that authorization checks for include access to a web page; invocation of a service method; or performance of an operation, such as reading, creating, updating, or deleting a domain object.

Authorizing Web Requests

One of the most common authorization requirements of web applications is to protect web pages or web resources, in general, from unauthorized access. The following Try It Out shows you how it is achieved using Spring Security Framework.

TRY IT OUT Authorizing Web Requests

In this Try It Out, you configure the Spring Security so that it will authorize web requests made to some protected web pages. You can continue from where you left off in the preceding Try It Out, and you can find the source code within the project named `authorizing-web-requests` in the code downloads. To begin, follow these steps:

1. Create the `editor.jsp` page in the `src/main/webapp` folder:

```
<%@ page language="java" contentType="text/html; charset=ISO-8859-1"
    pageEncoding="ISO-8859-1"%>
<!DOCTYPE html PUBLIC "-//W3C//DTD HTML 4.01 Transitional//EN"
"http://www.w3.org/TR/html4/loose.dtd">
<html>
<head>
<meta http-equiv="Content-Type" content="text/html; charset=ISO-8859-1">
<title>Insert title here</title>
</head>
<body>
editors only page
</body>
</html>
```

2. Add the following `<security:intercept-url>` to protect `editor.jsp`:

```
<security:http auto-config="true">
    <security:intercept-url pattern="/editor.jsp" access="ROLE_EDITOR"/>
    <security:intercept-url pattern="/**" access="ROLE_USER"/>
</security:http>
```

3. Run the application with `jetty:run`.

4. Log in to the application with **user1** and the password **secret**. Then try to access `editor.jsp` by typing **http://localhost:8080/editor.jsp** in the browser address bar. You should see a 403 access denied page.

5. Log out from the application by typing **http://localhost:8080/j_spring_security_logout**.

6. Log in to the application again, but this time use **user2** and the password **secret**. Again try to access `editor.jsp`. You should now see the `editor.jsp` page.

How It Works

You created an `editor.jsp` page in the `src/main/webapp` folder and placed the `<security:intercept-url/>` element in `<security:http>` so that it can only be accessed by users defined as `ROLE_EDITOR`. The important point here is that there can be several `<security:intercept-url>` elements defining roles for different resource patterns, and their order is important. Here the `<security:intercept-url>` element with `pattern="/editor.jsp"` should come before other elements with `pattern="/**"`. If it was the other way around, because `pattern="/**"` matches requests to the `/editor.jsp` page as well, the page would be accessible to users without the `ROLE_EDITOR` authority. Figure 12-7 shows what is going on when a request is performed by `user1`.

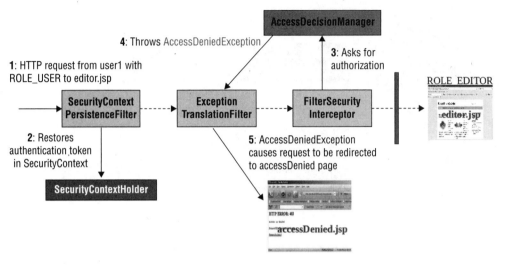

FIGURE 12-7

When the request arrives at the web application, `SecurityContextPersistenceFilter` restores the `Authentication` token by grabbing it from `HttpSession` and putting it into `SecurityContext` via `SecurityContextHolder`. Then it lets the request flow in. When the request comes at `FilterSecurityInterceptor`, it asks for `AccessDecisionManager` to authorize the request. `AccessDecisionManager` checks the rights for `user1` and decides that she has not been granted access to `editor.jsp`. It throws `AccessDeniedException`. At this point `ExceptionTranslationFilter` comes in to the scene to catch the exception and show the access denied page.

When `user2` performs the same request, the same thing happens until the `AccessDecisionManager` bean's decision. At this point, it allows the user to access the resource. As a result, `FilterSecurityInterceptor` lets the request arrive at the `editor.jsp` page.

How Does Authorization Work?

The main object of the authorization process is `AccessDecisionManager`. It decides whether the attempted action by the current user will be allowed. Figure 12-8 shows a general flowchart of the authorization process.

Delegation of access control checks to `AccessDecisionManager` is handled by a proxy object that intercepts the request or method call to the secure resource. The proxy object for web resources is `FilterSecurityInterceptor`. It is a servlet filter that is the last element in the security filter chain. For service method calls, the proxy object is `MethodSecurityInterceptor`. Both extend from `AbstractSecurityInterceptor`.

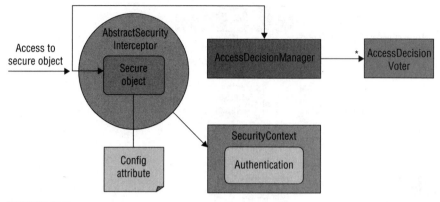

FIGURE 12-8

During configuration time, it is expected that you define what roles are allowed to access or perform a specific operation on the secure resource. Those definitions are called `org.springframework.security.access.ConfigAttribute`. In other words, secure objects are associated with several `ConfigAttribute` instances. At run time, when access occurs to the secure resource, `AbstractSecurityInterceptor` obtains `ConfigAttribute` values associated with the secure object, and it also obtains the current `Authentication` token that resides in `SecurityContext`.

The next step is to delegate the task to `AccessDecisionManager`, which handles `ConfigAttribute` objects and the `Authentication` to perform authorization. `AccessDecisionManager` is actually in the coordinator position. It contains several `org.springframework.security.access.AccessDecisionVoter` objects. Each `AccessDecisionVoter` is asked if it grants or denies access to a secure object by examining available `ConfigAttribute` values and a current `Authentication` token. `AccessDecisionVoter` beans can be of different types. They are classified according to the type of `ConfigAttribute` values they can handle. If `AccessDecisionVoter` cannot process `ConfigAttribute`, it just returns `ACCESS_ABSTAIN`. If it can process `ConfigAttribute`, it then checks whether the current `Authentication` token satisfies `ConfigAttribute`. If the check is successful, it returns `ACCESS_GRANTED`; otherwise it returns `ACCESS_DENIED`. `AccessDecisionManager` performs the final decision according to those answers returned by `AccessDecisionVoter` beans.

The three built-in implementations of the `AccessDecisionManager` interface are

➤ `org.springframework.security.access.vote.AffirmativeBased`, which allows access when at least one `AccessDecisionVoter` returns `ACCESS_GRANTED`

➤ `org.springframework.security.access.vote.UnanimousBased`, which allows access when all the voters return `ACCESS_GRANTED`

➤ `org.springframework.security.access.vote.ConsensusBased`, which compares the sum of `ACCESS_GRANTED` answers with the sum of `ACCESS_DENIED` answers, and it decides according to the result

> **NOTE** `AffirmativeBased` *allows access when at least one* `AccessDecicionVoter` *returns* `ACCESS_GRANTED`. `UnanimousBased`, *on the other hand, allows access when all the voters return* `ACCESS_GRANTED`. *If any one of them returns* `ACCESS_DENIED`, `UnanimousBased` *will throw* `AccessDeniedException`. *The last one,* `ConsensusBased`, *compares the sum of* `ACCESS_GRANTED` *answers with the sum of* `ACCESS_DENIED` *answers, and it decides according to the result.*

By default, the `<security:http>` element registers the `AffirmativeBased AccessDecisionManager` implementation with two `AccessDecisionVoter` implementations: `org.springframework.security` `.access.vote.RoleVoter` and `org.springframework.security.access.vote.AuthenticatedVoter`.

The `RoleVoter` implementation understands `ConfigAttribute` objects whose `getAttribute()` method returns a `String` value starting with the `ROLE_` prefix. Unless the `ConfigAttribute` value starts with `ROLE_`, it returns `ACCESS_ABSTAIN`. If a given `ConfigAttribute` returns such a `String` value, it then tries to compare it with names of `GrantedAuthority` objects available in the current `Authentication` token. If the match occurs, it returns `ACCESS_GRANTED`; otherwise it returns `ACCESS_DENIED`.

The second one defined by default is `AuthenticatedVoter`. It understands special keywords that represent the current `Authentication` status: `IS_AUTHENTICATED_REMEMBERED`, `IS_AUTHENTICATED_ANONYMOUSLY`, and `IS_AUTHENTICATED_FULLY`. If the access attribute of `<security:intercept-url>` contains any of those keywords, `AuthenticatedVoter` checks the type of the `Authentication` token. If the `ConfigAttribute` value is `IS_AUTHENTICATED_FULLY`, it then expects the `Authentication` token to be only `UsernamePasswordAuthenticationToken`. Otherwise it returns `ACCESS_DENIED`. In other words, it disallows logins with the remember-me feature and forces the user to log in interactively. If the value is `IS_AUTHENTICATED_REMEMBERED`, it then accepts either `UsernamePasswordAuthenticationToken` or `RememberMeAuthenticationToken`, but it denies `AnonymousAuthenticationToken`. As previously stated, conceptually, anonymous authentication is no different than being unauthenticated. Finally, if the attribute value is `IS_AUTHENTICATED_ANONYMOUSLY`, it accepts any valid `Authentication` token present in the `SecurityContext`.

Expression-Based Authorization

It is possible to employ Spring Expression Language (SpEL) in defining `ConfigAttribute` values. This is called *expression-based authorization.* It is disabled by default. To enable it, add the `use-expressions="true"` attribute to the `<security:http>` element as follows:

```
<security:http auto-config="true" use-expressions="true">
    <security:intercept-url pattern="/**"
        access="hasRole('ROLE_USER') and hasIpAddress(192.168.1.0/24)"/>
</security:http>
```

It then becomes possible to use a SpEL expression in access attributes of `<security:intercept-url>`. Spring Security provides some built-in functions for authorization checks and for specifying the expected type of `Authentication` token. Table 12-1 lists some common expressions available for use.

TABLE 12-1: Common Built-In Expressions

EXPRESSION	DESCRIPTION
hasRole('ROLE_USER')	Returns true if current Authentication has the specified role
hasAnyRole('ROLE_USER','ROLE_EDITOR')	Returns true if current Authentication has at least one of the specified roles
hasAuthority('ROLE_USER')	Same as hasRole()
hasAnyAuthority('ROLE_USER','ROLE_EDITOR')	Same as hasAnyRole()
hasIpAddress ('192.168.1.0/24')	Returns true if the current user accesses from a specified IP address or address range
principal	Allows access to the principal object representing the current user within the current Authentication token
authentication	Allows access to the current Authentication token in SecurityContext
permitAll	Always evaluates to true
denyAll	Always evaluates to false
isAnonymous()	Returns true if the principal is an anonymous user
isRememberMe()	Returns true if the principal is a remember-me user
isAuthenticated()	Returns true if the principal is not an anonymous user
isFullyAuthenticated()	Returns true if the principal is not an anonymous or remember-me user

> **NOTE** When you enable an expression in the <security:http> element, an org.springframework.security.web.access.expression .WebExpressionVoter is registered at AccessDecisionManager instead of RoleVoter and AuthenticatedVoter.

Using JSP Security Tags

Spring Security has its own JavaServer Pages (JSP) tag library that provides basic support for displaying current authentication information and applying authorization checks within JSP pages. To use the security tag library, after adding the spring-security-taglibs dependency in your pom.xml file, you must also declare it in the JSP page as follows:

```
<%@ taglib prefix="sec" uri="http://www.springframework.org/security/tags" %>
```

Authorize Tag

The `authorize` tag is used to determine whether the content written between the `<sec:authorize>` tags should be evaluated by the JSP. It can be used to display individual HTML elements—such as buttons—in the page, according to the granted authorities of the current user. The following code snippet shows how an HTML link can be made available in the web page if the current user has specified authorities:

```
<sec:authorize ifAllGranted="ROLE_EDITOR">
        <a href="editor.jsp">Editors only</a>
</sec:authorize>
```

If all roles listed in the `ifAllGranted` attribute are available among granted authorities of the current user, the Editors Only link is visible. It also has the `ifAnyGranted` and `ifNotGranted` attributes that can be used similarly. It is possible to use expressions with an access attribute. For this feature to work, you must enable expression support in the `<security:http>` element. Actually, the `ifAllGranted`, `ifAnyGranted`, and `ifNotGranted` attributes were recently deprecated in favor of `access` attribute, which has support for SpEL expressions as well. The following code shows how the `access` attribute can be used:

```
<sec:authorize access="hasRole('ROLE_EDITOR')">
        <a href="editor.jsp">Editors only</a>
</sec:authorize>
```

The `authorize` tag also has a `url` attribute. If you place a URL in that attribute, Spring Security tries to check the URL against the `<security:intercept-url/>` elements. If the current user is allowed to access the specified URL, the content of the tag is visible. Here's an example:

```
<sec:authorize url="/editor.jsp">
        <a href="editor.jsp">Editors only</a>
</sec:authorize>
```

Authenticate Tag

The `authenticate` tag is used to access the contents of the current `Authentication` token in `SecurityContext`. It can be used to display information about the current user in the page as shown here:

```
<sec:authentication property="principal.username"/>
```

`principal.username` is resolved through the `Authentication` token's `principal` property.

```
<sec:authentication property="name"/>
```

The `name` value is resolved directly from the `Authentication` token.

Authorizing Service Methods

You can secure your service layer methods using Spring Security. It provides support for various annotations that can be used to specify who is allowed to execute the service method. First of all, it has always been possible to secure method calls with the `@Secured` annotation. Pre/post authorize annotations are added to the security framework for supporting expression based security in version 3. It is also possible to use JSR-250 annotations as well.

Method-level security is enabled by adding the following namespace element in the bean configuration file. By default, neither of the supported annotation methods is enabled. You can enable them as follows:

```
<security:global-method-security
    jsr250-annotations="enabled" secured-annotations="enabled"
    pre-post-annotations="enabled">
</security:global-method-security>
```

JSR-250 security annotations consist of `@RolesAllowed`, `@PermitAll`, and `@DenyAll`. The `@Secured` annotation is the framework's own annotation, which is similar to JSR-250 `@RolesAllowed`. Pre/post annotations are `@PreAuthorize`, `@PostAuthorize`, `@PreFilter`, and `@PostFilter`. Except for `@PreAuthorize`, the annotations are usually used with access control list (ACL) domain object security. It is possible to use these annotations both on the class and method levels, as well as mix them in the same bean. The following Try It Out shows how method-level security can be configured in Spring Security and used to secure service bean method calls.

TRY IT OUT Authorizing Service Methods

In this Try It Out, you configure the method-level security feature of Spring Security to secure service bean method calls. You then test whether it works using JUnit tests in a standalone environment. You can find the source code within the project named `authorizing-service-methods` in the code downloads. To begin follow these steps:

1. Create a simple Maven Java project.

2. Add the following dependencies to the `pom.xml` file:

```
<dependency>
    <groupId>org.springframework.security</groupId>
    <artifactId>spring-security-web</artifactId>
    <version>3.2.5.RELEASE</version>
</dependency>
<dependency>
    <groupId>org.springframework.security</groupId>
    <artifactId>spring-security-config</artifactId>
    <version>3.2.5.RELEASE</version>
</dependency>

<dependency>
    <groupId>commons-logging</groupId>
    <artifactId>commons-logging</artifactId>
    <version>1.1.1</version>
</dependency>

<dependency>
    <groupId>javax.servlet</groupId>
    <artifactId>javax.servlet-api</artifactId>
    <version>3.1.0</version>
</dependency>
```

```
</dependency>

<dependency>
    <groupId>junit</groupId>
    <artifactId>junit</artifactId>
    <version>4.11</version>
    <scope>test</scope>
</dependency>
<dependency>
    <groupId>org.springframework</groupId>
    <artifactId>spring-test</artifactId>
    <version>4.0.5.RELEASE</version>
    <scope>test</scope>
</dependency>
```

3. Create a Spring bean configuration file called `applicationContext.xml` in the `src/main/resources` folder:

```xml
<?xml version="1.0" encoding="UTF-8"?>
<beans xmlns="http://www.springframework.org/schema/beans"
    xmlns:xsi="http://www.w3.org/2001/XMLSchema-instance"
    xmlns:security="http://www.springframework.org/schema/security"
    xsi:schemaLocation="http://www.springframework.org/schema/security
    http://www.springframework.org/schema/security/spring-security-3.2.xsd
        http://www.springframework.org/schema/beans
    http://www.springframework.org/schema/beans/spring-beans.xsd">

</beans>
```

4. Add the following bean configurations to the `applicationContext.xml` file:

```xml
<security:authentication-manager>
    <security:authentication-provider ref="testingAuthenticationProvider"/>
</security:authentication-manager>

<bean id="testingAuthenticationProvider"
class="org.springframework.security.authentication.TestingAuthenticationProvider"/>

<security:global-method-security secured-annotations="enabled"/>
```

5. Create the `com.wiley.beginningspring` package and create the following class in it:

```java
public class BusinessService {
    @Secured("ROLE_USER")
    public void secureMethod() {
        System.out.println("secure method");
    }
}
```

6. Create a bean definition for the `BusinessService` class:

```xml
<bean id="businessService" class="com.wiley.beginningspring.BusinessService"/>
```

7. Create the `com.wiley.beginningspring` package in the `src/test/java` source folder and create the following class in it:

```
@RunWith(SpringJUnit4ClassRunner.class)
@ContextConfiguration("/applicationContext.xml")
public class MethodLevelSecurityTests {
    @Autowired
    private BusinessService businessService;

    @After
    public void tearDown() {
        SecurityContextHolder.clearContext();
    }


    @Test(expected=AuthenticationCredentialsNotFoundException.class)
    public void testSecureMethodWithoutAuthentication() {
        businessService.secureMethod();
    }

    @Test(expected=AccessDeniedException.class)
    public void testSecureMethodWithoutAppropriateAuthority() {
        TestingAuthenticationToken authentication =
            new TestingAuthenticationToken("user1", "secret");
        SecurityContextHolder.getContext().setAuthentication(authentication);

        businessService.secureMethod();
    }

    @Test
    public void testSecureMethodWithAppropriateAuthority() {
        TestingAuthenticationToken authentication =
            new TestingAuthenticationToken("user1", "secret","ROLE_USER");
        SecurityContextHolder.getContext().setAuthentication(authentication);

        businessService.secureMethod();
    }

}
```

8. Run the tests using JUnit.

How It Works

You created a simple Java project and added the necessary dependencies to configure and run Spring Security for method-level security. Afterward, you created a bean configuration file and enabled the security namespace in it.

You added the `<security:global-method-security/>` element with the `secured-annotations="enabled"` attribute. That way, you can use the `@Secured` annotation over your Spring-managed beans' classes or their methods. This element causes Spring Security to configure an `AccessDecisionManager` bean of `AffirmativeBased`, including the `RoleVoter` and `AuthenticatedVoter` voter instances.

Spring Security expects an `Authentication` token to be presented in `SecurityContext` to assume that authentication is performed but doesn't care who put it there. It provides an `org.springframework.security.authentication.TestingAuthenticationProvider` for this purpose. If you create an `Authentication` token of type `org.springframework.security.authentication.Testing AuthenticationToken` and place it into `SecurityContext`, `TestingAuthenticationProvider`—assuming it is among the configured `AuthenticationProvider` instances of `AuthenticationManager`—automatically validates it and authentication finishes with success. Hence, it is easy to test method-level security features within standalone test environments.

You can just create a `TestingAuthenticationToken` with the necessary `principal` and `GrantedAuthority` objects for the test case, and the rest is handled by `TestingAuthenticationProvider`. Therefore, you created a bean called `testingAuthenticationProvider` from the `TestingAuthenticationProvider` class and referenced it via the `<security:authentication-provider>` element within `<security:authentication-manager>`. It is advisable to remove the `TestingAuthenticationProvider` bean from among the configured `AuthenticationProvider` instances in production because of security reasons. It is solely for testing purposes.

After finishing the bean configuration in the `ApplicationContext` file, you created a class called `BusinessService` and defined a bean for it. Within that class, you added a method with the `@Secured` annotation on it. The `@Secured` annotation has a value of `ROLE_USER`. This means that this method is only accessible for users who have `ROLE_USER` among their `GrantedAuthority` instances.

Then you created a test method and configured it with Spring `TestContext` so that it loads the `ApplicationContext` when tests are run. You injected `BusinessService` within the test class using the `@Autowired` annotation.

Within the test class, you created three test methods. Let's look at them in detail:

➤ `testSecureMethodWithoutAuthentication()` just invokes `businessService.secureMethod()` without creating an `AuthenticationToken` and putting it into `SecurityContext`. When the test method is run using JUnit, Spring Security throws `AuthenticationCredentialsNotFoundException`.

➤ `testSecureMethodWithoutAppropriateAuthority()` creates a `TestingAuthenticationToken` and places it into `SecurityContext` through `SecurityContextHolder`. However, the created token doesn't contain an `Authority` with the value `ROLE_USER`. Therefore, when you run the test method, Spring Security throws `AccessDeniedException`.

➤ `testSecureMethodWithAppropriateAuthority()` creates a `TestingAuthenticationToken` object providing it with `Authority` information. Therefore, that test method is able to invoke `secureMethod()` when it is run.

One important thing while coding those test methods is that you should clear `SecurityContext` after each test method runs. Otherwise, the `Authentication` token will stay in `SecurityContext` after the test method finishes, and this may cause a side effect to other methods that run together as a test suite. Therefore, we have added a `tearDown()` method that has the JUnit `@After` annotation and we have cleared `SecurityContext` within it.

You can also secure service beans in which you cannot employ Java annotations using the
`<security:protect-pointcut>` element in `<security:global-method-security>` as shown here:

```
<security:global-method-security>
  <security:protect-pointcut access="ROLE_USER" expression=
    "execution(* com.wiley.beginningspring.BusinessService.secureMethod(..))"/>
</security:global-method-security>
```

Assume that you don't or can't use any of those annotations supported by Spring Security in your
`BusinessService` class. In that case, you can add the `<security:protect-pointcut>` element, with the
roles listed in the access attribute. The expression attribute of the `<security:protect-pointcut>`
element expects an AspectJ pointcut expression. Therefore, you must add the `spring-aspects.jar`
dependency into your classpath to be able to run this feature.

SUMMARY

This chapter first quickly showed you the security features provided by Spring Security Framework
for web applications. Then you examined the Spring Security filter chain and its constituting elements by which those features are provided. The first Try It Out demonstrated how you can configure Spring Security within a web application. The chapter explained that Spring Security can be
configured with some of its features enabled by default so that web applications can satisfy some of
the most common, basic security requirements, and then developers can gradually customize those
features and add new ones as well.

The chapter talked about primary building blocks of the framework, such as `Authentication`,
`UserDetails`, `UserDetailsService`, `SecurityContext`, and `SecurityContextHolder`,
and then it walked through successful and unsuccessful login flows to explain in detail
how the authentication process works. During this part, you delved into the details of
`AuthenticationManager`, which is the coordinator of the authentication process. You also read
about the role of `AuthenticationProvider` objects and how `Authentication` tokens are related to
`AuthenticationProvider` implementations. After discovering how to successfully protect the application via an autogenerated login form, you found out how to customize the login page. The chapter
explained how logout works and talked about how its parts can be customized as well.

The chapter provided an explanation of how authorization works and discussed the fundamental
building blocks of the authorization process. The chapter focused on `AccessDecisionManager`, which
is the main actor of the authorization process, and its voters to which it asks if the `ConfigAttribute`
values of the currently accessed secure object can be satisfied by the granted authorities of the authenticated user. The second part of the authorization process was about how to secure service method
calls of Spring-managed beans in the `ApplicationContext`. The chapter explained the different annotations that you can use to specify the `ConfigAttribute` values of method call, and what you can do
to secure methods if it is not possible to employ those annotations over them. You learned that Spring
Security introduced expression-based access control so that access to secure resources can be protected
by employing SpEL expressions as `ConfigAttribute` values.

The chapter finished with a look at how service method calls can be tested within a standalone environment and how integration tests can be run in which `SecurityContext` is populated with a valid

`Authentication` token. As a result, developers can check method-level security features without deploying the whole application into the application server.

EXERCISES

You can find possible solutions to these exercises in Appendix A.

1. Configure concurrent session management so that a user can open at most one session in the application, and any other login attempt from the same user should result in an error message.

2. Configure Spring Security to use a basic authentication method (instead of form-based authentication) to protect access to URL resources.

3. Instead of using the `@Secured` annotation to protect access to `BusinessService`
`.secureMethod()`, enable pre/post annotations and use `@PreAuthorize` to protect it.

▶ **WHAT YOU LEARNED IN THIS CHAPTER**

TOPIC	KEY POINTS
springSecurityFilterChain	Filter chain that consists of several security filters
DelegatingFilterProxy	Filter implementation class defined in the web.xml file so that actual Filter beans can be defined within the Spring ApplicationContext
Authentication	Token that represents authentication information in the system
UserDetails	Principal information that represents the current user
UserDetailsService	UserDetails access interface that allows different user repositories to be used to manage user information
SecurityContext	Data structure in which the Authentication object is stored
SecurityContextHolder	Data structure in which SecurityContext is held and the current Authentication token is made accessible during the request
AuthenticationManager	Coordinator bean of the authentication process
AuthenticationProvider	Beans that are used to validate various types of Authentication tokens during the authentication process
DaoAuthenticationProvider	AuthenticationProvider implementation that validates UsernamePasswordAuthenticationToken
UsernamePasswordAuthenticationToken	Authentication token implementation that contains the username and password information submitted by the user during authentication, and also the GrantedAuthority objects of the current user when authentication is successful
UsernamePasswordAuthenticationFilter	Concrete subclass of AuthenticationProcessingFilter that handles login form submission, creates the Authentication token, and triggers the authentication process
SecurityContextPersistenceFilter	Security filter that saves the Authentication token between web requests

TOPIC	KEY POINTS
`FilterSecurityInterceptor`	Authorization filter that protects access to URL resources
`LogoutFilter`	Security filter that performs logout
`PasswordEncoder`	Interface to create encoded form of user passwords
`SaltSource`	Interface to provide a salt value during the password-encoding process to complicate dictionary attacks
`BasicAuthenticationFilter`	Security filter that manages the HTTP basic authentication process
`RememberMeAuthenticationToken`	`Authentication` token that represents the remember-me token
`RememberMeAuthenticationFilter`	Security `Filter` that handles the remember-me cookie and creates an `Authentication` token out of it
`RememberMeAuthenticationProvider`	`AuthenticationProvider` implementation that handles the `RememberMeAuthenticationToken`
`ConcurrentSessionFilter`	Security filter that manages session replacement or migration during the login process and concurrent session management of users from different locations
Session fixation attacks	Security attack that tries to exploit keeping `HttpSession` open after the login process
`HttpSessionEventPublisher`	Servlet listener that helps to track `HttpSession` timeouts and to update `SessionRegistry` to manage concurrent sessions
`AccessDecisionManager`	Coordinator bean of the authorization process
`AffirmativeBased`	Default implementation of `AccessDecisionManager` that allows access if at least one `ACCESS_GRANT` is issued by `AccessDecisionVoters`
`AccessDecisionVoter`	Interface to create voters that are consulted by `AccessDecisionManager` to evaluate `ConfigAttribute` values of secure objects against granted `Authority` objects of the current user

continues

(continued)

TOPIC	KEY POINTS
`RoleVoter`	Implementation of `AccessDecisionVoter` that handles `ConfigAttribute` values starting with the `ROLE_` prefix
`AuthenticatedVoter`	Implementation of `AccessDecisionVoter` that handles `ConfigAttribute` values of `IS_AUTHENTICATED_FULLY`, `IS_AUTHENTICATED_REMEMBERED`, and `IS_AUTHENTICATED_ANONYMOUSLY`
`MethodSecurityInterceptor`	Concrete subclass of `AbstractSecurityInterceptor` that is used to secure service method calls
`@Secured, @PreAuthorize`	Security annotations that are used to specify `ConfigAttribute` values of service methods
`TestingAuthenticationToken`	Implementation of `Authentication` token that is used to create a valid authentication object that expects principal, credential, and `GrantedAuthority` objects during its construction. It is used in standalone integration tests.
`TestingAuthenticationProvider`	Implementation of `AuthenticationProvider` that is used to handle `TestingAuthenticationToken` instances

Next Stop: Spring 4.0

WHAT YOU WILL LEARN IN THIS CHAPTER:

➤ Keeping up with the latest: Java 8 and Java EE7 support

➤ Configuring injection with conditional dependency

➤ Ordering the elements of autowired collections

➤ Repeating annotations

➤ Introducing new annotations

> **CODE DOWNLOAD** *The wrox.com code downloads for this chapter are found at* www.wrox.com/go/beginningspring *on the Download Code tab. The code is in the Chapter 13 download and individually named according to the names throughout the chapter.*

It's been more than four years since the last major release of the Spring Framework, which was version 3.0. Versions 3.1 and 3.2 followed up by bringing features such as Java 7 and Java EE6 support into the enterprise world. Now the producers of Spring offer the best of the breed with version 4.0, which offers full support of Java 8 and Java EE7. This chapter covers the new features introduced by the framework as well as the features added for supporting the new versions of Java.

Even though Spring 4.0 is compatible with the latest versions of Java SE and Java EE, it still supports the older versions. Going back to JDK6 update 18 and Java EE6, the framework offers the functionality for former versions. Servlet 2.5 is also supported especially for deployment on Google App Engine, which means that Java EE5 support is also on board. But developers of the framework strongly suggest that you move onto at least Java EE6 so that you can experience better testing integration.

KEEPING UP WITH THE LATEST: JAVA 8 AND JAVA EE7 SUPPORT

The codebase has been pruned with Spring 4, and deprecated methods, classes, and packages have been removed. The specifications supported by the framework have also been incremented by version, so the latest features of Java 8 and Java EE 7—such as JPA 2.1, JSR 349 – Bean Validation 1.1, JTA 1.2, and JMS 2.0—are now supported with version 4.0.

This section goes through these features and details them with examples so you get to know them with real-world working samples.

Lambda Expressions

Lambda expressions are anonymous function code blocks with parameters that can be executed once or multiple times. The benefits of lambda expressions include reduced typing and increased code readability. With version 4, the Spring classes within the application programming interface (API), such as `JdbcTemplate`, `MessageTemplate`, and `TransactionTemplate`, provide integration with lambda expressions.

The Try It Out in this section demonstrates the use of lambda expressions with the new version of `JdbcTemplate`. For the sake of simplicity, we have rewritten the activity from the "Configuring and Using Spring Jdbctemplate" Try It Out in Chapter 4 using lambda expressions.

TRY IT OUT   Integrating JdbcTemplate with Lambda Expressions

Use the following steps to create a domain class, its DAO, and the database configurations to use the lambda expressions in the DAO implementation to fetch data through `JdbcTemplate`. You can find the source of the project named as `lambdaexpressions` within the zip file of the code downloads.

1. Create an empty Maven application project from the archetype `maven-archetype-quickstart`. Add the `spring-core`, `spring-context`, and `spring-jdbc` dependencies to your `pom.xml` file. At the time of writing this book, the latest version of Spring subprojects was the `4.0.5.RELEASE`:

```
<dependency>
    <groupId>org.springframework</groupId>
    <artifactId>spring-core</artifactId>
    <version>4.0.5.RELEASE</version>
</dependency>
<dependency>
    <groupId>org.springframework</groupId>
    <artifactId>spring-context</artifactId>
    <version>4.0.5.RELEASE</version>
</dependency>
<dependency>
    <groupId>org.springframework</groupId>
    <artifactId>spring-jdbc</artifactId>
    <version>4.0.5.RELEASE</version>
</dependency>
```

2. Add the H2 database driver class dependency. At the time of writing this book the latest version of it was 1.3.175:

```
<dependency>
    <groupId>com.h2database</groupId>
    <artifactId>h2</artifactId>
    <version>1.3.175</version>
</dependency>
```

3. Create the files create.sql and populate.sql under the src/main/resources folder:

create.sql

```sql
CREATE TABLE ACCOUNT (
    ID BIGINT IDENTITY PRIMARY KEY,
    OWNER_NAME VARCHAR(255),
    BALANCE DOUBLE,
    ACCESS_TIME TIMESTAMP,
    LOCKED BOOLEAN
);
```

populate.sql

```sql
insert into account(id, owner_name,balance,access_time,locked)
        values(100, 'mertcaliskan',10000,CURRENT_DATE ,1);
```

4. Create the Account class under the com.wiley.beginningspring.ch13 package:

```java
public class Account {

    private long id;
    private String ownerName;
    private double balance;
    private Date accessTime;
    private boolean locked;

    public Account(long id, String owner_name, double balance,
                    Timestamp access_time, boolean locked) {
        this.id = id;
        this.ownerName = owner_name;
        this.balance = balance;
        this.accessTime = access_time;
        this.locked = locked;
    }

    @Override
    public String toString() {
        return "Account{" +
                "id=" + id +
                ", ownerName='" + ownerName + '\'' +
                ", balance=" + balance +
                ", accessTime=" + accessTime +
                ", locked=" + locked +
                '}';
    }
}
```

5. Create the `AccountDao` interface under the `com.wiley.beginningspring.ch13` package:

```
public interface AccountDao {
    Account find(long accountId);
}
```

6. Create the `AccountDaoJdbcImpl` class under the `com.wiley.beginningspring.ch13` package:

```
public class AccountDaoJdbcImpl implements AccountDao {

    private JdbcTemplate jdbcTemplate;

    public void setJdbcTemplate(JdbcTemplate jdbcTemplate) {
        this.jdbcTemplate = jdbcTemplate;
    }

    public Account find(long accountId) {
        return jdbcTemplate.queryForObject("select id, owner_name, balance,
    access_time,locked from account where id = " + accountId,
                (rs, rowNum) -> new Account(rs.getLong("id"),
                            rs.getString("owner_name"),
                            rs.getDouble("balance"),
                            rs.getTimestamp("access_time"),
                            rs.getBoolean("locked")));
    }
}
```

7. Create the `ApplicationConfig` class under the `com.wiley.beginningspring.ch13` package:

```
@Configuration
public class ApplicationConfig {

    @Bean
    public DataSource dataSource() {
        DriverManagerDataSource dataSource = new DriverManagerDataSource();
        dataSource.setDriverClassName("org.h2.Driver");
        dataSource.setUrl("jdbc:h2:mem:test;INIT=runscript from ~CA
            'classpath:create.sql'\\;runscript from 'classpath:populate.sql'");
        dataSource.setUsername("sa");
        dataSource.setPassword("");
        return dataSource;
    }
```

```
        cTemplate() {
        emplate = new JdbcTemplate();
        taSource(dataSource());
        e;
```

```
        countDao() {
        mpl accountDao = new AccountDaoJdbcImpl();
        JdbcTemplate(jdbcTemplate());
```

```
            return accountDao;
        }
    }
```

8. Create the `Main` class under the `com.wiley.beginningspring.ch13` package:

```java
public class Main {
    public static void main(String... args) throws SQLException {
        AnnotationConfigApplicationContext applicationContext =
            new AnnotationConfigApplicationContext(ApplicationConfig.class);

        AccountDao accountDao = applicationContext.getBean(AccountDao.class);
        Account account = accountDao.find(100L);

        System.out.println(account);
    }
}
```

9. Execute the `main` method of the `Main` class and you should see output similar to what's shown here (the date may differ):

```
Account{id=100, ownerName='mertcaliskan', balance=10000.0,
                        accessTime=2014-10-29 00:00:00.0, locked=true}
```

How It Works

First you created an empty Java project with the quick-start Maven archetype. Then you added the dependencies for `spring-core`, `spring-context`, and `spring-jdbc`.

You used the `H2` database for creating tables and putting sample data into it. Thus, you also added its Maven dependency. `H2` offers table creation and sample data creation while connecting via JDBC. So you defined two files: `create.sql` and `populate.sql`. They are provided as the URL parameter in the `dataSource` bean creation method of the `ApplicationConfig` class.

As the domain object, you created the `Account` class that contains fields such as the name of the owner, the balance, and so on. You then created a DAO interface and JDBC implementation of that interface class that contains the `find` method, which finds an account according to a given ID.

You rewrote the `find` method with lambda expressions so that you can easily parse a `ResultSet` and create the `Account` object. The syntax of the expression `(rs, rowNum)` maps to the `mapRow` method's signature stated in the `RowMapper` interface, which is `T mapRow(ResultSet rs, int rowNum)`. So you can say that you're creating an anonymous row mapper to map your result set into the fields of the `Account` class by instantiating that row mapper.

Method References

The new *method reference* feature introduced by Java 8 offers the same feature as lambda expressions, but it makes it possible to reuse any existing methods you have. The `find` method stated in the following snippet is a rewrite of the one in the `AccountDaoJdbcImpl` class given in the previous Try It Out activity:

```
public Account find(long accountId) {
    return jdbcTemplate.queryForObject("select id, owner_name, balance,
                access_time,locked from account where id = " + accountId,
            this::mapAccount);
}

private Account mapAccount(ResultSet rs, int rowNum) throws SQLException {
    return new Account(rs.getLong("id"),
                        rs.getString("owner_name"),
                        rs.getDouble("balance"),
                        rs.getTimestamp("access_time"),
                        rs.getBoolean("locked"));
}
```

Here, you are using your existing `mapAccount` row mapping method and referring to it within the `queryForObject` method with the *ContainingClass :: MethodName* syntax.

Bean Validation Integration

JSR 349 – Bean Validation 1.1 is officially supported with Spring 4. You can easily use Hibernate Validator as the reference implementation of JSR 349 – Bean Validation 1.1 as described in the "Validating User Input" section of Chapter 3.

JSR 310: Date Time Value Type Support

Because Java 8 is supported with the latest version of Spring, it's now possible to use the `@DateTimeFormat` annotation on top of classes coming from the `java.time` package of the Java Development Kit (JDK), such as `LocalDate`, `LocalTime`, `LocalDateTime`, and so on. You can find the details of this in the "Handling Forms with JSP" section of Chapter 3.

CONFIGURING INJECTION WITH CONDITIONAL DEPENDENCY

Spring 4 offers the *Conditional Bean Definition Model*, which interacts with the container to provide dynamic composition of an application's configuration. With the `@Conditional` annotation and the `Condition` interface, it's possible to handle creation of a bean and its dependency injection under certain circumstances, as shown in the following Try It Out.

TRY IT OUT   Conditional Bean Autowiring According to a Given System Property

Use the following steps to create an application that demonstrates dynamic bean injection according to a specified argument. You can find the source of the project named as `conditional` within the zip file in the code downloads.

1. Create an empty Maven application project from the archetype `maven-archetype-quickstart`. Add the `spring-core` and `spring-context` dependencies to your `pom.xml` file. At the time of writing this book, the latest version of Spring subprojects was the `4.0.5.RELEASE`:

```
<dependency>
    <groupId>org.springframework</groupId>
```

```
        <artifactId>spring-core</artifactId>
        <version>4.0.5.RELEASE</version>
    </dependency>
    <dependency>
        <groupId>org.springframework</groupId>
        <artifactId>spring-context</artifactId>
        <version>4.0.5.RELEASE</version>
    </dependency>
```

2. Create the `EmailNotificationCondition` class under the `com.wiley.beginningspring.ch13` package:

```java
public class EmailNotificationCondition implements Condition {

    @Override
    public boolean matches(ConditionContext context,
                           AnnotatedTypeMetadata metadata) {
        return context.getEnvironment().
            getProperty("notificationSystem").contains("email");
    }
}
```

3. Create the `SmsNotificationCondition` class under the `com.wiley.beginningspring.ch13` package:

```java
public class SmsNotificationCondition implements Condition {

    @Override
    public boolean matches(ConditionContext context,
                           AnnotatedTypeMetadata metadata) {
        return context.getEnvironment().
            getProperty("notificationSystem").contains("sms");
    }
}
```

4. Create the `NotificationService` interface under the `com.wiley.beginningspring.ch13` package:

```java
public interface NotificationService {

    void notify(String username);
}
```

5. Create the `EmailNotificationService` class under the `com.wiley.beginnir` package:

```java
public class EmailNotificationService implements Notificatior

    @Override
    public void notify(String username) {
        System.out.print("Notifying user: " + username + "
    }
}
```

6. Create the `SmsNotificationService` class under the `com.wiley.beginningspring.ch13` package:

```java
public class SmsNotificationService implements NotificationService {

    @Override
    public void notify(String username) {
        System.out.print("Notifying user: " + username + " with SMS.");
    }
}
```

7. Create the `ApplicationConfig` class under the `com.wiley.beginningspring.ch13` package:

```java
@Configuration
@ComponentScan(basePackages = {"com.wiley.beginningspring.ch13"})
public class ApplicationConfig {

    @Bean(name="notificationService")
    @Conditional(EmailNotificationCondition.class)
    public NotificationService emailNotifier() {
        return new EmailNotificationService();
    }

    @Bean(name="notificationService")
    @Conditional(SmsNotificationCondition.class)
    public NotificationService smsNotifier() {
        return new SmsNotificationService();
    }
}
```

8. Create the `Main` class under the `com.wiley.beginningspring.ch13` package:

```java
public class Main {

    public static void main(String... args) {
        ApplicationContext context =
            new AnnotationConfigApplicationContext(ApplicationConfig.class);
        NotificationService notificationService =
            (NotificationService) context.getBean("notificationService");
        notificationService.notify("johndoe");
    }
}
```

Execute the `main` method by providing the virtual machine (VM) argument as shown here:

```
-DnotificationSystem=sms
```

ee the following output:

```
tifying user: johndoe with SMS.
```

orks

ted an empty Java project with the quick-start Maven archetype. Then you added the
or spring-core and spring-context.

Then you implemented your condition classes that predicate the matching. The EmailNotificationCondition class checks for the system property notificationSystem, and if it's set to email it returns true. The SmsNotificationCondition class returns true by checking against the same system property (notificationSystem) as set to sms.

For the notification services, you first created the NotificationService interface with the notify method. The EmailNotificationService and SmsNotificationService classes just implemented this interface and printed out a notification message for the purposes of demonstration. Both of the notification service beans were configured within the ApplicationConfig class by an @Bean annotation. And both definitions contain the same bean name, so you can think of it like this: You have one notification service, and it can easily be configured according to the value of the notificationSystem system property. It can either be an e-mail notification service or an SMS notification service.

The Main class just accesses the notification service it has abstracted from the underlying bean, so it makes the notify method invocation regardless of the bean definition.

> **NOTE** *You can also use Spring Bean Profiles as an alternative to the Conditional Bean Definition Model.*

ORDERING THE ELEMENTS OF AUTOWIRED COLLECTIONS

It's possible to autowire all the beans of a specified type into a collection or an array with the @Autowired annotation in Spring. While doing this wiring, the order of injection was disregarded until version 4.0. Now, by applying @Order on the bean, you can provide an injection order for the collection. The following Try It Out demonstrates an example of this.

TRY IT OUT Ordering Elements on Autowired Collections

Use the following steps to create an application that instantiates multiple beans and injects them according to a specified order. You can find the source of the project named as beanorder within the zip file in the code downloads.

1. Create an empty Maven application project from the archetype maven-archetype-quickstart. Add the spring-core and spring-context dependencies to your pom.xml file. At the time of writing this book, the latest version of Spring subprojects was the 4.0.5.RELEASE:

```
<dependency>
    <groupId>org.springframework</groupId>
    <artifactId>spring-core</artifactId>
    <version>4.0.5.RELEASE</version>
</dependency>
<dependency>
    <groupId>org.springframework</groupId>
    <artifactId>spring-context</artifactId>
    <version>4.0.5.RELEASE</version>
</dependency>
```

2. Create the `Person` abstract class under the `com.wiley.beginningspring.ch13` package:

```
public abstract class Person {
}
```

3. Create the `Instructor` class under the `com.wiley.beginningspring.ch13` package:

```
@Component
@Order(value = 1)
public class Instructor extends Person {
}
```

4. Create the `StudentOne` class under the `com.wiley.beginningspring.ch13` package:

```
@Component
@Order(value = 3)
public class StudentOne extends Person {
}
```

5. Create the `StudentTwo` class under the `com.wiley.beginningspring.ch13` package:

```
@Component
@Order(value = 2)
public class StudentTwo extends Person {
}
```

6. Create the `Classroom` class under the `com.wiley.beginningspring.ch13` package:

```
@Component
public class Classroom {

    @Autowired
    private List<Person> classroomList;

    public List<Person> getClassroomList() {
        return classroomList;
    }
}
```

7. Create the `ApplicationConfig` class under the `com.wiley.beginningspring.ch13` package:

```
@Configuration
@ComponentScan(basePackages = {"com.wiley.beginningspring.ch13"})
public class ApplicationConfig {
}
```

8. Create the `Main` class under the `com.wiley.beginningspring.ch13` package and execute the `main` method:

```
public class Main {

    public static void main(String... args) {
        ApplicationContext context =
            new AnnotationConfigApplicationContext(ApplicationConfig.class);
```

```
            Classroom classroom = context.getBean(Classroom.class);

            System.out.println(classroom.getClassroomList());
        }
    }
```

How It Works

First you created an empty Java project with the quick-start Maven archetype. Then you added the dependencies for spring-core and spring-context.

You created the Person abstract class and then implemented Instructor, StudentOne, and StudentTwo as subclasses of it by defining them as Spring beans. The beans are also annotated with @Order to specify an order with an integer value as follows:

1. Instructor

2. StudentTwo

3. StudentOne

Your final domain object is Classroom, which contains a list of Person objects injected into it.

After doing the application context configuration, you retrieved the Classroom bean from the context and accessed its classroom list. The output should be similar to the bean order given and resemble the following:

```
[com.wiley.beginningspring.ch13.bean.Instructor@52525845,
    com.wiley.beginningspring.ch13.bean.StudentTwo@3b94d659,
    com.wiley.beginningspring.ch13.bean.StudentOne@24b1d79b]
```

REPEATING ANNOTATIONS

With the former versions of Spring, it was impossible to declare @Scheduled annotations more than once on a method. Because version 4.0 tightly integrates itself with Java 8, it brings support for the @Repeatable annotation, which enables the declaration of one annotation multiple times on a given method. The Try It Out in this section demonstrates the repeating annotations with a simple application.

TRY IT OUT   Using @Scheduled Multiple Times on a Method

Use the following steps to create an application that contains multiple @Scheduled annotations on a method with the help of Java 8. You can find the source of the project named as repeatableannotations within the zip file in the code downloads.

1. Create an empty Maven application project from the archetype maven-archetype-quickstart. Add the spring-core and spring-context dependencies to your pom.xml file. At the time of writing this book, the latest version of Spring subprojects was the 4.0.5.RELEASE:

```
<dependency>
    <groupId>org.springframework</groupId>
    <artifactId>spring-core</artifactId>
    <version>4.0.5.RELEASE</version>
```

```
    </dependency>
    <dependency>
        <groupId>org.springframework</groupId>
        <artifactId>spring-context</artifactId>
        <version>4.0.5.RELEASE</version>
    </dependency>
```

2. Create the `SchedulerBean` class under the `com.wiley.beginningspring.ch13` package:

```
@Service
public class SchedulerBean {

    @Scheduled(fixedDelay = 3000)
    @Scheduled(cron="0 00 01 * * *")
    public void doStuff() {
        System.out.println("Hi there!");
    }
}
```

3. Create the `ApplicationConfig` class under the `com.wiley.beginningspring.ch13` package:

```
@Configuration
@ComponentScan(basePackages = {"com.wiley.beginningspring.ch13"})
@EnableScheduling
public class ApplicationConfig {
}
```

4. Create the `Main` class under the `com.wiley.beginningspring.ch13` package and execute the `main` method:

```
public class Main {

    public static void main(String... args) {
        new AnnotationConfigApplicationContext(ApplicationConfig.class);
        while(true);
    }
}
```

How It Works

First you created an empty Java project with the quick-start Maven archetype. Then you added the dependencies for `spring-core` and `spring-context`.

You created a singleton service class named `SchedulerBean` that contains the `doStuff` method marked with two `@Scheduled` annotations. So according to the definitions given, this method will be fired every three seconds after each execution ends, and also it will be fired at 1:00 a.m. every morning.

You did the application context configuration with the `ApplicationConfig` class. It enables the component scan under the `com.wiley.beginningspring.ch13` package and then also enables the scheduling of specified methods with the `@EnableScheduling` annotation.

In the `Main` class, you first configured the application context, and then that went into an infinite loop to get the scheduling on the method to work. So every three seconds you see the output `Hi there!` along with the output `Hi there!` at 1:00 a.m.

> **NOTE** The @Scheduled *annotation refers to the* @Schedules *annotation as its container with the* @Repeatable *annotation. So if you are not using Java 8, you can still define multiple* @Scheduled *annotations with the help of this container as shown here:*
>
> ```
> @Schedules(value = {
>         @Scheduled(fixedDelay = 3000),
>         @Scheduled(cron="0 00 01 * * *")
> })
> public void doStuff() {
>     System.out.println("Hi there!");
> }
> ```
>
> *With Java 8, this container annotation is being created implicitly when multiple* @Scheduled *annotations are declared more than once on a method.*

> **NOTE** *If you experience a problem like the following error while you're compiling the source code of the example,*
>
> ```
> SchedulerBean.java:[15,4] error: repeated annotations are not
> supported in -source {0}
> ```
>
> *it might be because the* JAVA_HOME *environment is not set on your machine. Even if you installed Java 8 on your local, you also need to set the environment variable because it's directly being used by Maven.*

INTRODUCING NEW ANNOTATIONS

Spring 4.0 introduced new annotations into the framework. Aside from the annotations introduced in the previous section, a couple of others also exist, which are described in this section.

Documenting with @Description

The @Description annotation enables defining a textual description for the beans defined with the @Component or @Bean annotations. It's useful for documentation and to improve the code readability. A sample definition for a bean annotated with both @Component and @Order follows:

```
@Component
@Order(value = 1)
@Description("Instructor for the lecture BBM490 - Enterprise Web Architecture")
public class Instructor extends Person {
}
```

Using the @RestController Annotation

For creating REST-based web services, you can use the new `@RestController` annotation on controller classes. It's a convenience annotation that composes the `@Controller` and `@ResponseBody` annotations together in one place. You can find details in the "Creating Your First REST Web Service" section of Chapter 11.

SUMMARY

This chapter described what Spring 4.0 brought to the developers with the latest integration with Java 8 and Java EE7. You learned about lambda expressions and how they improved the use of row mappers in the JDBC template mechanism. You also saw the method reference version of the lambda expression to elaborate the usage of the Java 8.

The chapter then defined what the Conditional Bean Definition Model is and how you declare bean autowiring based on given conditions. You examined a scenario of applying order on the autowiring of the same types into collections. A Try It Out demonstrated the repeatable annotations with an example that defined multiple `@Scheduled` annotations on the same method.

> **TIP** It's highly recommended that you upgrade to Spring 4 because the version 3.2 branch has been moved to the maintenance state.

EXERCISES

You can find possible solutions to these exercises in Appendix A.

1. What are the two alternative methods that are introduced with Spring 4 for mapping row elements instead of by implementing a `RowMapper`?

2. Instead of defining a wrapper annotation for the repeating annotations, what is a better way offered by Spring 4?

▶ WHAT YOU LEARNED IN THIS CHAPTER

TOPIC	KEY POINTS
Lambda expression	An anonymous function code block with parameters that can be executed once or multiple times.
Method reference	A feature that is similar to lambda expressions but makes it possible to reuse the existing methods in the code.
Conditional Bean Definition Model	Implementation that interacts with the container to provide dynamic composition of an application's configuration.
@Conditional	Annotation that indicates that a component is only eligible for registration to the application context when all given conditions match.
@Repeatable	Annotation that enables the declaration of one annotation multiple times on a given method.
@Description	Annotation that enables defining a textual description for the beans defined with the @Component or @Bean annotations. It's useful for documentation and code readability.

APPENDIX

Solutions to Exercises

This chapter gathers the solutions to the exercises given in the chapters. We have recapped the exercises along with their possible solutions. You can also download the working code samples as stated in the Code Download section.

> **CODE DOWNLOAD** *The wrox.com code downloads for this appendix are found at* www.wrox.com/go/beginningspring *on the Download Code tab. The code is in the Appendix A download and individually named according to the names throughout the appendix.*

CHAPTER 1

Exercise 1

Investigate the in-container test frameworks available today. What are their biggest advantages and disadvantages compared to testing outside the container?

Solution to Exercise 1

Few in-container server-side testing frameworks are available. One of them is Arquillian, developed at JBoss.org. It enables developers to write integration tests for business objects executed inside a container. The container may be a Java EE application server, or a Servlet/Web Container. You can find more information about Arquillian at http://arquillian.org/.

The other in-container test framework available is the Jersey Test Framework. Jersey is the reference implementation of the JAX-RS specification, and the Jersey Test Framework is used to test RESTful web applications developed using Jersey remotely. You can find more information about the Jersey Test Framework at `https://jersey.java.net/documentation/latest/` `test-framework.html`.

Advantages of in-container testing include the following:

➤ You deploy the application and run the tests in the actual full stack environment compared to a mocked-up environment that is partly built during test setup.

➤ Tests written for and run within the target environment enable you to check real usage scenarios as opposed to mocked-up tests that might be totally unrelated to actual user experiences.

Disadvantages of in-container testing include the following:

➤ It is much slower than running tests out of the container, because it takes time to deploy and run the application in the target environment.

➤ It might consume more resources like CPU time and memory space because it brings up the entire application at run time.

➤ It is easy to get distracted from test-driven programming because you are more inclined to first code up the components and then bring them together to test in the container.

Exercise 2

What IoC method is used by the new EJB programming model today?

Solution to Exercise 2

Java EE uses Context and Dependency Injection (CDI) as its dependency injection method. It has been standardized via JSR-299. CDI provides type-safe and annotation-driven dependency injection capabilities for the Java EE platform. Besides dependency injection features, CDI enhances the Java EE programming model in two more important ways. First, it allows you to use EJBs directly as JSF backing beans. Second, CDI allows you to manage the scope, state, life cycle, and context for objects in a declarative way. JSR 299 utilizes the Dependency Injection for Java (JSR 330) specification as its foundational API, primarily by using JSR 330 annotations such as `@Inject`, `@Qualifier`, and `@ScopeType`. You can find more information about CDI at `https://docs.oracle.com/` `javaee/6/tutorial/doc/giwhl.html`.

Exercise 3

Which dependency injection method can handle "circular dependencies" and which cannot?

Solution to Exercise 3

Constructor injection cannot handle circular dependencies. Assume you have the following bean configuration:

```
<bean id="foo" class="com.wiley.beginningspring.exercises.ch1.Foo">
    <constructor-arg ref="bar"/>
</bean>

<bean id="bar" class="com.wiley.beginningspring.exercises.ch1.Bar">
    <constructor-arg ref="foo"/>
</bean>
```

When the `foo` bean is being created, Spring Container tries to obtain the `bar` bean to inject it into the `foo` bean via constructor of the `Foo` class. It then tries to create the `bar` bean, but this time it tries to obtain the `foo` bean in order to inject it into the `bar` bean similar to `Foo` class. At this point the `foo` bean cannot be obtained for injection because it is not ready for dependency injection yet. As a result, Spring throws `BeanCurrentlyInCreationException` to indicate the circular dependency problem.

Setter injection, on the other hand, can handle it. Let's examine the following bean configuration:

```
<bean id="foo" class="com.wiley.beginningspring.exercises.ch1.Foo">
    <property name="bar" ref="bar"/>
</bean>

<bean id="bar" class="com.wiley.beginningspring.exercises.ch1.Bar">
    <property name="foo" ref="foo"/>
</bean>
```

Spring Container first creates the `foo` bean by calling the default constructor of the `Foo` class and then it attempts to inject its `bar` dependency. It then goes to the `bar` bean definition and starts creating the `bar` bean to perform dependency injection on the `foo` bean. This time Spring Container is able to create the `bar` bean by calling the default constructor of the `Bar` class and tries to inject its `foo` dependency. The `foo` bean is already created at the first step, so Spring Container obtains it and injects it into the `bar` bean. Now the `bar` bean is ready for dependency injection, and it is obtained by the container and injected into the `foo` bean as the last step.

However, many Spring features won't be available on your circularly dependent beans even if you are able to create and inject their dependencies using setter injection because many of the middleware features, such as transaction, validation, caching, and security, provided by the Spring Container depend on `BeanPostProcessors`, which are special infrastructural beans of Spring itself. Those infrastructural beans postprocess application-level beans, such as the `foo` and `bar` beans, after they are created and their dependencies are injected so that middleware features are applied before those application-level beans become ready to be injected as dependencies to the other beans in the container. As you may have already noticed in the preceding example, the `foo` bean is not fully initialized for postprocessing when it is injected into the `bar` bean. Therefore, if it is configured to have such middleware features, they won't be available on the `foo` bean instance that is injected into the `bar` bean.

Therefore, it is almost always preferable to break circular dependencies in your application so that your beans will be able to benefit from those middleware features provided by the Spring Container. You can also disable cyclic dependency resolution with `AbstractRefreshableApplicationContext.setAllowCircularReferences(false)` to prevent such problems.

CHAPTER 2

Exercise 1

The `<context:component-scan>` element supports extending the bean-scanning mechanism outside the `@Component` annotations. The `<context:include-filter/>` child element is available for this purpose. Create a sample application in which beans are defined with `<context:component-scan/>`, but without using the `@Component` annotation. Instead beans should be discovered by scanning packages in which bean classes are placed.

Solution to Exercise 1

Use the following steps:

1. Use the following Maven command to create a project:

    ```
    mvn archetype:generate -DarchetypeGroupId=org.apache.maven.archetypes
        -DgroupId=com.wiley.beginningspring -DartifactId=spring-book-ch2-exercise1
    ```

2. Add the following dependencies to your `pom.xml` file:

    ```xml
    <dependency>
        <groupId>org.springframework</groupId>
        <artifactId>spring-context</artifactId>
        <version>4.0.5.RELEASE</version>
    </dependency>
    ```

3. Create the `com.wiley.beginningspring.exercises.ch2` package in the `src/main/java` folder.

4. Create the `Foo` class in that package:

    ```java
    public class Foo {
    }
    ```

5. Create an `applicationContext.xml` file with the following content in the `src/main/resources` folder:

    ```xml
    <?xml version="1.0" encoding="UTF-8"?>
    <beans xmlns="http://www.springframework.org/schema/beans"
        xmlns:xsi="http://www.w3.org/2001/XMLSchema-instance"
        xmlns:context="http://www.springframework.org/schema/context"
        xsi:schemaLocation="http://www.springframework.org/schema/beans
        http://www.springframework.org/schema/beans/spring-beans.xsd
            http://www.springframework.org/schema/context
            http://www.springframework.org/schema/context/spring-context.xsd">

        <context:component-scan base-package="com.wiley.beginningspring">
            <context:include-filter type="assignable" expression="java.lang.Object"/>
        </context:component-scan>
    </beans>
    ```

6. Create a `Main` class with the following `main` method contents in the same package:

```
public class Main {
    public static void main(String[] args) {
        ClassPathXmlApplicationContext applicationContext =
            new ClassPathXmlApplicationContext("/applicationContext.xml");
        boolean containsFoo = applicationContext.containsBean("foo");
        System.out.println(containsFoo);
    }
}
```

7. Run the `main` method and observe the result from your console.

The `component-scan` element is configured to search within the `com.wiley.beginningspring` package and all of its subpackages for candidate components. However, we also added the `include-filter` child element to make it consider any class extending from `java.lang.Object` as a candidate besides the `@Component` annotation and its stereotypes. Because the `Foo` class, actually any Java class, extends from `java.lang.Object`, it is used to create a bean in the container. Note that we haven't used any `@Component` annotations on the `Foo` class.

Exercise 2

Create a bean class that implements the `InitializingBean` interface, and also create two other methods—one of them named `init` and annotated with `@PostConstruct` and the other named `initialize` and defined as `init-method` in the XML configuration. Examine in which order those methods will be invoked while the bean is being instantiated.

Solution to Exercise 2

Use the following steps:

1. Use the following Maven command to create a project:

```
mvn archetype:generate -DarchetypeGroupId=org.apache.maven.archetypes
    -DgroupId=com.wiley.beginningspring -DartifactId=spring-book-ch2-exercise2
```

2. Add the following dependencies to your `pom.xml` file:

```
<dependency>
    <groupId>org.springframework</groupId>
    <artifactId>spring-context</artifactId>
    <version>4.0.5.RELEASE</version>
</dependency>
```

3. Create the `com.wiley.beginningspring.exercises.ch2` package in the `src/main/java` folder.

4. Create a `Foo` class so that it implements `InitializingBean` as follows:

```
public class Foo implements InitializingBean {
    @Override
```

```
public void afterPropertiesSet() throws Exception {
    System.out.println("afterPropertiesSet method is called");
}
}
```

5. Create an `init` method within the `Foo` class and annotate the method with the `@PostConstruct` annotation:

```
@PostConstruct
public void init() {
    System.out.println("init method is called");
}
```

6. Create a second method with the name `initialize` and define it as `default-init-method` in the `applicationContext.xml` file. The `initialize` method should be invoked automatically during bean creation:

```
public void initialize() {
    System.out.println("initialize method is called");
}
```

7. Create an `applicationContext.xml` file with the following content in the `src/main/resources` folder:

```xml
<?xml version="1.0" encoding="UTF-8"?>
<beans xmlns="http://www.springframework.org/schema/beans"
    xmlns:xsi="http://www.w3.org/2001/XMLSchema-instance"
    xmlns:context="http://www.springframework.org/schema/context"
    xsi:schemaLocation="http://www.springframework.org/schema/beans
    http://www.springframework.org/schema/beans/spring-beans.xsd
        http://www.springframework.org/schema/context
        http://www.springframework.org/schema/context/spring-context.xsd"
            default-init-method="initialize">
    <context:component-scan base-package="com.wiley.beginningspring">
        <context:include-filter type="assignable" expression="java.lang.Object"/>
    </context:component-scan>
</beans>
```

8. Create a `Main` class with a `main` method containing the following content:

```java
public class Main {
    public static void main(String[] args) {
        ClassPathXmlApplicationContext applicationContext =
            new ClassPathXmlApplicationContext("/applicationContext.xml");
    }
}
```

9. Run the `main` method and observe the result from your console. You should see a console output similar to the following:

```
init method is called
afterPropertiesSet method is called
initialize method is called
```

Initialization of a bean is performed after its dependencies are injected by the Spring Container. There may be several initialization methods defined in a bean class. Spring invokes them in a specific order. First the initialization method specified with the `@PostConstruct` annotation is invoked. Then the `afterPropertiesSet()` method is called if the bean implements the `InitializingBean` interface. Finally, the initialization method specified within the bean configuration file is invoked. We specified the initialization method in the `<beans>` element that applies to all beans defined in that XML file. It is equally possible to specify the initialization method on each `bean` element.

Exercise 3

Try to create two beans that depend on each other with Java-based configuration using setter injection. What happens?

Solution to Exercise 3

Use the following steps:

1. Use the following Maven command to create a project:

    ```
    mvn archetype:generate -DarchetypeGroupId=org.apache.maven.archetypes
        -DgroupId=com.wiley.beginningspring -DartifactId=spring-book-ch2-exercise3
    ```

2. Add the following dependencies to your `pom.xml` file:

    ```
    <dependency>
        <groupId>org.springframework</groupId>
        <artifactId>spring-context</artifactId>
        <version>4.0.5.RELEASE</version>
    </dependency>
    ```

3. Create the `com.wiley.beginningspring.exercises.ch2` package in the `src/main/java` folder.

4. Create the `Foo` and `Bar` classes in the `com.wiley.beginningspring.exercises.ch2` package as follows:

    ```
    public class Foo {
        private Bar bar;

        public void setBar(Bar bar) {
            this.bar = bar;
        }
    }

    public class Bar {
        private Foo foo;

        public void setFoo(Foo foo) {
            this.foo = foo;
        }
    }
    ```

5. Create a `Configuration` class as follows:

```
@Configuration
public class Ch2Exercise3Configuration {
    @Bean
    public Foo foo() {
        Foo foo = new Foo();
        foo.setBar(bar());
        return foo;
    }

    @Bean
    public Bar bar() {
        Bar bar = new Bar();
        bar.setFoo(foo());
        return bar;
    }
}
```

6. Create a `Main` class with a `main` method as follows:

```
public class Main {
    public static void main(String[] args) {
        AnnotationConfigApplicationContext applicationContext =
            new AnnotationConfigApplicationContext();
        applicationContext.register(Ch2Exercise3Configuration.class);
        applicationContext.refresh();
    }
}
```

7. Run the `main` method and observe the result from your console.

When you run the `main` method, you get an exception because of the circular bean factory method invocations in the configuration class. You can fix this error by employing autowiring as follows:

```
@Configuration
public class Ch2Exercise3Configuration {
    @Bean
    @Autowired
    public Foo foo() {
        Foo foo = new Foo();
        //foo.setBar(bar());
        return foo;
    }

    @Bean
    @Autowired
    public Bar bar() {
        Bar bar = new Bar();
        //bar.setFoo(foo());
        return bar;
    }
}
```

CHAPTER 3

Exercise 1

Which Spring annotation should be used to support Java 8's `java.time.LocalDateTime`?

Solution to Exercise 1

The `@DateTimeFormat` annotation should be used with `iso` format as `@DateTimeFormat(iso = ISO.DATE_TIME)`.

Exercise 2

What's the best approach for handling locale changes in a Spring MVC–based application that doesn't manage user sessions and works as stateless?

Solution to Exercise 2

Using the bean of class `org.springframework.web.servlet.i18n.CookieLocaleResolver` that depends on a cookie on the client enables setting the locale with the help of a cookie as a locale resolver.

Exercise 3

Define a global exception handler that will handle all exceptions that would derive from the `RuntimeException` class and that will redirect to the view `uppsie.mvc`.

Solution to Exercise 3

The following code gives the `GlobalExceptionHandler` class definition annotated with the `@ControllerAdvice`:

```
@ControllerAdvice
public class GlobalExceptionHandler {

    @ExceptionHandler(RuntimeException.class)
    public ModelAndView handleException() {
        return new ModelAndView("uppsie");
    }
}
```

CHAPTER 4

Exercise 1

Define a new method called `List<Account> findByOwnerAndLocked(String ownerName, boolean locked)` in the `AccountDao` interface and implement it within the `AccountDaoJdbcImpl` class using the named parameter support of Spring.

Solution to Exercise 1

You can continue with the project you started in the "Configuring and Using Spring JdbcTemplate" Try It Out in Chapter 4. Use the following steps:

1. Modify the `AccountDaoJdbcImpl` class so that it creates a `NamedParameterJdbcTemplate` object using the `JdbcTemplate` bean injected into it as follows:

```
public class AccountDaoJdbcImpl implements AccountDao {

    private JdbcTemplate jdbcTemplate;
    private NamedParameterJdbcTemplate namedParameterJdbcTemplate;

    public void setJdbcTemplate(JdbcTemplate jdbcTemplate) {
        this.jdbcTemplate = jdbcTemplate;
        namedParameterJdbcTemplate = new NamedParameterJdbcTemplate(jdbcTemplate);
    }
    //other method implementations...
}
```

2. Use the `NamedParameterJdbcTemplate` object to perform the query in the `findByOwnerAndLocked(..)` method as follows:

```
@Override
public List<Account> findByOwnerAndLocked(String ownerName, boolean locked) {
    Map<String, Object> paramMap = new HashMap<String, Object>();
    paramMap.put("ownerName", ownerName);
    paramMap.put("locked", locked);
    return namedParameterJdbcTemplate.query(
"select id,owner_name,balance,access_time,locked from account where owner_name = ↵
    :ownerName and locked = :locked",
            paramMap,
            new RowMapper<Account>() {
                @Override
                public Account mapRow(ResultSet rs, int rowNum)
                    throws SQLException {
                    Account account = new Account();
                    account.setId(rs.getLong("id"));
                    account.setOwnerName(rs.getString("owner_name"));
                    account.setBalance(rs.getDouble("balance"));
                    account.setAccessTime(rs
                            .getTimestamp("access_time"));
                    account.setLocked(rs.getBoolean("locked"));
                    return account;
                }
            });
}
```

Exercise 2

Define beans for the `AccountInsert`, `AccountUpdate`, and `AccountDelete` classes, inject them into the `accountDao` bean, and then change the implementation of the insert, update, and delete methods of `AccountDaoJdbcImpl` so that it will use those new beans for its SQL operations.

Solution to Exercise 2

You can continue with the project you started in the "Encapsulating SQL Queries Using `MappingSqlQuery`" Try It Out in Chapter 4. Use the following steps:

1. Create the following classes:

```java
public class AccountInsert extends SqlUpdate {
    public AccountInsert(DataSource dataSource) {
     super(dataSource,
     "insert into account(owner_name,balance,access_time,locked) values(?,?,?,?)");
     setParameters(new SqlParameter[] {
                new SqlParameter(Types.VARCHAR),
                new SqlParameter(Types.DOUBLE),
                new SqlParameter(Types.TIMESTAMP),
                new SqlParameter(Types.BOOLEAN) });
     setReturnGeneratedKeys(true);
     setGeneratedKeysColumnNames(new String[]{"id"});
     compile();
     }
}

public class AccountUpdate extends SqlUpdate {
    public AccountUpdate(DataSource dataSource) {
        super(dataSource,
    "update account set (owner_name,balance,access_time,locked)=(?,?,?,?) where id=?");
        setParameters(new SqlParameter[] {
                new SqlParameter(Types.VARCHAR),
                new SqlParameter(Types.DOUBLE),
                new SqlParameter(Types.TIMESTAMP),
                new SqlParameter(Types.BOOLEAN),
                new SqlParameter(Types.BIGINT)});
        compile();
    }
}

public class AccountDelete extends SqlUpdate {
    public AccountDelete(DataSource dataSource) {
        super(dataSource, "delete account where id = ?");
        setParameters(new SqlParameter[]{new SqlParameter(Types.BIGINT)});
        compile();
    }
}
```

2. Modify the `AccountDaoJdbcImpl` class as follows:

```java
public class AccountDaoJdbcImpl implements AccountDao {

    private SqlUpdate accountInsert;
    private SqlUpdate accountUpdate;
    private SqlUpdate accountDelete;

    public void setAccountInsert(SqlUpdate accountInsert) {
        this.accountInsert = accountInsert;
    }
```

```
        public void setAccountUpdate(SqlUpdate accountUpdate) {
            this.accountUpdate = accountUpdate;
        }

        public void setAccountDelete(SqlUpdate accountDelete) {
            this.accountDelete = accountDelete;
        }

        //...
    }
```

3. Define the Spring-managed `accountInsert`, `accountUpdate`, and `accountDelete` beans for those classes created in the first step and inject them into the `accountDao` bean as follows:

```
@Configuration
public class Ch4Configuration {
    @Bean
    public SqlUpdate accountInsert() {
        AccountInsert accountInsert = new AccountInsert(dataSource());
        return accountInsert;
    }

    @Bean
    public SqlUpdate accountUpdate() {
        AccountUpdate accountUpdate = new AccountUpdate(dataSource());
        return accountUpdate;
    }

    @Bean
    public SqlUpdate accountDelete() {
        AccountDelete accountDelete = new AccountDelete(dataSource());
        return accountDelete;
    }

    @Bean
    public AccountDao accountDao() {
        AccountDaoJdbcImpl accountDao = new AccountDaoJdbcImpl();
        accountDao.setJdbcTemplate(jdbcTemplate());
        accountDao.setAccountByIdQuery(accountByIdQuery());
        accountDao.setAccountInsert(accountInsert());
        accountDao.setAccountUpdate(accountUpdate());
        accountDao.setAccountDelete(accountDelete());
        return accountDao;
    }

    //...
}
```

4. Use those beans within the related methods of `AccountDaoJdbcImpl` to perform JDBC operations:

```
public class AccountDaoJdbcImpl implements AccountDao {
    public void insert(Account account) {
        GeneratedKeyHolder keyHolder = new GeneratedKeyHolder();
```

```
            int count = accountInsert.update(new Object[]{
                account.getOwnerName(),account.getBalance(),
                account.getAccessTime(),account.isLocked()},keyHolder);
            if (count != 1)
                throw new InsertFailedException("Cannot insert account");
            account.setId(keyHolder.getKey().longValue());
        }

        public void update(Account account) {
            int count = accountUpdate.update(
                account.getOwnerName(),account.getBalance(),
                account.getAccessTime(),account.isLocked(),account.getId());
            if (count != 1)
                throw new UpdateFailedException("Cannot update account");
        }

        public void delete(long accountId) {
            int count = accountDelete.update(accountId);
            if (count != 1)
                throw new DeleteFailedException("Cannot delete account");
        }

        //...
    }
```

Exercise 3

Add a new property called `byte[] ownerPhoto` into the `Account` domain class, and a corresponding BLOB column with the name `owner_photo`. Modify the `AccountByIdQuery`, `AccountInsert`, and `AccountUpdate` classes so that they handle this new property.

Solution to Exercise 3

You can continue with the code of Exercise 2. Use the following steps:

1. Modify the `Account` class as follows:

```
public class Account {
    private byte[] ownerPhoto;

    public byte[] getOwnerPhoto() {
        return ownerPhoto;
    }
    public void setOwnerPhoto(byte[] ownerPhoto) {
        this.ownerPhoto = ownerPhoto;
    }

    //...
}
```

2. Execute the following DDL SQL statement to alter the account table:

```
ALTER TABLE ACCOUNT ADD OWNER_PHOTO BLOB
```

3. Modify the `AccountByIdQuery`, `AccountInsert`, and `AccountUpdate` classes as follows:

```
public class AccountByIdQuery extends MappingSqlQuery<Account> {

    private LobHandler lobHandler = new DefaultLobHandler();

    public AccountByIdQuery(DataSource dataSource) {
        super(dataSource,
"select id,owner_name,balance,access_time,locked,owner_photo from account ⏎
    where id = ?");
        declareParameter(new SqlParameter(Types.BIGINT));
        compile();


    }

    @Override
    protected Account mapRow(ResultSet rs, int rowNum) throws SQLException {
        Account account = new Account();
        account.setId(rs.getLong("id"));
        account.setOwnerName(rs.getString("owner_name"));
        account.setBalance(rs.getDouble("balance"));
        account.setAccessTime(rs.getTimestamp("access_time"));
        account.setLocked(rs.getBoolean("locked"));
        account.setOwnerPhoto(lobHandler.getBlobAsBytes(rs, "owner_photo"));
        return account;
    }
}

public class AccountInsert extends SqlUpdate {

    public AccountInsert(DataSource dataSource) {
        super(dataSource,
        "insert into account(owner_name,balance,access_time,locked,owner_photo) ⏎
            values(?,?,?,?,?)");
        setParameters(new SqlParameter[] {
                new SqlParameter(Types.VARCHAR),
                new SqlParameter(Types.DOUBLE),
                new SqlParameter(Types.TIMESTAMP),
                new SqlParameter(Types.BOOLEAN),
                new SqlParameter(Types.BLOB)});
        setReturnGeneratedKeys(true);
        setGeneratedKeysColumnNames(new String[]{"id"});
        compile();
    }
}

public class AccountUpdate extends SqlUpdate {
    public AccountUpdate(DataSource dataSource) {
        super(dataSource,
"update account set (owner_name,balance,access_time,locked, owner_photo) = ⏎
    (?,?,?,?,?) where id=?");
        setParameters(new SqlParameter[] {
                new SqlParameter(Types.VARCHAR),
                new SqlParameter(Types.DOUBLE),
```

```
                    new SqlParameter(Types.TIMESTAMP),
                    new SqlParameter(Types.BOOLEAN),
                    new SqlParameter(Types.BIGINT),
                    new SqlParameter(Types.BLOB)});
            compile();
        }
    }
```

CHAPTER 5

Exercise 1

Try to configure your environment so that it uses a different JPA vendor—for example, Eclipselink—to perform persistence operations.

Solution to Exercise 1

Use the following steps:

1. Use the following Maven command to create a project:

    ```
    mvn archetype:generate -DarchetypeGroupId=org.apache.maven.archetypes
        -DgroupId=com.wiley.beginningspring -DartifactId=spring-book-ch5-exercise1
    ```

2. Add the following dependencies to your pom.xml file:

    ```
    <dependency>
    <groupId>org.eclipse.persistence</groupId>
    <artifactId>org.eclipse.persistence.jpa</artifactId>
    <version>2.5.2</version>
    </dependency>
    <dependency>
        <groupId>com.h2database</groupId>
        <artifactId>h2</artifactId>
        <version>1.3.175</version>
    </dependency>
    ```

3. Create a META-INF/persistence.xml file with the following content in the src/main/resources source folder:

    ```
    <?xml version="1.0" encoding="UTF-8"?>
    <persistence version="2.0"
        xmlns="http://java.sun.com/xml/ns/persistence"
        xmlns:xsi="http://www.w3.org/2001/XMLSchema-instance"
        xsi:schemaLocation="http://java.sun.com/xml/ns/persistence
        http://java.sun.com/xml/ns/persistence/persistence_2_0.xsd">
        <persistence-unit name="test-jpa" transaction-type="RESOURCE_LOCAL">
            <properties>
                <property name="javax.persistence.jdbc.url"
                        value="jdbc:h2:tcp://localhost/~/test" />
                <property name="javax.persistence.jdbc.driver"
                        value="org.h2.Driver" />
    ```

```
                    <property name="javax.persistence.jdbc.username" value="sa" />
                    <property name="javax.persistence.jdbc.password" value="" />
                </properties>
            </persistence-unit>
        </persistence>
```

4. Create the `com.wiley.beginningspring.ch5` package in the `src/main/java` source folder.

5. Create a `Main` class with the following content in that package:

```
public class Main {
    public static void main(String[] args) {
        EntityManagerFactory entityManagerFactory =
            Persistence.createEntityManagerFactory("test-jpa");
        System.out.println(entityManagerFactory.isOpen());
    }
}
```

6. Run `org.h2.tools.Console` to start H2 Server if it is not already started. After that, run the `main` method and observe the result.

Exercise 2

Create `EntityManagerFactory` using `LocalContainerEntityManagerFactoryBean`, which will load a `META-INF/my-persistence.xml` file as its only JPA configuration.

Solution to Exercise 2

Use the following steps:

1. Use the following Maven command to create a project:

```
mvn archetype:generate -DarchetypeGroupId=org.apache.maven.archetypes
    -DgroupId=com.wiley.beginningspring -DartifactId=spring-book-ch5-exercise2
```

2. Add the following dependencies to your `pom.xml` file:

```
<dependency>
    <groupId>org.springframework</groupId>
    <artifactId>spring-orm</artifactId>
    <version>4.0.5.RELEASE</version>
</dependency>

<dependency>
    <groupId>org.springframework</groupId>
    <artifactId>spring-context</artifactId>
    <version>4.0.5.RELEASE</version>
</dependency>

<dependency>
    <groupId>org.hibernate</groupId>
    <artifactId>hibernate-core</artifactId>
    <version>4.3.1.Final</version>
</dependency>
```

```
<dependency>
    <groupId>org.hibernate</groupId>
    <artifactId>hibernate-entitymanager</artifactId>
    <version>4.3.1.Final</version>
</dependency>

<dependency>
    <groupId>com.h2database</groupId>
    <artifactId>h2</artifactId>
    <version>1.3.175</version>
</dependency>
```

3. Create the `META-INF/my-persistence.xml` file in the `src/main/resources` folder with the following content:

```xml
<?xml version="1.0" encoding="UTF-8"?>
<persistence version="2.0"
    xmlns="http://java.sun.com/xml/ns/persistence"
    xmlns:xsi="http://www.w3.org/2001/XMLSchema-instance"
    xsi:schemaLocation="http://java.sun.com/xml/ns/persistence
    http://java.sun.com/xml/ns/persistence/persistence_2_0.xsd">
    <persistence-unit name="test-jpa" transaction-type="RESOURCE_LOCAL">
    <provider>
        org.hibernate.jpa.HibernatePersistenceProvider
    </provider>
        <properties>
            <property name="hibernate.connection.driver_class"
                    value="org.h2.Driver" />
            <property name="hibernate.connection.url"
                    value="jdbc:h2:tcp://localhost/~/test" />
            <property name="hibernate.connection.username" value="sa" />
            <property name="hibernate.connection.password" value="" />
            <property name="hibernate.dialect"
                    value="org.hibernate.dialect.H2Dialect" />
            <property name="hibernate.hbm2ddl.auto" value="update" />
        </properties>
    </persistence-unit>
</persistence>
```

4. Create the `com.wiley.beginningspring.exercises.ch5` package in the `src/main/java` folder.

5. Create a `Configuration` class in that package with the following content:

```java
@Configuration
public class Ch5Configuration {
    @Bean
    public LocalContainerEntityManagerFactoryBean entityManagerFactory() {
        LocalContainerEntityManagerFactoryBean factoryBean =
            new LocalContainerEntityManagerFactoryBean();
        factoryBean.setPersistenceXmlLocation(
            "classpath:/META-INF/my-persistence.xml");
        return factoryBean;
    }
}
```

6. Create a `Main` class as follows:

```
public class Main {
    public static void main(String[] args) {
        AnnotationConfigApplicationContext applicationContext =
            new AnnotationConfigApplicationContext(Ch5Configuration.class);
        EntityManagerFactory entityManagerFactory =
            applicationContext.getBean(EntityManagerFactory.class);
        System.out.println(entityManagerFactory.isOpen());
    }
}
```

Exercise 3

Try to perform a persistence operation using JPA outside of an active transaction and observe the exception thrown.

Solution to Exercise 3

You can continue with the project you created for Exercise 2. Use the following steps:

1. Create the following persistent domain class in the `com.wiley.beginningspring .exercises.ch5` package:

```
@Entity
public class Foo {
    @Id
    @GeneratedValue
    private Long id;
}
```

2. Modify the `main` method as follows to insert a new `Foo` instance without an active transaction and then run the method:

```
public class Main {
    public static void main(String[] args) {
        AnnotationConfigApplicationContext applicationContext =
            new AnnotationConfigApplicationContext(Ch5Configuration.class);
        EntityManagerFactory entityManagerFactory =
            applicationContext.getBean(EntityManagerFactory.class);
        System.out.println(entityManagerFactory.isOpen());
        EntityManager entityManager = entityManagerFactory.createEntityManager();

        Foo foo = new Foo();

        entityManager.persist(foo);

        entityManager.flush();
        entityManager.close();
    }
}
```

CHAPTER 6

Exercise 1

Configure your system using JpaTransactionManager and implement the depositMoney(long accountId, double amount) method of the AccountServiceImpl class using JPA. The AccountServiceImpl class is written in the "Using @Transactional on Class Level" section of Chapter 6.

Solution to Exercise 1

You can continue with the project you created for Exercise 2 of Chapter 5. Use the following steps:

1. Add the following dependency element into the pom.xml file:

```
<dependency>
    <groupId>org.springframework</groupId>
    <artifactId>spring-tx</artifactId>
    <version>4.0.5.RELEASE</version>
</dependency>
```

2. Create the com.wiley.beginningspring.ch6 package in the src/main/java source folder.

3. Create the following Account class in that package:

```
@Entity
public class Account {
    @Id
    @GeneratedValue
    private long id;
    private String ownerName;
    private double balance;
    private Date accessTime;
    private boolean locked;
    private byte[] ownerPhoto;

    //getters & setters...
}
```

4. Create the following AccountService interface and AccountServiceImpl class in the same package:

```
public interface AccountService {
    public void transferMoney(long sourceAccountId, long targetAccountId,
            double amount);
    public void depositMoney(long accountId, double amount) throws Exception;
    public Account getAccount(long accountId);
}

@Transactional
public class AccountServiceImpl implements AccountService {

    @PersistenceContext
```

```
    private EntityManager entityManager;

    @Override
    public void transferMoney(
        long sourceAccountId, long targetAccountId, double amount) {
        //...
    }

    @Override
    @Transactional(rollbackFor=Exception.class)
    public void depositMoney(long accountId, double amount) throws Exception {
        Account account = entityManager.find(Account.class, 100L);
        account.setBalance(account.getBalance() + amount);
    }

    @Override
    @Transactional(readOnly=true)
    public Account getAccount(long accountId) {
        return null;
    }
}
```

5. Create the following `Configuration` class in the same package:

```
@Configuration
@EnableTransactionManagement
public class Ch6Configuration {

    @Autowired
    private EntityManagerFactory entityManagerFactory;

    @Bean
    public PlatformTransactionManager transactionManager() {
        JpaTransactionManager transactionManager = new JpaTransactionManager();
        transactionManager.setEntityManagerFactory(entityManagerFactory);
        return transactionManager;
    }

    @Bean
    public AccountService accountService() {
        AccountServiceImpl accountService = new AccountServiceImpl();
        return accountService;
    }
}
```

6. Execute the following DDL and DML SQLs in order to populate the database:

```
create table Account (
    id bigint generated by default as identity,
    accessTime timestamp, balance double not null,
    locked boolean not null, ownerName varchar(255),
    ownerPhoto binary(255), primary key (id));

insert into Account
    values(100,'2014-01-01 00:00:00',10.0,false,'John Doe',null);
```

7. Create the following `Main` class in the `com.wiley.beginningspring.ch6` package in which you obtain the `accountService` bean and use it to deposit money to an account:

```
public class Main {
    public static void main(String[] args) throws Exception {
        AnnotationConfigApplicationContext applicationContext =
            new AnnotationConfigApplicationContext(
                Ch5Configuration.class, Ch6Configuration.class);
        AccountService accountService =
            applicationContext.getBean(AccountService.class);
        accountService.depositMoney(100, 10.0);
    }
}
```

Exercise 2

What needs to be done to switch from local transactions to JTA—that is, global transactions?

Solution to Exercise 2

It is enough to configure the `transactionManager` bean as follows:

```
<bean id="transactionManager"
        class="org.springframework.transaction.jta.JtaTransactionManager"/>
```

Exercise 3

Implement a `TransactionSyncronization` class containing a logic that will be executed after a transaction rolls back. This logic can be a simple `System.out.println()` statement that prints the current transaction status to the console.

Solution to Exercise 3

You can continue from where you left off in Exercise 2 of Chapter 6. Use the following steps:

1. Create the following class:

```
public class MyTxSync implements TransactionSynchronization {

    //other methods of TransactionSynchronization interface

    @Override
    public void afterCompletion(int status) {
        switch (status) {
        case TransactionSynchronization.STATUS_COMMITTED:
            System.out.println("tx commited");
            break;
        case TransactionSynchronization.STATUS_ROLLED_BACK:
            System.out.println("tx rollbacked");
            break;
        default:
            System.out.println("unknown status :" + status);
        }
    }
}
```

2. Modify the `depositMoney(..)` method of `AccountServiceImpl` as follows:

```
@Override
@Transactional(rollbackFor=Exception.class)
public void depositMoney(long accountId, double amount) throws Exception {
    TransactionSynchronizationManager.registerSynchronization(new MyTxSync());

    Account account = entityManager.find(Account.class, 100L);
    account.setBalance(account.getBalance() + amount);

    if(true) throw new RuntimeException("thrown to test tx sync");
}
```

3. Run the `main` method, and observe the result. You can also test it after commenting the statement at which `RuntimeException` is thrown so that the transaction commits.

CHAPTER 7

Exercise 1

How can you disable `TestExecutionListeners` configured by default and see that no dependency injection is performed at all?

Solution to Exercise 1

Use the following steps:

1. Use the following Maven command to create a project:

```
mvn archetype:generate -DarchetypeGroupId=org.apache.maven.archetypes
    -DgroupId=com.wiley.beginningspring -DartifactId=spring-book-ch7-exercise1
```

2. Add the following dependencies to your `pom.xml` file:

```
<dependency>
    <groupId>org.springframework</groupId>
    <artifactId>spring-context</artifactId>
    <version>4.0.5.RELEASE</version>
</dependency>
<dependency>
    <groupId>org.springframework</groupId>
    <artifactId>spring-test</artifactId>
    <version>4.0.5.RELEASE</version>
</dependency>
<dependency>
    <groupId>junit</groupId>
    <artifactId>junit</artifactId>
    <version>4.11</version>
</dependency>
```

3. Create the `com.wiley.beginningspring.ch7` package in the `src/main/java` source folder and add the following class to it:

```
public class Foo {
}
```

4. Create the `com.wiley.beginningspring.ch7` package in the `src/test/java` source folder and add the following test class to it:

```
@RunWith(SpringJUnit4ClassRunner.class)
@ContextConfiguration
@TestExecutionListeners(listeners={})
public class Ch7Exercise1Tests {
    @Autowired
    private Foo foo;

    @Test
    public void testFooIsNotAvailable() {
        Assert.assertNull(foo);
    }
}
```

5. Create the `com.wiley.beginningspring.ch7` package in the `src/test/resources` source folder and a Spring bean configuration file called `Ch7Exercise1Tests-context.xml` in that package with the following content:

```
<?xml version="1.0" encoding="UTF-8"?>
<beans xmlns="http://www.springframework.org/schema/beans"
    xmlns:xsi="http://www.w3.org/2001/XMLSchema-instance"
    xsi:schemaLocation="http://www.springframework.org/schema/beans
    http://www.springframework.org/schema/beans/spring-beans.xsd">

    <bean id="foo" class="com.wiley.beginningspring.ch7.Foo"/>

</beans>
```

6. Run the test method using JUnit to see the result. You can also comment `@TestExecutionListeners(listeners={})` and observe that the test fails, indicating that the `foo` bean is injected.

Exercise 2

Create a test class that loads both XML-based and Java-based bean configurations.

Solution to Exercise 2

You can continue with the project you already created for Exercise 1. Use the following steps:

1. Create the following classes in the `com.wiley.beginningspring.ch7` package in the `src/main/java` source folder:

```
public class Bar {
}

@Configuration
public class Ch7Configuration {
    @Bean
    public Bar bar() {
        return new Bar();
    }
}
```

2. Create a Spring bean configuration file named `applicationContext.xml` in the `src/main/resources` source folder with the following content:

```
<?xml version="1.0" encoding="UTF-8"?>
<beans xmlns="http://www.springframework.org/schema/beans"
    xmlns:xsi="http://www.w3.org/2001/XMLSchema-instance"
    xsi:schemaLocation="http://www.springframework.org/schema/beans
    http://www.springframework.org/schema/beans/spring-beans.xsd">
    <bean id="foo" class="com.wiley.beginningspring.ch7.Foo"/>
</beans>
```

3. Create the following test class in the `com.wiley.beginningspring.ch7` package in the `src/test/java` source folder:

```
@RunWith(SpringJUnit4ClassRunner.class)
@ContextConfiguration(
classes={Ch7Configuration.class, Ch7Exercise2Tests.Config.class})
public class Ch7Exercise2Tests {

    @Configuration
    @ImportResource("classpath:/applicationContext.xml")
    static class Config {
    }

    @Autowired
    private Foo foo;

    @Autowired
    private Bar bar;

    @Test
    public void testDependenciesAreInjected() {
        Assert.assertNotNull(foo);
        Assert.assertNotNull(bar);
    }
}
```

4. Run the test method using JUnit to see the result.

Exercise 3

Register a Java object into JNDI Context using `SimpleNamingContextBuilder` and then look it up using `javax.naming.InitialContext` in your test class.

Solution to Exercise 3

You can continue with the project you already created for Exercise 1. Use the following steps:

1. Create the following test class in the `com.wiley.beginningspring.ch7` package of the `src/test/java` source folder:

```
@RunWith(SpringJUnit4ClassRunner.class)
@ContextConfiguration(classes=Ch7Exercise3Tests.Config.class)
```

```
public class Ch7Exercise3Tests {

    @Autowired
    private Foo foo;

    @Configuration
    static class Config {
        @Bean
        public Foo foo() {
            return new Foo();
        }
    }

    @Before
    public void setUp() throws NamingException {
        SimpleNamingContextBuilder builder = new SimpleNamingContextBuilder();
        builder.bind("foo", foo);
        builder.activate();
    }

    @Test
    public void testJNDIContextAccess() throws NamingException{
        InitialContext initialContext = new InitialContext();
        Foo foo2 = (Foo) initialContext.lookup("foo");

        Assert.assertSame(foo, foo2);
    }
}
```

2. Run the test method using JUnit to see the result.

CHAPTER 8

Exercise 1

Define an aspect that pointcuts before the methods that are annotated with @MyAnnotation.

Solution to Exercise 1

Use the following steps:

1. Use the following Maven command to create a project:

```
mvn archetype:generate -DarchetypeGroupId=org.apache.maven.archetypes
    -DgroupId=com.wiley.beginningspring -DartifactId=spring-book-ch2-exercise1
```

2. Add the following dependencies to the pom.xml file and remove all the previously declared dependencies that exist:

```
<dependency>
    <groupId>org.springframework</groupId>
    <artifactId>spring-core</artifactId>
    <version>4.0.5.RELEASE</version>
```

```
    </dependency>
    <dependency>
        <groupId>org.springframework</groupId>
        <artifactId>spring-beans</artifactId>
        <version>4.0.5.RELEASE</version>
    </dependency>
    <dependency>
        <groupId>org.springframework</groupId>
        <artifactId>spring-context</artifactId>
        <version>4.0.5.RELEASE</version>
    </dependency>
    <dependency>
        <groupId>org.springframework</groupId>
        <artifactId>spring-aop</artifactId>
        <version>4.0.5.RELEASE</version>
    </dependency>
    <dependency>
        <groupId>org.aspectj</groupId>
        <artifactId>aspectjweaver</artifactId>
        <version>1.8.1</version>
    </dependency>
```

3. Create the following classes under the com.wiley.beginningspring package in the
    src/main/java source folder:

```
@Target(value = {ElementType.METHOD, ElementType.TYPE})
@Retention(value = RetentionPolicy.RUNTIME)
public @interface MyAnnotation {
}

public interface MyBean {
    void sayHi();
}

@Component
public class MyBeanImpl implements MyBean {

    @MyAnnotation
    public void sayHi() {
        System.out.println("Hi..!");
    }
}

@Component
@Aspect
public class AfterPointcut {

    @Pointcut("@annotation(com.wiley.beginningspring.MyAnnotation)")
    public void annotatedWithMyAnnotation()  {
    }

    @After(value = "annotatedWithMyAnnotation()")
    public void afterWithMultiplePointcut() {
        System.out.println("Method intercepted with @MyAnnotation");
```

```
        }
    }

    public class App {
        public static void main(String... args) {
            ApplicationContext context =
                new AnnotationConfigApplicationContext(ApplicationConfig.class);

            MyBean myBean = context.getBean(MyBean.class);
            myBean.sayHi();
        }
    }
```

4. Run the `main` method in the `App` class. You see the following output:

```
Hi..!
Method intercepted with @MyAnnotation
```

Exercise 2

Create a pointcut expression where all beans under the `com.wiley.beginningspring.ch8` `.service` package are intercepted but only the ones that have the class name suffixed as `Bean`.

Solution to Exercise 2

The pointcut definition would be as follows:

```
@Pointcut("within(com.wiley.beginningspring.ch8.service.*)
        && execution(public * com.wiley.beginningspring.*Bean.*(..))")
```

Here we used the `&&` operator to join two match cases. It's possible to blend the expressions with grammatical operators such as and, or, and not (or with corresponding `&&`, `||`, and `!`).

CHAPTER 9

Exercise 1

Inject the `user.country` system property into a property of a Spring bean with the `@Value` annotation.

Solution to Exercise 1

Use the following steps:

1. Use the following Maven command to create a project:

```
mvn archetype:generate -DarchetypeArtifactId=maven-archetype-quickstart
    -DgroupId=com.wiley.beginningspring -DartifactId=ch9-exercise1
```

2. Add the following dependencies to the `pom.xml` file and remove all the previously declared dependencies that exist:

```
<dependency>
    <groupId>org.springframework</groupId>
    <artifactId>spring-core</artifactId>
    <version>4.0.5.RELEASE</version>
</dependency>
<dependency>
    <groupId>org.springframework</groupId>
    <artifactId>spring-context</artifactId>
    <version>4.0.5.RELEASE</version>
</dependency>

<dependency>
    <groupId>org.springframework</groupId>
    <artifactId>spring-expression</artifactId>
    <version>4.0.5.RELEASE</version>
</dependency>
```

3. Create the following classes under the `com.wiley.beginningspring` package in the `src/main/java` source folder:

```java
@Component
public class MyBean {

    @Value("#{systemProperties['user.country']}")
    private String message;

    public String getMessage() {
        return message;
    }
}


@Configuration
@ComponentScan(basePackages = {"com.wiley.beginningspring"})
public class ApplicationConfig {
}

public class App {

    public static void main(String... args) {
        ApplicationContext context =
            new AnnotationConfigApplicationContext(ApplicationConfig.class);
        MyBean myBean = context.getBean(MyBean.class);
        System.out.println(myBean.getMessage());
    }
}
```

4. Run the `main` method in the `App` class.

Exercise 2

Implement a method that reverses a given string and registers it as an Expression Language (EL) function. Demonstrate the code within a test method by providing a sample string.

Solution to Exercise 2

Use the following steps:

1. Use the following Maven command to create a project:

    ```
    mvn archetype:generate -DarchetypeArtifactId=maven-archetype-quickstart
        -DgroupId=com.wiley.beginningspring -DartifactId=ch9-exercise2
    ```

2. Add the following dependencies to the `pom.xml` file and remove all the previously declared dependencies that exist:

    ```xml
    <dependency>
        <groupId>org.springframework</groupId>
        <artifactId>spring-core</artifactId>
        <version>4.0.5.RELEASE</version>
    </dependency>
    <dependency>
        <groupId>org.springframework</groupId>
        <artifactId>spring-context</artifactId>
        <version>4.0.5.RELEASE</version>
    </dependency>

    <dependency>
        <groupId>org.springframework</groupId>
        <artifactId>spring-expression</artifactId>
        <version>4.0.5.RELEASE</version>
    </dependency>

    <dependency>
        <groupId>junit</groupId>
        <artifactId>junit</artifactId>
        <version>4.11</version>
        <scope>test</scope>
    </dependency>
    ```

3. Create the following classes under the `com.wiley.beginningspring` package in the `src/main/java` source folder:

    ```java
    public class MyStringUtils {

        public static String reverse(String str) {
            return new StringBuilder(str).reverse().toString();
        }
    }
    ```

4. Create the following classes under the `com.wiley.beginningspring` package in the `src/test/java` source folder:

    ```java
    public class ReverseFunctionTests {

        ExpressionParser parser;

        @Before
        public void setup() {
    ```

```
        parser = new SpelExpressionParser();
    }

    @Test
    public void reverseFunctionRegisteredOK() throws NoSuchMethodException {
        StandardEvaluationContext context = new StandardEvaluationContext();
        context.registerFunction("reverse",
                MyStringUtils.class.getDeclaredMethod("reverse",
                                            new Class[] { String.class }));

        String value = parser.
            parseExpression("#reverse('hello')").getValue(context, String.class);
        assertThat(value, is("olleh"));
    }
}
```

5. Run the test method using JUnit to see the passing test result.

CHAPTER 10

Exercise 1

Create domain class `Course` with properties `id` and `name`. Create a cache manager in Spring configuration and use Hazelcast as your cache provider. Create a `CourseService` bean and implement the `findById` service that returns the course for a given ID. Within the service, cache all the courses that have the name starting with the `BBM` keyword.

Solution to Exercise 1

Use the following steps:

1. Use the following Maven command to create a project:

```
mvn archetype:generate -DarchetypeArtifactId=maven-archetype-quickstart
    -DgroupId=com.wiley.beginningspring -DartifactId=ch10-exercise1
```

2. Add the following dependencies to the `pom.xml` file and remove all the previously declared dependencies that exist:

```
<dependency>
    <groupId>org.springframework</groupId>
    <artifactId>spring-core</artifactId>
    <version>4.0.5.RELEASE</version>
</dependency>
<dependency>
    <groupId>org.springframework</groupId>
    <artifactId>spring-context</artifactId>
    <version>4.0.5.RELEASE</version>
</dependency>
<dependency>
    <groupId>org.springframework</groupId>
    <artifactId>spring-context-support</artifactId>
```

```
        <version>4.0.5.RELEASE</version>
    </dependency>

    <dependency>
        <groupId>com.hazelcast</groupId>
        <artifactId>hazelcast-all</artifactId>
        <version>3.3</version>
    </dependency>
```

3. Create the following classes under the `com.wiley.beginningspring` package in the `src/main/java` source folder:

```java
public class Course implements Serializable {

    private int id;
    private String name;

    public Course(int id, String name) {
        this.id = id;
        this.name = name;
    }

    public int getId() {
        return id;
    }

    public String getName() {
        return name;
    }

}

public class CourseService {

    private Map<Integer, Course> courses = new HashMap<>();
    {
        courses.put(1, new Course(1, "BBM490 - Enterprise Web Architecture"));
        courses.put(2, new Course(2, "ART101 - Introduction Photography"));
    }

    @Cacheable(value = "courses", condition = "#course.name.startsWith('BBM')")
    public Course getCourse(Course course) {
        System.out.println("Course with id " + course.getId() + " requested.");
        return courses.get(course.getId());
    }

}

public class App {

    public static void main(String... args) {
        ApplicationContext context =
            new ClassPathXmlApplicationContext("applicationContext.xml");
        CourseService courseService = context.getBean(CourseService.class);

        Course course1 = new Course(1, "BBM490 - Enterprise Web Architecture");
        Course courseFetch1 = courseService.getCourse(course1);
```

```
            System.out.println(courseFetch1);
            Course courseFetch2 = courseService.getCourse(course1);
            System.out.println(courseFetch2);

            Course course2 = new Course(2, "ART101 - Introduction Photography");
            Course courseFetch3 = courseService.getCourse(course2);
            System.out.println(courseFetch3);
            Course courseFetch4 = courseService.getCourse(course2);
            System.out.println(courseFetch4);
        }
    }
```

4. Create the following file under the `src/main/resources` source folder:

```xml
<?xml version="1.0" encoding="UTF-8"?>
<beans xmlns="http://www.springframework.org/schema/beans"
       xmlns:xsi="http://www.w3.org/2001/XMLSchema-instance"
       xmlns:cache="http://www.springframework.org/schema/cache"
       xmlns:hz="http://www.hazelcast.com/schema/spring"
       xsi:schemaLocation="http://www.springframework.org/schema/beans
       http://www.springframework.org/schema/beans/spring-beans-4.0.xsd
       http://www.springframework.org/schema/cache
       http://www.springframework.org/schema/cache/spring-cache-4.0.xsd
       http://www.hazelcast.com/schema/spring
       http://www.hazelcast.com/schema/spring/hazelcast-spring-3.3.xsd">

    <cache:annotation-driven />

    <hz:hazelcast id="hazelcast">
        <hz:config>
            <hz:map name="users">
                <hz:map-store enabled="true"
    class-name="com.wiley.beginningspring.Course" write-delay-seconds="0"/>
            </hz:map>
        </hz:config>
    </hz:hazelcast>

    <bean id="userService" class="com.wiley.beginningspring.CourseService" />

    <bean id="cacheManager"
          class="com.hazelcast.spring.cache.HazelcastCacheManager">
        <constructor-arg ref="hazelcast" />
    </bean>
</beans>
```

5. Run the `main` method in the `App` class to see an output similar to the following:

```
Course with id 1 requested.
com.wiley.beginningspring.Course@1f010bf0
com.wiley.beginningspring.Course@177bea38
Course with id 2 requested.
com.wiley.beginningspring.Course@7f132176
Course with id 2 requested.
com.wiley.beginningspring.Course@7f132176
```

Exercise 2

What's the main difference between the @Cacheable and @CachePut annotations? Will it be possible to use either of these annotations on methods with void return types?

Solution to Exercise 2

The @CachePut annotation always gets the method executed first compared to the @Cacheable annotation. So this is a feasible approach where you always want to update your cache storage with the method return value. Because @CachePut uses the method's return value as the cached value, it doesn't make sense to use it on methods with the void return type.

CHAPTER 11

Exercise 1

Is it possible to produce XML output with REST web services?

Solution to Exercise 1

Yes, Spring MVC provides message converters that will handle XML requests and responses. To achieve this you need to annotate your domain objects with JAXB annotations like @XmlRootElement and @XmlElement. Also there is no need to define any extra dependency because these annotations ship with the JDK.

Exercise 2

Create the User domain class with the properties id, name, and address. Create a REST web service that outputs a User domain object list as JSON. While doing JSON conversion, omit the address field from the output.

Solution to Exercise 2

Use the following steps:

1. Use the following Maven command to create a project:

   ```
   mvn archetype:generate -DarchetypeArtifactId=maven-archetype-webapp
       -DgroupId=com.wiley.beginningspring -DartifactId= ch11-exercise2
   ```

2. Add the following dependencies to the pom.xml file:

   ```
   <dependency>
       <groupId>org.springframework</groupId>
       <artifactId>spring-core</artifactId>
       <version>4.0.5.RELEASE</version>
   </dependency>
   ```

```
<dependency>
    <groupId>org.springframework</groupId>
    <artifactId>spring-beans</artifactId>
    <version>4.0.5.RELEASE</version>
</dependency>
<dependency>
    <groupId>org.springframework</groupId>
    <artifactId>spring-context</artifactId>
    <version>4.0.5.RELEASE</version>
</dependency>
<dependency>
    <groupId>org.springframework</groupId>
    <artifactId>spring-web</artifactId>
    <version>4.0.5.RELEASE</version>
</dependency>

<dependency>
    <groupId>org.springframework</groupId>
    <artifactId>spring-webmvc</artifactId>
    <version>4.0.5.RELEASE</version>
</dependency>

<dependency>
    <groupId>com.fasterxml.jackson.core</groupId>
    <artifactId>jackson-core</artifactId>
    <version>2.4.0</version>
</dependency>

<dependency>
    <groupId>com.fasterxml.jackson.core</groupId>
    <artifactId>jackson-databind</artifactId>
    <version>2.4.0</version>
</dependency>
```

3. Replace the content of the web.xml file with the following:

```
<web-app xmlns="http://xmlns.jcp.org/xml/ns/javaee"
     xmlns:xsi="http://www.w3.org/2001/XMLSchema-instance"
     xsi:schemaLocation="http://xmlns.jcp.org/xml/ns/javaee
     http://xmlns.jcp.org/xml/ns/javaee/web-app_3_1.xsd"
     version="3.1">

    <servlet>
        <servlet-name>springmvc</servlet-name>
        <servlet-class>
            org.springframework.web.servlet.DispatcherServlet
        </servlet-class>
        <load-on-startup>1</load-on-startup>
    </servlet>

    <servlet-mapping>
        <servlet-name>springmvc</servlet-name>
        <url-pattern>/*</url-pattern>
    </servlet-mapping>
</web-app>
```

4. Create `springmvc-servlet.xml` under the `src/main/webapp/WEB-INF` folder:

```xml
<?xml version="1.0" encoding="UTF-8"?>
<beans xmlns="http://www.springframework.org/schema/beans"
       xmlns:xsi="http://www.w3.org/2001/XMLSchema-instance"
       xmlns:context="http://www.springframework.org/schema/context"
       xmlns:mvc="http://www.springframework.org/schema/mvc"
       xsi:schemaLocation="http://www.springframework.org/schema/beans
    http://www.springframework.org/schema/beans/spring-beans-4.0.xsd
    http://www.springframework.org/schema/context
    http://www.springframework.org/schema/context/spring-context-4.0.xsd
    http://www.springframework.org/schema/mvc
    http://www.springframework.org/schema/mvc/spring-mvc-4.0.xsd">

    <context:component-scan base-package="com.wiley.beginningspring" />
    <context:annotation-config />

    <mvc:annotation-driven />
</beans>
```

5. Create the following classes under the `com.wiley.beginningspring` package in the `src/main/java` source folder:

```java
public class User {

    private int id;
    private String name;
    @JsonIgnore
    private String address;

    public User(int id, String name, String address) {
        this.id = id;
        this.name = name;
        this.address = address;
    }

    public int getId() {
        return id;
    }

    public String getName() {
        return name;
    }

    public String getAddress() {
        return address;
    }
}

@RestController
@RequestMapping("/rest")
public class UserRestController {

    @RequestMapping(value = "/users", method= RequestMethod.GET)
    public List<User> list() {
```

```
              List<User> users = new ArrayList<User>();
              users.add(new User(1, "Mert Caliskan", "Izmir"));
              users.add(new User(2, "Kenan Sevindik", "Ankara"));
              return users;
          }
      }
```

6. Add the following part as a child element of the `<build>` element in the `pom.xml` file:

```
<plugins>
    <plugin>
        <groupId>org.eclipse.jetty</groupId>
        <artifactId>jetty-maven-plugin</artifactId>
        <version>9.2.1.v20140609</version>
        <configuration>
            <scanIntervalSeconds>2</scanIntervalSeconds>
            <webApp>
                <contextPath>/</contextPath>
            </webApp>
        </configuration>
    </plugin>
</plugins>
```

7. Run the application using the Maven `jetty:run` goal and request the URL
   `http://localhost:8080/rest/users` in your browser.

   You should see the output of JSON as shown here with omitted address values:

   ```
   [{"id":1,"name":"Mert Caliskan"},{"id":2,"name":"Kenan Sevindik"}]
   ```

CHAPTER 12

Exercise 1

Configure the concurrent session management so that a user can open at most one session in the application, and any other login attempt from the same user results in an error message.

Solution to Exercise 1

Use the following steps:

1. Use the following Maven command to create a project:

   ```
   mvn archetype:generate -DarchetypeArtifactId=maven-archetype-webapp
       -DgroupId=com.wiley.beginningspring -DartifactId=spring-book-ch12-exercise1
   ```

2. Add the following dependencies to the `pom.xml` file:

   ```
   <dependency>
       <groupId>org.springframework.security</groupId>
       <artifactId>spring-security-web</artifactId>
   ```

```
        <version>3.2.5.RELEASE</version>
</dependency>
<dependency>
        <groupId>org.springframework.security</groupId>
        <artifactId>spring-security-config</artifactId>
        <version>3.2.5.RELEASE</version>
</dependency>
<dependency>
        <groupId>commons-logging</groupId>
        <artifactId>commons-logging</artifactId>
        <version>1.1.1</version>
</dependency>
<dependency>
        <groupId>javax.servlet</groupId>
        <artifactId>javax.servlet-api</artifactId>
        <version>3.1.0</version>
</dependency>
```

3. Add the following part as a child element of the `<build>` element in the pom.xml file:

```
<plugins>
    <plugin>
        <groupId>org.eclipse.jetty</groupId>
        <artifactId>jetty-maven-plugin</artifactId>
        <version>9.2.1.v20140609</version>
        <configuration>
            <scanIntervalSeconds>2</scanIntervalSeconds>
            <webApp>
                <contextPath>/</contextPath>
            </webApp>
        </configuration>
    </plugin>
</plugins>
```

4. Replace the content of the web.xml file with the following:

```
<web-app xmlns="http://xmlns.jcp.org/xml/ns/javaee"
        xmlns:xsi="http://www.w3.org/2001/XMLSchema-instance"
        xsi:schemaLocation="http://xmlns.jcp.org/xml/ns/javaee
        http://xmlns.jcp.org/xml/ns/javaee/web-app_3_1.xsd"
        version="3.1">
  <display-name>Archetype Created Web Application</display-name>
        <filter>
          <filter-name>springSecurityFilterChain</filter-name>
          <filter-class>org.springframework.web.filter.DelegatingFilterProxy
                </filter-class>
        </filter>

        <filter-mapping>
            <filter-name>springSecurityFilterChain</filter-name>
            <url-pattern>/*</url-pattern>
        </filter-mapping>

        <listener>
```

```
        <listener-class>
          org.springframework.web.context.ContextLoaderListener
        </listener-class>
      </listener>

      <listener>
        <listener-class>
          org.springframework.security.web.session.HttpSessionEventPublisher
        </listener-class>
      </listener>
    </web-app>
```

5. Create a Spring bean configuration file named `ApplicationContext.xml` in the `src/main/webapp/WEB-INF` folder with the following content:

```xml
<?xml version="1.0" encoding="UTF-8"?>
<beans xmlns="http://www.springframework.org/schema/beans"
    xmlns:xsi="http://www.w3.org/2001/XMLSchema-instance"
    xmlns:security="http://www.springframework.org/schema/security"
    xsi:schemaLocation="http://www.springframework.org/schema/security
    http://www.springframework.org/schema/security/spring-security-3.2.xsd
       http://www.springframework.org/schema/beans
       http://www.springframework.org/schema/beans/spring-beans.xsd">

    <security:user-service id="userService">
        <security:user name="user1" password="secret" authorities="ROLE_USER"/>
        <security:user name="user2" password="secret"
            authorities="ROLE_USER,ROLE_EDITOR"/>
    </security:user-service>

    <security:authentication-manager>
        <security:authentication-provider user-service-ref="userService"/>
    </security:authentication-manager>

    <security:http auto-config="true">
        <security:intercept-url pattern="/**" access="ROLE_USER"/>
        <security:session-management>
          <security:concurrency-control
              error-if-maximum-exceeded="true" max-sessions="1"/>
        </security:session-management>
    </security:http>

</beans>
```

6. Run the application using the Maven `jetty:run` goal and try to log in to it using a browser with the URL `http://localhost:8080`. You can use `user1/secret` as credentials. Open another browser and try to log in to the application with the same user and observe the result.

Exercise 2

Configure Spring Security to use the basic authentication method (instead of form-based authentication) to protect access to URL resources.

Solution to Exercise 2

You can continue with the project you created for Exercise 1. Use the following steps:

1. Modify the `<security:http>` element in `applicationContext.xml` as follows:

```
<security:http auto-config="false">
    <security:http-basic />
    <security:intercept-url pattern="/**" access="ROLE_USER" />
    <security:session-management>
        <security:concurrency-control
            error-if-maximum-exceeded="true" max-sessions="1" />
    </security:session-management>
</security:http>
```

2. Run the application using the Maven `jetty:run` goal and try to log in to it using a browser with the URL `http://localhost:8080`. You can use `user1/secret` as credentials.

Exercise 3

Instead of using the `@Secured` annotation to protect access to `BusinessService.secureMethod()`, enable pre-post annotations and use `@PreAuthorize` to protect it.

Solution to Exercise 3

You can continue with the project you created for the "Authorizing Service Methods" Try It Out in Chapter 12. Use the following steps:

1. Modify the `<security:global-method-security>` element in `applicationContext.xml` as follows:

```
<security:global-method-security
    secured-annotations="enabled" pre-post-annotations="enabled"/>
```

2. Modify the test methods in the `MethodLevelSecurityTests` class so that it will invoke `secureMethod2()`, which is already annotated with `@PreAuthorize`. Just be careful that you change the assigned role to `ROLE_EDITOR` in the last test as follows:

```
@Test
public void testSecureMethodWithAppropriateAuthority() {
    TestingAuthenticationToken authentication =
        new TestingAuthenticationToken("user1", "secret","ROLE_EDITOR");
    SecurityContextHolder.getContext().setAuthentication(authentication);

    businessService.secureMethod2();
}
```

CHAPTER 13

Exercise 1

What are the two alternative methods that are introduced with Spring 4 for mapping row elements instead of by implementing a `RowMapper`?

Solution to Exercise 1

The lambda expressions introduced with Java 8 are utilized by Spring 4 to enable creating row mappers with anonymous code blocks:

```
public Account find(long accountId) {
    return jdbcTemplate.queryForObject("select id, owner_name, balance,
            access_time,locked from account where id = " + accountId,
            (rs, rowNum) -> new Account(rs.getLong("id"),
                                    rs.getString("owner_name"),
                                    rs.getDouble("balance"),
                                    rs.getTimestamp("access_time"),
                                    rs.getBoolean("locked")));
}
```

The same implementation can be done with method references, which are also introduced by Java 8 and makes it possible to reuse the existing methods that you have. So you can easily do the row mapping within your custom method implementation:

```
public Account find(long accountId) {
    return jdbcTemplate.queryForObject("select id,owner_name, balance, access_time,
        locked from account where id = " + accountId, this::mapAccount);
}
private Account mapAccount(ResultSet rs, int rowNum) throws SQLException {
    return new Account(rs.getLong("id"),
        rs.getString("owner_name"),
        rs.getDouble("balance"),
        rs.getTimestamp("access_time"),
        rs.getBoolean("locked"));
}
```

Exercise 2

Instead of defining a wrapper annotation for the repeating annotations, what is a better way offered by Spring 4?

Solution to Exercise 2

Spring 4 supports the @Repeatable annotation, which ships with Java 8, and this annotation has already been integrated with the @Scheduled and @PropertySource annotations that are offered by version 4 of the framework. So you can just use multiple @Scheduled or @PropertySource annotations on the same method instead of wrapping them with another annotation.

INDEX

A

`AcceptHeaderLocaleResolver` bean, 95
`AccessDecisionManager`, 355–357
`accountDao( )` method, 25
`AccountDaoInMemoryImpl` class, 24
`AccountDaoJdbcImpl` class, 112–113
`AccountService` bean, 25
ACID acronym
   atomicity, 176
   consistency, 176
   durability, 176
   isolation, 176
advice in AOP, 238
   Before, 244, 245
   After (Finally), 244, 246–247
   After Returning, 244, 245
   After Throwing, 244, 245–246
   `AfterReturningAdvice`,
      242–244
   Around, 244, 247–248
   `MethodBeforeAdvice`, 242–244
   `ThrowsAdvice`, 244
After (Finally) advice type, 244
`@After` annotation, 252
After Returning advice type, 244
After Throwing advice type, 244
`@AfterReturning` annotation, 252
`AfterReturningAdvice`, 242–244
`@AfterThrowing` annotation,
   252–253
`<alias>` element, 44–45
aliases, 44–45
anemic domain model, 6

annotations
   AOP
      `@After`, 252
      `@AfterReturning`, 252
      `@AfterThrowing`, 252–253
      `@Around`, 253
      `@Aspect`, 253
      `@Before`, 250–251
      `@DeclareParents`, 254–255
      `@Pointcut`, 251–252
   `@Autowired`, 19
   `@Bean`, 20
   `@Cacheable`, 290–291
   `@CacheEvict`, 292
   `@CachePut`, 292
   `@Caching`, 293
   caching abstraction, 289–290
   `@Component`, 19, 266
   `@Configuration`, 20
   configuration, RESTful services, 319–320
   `@ContextConfiguration`, 213, 225
   `@Controller`, 84
   `@ControllerAdvice`, 85
   `@CreditCardNumber`, 86
   `@Description`, 381
   `@Email`, 86
   `@EnableTransactionManagement`, 186
   `@Entity`, 140
   `@ExceptionHandler`, 85, 93–95
   `@Id`, 140
   `@ImportResource`, 213
   `@InitBinder`, 85
   `@Inject`, 219
   `@JoinColumn`, 142

annotations *(continued)*
 @ManyToMany, 144
 @ManyToOne, 143
 @ModelAttribute, 84–85
 MVC configuration, 71–72
 @OneToMany, 143
 @OneToOne, 142
 @PathVariable, 85
 @Pattern, 86
 @PersistenceContext, 161
 @PersistenceUnit, 161
 @PostConstruct, 296–298
 @Qualifier, 219
 repeating, 379–381
 @Repository, 19
 @RequestMapping, 84, 317
 @Resource, 219
 @ResponseBody, 316
 @RestController, 316, 381
 @Service, 19
 @Size, 86
 @Table, 140
 testing and, 232–233
 @Transactional, 186, 190–191, 219
 @WebAppConfiguration, 226
anonymous authentication, 333, 344
AOP (aspect-oriented programming), 184, 237–239
 advice, 238
  AfterReturningAdvice, 242–244
  MethodBeforeAdvice, 242–244
  ThrowsAdvice, 244
 annotations
  @After, 252
  @AfterReturning, 252
  @AfterThrowing, 252–253
  @Around, 253
  @Aspect, 253
  @Before, 250–251
  configuration and, 259
  @DeclareParents, 254–255
  @Pointcut, 251–252
 AspectJ, 239
 caching and, 285–286
 CGLIB proxy mechanism, 239

configuration, annotations and, 259
JDK dynamic proxy mechanism, 239
join-point, 238
methods, logging execution times, 240–243
point-cut, 238
 alternative designators, 249
 method signature expressions, 249
 type signature expressions, 248–249
 wildcards, 250
proxy objects, 239
Proxy pattern, 239
quick-start Maven archetype, 242
target, 238
weaving, 238
AOP (aspected-oriented programming), advice
Before, 245
After (Finally), 246–247
After Returning, 245
After Throwing, 245–246
Around, 247–248
APIs (application programming interfaces)
EJB2, 3
JPA (Java Persistence API), 138
application exceptions, 186
ApplicationConfig class, 290
ApplicationContext, 21
 caching, 216–217
 configuration
  ApplicationContextInitializer
   interface, 214
  Java-based, 210–214
  XML-based, 210–214
 JUnit, 210–214
ApplicationContext interface, 25
ApplicationContextInitializer
 interface, 214
arithmetic operators, SpEL, 276
Around advice type, 244
@Around annotation, 253
@Aspect annotation, 253
AspectJ, 239
 methods, logging execution times, 255–258
association tables, 144
associations
 directionality, 142

multiplicity, 142
objects
    directionality, 144–145
    many-to-many, 143–144
    many-to-one, 142–143
    one-to-many, 143
    one-to-one, 142
atomicity (ACID), 176
attributes
    depends-on, 38
    destroy-method, 52–53
    init-method, 52–53
    lazy-init, 51
    mapping to columns, 141–142
authenticate tag, 359
authentication, 332, 341
    anonymous, 333, 344
    basic, 352–353
    CAS (Central Authentication Service), 333
    login flow, 342–243
        page customization, 344–345
    OAuth, 333
AuthenticationManager, 342
authorization, 332
    expression-based, 357–358
    service methods, 359–364
    web requests, 353–355
authorize tag, 359
automatic dirty checking, 154
@Autowired annotation, 19
autowired collections, 377–379
autowiring, 39–43

B

batch operations, JdbcTemplate, 126
batchUpdate( ) method, 126
@Bean annotation, 20
bean scope, 48–51
Bean Validation 1.1, 374
Bean Validation API, 86–90
beans, 18
    access, SpEL, 280–281
    configuration, constructor injection and,
        31–32

definition profiles, 54–56
definitions, overriding, 36–38
instantiation, 45–48
naming, 44–45
request-scoped, testing, 225–227
scopes, 25
session-scoped, testing, 225–227
<beans> element, 19
Before advice type, 244
@Before annotation, 250–251
between operator, 277
bidirectional associations, 138–139
BLOBs (binary large objects), 126–127
bootstrapping cache storage, 296–298
boundaries, transactions, 177–180
built-ins
    expressions, 358
    scopes, 50
buttons on MVC forms, 79

C

cache annotations
    @Cacheable, 290–291
        conditional caching, 291–292
        keys, 291
    @CacheEvict, 292
    @CachePut, 292
    @Caching, 293
cache managers, 298
    CompositeCacheManager, 294–295
    ConcurrentMapCacheManager, 294
    configuration, different name, 289
    Ehcache, 299–302
    Guava, 302
    Hazelcast, 302–303
    NoOpCacheManager, 294
    SimpleCacheManager, 293–294
@Cacheable annotation, 290–291
    conditional caching, 291–292
    keys, 291
@CacheEvict annotation, 292
cacheManager, 286–289
@CachePut annotation, 292

427

caching, 285
  abstraction, annotations and configuration,
    289–290
  application building
    annotations and, 289–290
    cache manager name, 289
    service layer method caching, 286–289
  ApplicationContext, 216–217
  expressions in, 281
  initialization, programmatically, 296–298
  SpEL, 281
    expressions, 295–296
  storage bootstrapping, 296–298
@Caching annotation, 293
callback methods, life cycle callback methods, 52–53
callback objects, 116
capitalize method, 274–275
CAS (Central Authentication Service), 333
CGLIB proxying, 239
checkboxes in MVC forms, 78
checked exceptions, 186
circular dependencies, 34–35
CLOBs (character large objects), 126–127
collections
  autowired, 377–370
  operators, 279–280
    first and last element, 280
Command object, 74
Commons FileUpload, 90–93
@Component annotation, 19, 266
CompositeCacheManager, 294–295
conditional caching, @Cacheable annotation,
  291–292
conditional dependency, injection and, 374–377
conditional operators, SpEL, 277–278
configuration
  annotations, RESTful services, 319–320
  AOP, annotations and, 259
  ApplicationContext
    ApplicationContextInitializer
      interface, 214
  beans, constructor injection, 31–32
  cache manager, different name, 289
  context, 214
    inheriting, 214–216

environments, at runtim, 56–59
MVC
  annotations and, 71–72
  form tag library, 73–74
  PlatformTransactionManager bean,
    180–182
SpEL and, 264–266
Spring Container, 21–25
Spring Security, 334–340
@Configuration annotation, 20
configuration metadata, 18–20
consistency (ACID), 176
constructor injection, 11–12, 31–34
  bean configuration, 31–32
<constructor-arg> element, 32–33
constructors, calling, 272
containers. See also Spring Container
  lightweight, 8–9
context configuration, 214
  inheriting, 214–216
context hierarchies, 225
@ContextConfiguration annotation, 213, 225
ContextLoaderListener, 225
@Controller annotation, 84
@ControllerAdvice annotation, 85
controllers, MVC, testing, 230
@CreditCardNumber annotation, 86
CRUD (Create, Read, Update, Delete), 139
  objects and, 150–153
  RESTful services and, 307–318

D

data access, queries, 114–116
databases
  embedded, 108–109
  initializing, 111
  queries
    IN clause, 118–119
    JdbcTemplate, 114–116
    named parameters, 116–118
  records
    deleting, 121–124
    inserting, 121–124
    updating, 121–124

stored functions, calling, 124–125
stored procedures, calling, 124–125
DataNucleus, 139
DataSource, 110–111
DataSource object, 106–108
dates, MVC forms, 76–77
DDL operations, 127–128
Declarative Transaction Management, 183–186, 238
@DeclareParents annotation, 254–255
DELETE method, 306
dependency injection, 10–11, 18
   autowiring, 39–43
   bean
      lookups, 43–44
      overriding definitions, 36–38
   circular dependencies, 34–35
   conditional dependency, 374–377
   constructor injection, 31–34
   dependency resolution process, 35
   depends-on attribute, 38
   MVC and, 65
   setter injection, 29–31
   test fixtures, 217–219
dependency lookup, 10
depends-on attribute, 38
deployment, EJB model, 4
@Description annotation, 381
destroy-method attribute, 52–53
devFoo( ) method, 58
directionality associations, 142, 144–145
Dispatcher Servlet, 65–66, 306
   definition, 66–67
   Servlet Context, 67
domain objects, anemic domain model, 6
DriverManagerDataSource class, 107–108
drop-downs, forms, 77
DRY (Don't Repeat Yourself), 238
durability (ACID), 176

E

eager initialization, 18, 51
EBJ2 API, 3
EclipseLink, 139

Ehcache cache manager, 299–302
EJB (Enterprise JavaBeans), 1–2
   definitions, 4–5
   deployment, 4
EL (expression language), 263
   operators, 275
   SpEL (Spring Expression Language), 264
@Email annotation, 86
EmbededDatabase interface, 108–109
@EnableTransactionManagement annotation, 186
encapsulation, SQL queries, MappingSqlQuery class and, 128–132
encryption
   passwords, 349–350
   Spring Security, 334
entities, ORM, 140–141
@Entity annotation, 140
EntityManager, 163
EntityManagerFactory, 161–163
environments, configuration, at runtime, 56–59
exception handling, 166–167
   JDBC, 132–133
   MVC, 93–95
      testing, 230
   RESTful services, 322–326
@ExceptionHandler annotation, 85, 93–95
exceptions
   application, 186
   checked, 186
   system, 186
   unchecked, 186
execution keyword, 249
exercise solutions, 385–425
expression templates, 267
expression-based authorization, 357–358
expressions
   built-in, 358
   caching, 281
   lambda expressions, 370–374
ExpressParser interface, 267

F

FactoryBean interface, 47–48
files, uploading, 90–93

filters, Spring Security, 338

fixation attacks, Spring Security, 334

foo( ) method, 37

Form object, 74

form tab library (MVC), 73–74

form tag, 74–75

Form-Backing object, 74

forms, submitting, testing, 230

Front Controller, 65–66

functions

registering, 274–275

SpEL, 273–275

stored, calling, 124–125

G

GET method, 306

getBean( ) method, 37

getConnection( ) method, 107

getRemoteUser( ) method, 333–334

getValue( ) method, 267

global transactions, 182

Guava cache manager, 302

H

handler mappings, 66

HandlerMapping interface, 66

Hazelcast cache manager, 302–303

Hello World

MVC, 68–71

parsing, SpEL and, 268–270

Hibernate, 139, 147–150

HibernateTemplate class, 161–166

hierarchies, context, testing and, 225

HTML (HyperText Markup Language), 64

HTTP (HyperText Transfer Protocol), 64

status codes, RESTful services, 318

I

@Id annotation, 140

@ImportResource annotation, 213

IN clause, 118–119

inheritance, context configuration, 214–216

@InitBinder annotation, 85

initialization

caches, 296–298

eager initialization, 18, 51

lazy, 18, 51–52

init-method attribute, 52–53

@Inject annotation, 219

injection

conditional dependency and, 374–377

constructor injection, 11–12

dependency injection, 10, 18

test fixtures, 217–219

setter methods, 11, 12

system properties, SpEL and, 264–266

inline lists, 274

input, validation, 86–90

input elements, MVC forms, 75–76

instanceof operator, 277

instantiation, beans, 45–48

interfaces

ApplicationContext, 25

ApplicationContextInitializer, 214

EmbededDatabase, 108–109

ExpressParser, 267

FactoryBean, 47–48

HandlerMapping, 66

JpaDialect, 168

JpaVendorAdapter, 168

MethodInterceptor, 204

ServletContextAware, 67

UserDetailsService, 340–341

internationalization, MVC, 95–97

IoC (Inversion of Control), 8, 9–10

configuration metadata, 18–20

isolation (ACID), 176

isUserInRole( ) method, 333–334

J

JAAS (Jave Authentication and Authorization
Service), 332

Java

EJB (Enterprise JavaBeans), 1–2

JNDI (Java Naming and Directory Interface), 5

JSP (JavaServer Pages), 6

mapping Java types to SQL types, 145–147
POJO (Plain Old Java Object), 1–2
Java 8, 370–374
Java Annotation-based configuration, 27–29
Java EE7, 370–374
Java-based configuration, 21–26
JDBC (Java Database Connectivity)
  batch operations, 126
  BLOBs (binary large objects), 126–127
  callback objects, 116
  classes
     JdbcTemplate, 105
     MappingSqlQuery, 105
     NamedParameterJdbcTemplate, 105
     SimpleJdbcCall, 105
     SimpleJdbcInsert, 105
     SqlUpdate, 105
     StoredProcedure, 105
  CLOBs (character large objects), 126–127
  connection management, 105–111
  databases
     deleting records, 121–124
     inserting records, 121–124
     updating records, 121–124
  DataSource instance, 110–111
  DataSource object, 106–108
  DDL operations, 127–128
  embedded databases, 108–109
  EmbededDatabase interface, 108–109
  exception handling, 132–133
  initializing databases, 111
  JdbcTemplate, configuration, 112–113
  methods, vendor-specific, 127
  operations as Java objects, 128–132
  problems with, 104–105
  queries, 114–116
     IN clause, 118–119
     named parameters, 116–118
  stored functions, calling, 124–125
  stored procedures, calling, 124–125
  transactions, boundaries, 177–180
JdbcTemplate, 370–374
  batch operations, 126
  callback objects, 116
  configuration, 112–113

deleting records, 121–124
inserting records, 121–124
PreparedStatement, 119–121
queries, 114–116
updating records, 121–124
JdbcTemplate class, 105
JDK (Java Development Kit)
  caching, 286–289
  proxying, 239
JNDI (Java Naming and Directory Interface), 5
  mock objects for testing, 232
@JoinColumn annotation, 142
join-point in AOP, 238
JPA (Java Persistence API), 138
  associations, 150–153
  configuration, 147–156
  container setup, 156–160
  DAO implementation, 161–166
  deleting entities, 153–154
  finding entities, 153–154
  Hibernate, 147–150
  implements, 139
  load time weaving, 169–170
  persistence, 150–153
  QL (Query Language), 155–156
  updating entities, 153–154
JpaDialect interface, 168
JpaTemplate class, 161–166
JpaVendorAdapter interface, 168
JRE (Java Runtime Environment), 332
JSON (JavaScript Object Notation), 320
JSP (JavaServer Pages), 6
  MVC forms, 73
     binding, 74
     buttons, 79
     checkboxes, 78
     classes, 76–77
     dates, 76–77
     drop-downs, 77
     form tab library, 73–74
     input elements, 75–76
     labels, 78
     radio buttons, 78
     styles, 79–84
  security tags, 358–359

JUnit, 3–4
    `ApplicationContext`, 210–214
    runner class, 212

K

keys, primary keys
    natural primary keys, 141
    surrogate primary keys, 141
    synthetic primary keys, 141
keywords
    `within`, 248–249
    `execution`, 249

L

labels, MVC forms, 78
lambda expressions, 370–374
lazy initialization, 18, 51–52
`lazy-init` attribute, 51
life cycle callback methods, 52–53
lightweight containers, 8–9
lists, inline lists, 274
load time weaving, 169–170
local transactions, 182
`LocalEntityManagerFactoryBean`, 156–160
logical operators, SpEL, 276–277
login
    authentication, 342–243
    customization, 344–345
logout, 346
lookups
    bean lookups, 43–44
    dependency lookups, 10

M

`Main` class, 24
`main` method, 24
MANDATORY propagation, 192
`@ManyToMany` annotation, 144
many-to-many associations, 143–144
`@ManyToOne` annotation, 143
many-to-one associations, 142–143
`MappingSqlQuery` class, 105
    query encapsulation, 128–132

Maven project, 242
    creating, 21–22
metadata, configuration metadata, 18–20
method references, 373–374
method signature expressions (AOP), 249
`MethodBeforeAdvice`, 242–244
`MethodInterceptor` interface, 204
methods
    `accountDao( )`, 25
    `batchUpdate( )`, 126
    callbacks, life cycle callback methods,
        52–53
    `capitalize`, 274–275
    `DELETE`, 306
    `devFoo( )`, 58
    `foo( )`, 37
    `GET`, 306
    `getBean( )`, 37
    `getConnection( )`, 107
    `getRemoteUser( )`, 333–334
    `getValue( )`, 267
    `isUserInRole( )`, 333–334
    logging execution times
        AOP, 240–243
        AspectJ, 255–258
    `main`, 24
    `parseExpression`, 267
    `POST`, 306
    `prodFoo( )`, 58
    `PUT`, 306
    `setRootObject( )`, 273
    setter methods, 11
    setup, 220–221
    `setValue( )`, 267
    SpEL, 270–273
    static, calling, 272–273
    teardown, 220–221
    vendor-specific, 127
mock objects, testing and, 231–232
`@ModelAttribute` annotation, 84–85
multiplicity associations, 142
MVC (Model View Controller), 64–65
    annotations
        `@Controller`, 84
        `@ControllerAdvice`, 85

@CreditCardNumber, 86
@Email, 86
@ExceptionHandler, 85, 93–95
@InitBinder, 85
@ModelAttribute, 84–85
@PathVariable, 85
@Pattern, 86
@RequestMapping, 84
@Size, 86
configuration, annotations and, 71–72
dependency injection and, 65
Dispatcher Servlet, 65–66
exception handling, 93–95
file uploads, 90–93
form tab library, 73–74
forms
    binding, 74
    buttons, 79
    checkboxes, 78
    classes, 76–77
    dates, 76–77
    drop-downs and, 77
    form tag, 74–75
    input elements, 75–76
    JSP and, 73–84
    labels, 78
    radio buttons, 78
    styles, 79–84
Front Controller, 65–66
handler mappings, 66
Hello World application, 68–71
input validation, 86–90
internationalization, 95–97
mock reqest/response, printing, 231
testing
    controllers, 227–228
    exception handlers, 230
    form submission, 228–230
themes, 97–100
view resolvers, 66

N

NamedParameterJdbcTemplate class, 105
naming beans, 44–45

natural primary keys, 141
navigation, safe navigation operator (SpEL), 278–279
NESTED propagation, 192
NEVER propagation, 192
NoOpCacheManager, 294
NOT_SUPPORTED propagation, 192

O

OAuth, 333
object query language, 139
objects
    associations, 138–139
        directionality, 144–145
        many-to-many, 143–144
        many-to-one, 142–143
        one-to-many, 143
        one-to-one, 142
    BLOBs (binary large objects), 126–127
    callback objects, 116
    CLOBs (character large objects), 126–127
    Command, 74
    CRUD operations, 150–153
    Form, 74
    Form-Backing, 74
    mock objects for testing, 231–232
    TransactionSynchronization, 204–205
OGNL (Object Graph Navigation Language), 264
@OneToMany annotations, 143
one-to-many associations, 143
@OneToOne annotation, 142
one-to-one associations, 142
OpenID, 333
OpenJPA, 139
operators
    between, 277
    EL (expression language), 275
    instanceof, 277
    SpEL
        arithmetic, 276
        collection, 279–280
        conditional, 277–278
        logical, 276–277
        projection, 279–280

operators *(continued)*
>   regular expression, 278
>   relational, 276
>   safe navigation, 278–279
>   selection, 279–280
>   T( ), 272–273
ORM (object-relational mapping), 138
>   associations between objects, 142–145
>   entities, 140–141
>   framework, 139
>   Jave types to SQL types, 145–147
>   mapping attributes to columns, 141–142
>   mapping Java types to SQL types, 145–147

P

PAM (pluggable authentication module), 332
parameters, queries, 116–118
parseExpression method, 267
parsing, SpEL and, 267–270
passwords
>   encryption, 349–350
>   Spring Security, 334
@PathVariable annotation, 85
@Pattern annotation, 86
patterns, Template Method, 115
persistence, 153
persistence context, 150
persistence unit, 149
>   multiple, 170–171
@PersistenceContext annotation, 161
@PersistenceUnit annotation, 161
PlatformTransactionManager, 201–203
PlatformTransactionManager API, 180
>   implementations, 182–183
PlatformTransactionManager bean,
>   configuration, 180–182
@Pointcut annotation, 251–252
point-cut in AOP, 238
>   alternative designators, 249
>   method signature expressions, 249
>   type signature expressions, 248–249
>   wildcards, 250
POJO (Plain Old Java Object), 1–2
>   programming model

benefits, 7–8
>   problems, 2–7
POST method, 306
@PostConstruct annotation, 296–298
PreparedStatement, 119–121
primary keys
>   natural primary keys, 141
>   surrogate primary keys, 141
>   synthetic primary keys, 141
procedures, stored, calling, 124–125
prodFoo( ) method, 58
profiles, beans, 54–56
projection, operators, 279–280
projects, Maven, creating, 21–22
propagation rules
>   MANDATORY, 192
>   NESTED, 192
>   NEVER, 192
>   NOT_SUPPORTED, 192
>   REQUIRED, 191–-192
>   REQUIRED_NEW, 192
>   SUPPORTS, 192
<property> element, 30
proxy objects, 239
Proxy pattern, 239
PUT method, 306

Q

QL (Query Language), 155–156
@Qualifier annotation, 219
queries
>   IN clause, 118–119
>   JdbcTemplate, 114–116
>   parameters, named, 116–118
>   SQL
>   encapsulation, 128–132
>   MappingSqlQuery class and,
>   128–132

R

radio buttons, MVC forms, 78
records (databases)
>   deleting, 121–124

inserting, 121–124
updating, 121–124
regular expression operator, SpEL, 278
relational operators, SpEL, 276
remember-me support, 350–351
@Repository annotation, 19
@RequestMapping annotation, 84, 317
request-scoped beans, testing, 225–227
REQUIRED propagation, 191–192
REQUIRED_NEW propagation, 192
@Resource annotation, 219
@ResponseBody annotation, 316
REST (REpresentational State Transfer), 305
    DELETE method, 306
    GET method, 306
    POST method, 306
    PUT method, 306
@RestController annotation, 316
RestException class, 324
RestExceptionHandler class, 325
RESTful services, 306
    annotation configuration, 319–320
    CRUD operations, 307–318
    exception handling, 322–326
    HTTP, status codes, 318
    unit testing, 326–328
    web services, creating, 306–318
    XML and, 320–322
RestTemplate class, 326–328
RMI (remote method invocation), 6
#root, 273
RowMapper, 116
runtime, environment configuration, 56–59

S

safe navigation operator (SpEL), 278–279
savepoints, 192
scopes
    bean scope, 48–51
    built-in, 50
    singleton, 25
security, 331–332
    authentication, 332
    authorization, 332

CAS (Central Authentication Service), 333
    OAuth, 333
    OpenID, 333
    Siteminder, 333
    web.xml, 332–333
SecurityContext object, 341
selection, operators, 279–280
    first and last element, 280
@Service annotation, 19
service layers, caching methods, 286–289
Servlet Context, 67
Servlet Specification, web.xml security, 332–333
ServletContextAware interface, 67
session management in Spring Security, 351–352
SessionLocalResolver class, 95
session-scoped beans, testing, 225–227
setRootObject( ) method, 273
setter injection, 31–34
setter methods, 11, 12
setup methods, 220–221
setValue( ) method, 267
SimpleCacheManager, 293–294
SimpleJdbcCall, 124–125
SimpleJdbcCall class, 105
SimpleJdbcInsert class, 105
singleton scope, 24
Siteminder, 333
@Size annotation, 86
SoapUI, service methods, 306–307
SpEL (Spring Expression Language), 226, 264
    authorization and, 357–358
    caching, 281
        expressions, 295–296
    configuration and, 264–266
    functions, 273–275
        registering, 274–275
    Hello World, parsing, 268–270
    inline lists, 274
    methods, invoking, 270–273
    operators, 275
        arithmetic, 276
        collection, 279–280
        conditional, 277–278
        logical, 276–277
        projection, 279–280

SpEL (Spring Expression Language) *(continued)*
    regular expression, 278
    relational, 276
    safe navigation, 278–279
    selection, 279–280
  parsers, creating, 267–270
  <spring:eval>, 281
  system properties, 274
  system property injection, 264–266
  utilities, bean access, 280–281
  variables, 273–275
    environment, 274
    #root, 273
    system properties, 274
    #this, 274
SpelExpressionParser, 267
Spring 4.0, 369
  Java 8, 370–374
  Java EE7, 370–374
Spring Container
  configuration, 21–25
    Java Annotation-based configuration, 27–29
  standalone environment
    Java-based configuration, 21–26
    XML-based configuration, 26–27
Spring Security
  authentication, 333, 341
    anonymous, 333
    basic, 352–353
    login, 342–243
  authorization, service methods, 359–364
  CAS (Central Authentication Service), 333
  configuration, 334–340
  encryption, 334
    passwords, 349–350
  features, 333–334
  filters, 338
  fixation attacks, 334
  integration support, 333–334
  JSP tags, 358–359
  logout, 346
  OAuth, 333
  OpenID, 333

  passwords, 334
    encrypting, 349–350
  remember-me support, 333, 350–351
  secure HTTP, 334
  service method authorization, 359–364
  session management, 351–352
  Siteminder, 333
  SSO solutions, 333
  UserDetails, 346–347
  UserDetailsService interface, 340
  web requests, authorization, 353–355
<spring:eval>, 281
SQL (Structured Query Language)
  DML operations, encapsulation, 130–131
  mapping Java types to, 145–147
  queries
    encapsulation, 128–132
    MappingSqlQuery class and, 128–132
  stored procedures, encapsulations, 131–132
SqlUpdate class, 105, 130–131
SSO (single sign-on) solutions, 333
static methods, calling, 272–273
storage, cache bootstrapping, 296–298
stored functions, calling, 124–125
stored procedures, calling, 124–125
StoredProcedure class, 105
styles, MVC forms, 79–84
SUPPORTS propagation, 192
surrogate primary keys, 141
synthetic primary keys, 141
system exceptions, 186
system properties, injecting, SpEL and, 264–266
systemEnvironment variable, 274
systemProperties variable, 274

T

T( ) operator, 272–273
@Table annotation, 140
target in AOP, 238
teardown methods, 220–221
Template Method pattern, 115
templates, expression templates, 267
TestContext framework, 219–225

testing
    annotations, 232–233
    context hierarchies and, 225
    dependency injection, 217–219
    mock objects, 231–232
    MVC
        controllers, 227–228
        exception handlers, 230
        form submission, 228–230
    request-scoped beans, 225–227
    RESTful services and, 326–328
    session-scoped beans, 225–227
    transaction management, 219–222
    utilities, 232–233
    web applications, 222–223
        WebApplicationContext, 222–224
TextContext Framework, 204–205
themes, MVC, 97–100
#this, 274
ThrowsAdvice, 244
transaction abstraction model, 180–182
    advantages, 183
transaction management
    ACID acronym, 176
    boundaries, 177–180
    data access layer separation, 186–189
    declarative, 183–186
    default behavior, 189–190
    layer isolation, 186–189
    programming
        PlatformTransactionManager,
          201–203
        TransactionTemplate, 198–200
    propagation rules
        MANDATORY, 192
        NESTED, 192
        NEVER, 192
        NOT_SUPPORTED, 192
        REQUIRED, 191–-192
        REQUIRED_NEW, 192
        SUPPORTS, 192
    service layer separation, 186–189
    <tx:advice>, 195–197
@Transactional annotation, 186, 219
    class level, 190–191

transactions, 176
    local *versus* global, 182
    logic execution, 203–205
    PlatformTransactionManager bean,
        configuration, 180–182
    transaction demarcation, 180–182
TransactionSynchronization object,
    204–205
TransactionTemplate,
    198–200
transferMoney method, 24
transitive persistence, 153
transparent persistence, 154
<tx:advice>, 195–197

U

UEL (Unified Expression Language), 264
unchecked exceptions, 186
unidirectional associations, 138–139
unit testing, RESTful services, 326–328
uploading files, 90–93
URI (Uniform Resource Identifier), 64
user input, validation, 86–90
UserDetails, 346–347
UserDetailsService, 340–341, 348
UserRestController class, 316
utilities
    SpEL, bean access, 280–281
    for testing, 232–233

V

validation, user input, 86–90
variables, SpEL, 273–275
vendor-specific methods, 127
view resolvers, 66

W

weaving in AOP, 238
web applications, testing
    222-223
    WebApplicationContext,
        222–224

web requests, authorization, 353–355

web services, creating, 306–318

@WebAppConfiguration annotation, 226

WebApplicationContext, loading, 222–224

web.xml security, 332–333

wildcards, AOP, 250

within keyword, 248–249

World Wide Web, 64

X-Y-Z

XML (eXtensible Markup Language), 19
  RESTful services and, 320–322

XML-based configuration, 26–27